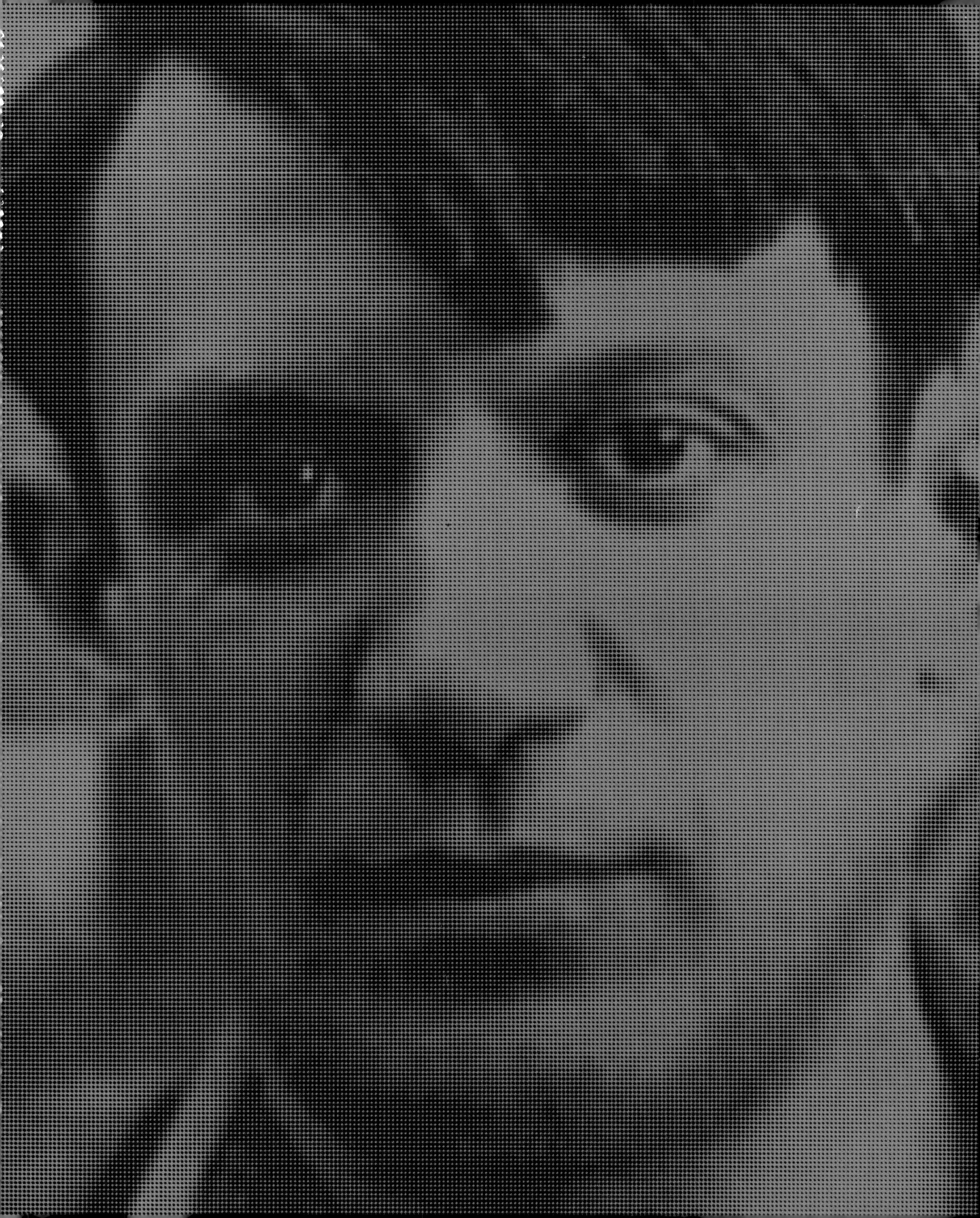

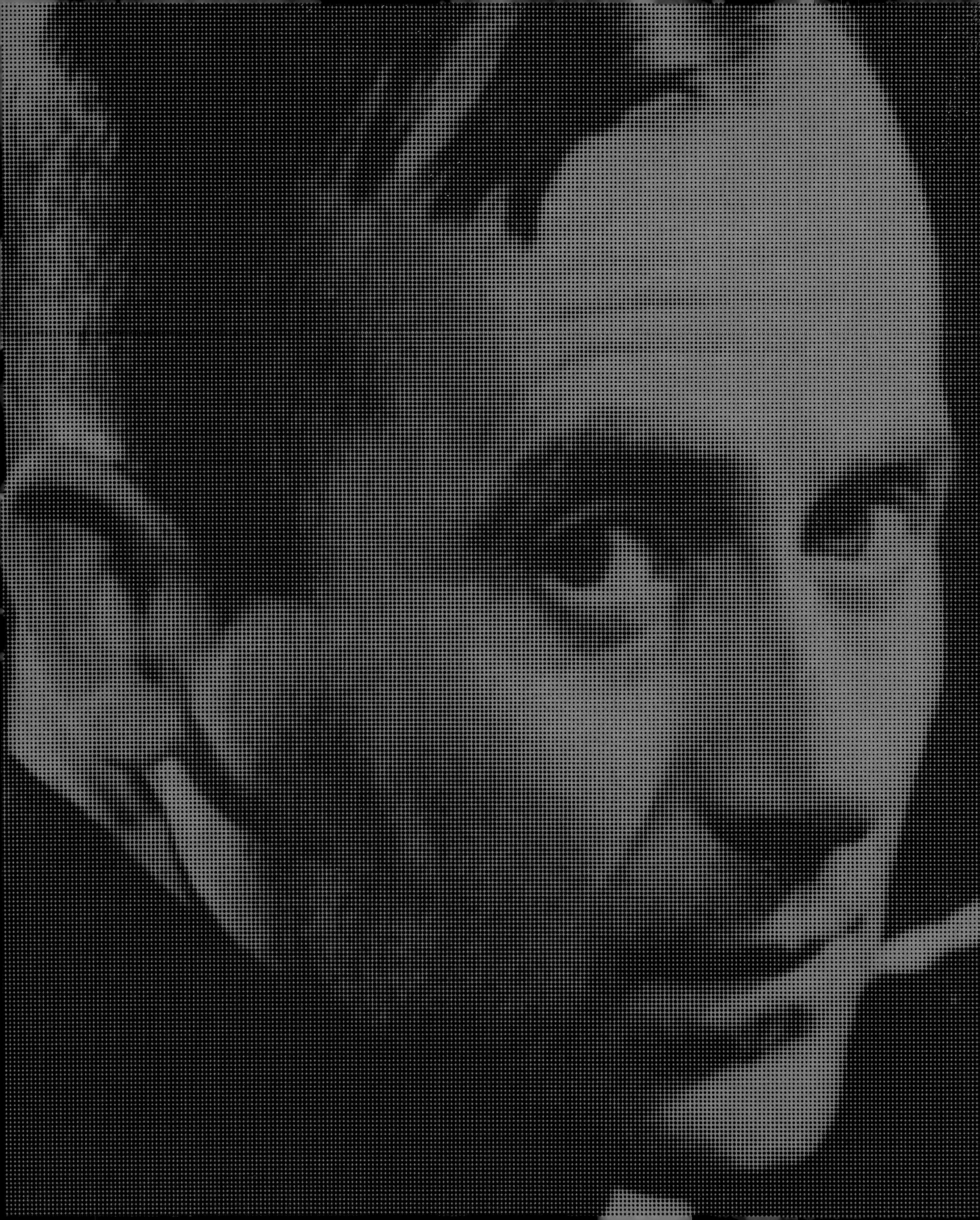

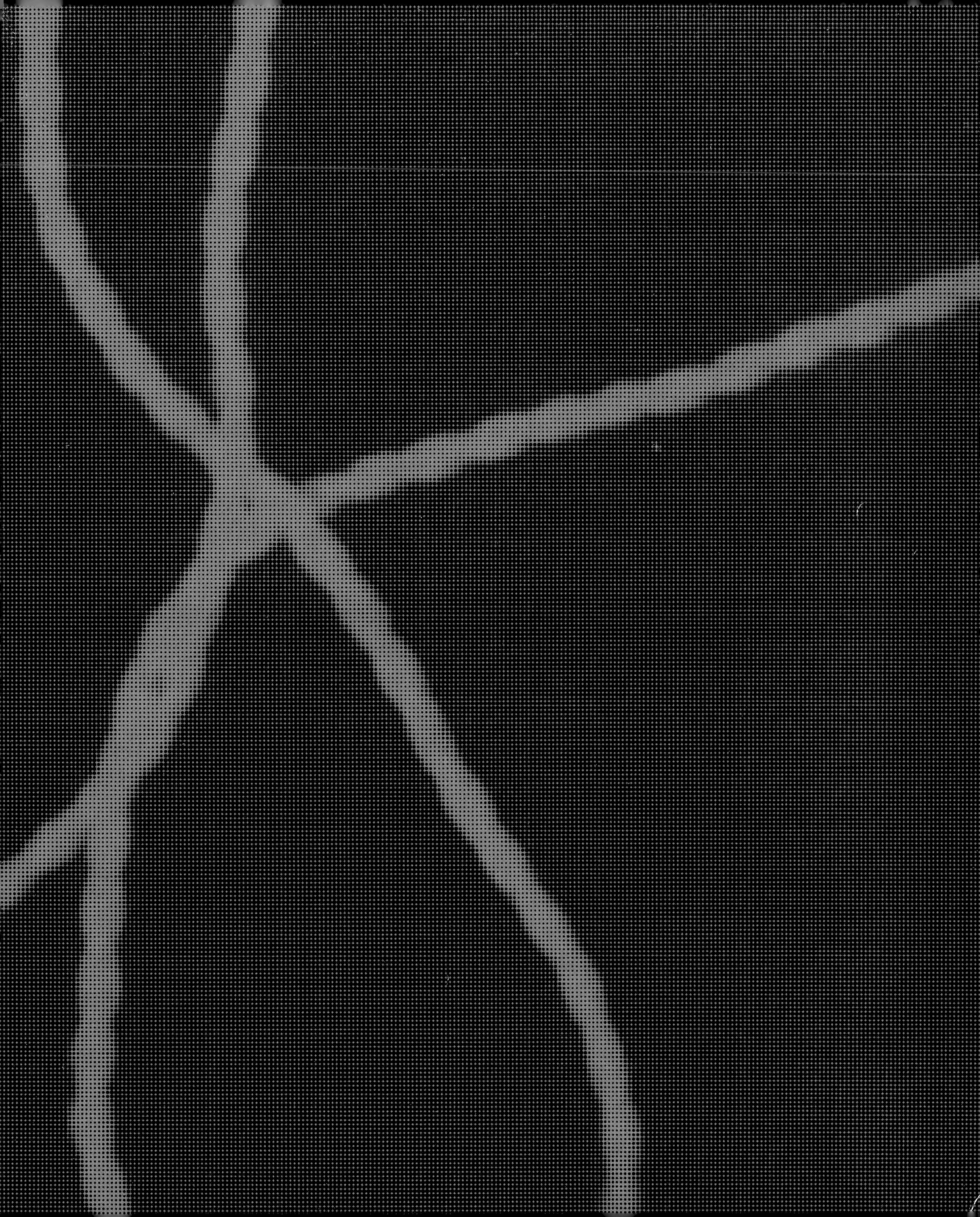

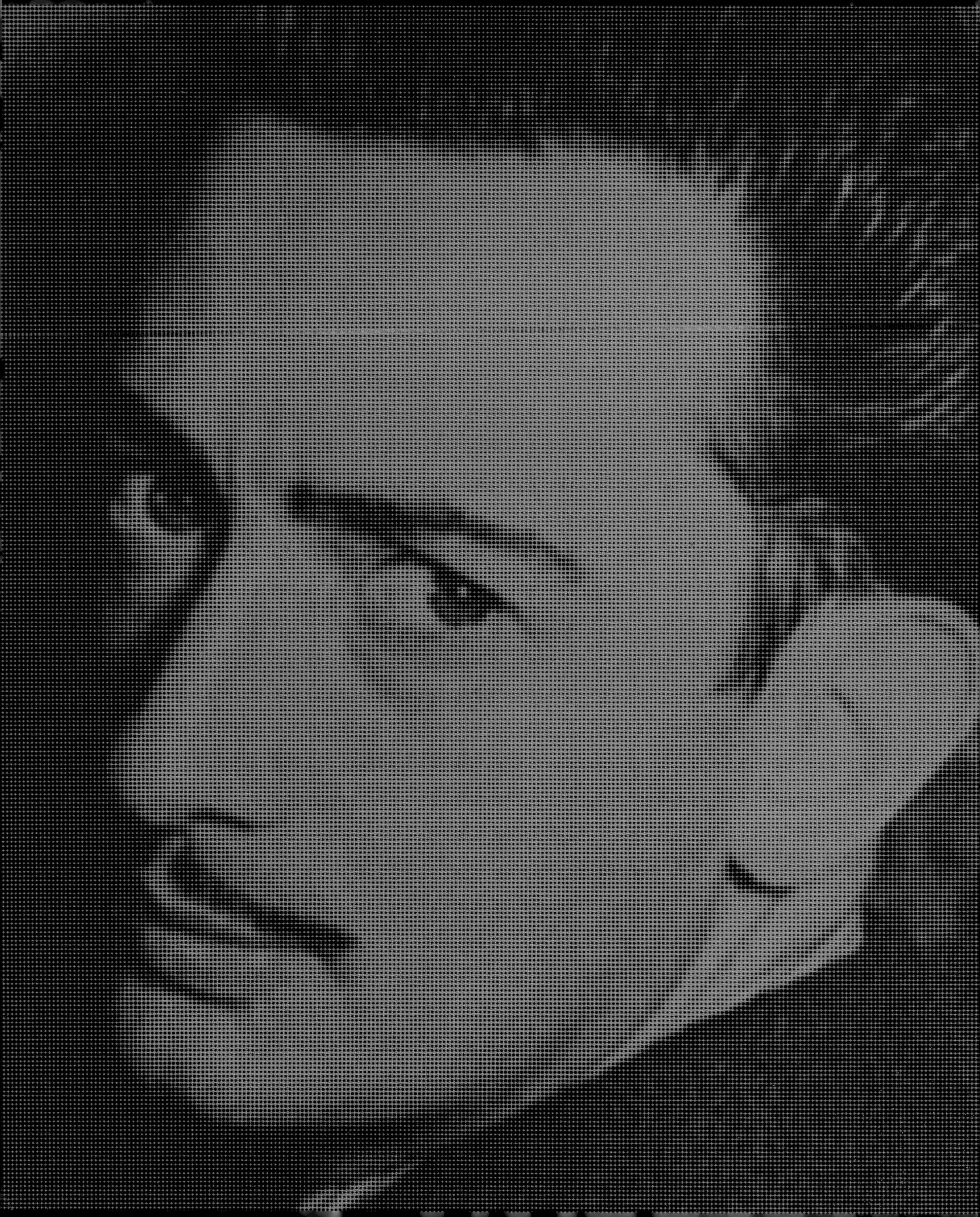

PICASSO, MIRÓ, DALÍ

Picasso
Dalí

Miró

ANGRY YOUNG MEN: THE BIRTH OF MODERNITY

edited by Eugenio Carmona

SKIRA

Cover
The Two Acrobats (Harlequin and his Companion)
[*Les Deux saltimbanques (Arlequin et Arlequin et sa compagne)*]
September–October 1901
Moscow, The State Pushkin Museum of Fine Arts

Design
Studio Fernando Gutiérrez

Editorial Coordination
Vincenza Russo

Editing
Michele Abate

Translations
Leslie Ray for Language Consulting Congressi, Milano

Iconographical Research
Paola Lamanna

First published in Italy in 2011
by Skira Editore S.p.A.
Palazzo Casati Stampa
via Torino 61
20123 Milano
Italy

www.skira.net

Printed and bound in Italy. First edition

ISBN: 978-88-572-0978-4

Distributed in USA, Canada, Central & South America by
Rizzoli International Publications, Inc., 300 Park Avenue
South, New York, NY 10010, USA.
Distributed elsewhere in the world by Thames and Hudson
Ltd., 181A High Holborn, London WC1V 7QX, United Kingdom.

Under the High Patronage of the President of the Italian Republic

PICASSO, MIRÓ, DALÍ.
Angry Young Men: the Birth of Modernity

Florence, Palazzo Strozzi, 12 March-17 July 2011

With the sponsorship of
Ministero per i Beni e le Attività Culturali
Ministero degli Affari Esteri
The Spanish Embassy in Italy
The Municipality of Barcelona
The Municipality of Malaga

PROMOTED AND ORGANISED BY

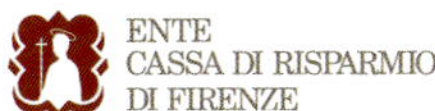

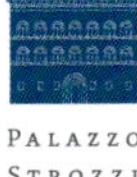

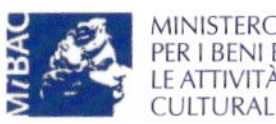

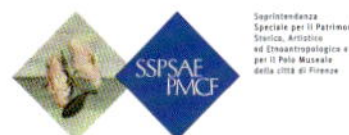

WITH

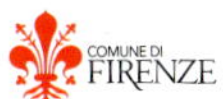

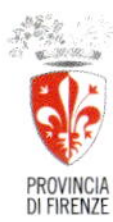

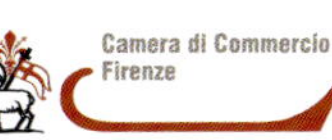

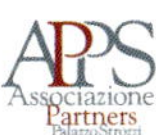

AND

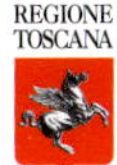

Exhibition curated by
Eugenio Carmona
Christoph Vitali

Exhibition realised by
Fondazione Palazzo Strozzi

Installation design
Luigi Cupellini
with the collaboration of
Carlo Pellegrini
Stage
Mariangela Lo Sasso

Graphic design for communication and exhibition
Rovai Weber design

Exhibition installation
Galli Allestimenti
Atlas e Livelux Light Designers
Stampa in Stampa
Alessandro Terzo
Franco Bianchi
Julie Guilmette
MMG Multimedia Meeting Group

Head of security
Ulderigo Frusi

Electrician
Simone Bagnoli

Alarm systems assistance and maintenance
Professional Security srl

Realisation of multimedia applications
Culturanuova
(Massimo Chimenti)

Accompanying texts in the exhibition
Ludovica Sebregondi

Translation of accompanying texts in the exhibition
Stephen Tobin
Lara Fantoni
Sisi Velloso Mata
Mireia Carol Gres

Communication and promotion
Susanna Holm
Sigma CSC

Press Office
Antonella Fiori
(national press)
Sue Bond Public Relation
(international press)

Website
Netribe

Preventive conservation and climate control
Opificio delle Pietre Dure
Preventive conservation and climate control department

Director
Roberto Boddi

Assistant
Sandra Cassi

Inspection of the conservational status of the works
Opificio delle Pietre Dure
Easel painting department

Director
Marco Ciatti

Technical Director
Chiara Rossi Scarzanella

Condition reports
Oriana Sartiani
Caterina Toso
Francesca Bettini
Diane Kunzelman
Luisa Gusmaroli
Isabella Sicoli

Family itinerary
Texts
James M. Bradburne
Devorah Block
Illustrations
Elisabet Ribera

Programming for "Picasso's Cube"
L'immaginario

Programming for families, youth and adults
Fondazione Palazzo Strozzi

Programming for school
Sigma CSC

Exhibition reservation office
Sigma CSC

Exhibition and ticketing personnel
TML Service

Ticketing
Vivaticket by Charta

Audio guides
START

Insurance
AON Artscope

Transportation
Arterìa

SPONSORS

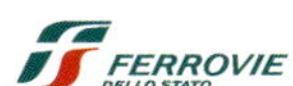

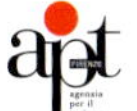

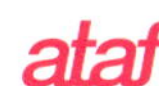

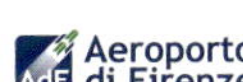

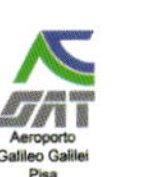

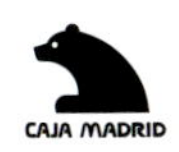

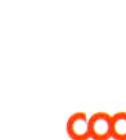

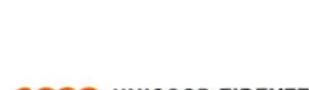

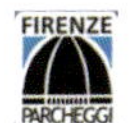

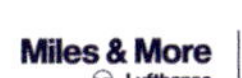

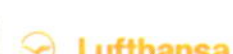

Photographic credits for works in the exhibition

p. 97
© 2010 foto Gonzalo de la Serna

pp. 87, 107, 109
© 2010. Digital Image, The Museum of Modern Art New York/Scala, Florence

pp. 179, 184
© 2010. Image copyright The Metropolitan Museum of Art/Art Resource/Scala, Florence

p. 90
© MNAC - Museu Nacional d'Art de Catalunya. Barcelona Photographers: Calveras/ Mérida/Sagristà

pp. 51, 52, 57, 58-59, 92, 112, 113
Archivio Fotográfico Museo National Centro de Arte Reina Sofía, Madrid

p. 197
Colleción Caixa Galicia, La Coruña

p. 187
Courtesy Acquavella Gallery

p. 186
E.W.K., Bern

pp. 100-101
Fabian Restauratoren GmbH

pp. 171, 172
Fundación Pablo Ruiz Picasso - Museo Casa Natal, Malaga

pp. 193, 195
Fondation Beyeler, Riehen/Basel

pp. 94, 104
Fundació Gala-Salvador Dalí, Figueres

p. 181
Image courtesy National Gallery of Art, Washington

p. 140
IVAM - Institut Valencià d'Art Modern, Valencia

p. 134
José A. Carrillo Castán

pp. 98, 99, 110, 178
Kunstmuseum Bern, Bern

p. 89
Mildred Lane Kemper Art Museum, Washington University in St. Louis

p. 139
Milwaukee Art Museum, Photo by John Nienhuis

pp. 53, 54, 55, 175
Museu de Montserrat

p. 173
Museo de Málaga, Malaga

pp. 105, 137, 138, 180, 183
Nahmad Collection, Switzerland

pp. 141, 142, 143
Sigrid Colomyès

p. 103
TEA - Tenerife Espacio de las Artes, Cabildo Insular de Tenerife

pp. 177, 189
The State Pushkin Museum of Fine Arts, Moscow

pp. 60-61
Thyssen-Bornemisza Collections

p. 63
Volkart Foundation, Switzerland

pp. 182, 188
Photographer Volker Naumann, Schönaich

Photographic credits for texts

© 2009-2011 Les Musées de Strasbourg: p. 43 top
© 2011 – Fundació Gala-Salvador Dalí - All right Reserved: pp. 42 middle right, 42 bottom right, 43 middle, 84 top, 120 top, 120 top and bottom left
© 2011 Digital Image, The Museum of Modern Art, New York/Scala, Firenze: p. 37
© 2011 Foto Scala, Firenze – su concessione Ministero Beni e Attività Culturali: pp. 47 top left; 151 right
© 2011 National Gallery of Art, Washington DC: p. 39
© 2011 Rosengart Collection Museum Lucerne: p. 34 left
© 2011. Albright Knox Art Gallery/Art Resource, NY/ Scala, Firenze: p. 117 bottom
© 2011. BI, ADAGP, Paris / Scala, Firenze: p.120 bottom right
© Archivio dell'Arte Luciano Pedicini, Napoli /Museo Civico Gaetano Bangieri: p. 47 bottom
© DACS/Giraudon/The Bridgeman Art Library/ Archivi Alinari, Firenze: p. 79 bottom
© Foto Scala, Firenze: pp. 126 top centre, 151 centre
© Fundación Pan Club Museo Xul Solar All right Reserved: p. 38 left
© J. Paul Getty Trust Museum, Los Angeles: p. 47 top right
© Kunstsammlung Nordhein-Westfalen, Düsseldorf: p. 127 right
© Museu Picasso, Barcelona pp. 126 top right, 164, 165
© NICHIREKI Co., Ltd. All right Reserved: p. 45 centre
© Thyssen – Bornemisza, Madrid: p. 74 top
2011 © Foto Scala, Firenze/ BPK, Bildagentur fuer Kunst, Kultur und Geschichte, Berlin: p. 151 left
AISA/Archivi Alinari, Firenze: pp. 40 top, 101
Archivi Alinari – Archivi Alinari, Firenze, p. 151 bottom right
Archivo de la Residencia de Estudiantes, Madrid, © Residencia de Estudiantes. All right Reserved: p. 41 left
Biblioteca de Catalunya, Archivo Joan Maragall, Generalitat de Catalunya Department de Cultura: p. 74 bottom
Bibliotheque Musée de L'Opera, Paris: p. 126 bottom
Copyright © 2011 Seattle Art Museum. All right Reserved p. 127 left
Foundation Bayeler, Basel Photo, Peter Schibli, Basel: p. 36
Museo Casa de los Tiros, Granada,1925: p. 38 right
Museo de Bellas Artes, Bilbao p. 84 centre
Museo Nacional Centro de Arte Reina Sofía, Madrid: pp. 41 centre, 41 right, 85 centre and bottom, 117 centre
Pachot/Ullstein bild/Archivio Alinari, Firenze: (photo portrait of Dalì)
Photography © The Art Institute of Chicago, Chicago: p. 34 right
Saint Louis Art Museum, Saint Louis p. 127 centre
University of Michigan Museum of Art: p. 120 centre right

Lenders

Barcelona, MNAC - Museu Nacional d'Art de Catalunya

Bern, E.W.K.

Bern, Kunstmuseum Bern

Bordeaux, Opéra National de Bordeaux

Figueres, Fundació Gala-Salvador Dalí

Künzelsau, Würth Collection

La Coruña, Colleción Caixa Galicia

Madrid, José Lladó

Madrid, Museo Nacional Centro de Arte Reina Sofía

Malaga, Colleccíon Tribal Ready

Malaga, Fundación Pablo Ruiz Picasso - Museo Casa Natal

Malaga, Museo de Málaga

Milwaukee, Milwaukee Art Museum

Moscow, The State Pushkin Museum of Fine Arts

Naples, Soprintendenza Speciale per i Beni Archeologici di Napoli e Pompei

New York, The Metropolitan Museum of Art

New York, The Museum of Modern Art

Oviedo, Colleccion Masaveu

Paris, Collection Maeght

Riehen/Basel, Fondation Beyeler

Santa Cruz de Tenerife, TEA – Tenerife Espacio de las Artes

Shizuoka, Ikeda Museum of the 20th Century Art

St. Louis, Mildred Lane Kemper Art Museum, Washington University in St. Louis

Switzerland, Nahmad Collection

Switzerland, Volkart Foundation

Valencia, IVAM - Institut Valencià d'Art Modern

Washington, National Gallery of Art

Museu de Montserrat

Thyssen-Bornemisza Collections

We are also grateful to the private lenders

Restorations

p. 103
Cúrcuma, Santa Cruz de Tenerife

pp. 100-101
Fabian Restauratoren GmbH

pp. 53, 175
Museu de Montserrat

p. 54
Voravit Roonthiva, Barcelona

Acknowledgements

This iniziative has been made possible by the contribution of countless people, whom the Fondazione Palazzo Strozzi and the curators would like to thank. We are especially grateful to the museum directors, public and private lenders, and all those who have personally been involved in the loans of the work on display.

We are grateful to: Irina A. Antonova, Francesco Bigazzi, Francesca Colombo, Laura Desideri, Alice Goldet, Jorge Hevia, Jonathan Miller, Marie Moatti, Fabrizio Paolucci, Maria de Peverelli Luschi, Paola Rubino and to the Teatro del Maggio Musicale Fiorentino.
We also thanks the Director of the Fundación Pablo Ruiz Picasso, Lourdes Moreno Molina and her staff: Laura Gaviño, Elisa Quiles, Mario Virgilio Montañez, Carlos Ferrer, Gloria Rueda Chaves, Joaquín Laguna, Trinidad Vega, Mª Jesús Ruiz and the collector D. Francisco Santana.

Eugenio Carmona is especially grateful to Manuel Borja-Villel, Sofía Díez, Victoria Fernández-Layos, Carlos Ferrer, José Lebrero Stals, María Morente del Monte, Rosario Peiró, Daniel Restrepo.

Special thanks to Miel de Botton and to Walter and Lucille Rubin.

We are also grateful to: Wanny di Filippo - Il Bisonte for the "Picasso's Cube" for the family activities; Lorenzo Villoresi for the perfumes in the "Picasso's Cube"; Arrigo Berni and Roberto Di Puma for the Moleskine notebooks; Francesca D'Anselmo and Giulia Giuffrida of Saatchi & Saatchi Rome; Veronica Triolo and Cecilia Tessieri of Amedei Srl.

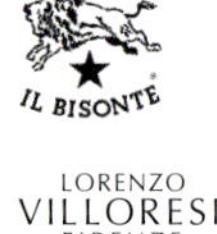

LORENZO
VILLORESI
FIRENZE

MOLESKINE®

We would like to thank Save the Queen for the uniforms of the Palazzo Strozzi staff.

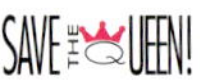

Tout l'intérêt de l'art se trouve dans le commencement. Apres le commencement, c'est déjà la fin.

PICASSO

CONTENTS

ACCORDING TO DALÍ, WHEN HE MET PICASSO IN 1926, THE FIRST THING HE RECALLS SAYING TO PICASSO WAS: "I have come to see you before visiting the Louvre." Picasso replied: "You're quite right." Although there is no independent evidence that this encounter ever took place, it certainly expresses the young Dalí's ambition, and after his 1926 visit, he became devoted to Picasso as a new paradigm, whom he regarded as a new "museum" for those who believed in modern art. In 1900, Pablo, Diego, José, Francisco de Paula, Juan Nepomuceno, María de los Remedios, Crispín, Crispiniano de la Santísima Trinidad, Ruiz Picasso, more simply Pablo Ruiz Picasso, and now known just as Picasso, arrived in Paris at the age of nineteen, already an innovative young artist. This was the year of the publication of Freud's *On the Interpretation of Dreams*, a year before Arnold Schönberg's groundbreaking *Pelleas und Melisande*, five years before Einstein's *anno mirabilis*, over a decade before the world was to be shattered by the First World War. But paradoxically, Dalí's visit of 1926 does not open a cycle. On the contrary, it closes a "story" that links the early works of Picasso, Miró and Dalí. Each of them was a young "emerging talent". Each of them was seeking to develop a unique visual language. Each of them looked to the known past in order to invent the unknown future. For Miró, and later Dalí, the "past" already included Picasso. Looking back now, almost a century later, we can see how all the dots connect. But seen from his own point of view, that of a young man in 1900, Picasso's dots all lay in the future, their eventual connections uncertain. For Picasso, modernity was yet to be born, and when it was, he would be among its most important parents.

The experience of youth and rebellion are not confined to the distant past. Picasso's father and uncle had decided to send the young artist to Madrid's Academy of San Fernando, the country's foremost art school in 1897, but Picasso disliked formal instruction and quit attending classes soon after enrolment. Some seventy-five years later, another angry young man, founder of Apple Computers Steve Jobs, similarly dropped out of Reed College at seventeen to make his own way. In a valedictory speech to graduating students of Stanford University in 2005, Jobs had much to say about what it meant to be young, hungry and foolish—but brave. He went on to tell the young graduates something as relevant in 2005 as it would have been to Picasso in 1897.

"Of course it was impossible to connect the dots looking forward when I was in college, but it was very, very clear looking backwards ten years later. Again, you can't connect the dots looking forward. You can only connect them looking backwards, so you have to trust that the dots will somehow connect in your future. You have to trust in something [...] because believing that the dots will connect down the road will give you the confidence to follow your heart, even when it leads you off the well-worn path, and that will make all the difference."

Picasso, Miró and Dalí—each of them—followed their heart, and this exhibition takes us into the heart of what it means to be young, to be full of ideas and enthusiasm, but not knowing how the dots will connect, what we will become—or what the world will become.

In addition to all the professionals—most of them young—who helped bring *Picasso, Miró, Dalí* to Florence, the Fondazione Palazzo Strozzi would like to thank the public and private collections which generously loaned important works to the exhibition. Our thanks once again go to the Ente Cassa di Risparmio di Firenze, the exhibition's main partner, who as always generously contributed to its success. We would like to thank the Founders of the Fondazione Palazzo Strozzi; the Province of Florence, the City of Florence, the Florentine Chamber of Commerce, and the Association of Partners of the Palazzo Strozzi, on whom the Fondazione depends in so many ways. We would like to thank all the exhibition's public and private sponsors, including the Regione Toscana, all of whom strongly supported the exhibition from the outset. Finally we would like to thank the entire Fondazione Palazzo Strozzi team—its Board of Trustees, its International Advisory Board, its Director and its staff—for having worked so hard to create an exhibition celebrating the youthful experimentation of three of the world's greatest artists, when they were themselves "emerging talents".

LORENZO BINI SMAGHI
Chairman of the Fondazione Palazzo Strozzi

FOR MANY YEARS NOW FLORENCE HAS BEEN KEEN TO VENTURE ONTO THE TERRAIN OF CONTEMPORARY art. This has happened precisely at Palazzo Strozzi, where the public has had the opportunity to enjoy some most delightful occasions, from the memorable experiences of Klimt, Chagall, Matisse and Miró, arriving, in more recent times, at Cézanne and de Chirico/Balthus.

The new proposal, *Picasso, Miró, Dalí*, adds a further element of reflection through three of the most representative exponents of the painting of Iberian origin.

The subtitle "the birth of modernity" is undoubtedly a demanding one at a time such as ours in which, from one retrospective to the next, we are still in search—and a search not without its anxieties and critical debates—of the authentic sense of "modernity", not only by critically investigating those, like Picasso, whose work did indeed act as a watershed and a point of no return, but also those who, while not denying the values of the past, proudly claimed their place in the sun in terms of the topical nature of their own artistic research.

Needless to say, it is pointless to worry ourselves over pre-constituted truths, but these periodic appointments at Palazzo Strozzi at least help us piece together a mosaic that is extremely stimulating and engaging.

MICHELE GREMIGNI
President of the Ente Cassa di Risparmio di Firenze

Se ha fabricado demasiado pintura y se hace muy poco ARTE

MIRÓ

¿No crees tú que los únicos
poetas, los únicos que realmente
realizamos poesía "nueva",
somos los pintores?

DALÍ

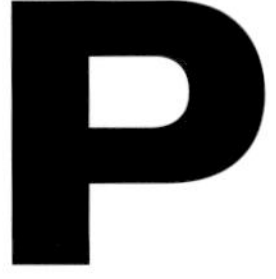ABLO PICASSO, JOAN MIRÓ AND SALVADOR DALÍ, THE THREE "ANGRY YOUNG MEN" OF THE EXHIBITION'S subtitle, are surely the most important artists of Spain—or rather of Catalonia—in the 20th century, and, at least as far as Picasso is concerned, possibly of the whole Western world. In the early work shown in the exhibition, which spans over thirty years, there are, however, noticeable differences between the three painters—Miró born twelve years after Picasso, and Dalí eleven years after Miró. Picasso, whose work of the late 19th century, from 1895 until the beginning of Cubism in 1907, is the most complete of the three, already in full command of all his artistic powers at an early age, even though throughout in his long life of ninety-two years he changed many times from one style to another, often quite different than the one before. Important loans from the Metropolitan Museum of Art, the Museum of Bern and many other public and private lenders fully document his earliest phases. The case of Joan Miró, whose early work of 1915 we are showing, is similar, although his artistic means are slightly more limited, and he develops his finest and broadest expression only with the advent of Surrealism. Magnificent works on loan from The Museum of Modern Art in New York, the museums of Milwaukee, Valencia and the Beyeler Foundation in Basel as well as many private lenders again give ample proof of the richness and beauty of Miró's early work. Salvador Dalí is, like Picasso, only sixteen years old, when he first shows his works, and his output from 1920 to 1926 is surely the most difficult to be put into context. In these early years he seems to be wandering through all manner of styles and modes of expression, heavily depending on older French artists like Cézanne and Matisse, of whose works some of his own seem to be direct copies. However Dalí's work, with loans from Reina Sofía in Madrid, the Dalí Museum in Figueres, the Museum of Montserrat and as with the other two artists many private lenders, proves to be a major figure even before he finds his own personality and style and becomes the great master of narrative Surrealism.

A similar exhibition was done twenty years ago, at Schirn Kunsthalle Frankfurt in 1991, which I then directed, and at the Museum Reina Sofía in Madrid. It was also called *Picasso, Miró, Dalí* and had the subtitle *The Origins of Spanish Modernism 1900–36*. As this indicates, the exhibition, which I developed together with Maria Corral, the director of Reina Sofía at the time, and to which Eugenio Carmona heavily contributed, included, besides the three great masters, forty-three other Spanish artists, among them Alberto Sánchez, Leandre Cristófol, Ernesto Giménez Caballero and Ernesto Palencia. The exhibition covered the period until the Spanish Civil War, which ended with Franco coming to power, marking the end of great modern art in Spain until his death in 1975.

I would like to extend my deepest thanks to all the lenders, public and private, for their generous support of the exhibition and to wish it a warm and attentive reaction and acceptance in Florence and in Italy.

CHRISTOPH VITALI
Curator of the exhibition

PICASSO, MIRÓ, DALÍ

Eugenio Carmona

YOUTH, IDENTITY AND MODERNITY

Legend has it that Dalí went to see Picasso in the spring of 1926. We could also begin by adopting another perspective and composing the sentence as follows: "Legend has it that, in the spring of 1926, Salvador Dalí was received by Pablo Picasso." The event is related by Dalí himself in his *La vida secreta de Salvador Dalí* [*The Secret Life of Salvador Dalí*], is drafted as a stylistic reworking of a 19th-century bourgeois book of memoires. Dalí's text is therefore intended to be presented from the space of *reality*. But the author (who parodies the autobiographical genre, even though he does so seriously) does not hesitate to comment that it is composed of a concatenation of both real and invented episodes. It is not surprising that Dalí's entire mature thought always gave prominence to the maxim in which André Breton, paraphrasing Freud, argued that reality is contained in the surreal, and vice versa. That is to say, according to this point of view, the real and the imaginary, understanding imaginary to be that which is the fruit of *desire*, operate on the same plane. When remembering his life, without wishing to be untruthful, for Dalí what was *not true was a good story*. Certain things he would have wanted to happen he had experienced with such intensity that, in fact, it was as if they had happened.

The dedication of the book to Gala-Gradiva is a story in itself. If Gala, as Gradiva, is *what she appears*, it is evident that she is invention and revelation at the same time. In any event, Gala's presence in the Dalí's imagination is not where we are interested in going right now. Gradiva was a constant reference for the Surrealists, at least for some time. But Gradiva immediately harkens back to the novel by Jensen that was commented upon by Freud; when analysing this novel Freud proposed an entire framework of analysis for the narration of the imaginary, for literary fantasy.

In any event, this is the account of the precise moment when Dalí describes his encounter with Picasso:

> "To go back a little, I spent another two months in Figueras[1], making my last preparations before pouncing on Paris. I have forgotten to mention that before Pierre Loeb's arrival I had already made a trip to Paris, which lasted just a week, in the company of my aunt and my sister. During this brief sojourn I did only three important things. I visited Versailles, the Musée Grevin, and Picasso. I was introduced to the latter by Manuel Angelo Ortiz, a cubist painter of Granada, who followed Picasso's work to within a centimetre. Ortiz was a friend of Lorca's and this is how I happened to know him. When I arrived at Picasso's on Rue la Boétie I was as deeply moved and as full of respect as thought I were having an audience with the Pope. 'I have come to see you,' I said, 'before visiting the Louvre.'
> 'You're quite right,' he answered.
>
> I brought a small painting, carefully packed, which was called *The Girl of Figueras*. He looked at it for at least fifteen minutes, and made no comment whatever. After which we went up to the next story, where for two hours Picasso showed me quantities of his paintings. He kept going back and forth, dragging out great canvases which he placed against the easel. Then he went to fetch others among an infinity of canvases stacked in rows against the wall. I could see that he was going to enormous trouble. At each new canvas, he cast me a glance filled with a vivacity and an intelligence so violent that it made me tremble. I left without in turn having made the slightest comment.
>
> At the end, on the landing of the stairs, just as I was about to leave we exchanged a glance which meant exactly:
> 'You get the idea?'
>
> 'I get it!'"[2]

Let us consider this in stages. In *Secret Life* the story of Dalí's encounter with Picasso is presented as an instant of revelation, as a *decisive* instant, but it is not an autonomous story, nor does it possess a title in its own right. It is a story contained within another story that is in turn contained within another story, developed with the technique—or with the rhetoric—of the multiple image developed by Dalí in the late 1920s. That is to say, Dalí reconsiders an essential fact of his life not by recourse to the simple listing of details nor to the conventional development of scenes, but by redefining the events from a certain perspective that is not inconsistent with the paranoiac-critical basis of narrative.

In the pages of *Secret Life* that interest us here, Dalí begins the *major* narration with his definitive expulsion as a student from the Academy of San Fernando in Madrid. Dalí gets the dates wrong. And when I say *wrong* I mean that he deliberately makes a mistake or that he makes an unconscious mistake that is no less deliberate. The shortcomings in Dalí's memory in the story are not simple disruptions of memory, but rather they have a certain sense or possess a certain meaning. Dalí gets the dates wrong at the outset. He affirms in *Secret Life* that he was expelled from the Academy on 20 October 1926. It may be that this was the date when the official document of his expulsion was signed. But the incident that brought about the expulsion took place on 14 June. In any event, Dalí places his expulsion from the Academy as the starting point for a story and

1. "Figueras" is the Spanish form of the Catalan "Figueres".

2. Salvador Dalí, *The Secret Life of Salvador Dalí*, 1942, translated by Haakon M. Chevalier, Vision, London 1948, p. 206.

for a personal transformation that nevertheless had a different starting point: that of the supposed visit to Picasso mentioned above. In Dalí's narrative strategy, this visit to Picasso would have to wait to make its appearance: that is to say, it would have to find its place strategically.

As is known, Dalí had already been expelled from the Academy of San Fernando previously. But on this occasion it happened because he dared to declare that the members of the tribunal, composed of professors, several of them artists themselves, were incompetent. It has always been thought that Dalí's reaction to his examiners was spontaneous and that it was provoked by events, particularly the Academy's refusal to give a teaching post to painter Daniel Vázquez Díaz, whom Dalí supported. But from reading *Secret Life* we deduce that Dalí had acted coolly and had meditated on it in advance. We could even see the anticipation of one of his *tricks* [*tretas*] included in it. Dalí says:

> "These tricks were various, and even contradictory, and were merely terroristic and paralyzing devices for imposing the ferociously authentic essence of my irrepressible ideas, by which I lived and thanks to which my "tricks" not only became dazzlingly effective, but emerged from the category of the episode and became incorporated into that of history. I have always had the gift of manipulating and of controlling with ease the slightest reaction of people who surround me, and it is always a voluptuous pleasure to feel at constant "attention" to my capricious orders all those who, in obeying me to the letter, will most likely go down into their own purgatory, without even suspecting their faithful and involuntary subordination"[3].

Dalí's *tricks* are part of the narcissistic aetiology of the perverse polymorph who had reached maturity. And they worked. The *trick* followed by the painter when declaring the members of the Academy incompetent sought something, and it found it: to stop living in Madrid, to stop living in the Student Hall of Residence, to move away from the rules for living and aesthetics of the Generation of '27[4] and to redefine (if this were possible) his relationship with Federico García Lorca and with Luis Buñuel. Being expelled from the Academy of San Fernando also meant rediscovering Figueres as his own *place*: as a *place* in the most profound psychological meaning of the term and the concept. And, in short, provoking his expulsion from the Academy meant challenging his father and the future that the latter had mapped out for him. At that moment the confrontation did not succeed in provoking a rupture, a rupture for which Dalí was undoubtedly ill-prepared, but it did have a certain symbolic value. Indeed, the following paragraph of Dalí's story is devoted to placing on record that, as soon as he returned home, his father posed for a pencil portrait that was—as Dalí himself says—"one of my most successful of this period"[5], adding that "the mark of the pathetic bitterness"[6] that the expulsion of his son from the Academy had caused him were visible in the expression on his father's face. Cynicism and cruelty dressed in a smiling childishness.

For Dalí the *father* was not only the figure of his own biological father. For Dalí the *father* was also the Academy of San Fernando, Madrid, the Student Hall of Residence and García Lorca. All are in the same sphere, on the same plane. All wanted to determine his future and guide his aesthetic and moral opinions in a direction in which he did not want them to be guided. And it was precisely at this

3. *Ibid.*, p. 207.

4. In this regard, Dalí himself wrote: "The motives for my action were simple: I wanted to have done with the School of Fine Arts and with the orgiastic life of Madrid once and for all; I wanted to be forced to escape all that and come back to Figueres to work for a year, after which I would try to convince my father that my studies should be continued in Paris. Once there, with the work I would bring I would definitely seize power!" Dalí, *The Secret Life*, cit. p. 204.

5. *Ibid.*

6. *Ibid.*

time of rebellion against the figure of the father—in the broadest sense of the term—that Dalí announces to us, in the story in his *Secret Life*, the appearance of an especially important moment in his work:

> "I executed a series of mythological paintings in which I tried to draw positive conclusions from my cubist experience, linking its lesson of geometric order to the eternal principles of tradition"[7].

Mythology, Cubism, tradition: and then Picasso appears. Although not the Picasso that we were expecting. Not the Picasso supposedly visited in the Rue la Boétie in the spring of 1926. Another Picasso appeared. Dalí tells us in *Secret Life*.

> "All this activity, which I carried on without stirring from my studio in Figueres for one second, produced a profound commotion, and the polemics aroused by my works reached the attentive ears of Paris. Picasso had seen my *Girl's Back* in Barcelona and praised it.
>
> I received on this subject a letter from Paul Rosenberg asking for photographs, which I failed to send, out of sheer negligence. I knew that the day I arrived in Paris I would put them all in my bag with one sweep"[8].

And next, following these statements, in the same paragraph, Miró appears seamlessly in Dalí's story: "One day I received a telegram from Juan Miró", says Dalí, "who at this period was already quite famous in Paris, announcing that he would come and visit me in Figueras, accompanied by his dealer, Pierre Loeb."[9] In the presence of Miró, Dalí's father transformed. But the truly important thing is that Dalí summoned Picasso and Miró to the same space at the same time. Both acknowledged him and paid spontaneous homage to him without palliatives, which is what the paranoiac narcissist always wants, and both were accompanied by their dealers. In contrast with the provincial idealism of the cultural reformers of Madrid, for Dalí artistic success is indissolubly linked, plainly and without false modesty, with trade and money.

In the story of *Secret Life*, Dalí's rebellion against *the name of the father*, which was not yet a complete rebellion, added the names of Picasso and Miró. Picasso and Miró appeared, full stop. But the sequences that Dalí joins together when referring to Picasso, to Miró and to their dealers, although they appear linked in time, do not have the same chronology. Picasso may *perhaps* have seen—and I will emphasise the *perhaps* for now—the painting entitled *Espalda de niña* (or *Figura de espaldas*[10]) in the first solo exhibition by Dalí at the Galeries Dalmau, in Barcelona, between 14 and 27 November 1925. But some of Picasso's biographers have their doubts about Picasso's presence in Barcelona on that date[11]. Perhaps Paul Rosenberg knew about Dalí soon after the artist's first solo exhibition in Dalmau. But, as we will see, it does not seem that Picasso was involved in it. And, despite the opinions of well-known biographers of the painter, it also seems that it was Dalí who took the initiative regarding the dealer and not the other way round. Miró would also not come into contact with Dalí until September 1927. This time it was actually Miró who, accompanied by Pierre Loeb, took the initiative. Both visited Dalí in Figueres. Miró was kind and positive in his comments on the young painter's latest works. Loeb, on the other

7. *Ibid.*, p. 205.

8. *Ibid.*.

9. *Ibid.*.

10. The painting is not exactly the same, since Dalí modified it after displaying it in Dalmau. In this regard, see: Rafael Santos Torroella, *El primer Dalí. 1918-1929*, Students' Residence and Instituto Valenciano de Arte Moderno, with the collaboration of Telefónica and the Fundación Gala-Salvador Dalí, Madrid 2005, pp. 234–6.

11. At least that is the opinion of Enrique Mallén in the biography that is included in the *Digital Catalogue Raissoné* on the website *Online Picasso Project*. This is how we find it in John Richardson, *A Life of Picasso. The Triumphant Years, 1917-1932*, Alfred A. Knopf, New York 2005.

hand, kept his enthusiasm for later, because in his opinion Dalí's works were still too influenced by those of other artists. It is not surprising, therefore, that Loeb does not come out very well in the story of *Vida secreta*.
Yet, in any event, Dalí is mixing together in the same temporal space episodes that happened over a period of two years. Neither did all the characters mentioned link their presences in the way that Dalí evoked them. In his memory Dalí suppresses the spatial and temporal coordinates to tell of himself and to make us, his readers, see his thoughts and see that in its memories his expulsion from the Academy of San Fernando—and therefore from Madrid, from the Hall of Residence and from the Generation of '27—was linked with the ideal of being praised and admired by Picasso, Miró and their dealers.

Indeed, in the story of *Secret Life* that we are following, Dalí locates in this same space his encounter with Luis Buñuel to make *Le Chien andalou*, an event that, as is known, did not take place until 1928 and involved the decisive integration—not without its own personal triumph—of Dalí in the Parisian Surrealist group.

It is then, and only then, when all these letters are placed on the table, when all these chronological alterations have been made in Dalí's narrative and when all the characters and circumstances that it was necessary to cite have been cited, that Dalí remembers his encounter with Picasso in 1926, telling us that *he had forgotten to mention it*. Dalí, a reader of Freud, hoped that his interlocutors also were and that they knew the importance the Viennese psychiatrist attached to slips and to apparent or unexpected episodes of forgetfulness as the expression of something that possesses a special meaning in the unconscious.

Anna María Dalí, who accompanied her brother on the trip to Paris in the spring of 1926, never provided any recollection of the visit to Picasso[12]. Manuel Ángeles Ortiz never had a clear memory of the facts. What is certain is that Manuel Ángeles Ortiz was the only one of the Spanish "renewers" who was really close to Picasso. Picasso taught him to be a Cubist and a Classical artist at the same time[13]. Picassian concomitances exist between the work of Manuel Ángeles Ortiz and that of Dalí that have never been highlighted. Is this *another way* in which Dalí could have been introduced to Picasso by Manuel Ángeles Ortiz? And above all a question: if Picasso had seen Dalí's works in 1925 and had been enthusiastic about them, then why did Dalí need someone to introduce him on a visit that was taking place just a few months later? Dalí affirms that Picasso interested Paul Rosenberg in his work. But we know of a letter[14], which is not easy to understand, but from which it may be deduced that Dalí sent photographs to Rosenberg regarding his exhibition in Dalmau in 1925. Rosenberg acknowledged receipt of the letter. But Dalí did not reply to this. Dalí later wrote to him again asking for the photographs and Rosenberg, with barely suppressed surprise at the young painter's attitude, replied to him again, after Dalí's second one man show in Dalmau, in 1927. On the other hand, can we imagine the mature and successful Picasso in 1926 contemplating a work by a young painter for more than a quarter of an hour? Can we imagine Picasso moving all his paintings around for more than two hours without his young interlocutor saying a single word? Can we imagine a final scene of absolute, fascinated and fascinating complicity between two creators feeling so much empathy for an instant, which would only be discussed again years later?

---

12. I have taken this comment from Ian Gibson, *La vida desaforada de Salvador Dalí*, translated by Daniel Najmías revised by the author, Anagrama, Barcelona 1998, pp. 183 *et seq.*

13. See Eugenio Carmona, "Manuel Ángeles Ortiz en los años del Arte Nuevo", in *Manuel Ángeles Ortiz*, edited by Lina Davidov and Eugenio Carmona, Museo Nacional Centro de Arte Reina Sofía, Madrid 1996, pp. 17-38.

14. The letter, dated 15 December 1927, reads as follows: "Monsieur, / Je vous écrivis, en effet, il y a déjà longtemps, au moment de votre exposition aux galeries Dalmau à Barcelona, e je fus très étonné de n'avoir pas eu votre réponse à cette lettre. / Je suis en possession et des photographies qu'elle renfermait. Je les examinerai à loisir. / Quand vous viendrez a Paris, je vous prie de bien vouloir me faire le plaisir de votre visite. Et, dans cette attente, veuillez agréer, Monsieur, mes salutations les plus distinguées." This letter was reproduced in the "Biography" offered by Montserrat Aguer and Fèlix Fanés in the catalogue of the exhibition *Dalí joven (1918-1930)*, Museo Nacional Centro de Arte Reina Sofía, Madrid 1994, p. 33.

In his *Vida secreta* Dalí affirms that he found Picasso's gaze so *full of vivacity* and with such *a keen intelligence* that it made him *tremble*. Only someone who has had direct experience of Picasso's gaze could state something so forthright. It is undoubtedly disconcerting to leave the encounter in 1926 between Dalí and Picasso so hazy, somewhere between the certain and the imaginary. But there is no doubt that this encounter *did* take place, even though on another plane, on another terrain. As an artist, Dalí visited Picasso. As an artist, Picasso paid attention to Dalí. When drafting his memoirs, Dalí could not separate his meetings with Picasso from his meetings with Miró. Dalí tells us something important: he tells us that there existed a way in which the works of Picasso, Miró and Dalí were related. The young Dalí could not grow as an artist until he had ensured that his work or his aspirations were in tune with those of Picasso and with those of Miró. The young Miró, who in his youthful work inhabited a cultural space that Dalí would inherit, always worked with Picasso on the horizon, not so much that of his creations, but certainly his looking to the future. Picasso was immediately able to recognise the transformational worth of the young Miró. And in his youthful work Picasso, after occupying a cultural space that he was to leave modified for Miró and Dalí, had to tackle some circumstances of the relationship between identity and the conquest of modernity that later Miró and Dalí would have to recapture and redirect.

There exists, therefore, a *story* that links the youthful works of Picasso, Miró and Dalí. It is a *story* that cannot be told like other stories. It is a story that does not have a climax, a plot and a happy ending, but it has filled the experiences of artistic modernity with indispensable aesthetic thoughts, episodes and chapters. These episodes can be related and shown. This story in episodes and thoughts that relates the moments of the formation of Picasso, Miró and Dalí—even if dominated by Catalonia and by the first three decades of the 20th century—could have several geographies and several chronologies. The young Picasso walked alone and it is not possible to locate a starting point that brings together the three names involved. Yet it *is* possible to locate a point of arrival: that of Dalí's *visit* to Picasso. In his memoire Dalí relates it to his getting to know Miró and, at the end the Surrealist group would end up bringing them together in Paris. This point of arrival enables us to travel back in time. It enables us first to see the psychomachic event in which Dalí becomes Picasso's interpreter against the backdrop of a totally renewed Miró. Then it enables us to gain access to a space shared between Miró and Dalí, in the first half of the 1920s, in which reflection on the *genius loci* acts as a mirror of the demands of the Modern era. And in turn, the question of the presence of the *genius loci* in Miró and Dalí gives us the key to interpret a previous moment: that of Picasso and Miró crossing paths in the Barcelona of 1917. This Picasso who returns to Barcelona in 1917 with *Parade* is very different from the artist that had invented a painting entitled *Les Demoiselles d'Avignon* ten years earlier. To what extent does our knowledge of the Picasso of 1917 illuminate the preparatory notebooks of the work of 1907? And does knowing the aesthetic premises of Picasso in 1907 not guide us decisively around the enormous production of a young Picasso who questions his origins in search of transformation? ■

WHEN DALÍ SAYS HE MET PICASSO

CATALONIA / PARIS, 1926

PSYCHOMACHIA

When we say that Dalí visited Picasso in the spring of 1926, in addition to leaving open the possibility that this visit did take place, what we are talking about is, in fact, the moment when Dalí *recognises* Picasso and locates him as a reference and a paradigm. Something that Dalí would also do immediately afterwards with Miró. But which Picasso did Dalí hope to find?

Spanish plastic renovation, this is, those in favour of what those involved called *arte nuevo* [new art], had two main artistic fields: the one located in Madrid and the one taking place in Catalonia. In principle, the Catalan environment was more peculiar, more adaptable and more active. With passing time both nuclei gained equal intensity and equally important contributions, but they were almost always independent from each other. From the late 19th century the cultural history of Catalonia had its own life, different from that of the rest of Spain. Picasso's father, a professor of art, was undoubtedly thinking of his son's future when he chose Barcelona as the final destination of his considerable academic career. But Picasso's father's choice was not common at that time. Another paternal decision, that of Don Salvador Dalí y Cusí, challenged the system of cultural independence between Catalonia and Madrid when he sent his son to study at the Academy of San Fernando and made him live at the Students' Residence. Dalí would not be the only case[1].

But the issue is that, being the great absentee, a step away from becoming the great myth of *the new*, prior to the spring of 1926, the *image* of Picasso in the renovating atmospheres of Madrid and Catalonia was perhaps different. It was a difference based on the distinct cultural strategies of each environment[2]. Natalia Bravo has studied this issue in depth. In Madrid, despite the early comments on the Cubist Picasso made by Ramiro de Maeztu[3] in 1911, we find *very little*. It would be necessary to wait until the brief homage to Picasso, in Pombo, due to the presentation of *Parade*, in 1917, organised by Ramón Gómez de la Serna, or until 1918—when Picasso had already had several cycles of relations with the Modern Movement—where, in the Ultraist magazine *Reflector*, the poet and literary critic Guillermo de Torre, made a small comment on the duality of Picasso the Cubist and the Classical artist. And even in this delay, in 1919, two well known intellectuals, who were highly influential at the time, namely Juan de la Encina and José Moreno Villa, denied Picasso all credibility in their art criticism. Soon afterwards they would change their position, and perhaps Dalí had something to do with this[4]. But, in any event, and taking into account that Moreno Villa was one of the tutors at the Students' Residence when Dalí arrived in Madrid in 1921, no later, Picasso was not exactly a generally positive point of reference in the intellectual media of the capital. This was the case with the exception of Eugeni d'Ors, who had moved to Madrid in 1920. However, d'Ors prior to 1920 had his opinions very much located in the Catalan context. And his were hugely influential opinions. Influential first in Catalonia, then in Madrid and even later throughout Europe through his influence on Waldemar George and other critics.

D'Ors soon encountered the *fin-de-siècle* transformation of Symbolism pushing for the recovery of Classicism, something that Morèas himself favoured[5]. Later he became closely acquainted with Cubism. But he interpreted

1. We could refer to the presence of Lorca in Catalonia, to the influence in Madrid—with different scope and differing presences—of Eugeni d'Ors and Sebastià Gasch, to the interaction between publications such as *La Gaceta Literaria* and *L'Amic de les Arts* or to the creation of ADLAN among other things.

2. Natalia Bravo Ruiz has studied this issue in depth in *Picasso y la crítica de arte en España (1900–1936)*, Malaga, Fundación Picasso, Malaga 2002.

3. Ramiro de Maeztu was then an influential writer connected with the Generation of '98; his essay "La idea platón-Picasso" appeared in *El Heraldo de Madrid* on 28 November 1911.

4. Of course, Dalí's arrival at the Students' Residence was one of the triggers for Moreno Villa to transform into one of the main promoters of *new art*. Moreno Villa's painting also gives us the means to understand the influence of Juan Gris on his own painting and on Dalí's.

5. See Michel Décaudin, *La Crise des valeurs symbolistes en France 1890–1914*, Privat, Toulouse 1960, republished in 1981 by Slatkine.

Cubism to his own advantage. D'Ors was interested in encoding for Catalonia a new art where Classicism and "Mediterraneanity" were the main references. His proposal was initially called *Estructuralisme*, but the term *Noucentisme* coined by him met with success and is the one we use today[6]. D'Ors saw in Cézanne not the final development of Impressionism but the beginning of a new Classicism, an opinion that is even now shared by the critics. Cubism, grasping this Cézannian possibility over all others, would become an art that, in principle, was anti-Impressionist. But it would also come to be a moment of transition; a *necessary* attempt at experimentation, a *Lent* of painting that, after many sacrifices and renunciations of the temptations of the plastically sensual, would lead to the *Easter of the Resurrection*, of a re-founded Classicism, new and modern. D'Ors outlined these approaches in principle as a solution for the Catalan art of the decade of 1910 and as a future premonition for the rest of European art. But in the evolution of Picasso he found the confirmation of his theories, no matter how much Picasso *resisted* being truly an artist with a language fully based on Classical art. Curiously, and even though they diverged in their *nuances* or in their acceptance or not of the various -isms, most Catalan commentators on art subscribed to these same assumptions or to very similar assumptions[7]. This was the case at least until 1926, and such observations arose with a certain independence from the surrounding artistic reality. Picassian Cubism never ceased to have a geographical reference in Catalonia[8]. And when Cubism appeared early in Barcelona in 1912, at the Galeries Dalmau, almost all the commentators on the event described a peculiar version of Cubism as a *state prior* to a reconsidered Classical art[9]. The opinion ended up appearing in the creative magazines for more than a decade. Perhaps for this reason no Catalan artist engaged in Cubism. Cubism remained as an *issue yet to be addressed*. In my opinion, in the middle of his studies at the Academy of San Fernando in Madrid, Dalí in fact wanted to address this issue.

But this is something that we will see later on, even though in this essay *to advance* is to go back in time. The issue is, then, that, on the dates that concern us here, for most of the renovating artistic environment in Catalonia, and to a certain extent also in Madrid, the *authentic* Picasso, the truly Modern or up-to-date Picasso was not the Cubist Picasso, but the Picasso that we call *Classical*.

Without a doubt, this conception of Picasso must have been the one that was deposited in the young Dalí. And perhaps for this reason the young Dalí—with his typical spirit of contradiction—did not attend to it immediately. Picasso did not truly become part of the repertoire of Dalí's references until 1924. A year later the transformation of the image of Picasso would begin in the spheres of plastic renovation of Catalonia and Madrid. As is known, Sebastià Gasch was not only the *discoverer* of Miró but was also very close to Dalí for some years. Dalí would in fact end up involving Gasch in some of his *tricks*. Gasch's opinions and Dalí's did not exactly coincide. But regarding Picasso they could be sufficiently close to be revealing. In 1925, talking about Miró, Gasch used expressions similar to those of *analytical Cubism* and *synthetic Cubism*[10], and he was perhaps one of the first art critics to do so internationally. But Gasch had the view, undoubtedly following d'Ors in part, that Cubism, despite having recovered the Classical tradition of art, could not be an artistic form in its own right, but a stage of transition either towards Abstract art or else towards Neoclassicism. A year later, Gasch continued this type of approach,

---

6. In this regard, see the studies by Laura Mercader, Martí Peran and Natalia Bravo in *Eugenio d'Ors del arte a la letra*, Museo Nacional Centro de Arte Reina Sofía, Madrid 1997.

7. In this regard we may consult the words of Eugenio Carmona in *Picasso, Miró, Dalí y los orígenes del arte contemporáneo en España, 1900–1936*, Shrin Kunsthalle and Museo Nacional Centro de Arte Reina Sofía, Frankfurt and Madrid 1991.

8. The Cubist experience, with a preamble by Gósol, is linked to names such Horta de Ebro, Cadaqués, etc. In this regard, see Josep Palau i Fabre, *Picasso à Catalunya*, Polígrafa, Barcelona 1966.

9. This is to a degree a controversial theme, but in my view it is the *Gordian knot* for understanding the meaning of the reception of Modern art in Catalonia. In support of a certain interaction between *Noucentisme* and Cubism or a reception on the plane of the identity of the two proposals, consult: Robert Lubar, "Miró before 'The Farm'. A Cultural Perspective", in the exhibition catalogue, *Joan Miró: A Retrospective*, Guggenheim Museum, New York 1987, pp. 8–28. Likewise see by Lubar, "Cubism, Classicism, and Ideology: The 1912 'Exposiciò d'Art Cubista' in Barcelona and French Cubism Criticism", in *On Classic Ground. Picasso, Léger, De Chirico and the new Classicism*, 1910–1930, Tate Gallery, London 1990, pp. 309–23. On the exhibition in Dalmau, see the book by Mercè Vida, *L'Exposició d'Art Cubista de les Galeries Dalmau*, Universitat de Barcelona, Barcelona 1996. For the subject of Junoy in those years, and regarding the comparison between Cubism and *Noucentisme* (which Junoy called *Mediterreanisme*) see: *Junoy, Josep María: Obra poética*, Study and editing by Jaume Vallcorba-Plana, Edicions des Quaderns Crema, Barcelona, 1984. I would also like to add that this topic was one of the chapters of my doctoral thesis: *La renovación plástica española del "momento vanguardista" al "retorno al orden". 1917–1925*, University of Malaga, 1989; the conclusions of which are in *Picasso, Miró, Dalí, cit.*, in 1991 and later in "Novecentismo y vanguardia en las artes plásticas españolas", in *La Generación del 14. Novecentismo y vanguardia en las artes plásticas españolas*, Instituto MAPFRE de Cultura, Madrid 2004.

10. He said that he used these terms following Raynal and undoubtedly he was one of the first writers on Modern art to raise this dichotomy. In "Els pintors d'avantguarda. Joan Miró", in *Gaseta de les Arts*, issue 39, Barcelona 15 December 1925.

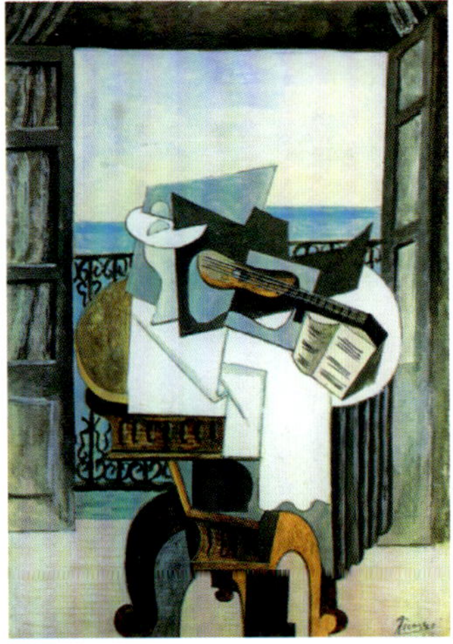

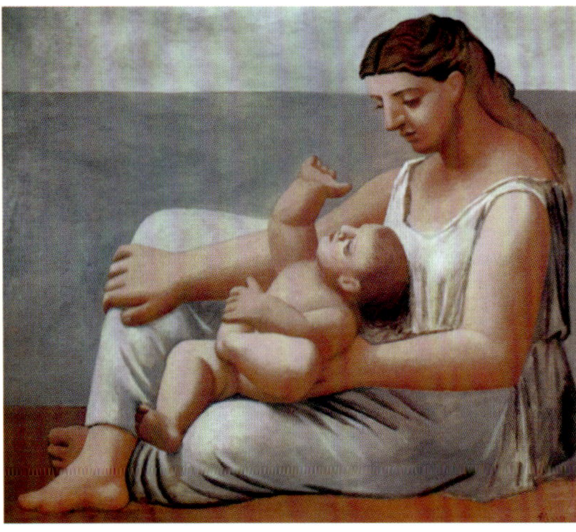

Pablo Picasso
Table in Front of the Window, 1919
LUCERNE, PICASSO-SAMMLUNG DER STADT LUZERN
SIEGFRIED UND ANGELA ROSENGART COLLECTION

Pablo Picasso
Mother and Child by the Sea, 1921
CHICAGO, THE ART INSTITUTE OF CHICAGO

but transforming it[11]. The dichotomy was now established between *cerebral art* and *instinctive art*. The former was that of Jeanneret, Ozenfant and the Purists. The latter, that of Miró and the Surrealists. Neither of the formulas was fully valid in Gasch's view. The true art of the moment was that which was able to combine intelligence and sensitivity, and Picasso was the main exponent of this solution or of this formula. But to which Picasso was Gasch referring in May 1926? The reproductions that accompanied his article—entitled, specifically, "Picasso"—are images of a Picasso that is predominantly *Classical*, that for their psychological intensity, their tendency towards the erotic or their pure virtuosity, go beyond the desire for limits that is characteristic of Classicism. The first is what we find in *Mother and Child by the Sea*, from 1921; the second is what we identify in *The Siesta* (*Sleeping Peasants*), from 1919; and the third is outlined in *Portrait of Sergej Diaghilev and Alfred Selisberg*, a drawing executed in 1919. These are, to a certain degree, set against *Table Before the Window*, also dated 1919, a variant on the series of well-known still lifes before the open window executed in Saint Raphaël.

All the photographic credits for these reproductions refer to Paul Rosenberg or to the gallery L'Effort Moderne. Was this the Picasso that could be discussed in 1926? When Gasch published his article the references to the latest Picasso had already appeared through Zervos and *Cahiers d'Art*[12] and an important text by Waldemar George on Picasso was about to appear in *L'Amour de l'Art*, which is decisive for this whole issue[13]. Comparing the dates, we may suppose that Gasch's text was prepared before these contributions appeared from Zervos and *Cahiers d'Art*. But there is something in the Gasch article that is like an optical effect. By placing the image of *Table Before the Window* and that of the female figure in *Mother and Child*... together, it seems that we are seeing the stylistic references (and perhaps something more than stylistic) of the *Neocubist Academy* that Dalí created, in fact, in 1926.

In June 1926, when the article by Gasch appeared, Dalí was already amply aware of the existence of *another* Picasso. As probably Gasch was too. And that is why we can ask ourselves to what extent certain doses of synergy between Dalí and Gasch are found in the text that we are commenting upon. Be that as it may, in his numerous texts that appeared in 1927, Gasch would begin to speak of a new Picasso, of the *plastic-poetic Picasso*. This was a Picasso who came to resolve the situation of modern art on this date, because he linked the inheritance of

11. In reality, it was not a year later, but just a few months. I am referring to the following articles by Gasch: "Picasso i el impresionisme", in *Gaseta de les Arts*, issue 44, Barcelona 1 March 1926; and "Picasso", in *D'Ací d'Allá*, issue 102, Barcelona June 1926.

12. Christian Zervos, "Œuvres recièntes de Picasso", in *Cahiers d'Art*, Year I, issue 5, Paris June 1926. In the following issue of the magazine, Zervos was to return to the topic and prior to this essay in *Cahiers d'Art* interesting texts by Elie Faure and by Jean Cassou were published that Gasch may have taken into account.

13. Waldemar George, "L'Exposition Picasso", *L'Amour de l'Art*, Year II, Issue 6, Paris, June 1926, pp. 190–4.

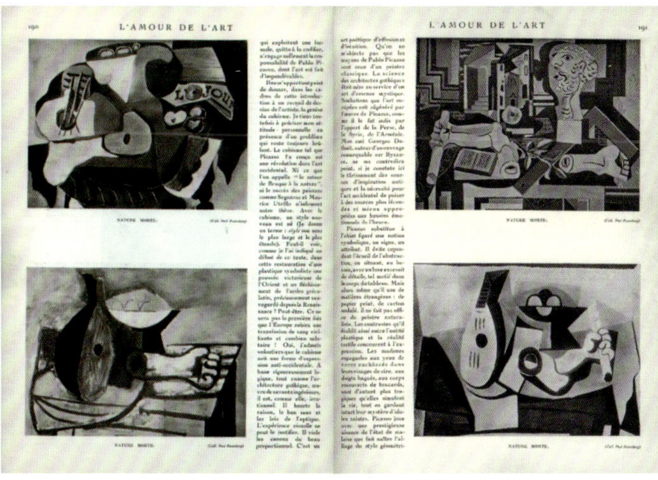

L'AMOUR DE L'ART

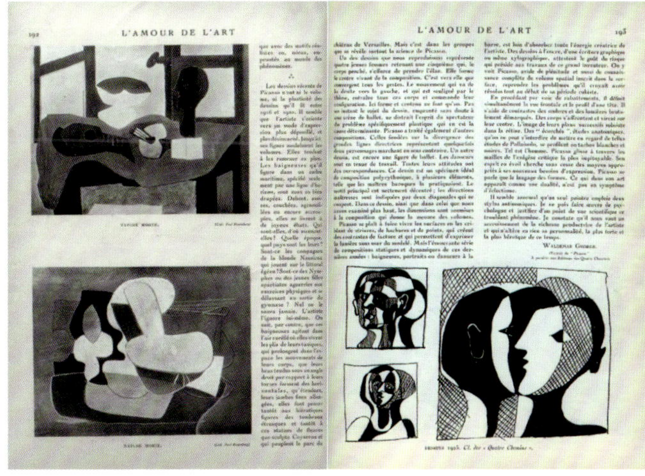

L'AMOUR DE L'ART

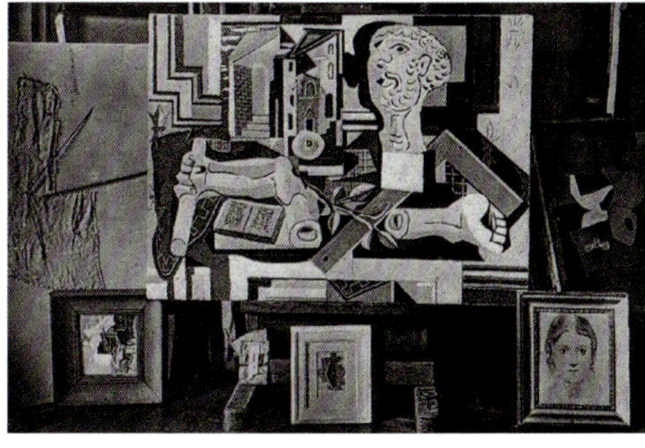

L'Amour de l'Art, no. 6, June 1926
Article by Waldemar George with reproductions of Pablo Picasso

L'Amour de l'Art, no. 6, June 1926
Article by Waldemar George with reproductions of Pablo Picasso

Reproductions of works by Picasso offered by Zervos in *Cahiers d'Art*, no. 5, June 1926

pure Cubist painting, without falling into abstraction or rationalism, and the versatility and force of the instinct of the Surrealists, without falling either into the arbitrary or into the literary[14]. *Musical Instruments on a Table* (today in the Museo Reina Sofía) executed by Picasso between 1925 and 1926, could be a fine example of the Picasso that Gasch calls *plastic-poetic*.

Gasch's theses came from his previous analyses, but they also took on board most of the opinions of Tériade[15] published in *Cahiers d'Art*. This *plastic-poetic* Picasso of Gasch would come to coincide with the *lyrical* Picasso that Dalí mentions in some of his youthful writings. Although the truth is that in the writings of his youth Dalí mentions Picasso little, and when he does so it is more to offer his name as the watchword for the authentically Modern and not so much to comment on his work. In any event, if in Gasch's writings there existed one Picasso in 1926 and another in 1927, then in 1928 we will find a third. This third Picasso appeared commented upon in the pages of *Gallo*[16], the magazine that Federico García Lorca published in Granada, and the magazine to which Dalí contributed graphics and published his important essay *San Sebastián* and the *Catalan Anti-Art Manifesto*.

Now Gasch does not present us with an "essentially mental" Picasso working in response to his "interior model". It is, he tells us, the "movements of his soul, tortured and disturbed" that Picasso depicts in his painting. In short, we are supposedly dealing with a Neo-Romantic[17] or Surreal Picasso, if it were not for the fact that the term Surrealism is carefully avoided. And it is avoided because, although Gasch continues proposing the existence of the *plastic-poetic tendency*, he speaks above all of an *ineffable* and *unclassifiable* Picasso. That is to say, Gasch allowed himself to be pulled along by the wave of mythologizing of Picasso that Zervos had begun in 1926. And one of the strong points of this mythologizing of Picasso was precisely to place Picasso systematically above the *mêlée* of any -ism, school or peremptory classification. According to this perspective, only Picasso nourished himself on his own proteic quality.

In Dalí, with passing time, the need would arise to be considered as this latest Picasso that Gasch had taken partly from Zervos, partly from Tériade, partly from himself. But in 1928 the painter from Cadaqués had his connection with the Surrealist group too much on his mind to want to be located beyond the palpitations of the present. Also, the moody, driven Picasso described by Gasch was perhaps no longer of interest to a Dalí who at the end of 1927 had undertaken

---

14. Gasch refers to the *plastic-poetic* Picasso on numerous occasions, some relating to Dalí's work. In order not to complicate this citation too much, it is worthwhile mentioning two texts by Gasch: "Del cubisme al superrealisme", *La Nova Revista*, Barcelona July 1927. This text, when translated in *La Gaceta Literaria* of Madrid, caused a major impact in the artistic spheres of the Generation of '27. The other article by Gasch to be considered is "Cop d'ull sobre l'evolució de l'art modern", *L'Amic de les Arts*, Year II, issue 18, Sitges, September 1927. He expressed some conclusions on the impact of the conception of this *plastic-poetic* Picasso in *Picasso, Miró, Dalí*, 1991, *cit*. Natalia Bravo corrected some of my proposals in *Bárbaros e italianos. Picasso en el pensamiento crítico de Sebastià Gasch y Eugenio d'Ors (1923–1931)*, Fundación Picasso, Malaga 1996. Subsequently I reconsidered the importance of Gasch's considerations in *Pintura-fruta. La figuración lírica española, 1926–1936*, Comunidad de Madrid, Madrid 1996.

15. In this regard, see Carmona, *Pintura fruta*, *cit*.

16. Sebastià Gasch, "Picasso", in *Gallo*, ▶

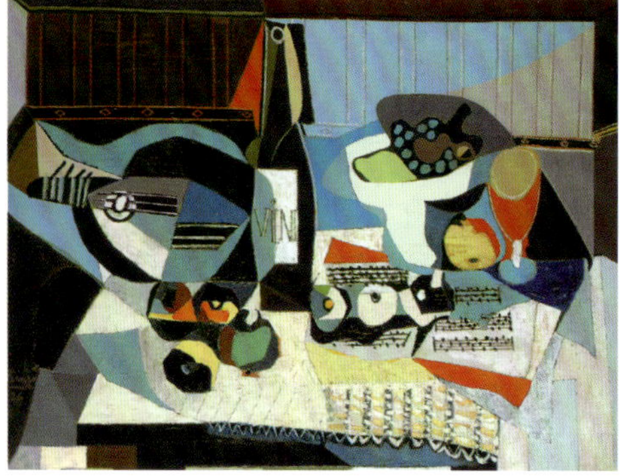

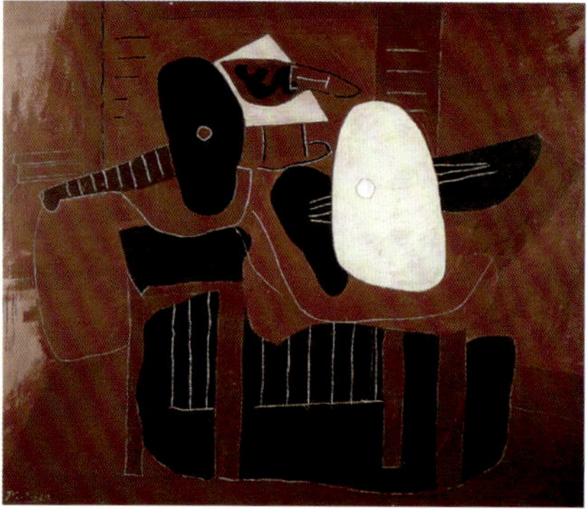

Pablo Picasso
Still-Life with Wine Bottle, 1926
BASEL, FONDATION BEYELER

Pablo Picasso
Musical Instruments on a Table, 1926
BASEL, FONDATION BEYELER

a new type of painting in which Picasso was no longer a point of reference. Dalí's supposed visit to Picasso in the spring of 1926 appears, however, as a kind of vortex valve regulating the work of the young Dalí. What happened then? How could such a high valuation of a possible "Picassian" Dalí exist for the critics, if this Picassian Dalí, who emerged in the spring of 1926, lasted just one year?

I believe that in some connoisseurs or scholars of Dalí's work, in recent years a strong focus on one aspect of his painting has existed that has avoided its complexity and variety. This focus has left the symbolic aspect of Dalí's visit to Picasso to one side and has underlined, in particular, Dalí's use of an *iconotema* [iconic theme][18] that the painter had borrowed from Picasso. It is the effigy of a head cut at the neck. He makes this physiognomy a *cut head* on some occasions and a *fragment* on others. But just as important as, or even more important than this feature is the multiform character of the head, which branches off or triples like old medieval tricephalic heads. It is agreed and accepted that Dalí took this iconographic concretion from a certain work by Picasso: *Workshop with Plaster Head and Arms* or *Plaster Head and Arms*[19], a work executed in 1925, probably in Juan-les-Pins in late summer. It is considered that Dalí may have seen the work on his visit to Picasso. It has also been suggested that he could at least have found out about it through its reproduction in *Cahiers d'Art* in early 1926[20]. This is very likely. Yet it is even more likely that Dalí had leafed through the monograph by Zervos, *Picasso. Œuvres. 1920–1926*, in what was perhaps the first publication by Éditions "Cahiers d'Art"[21]. Dalí could also have encountered articles and publications by Waldemar George and Léon Deshairs, among others[22].

In any event, Dalí's sources are not a problem. The issue is another. The crux of the issue is that Dalí, on appropriating this iconographic concretion, this *iconotema*, accomplished, at the same time, a whole *interpretation* of Picasso's work. And this interpretation involved both a powerful transformation of contents and the opening up of a new stylistic register in his production.

This stylistic choice involved embarking upon the path of one specific Picasso. In the reproductions of his recent work offered by *Cahiers d'Art*, both by the magazine itself and by the editorial, Picasso deliberately appeared as a multiple and versatile artist, without an option of plastic language that could be considered a priority. It undoubtedly reinforced the emergence of the mythical plane on which the artist wished to be located and on which some critics wanted, and managed, to locate him. Dalí's option came to underline what survived in Picasso of the inheritance of Cubism. A transformed Cubism, true, but Cubism after all. It was a Cubism that exchanged forms tending towards angular geometry for curved forms: *curvilinear Cubism* was what Alfred H.

◄ Year I, issue 2, Granada April 1928, pp. 1–3. On the location of this text by Gasch in the creative context, consult: Eugenio Carmona, "Ironía. Instinto. Las artes plásticas en *Gallo*", in *"Gallo". Interior de una revista. 1928*, edited by Luis Muñoz, sponsored by La Alhambra and General Life and Students' Residence, Granada and Madrid 2008, pp. 128–81.

17. Not only in the literal meaning of the term but also in the sense given by Charensol in the second half of the 1920s in commenting on the evolution of some creators linked to the first avant-gardes. Tériade and Gasch, in their writings, as well as Dalí in his text *Nous limits de la pintura*, took very much into account the presence of this *Neo-Romanticism* on the Parisian and European scene. Nevertheless, this tendency or possibility has been taken up on very few occasions by contemporary critics.

18. I am referring to an icon that closes a cycle of meanings on itself in the specific, chronologically determined field of the production of a creator.

19. In Spanish the work is usually entitled *Naturaleza muerta con cabeza de yeso* or *Bodegón con cabeza de yeso*. Zervos gives it number 445 in Volume V of his annotated catalogue of Picasso.

20. Zervos, "Œuvres recièntes de Picasso", *cit.*

21. From the information that appeared in the magazine *Cahiers d'Art*, the book must have appeared between late summer and early autumn 1926. It had been first announced, albeit with a different title, in the articles by Zervos mentioned above (note above). It was also indicated that it would be released by the publishers of Albert Morancé, where Zervos worked before founding *Cahiers d'Art*. In the articles by Zervos mentioned above it is stated that the photographs that illustrate them come from the book to be edited by Albert Morancé. But in Zervos' book edited by Éditions "Cahiers d'Art" these photographs were not published, but individual plates of each work.

22. Leon Deshairs, "Pablo Picasso", in *Art et Décoration*, Year I, issue 47, Paris 1925, pp. 73–84.

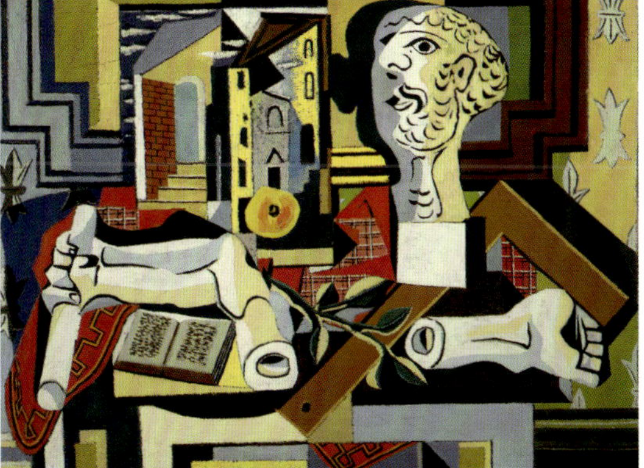
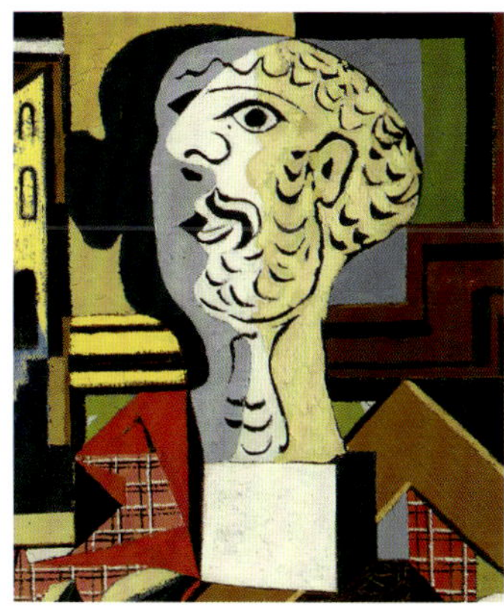

Pablo Picasso
Workshop with Plaster Head and Arms
(*Composition with Plaster Head and Arms*)
(full and detail), 1925
NEW YORK, THE MUSEUM OF MODERN ART

Barr was to call it[23]. But it was a Cubism that had reconsidered its relationship with the presence of the projective space and in perspective. And it was also a Cubism that plainly outlined its collision and integration with the tendency towards Classicism that Picasso had developed in recent years. The creators of the *new art* in Madrid—who gradually left to live in Paris—immersed themselves in this type of Cubism, and it is curious that Dalí could share with them, even if superficially and momentarily[24], plastic interests that he could not share with any other artist on the Catalan scene.

But it did not stop there. From its appearance in 1924, the graphic position of *La Revolution Surrèaliste* magazine, the official organ of the Surrealist movement, gave a special profile and special significance to certain aspects of Picasso's Cubism. The reconsideration of Picassian Cubism from the Surrealist perspective was clear in the texts of *Le Surrèalisme et la peinture* and reached its peak on the pages of *La Revolution Surrèaliste* with the publication of *Les Demoiselles d'Avignon* and *The Dance* in the same issue. There therefore existed a whole reinterpretation or, if one prefers, an entire Surrealist reconsideration of certain aspects of Picasso's Cubist production. Dalí was in this. And he was so even though he vehemently denied his links with Surrealism during the years 1925, 1926 and 1927.

In any event, what it is also significant to bear in mind is that Dalí's embracing of this *curvilinear, plastic-poetic* or *lyrical Cubism*, or whatever one wishes to call it, was momentary or episodic in his work. It was almost an *excursus*. The mature Dalí was to go back more in his style to the Neoclassical Dalí or to the champion of the New Objectivity (Neue Sachlichkeit) than to the Late Cubist Dalí. Nevertheless, and this being the case, two fundamental aspects were to emerge of the work and of the contribution to modern art of this Dalí who unexpectedly embraces the features of Late Cubism: *soft forms* and the *multiple image*.

The interpretation of Cubist faceting as *splitting apart* was not something exclusive to Dalí. Painters such as Moreno Villa or Xul Solar also did this. García Lorca also did this in his drawings. But to give the faceting game transformed into splitting an implementation of a psychological nature is something entirely different. In issue 4 of *La Révolution Surréaliste*, dated 15 July 1925, Breton began to publish "Le Surréalisme et la Peinture".

This first text begins with the famous sentence: "The eye exists in a savage state." A *Harlequin* by Picasso created in 1924 was reproduced above this sentence. The painting is very well-known today, as it is in the National

23. This expression was developed by Alfred H. Barr Jr. in *Picasso. Fifty years of His Art*, The Museum of Modern Art, New York 1946.

24. I say that this relationship was *superficial* and *momentary* because, even if it seems interesting for me to mention it, the interest of the renovators of Madrid in the latest Picassian Cubism, which Gasch called *plastic-poetic*, moved towards the creation of a whole tendency discussed by Tériade on the very pages of *Cahiers d'Art*. For this topic, see: Eugenio Carmona, *Pintura fruta. La figuración lírica española. 1926–1931*, Comunidad de Madrid, Madrid 1992.

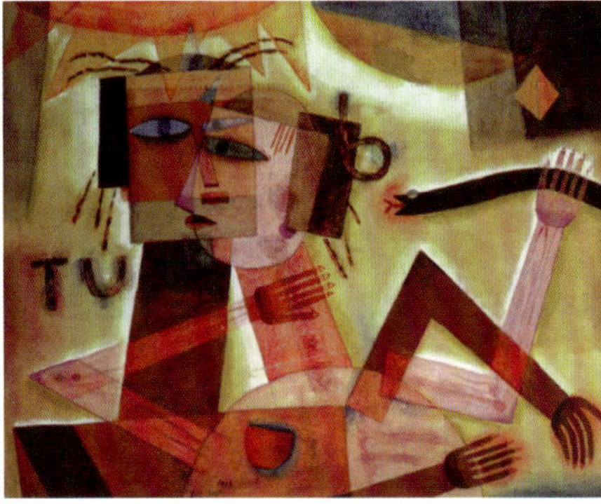

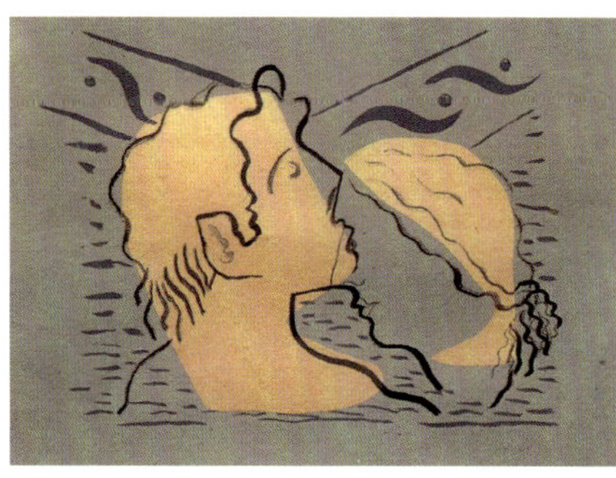

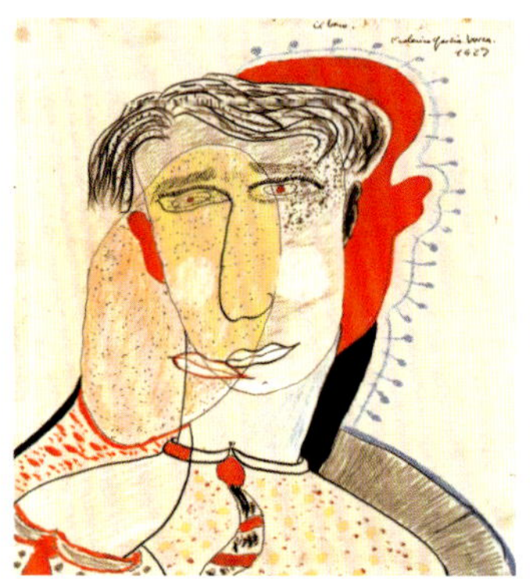

Xul Solar
You and I, 1923
COLECCIÓN FUNDACIÓN PAN CLUB

José Moreno Villa
Lovers, c. 1927
MADRID, COLECCIÓN ALFONSO EMILIO PÉREZ SÁNCHEZ

Federico García Lorca
The Kiss, 1925
GRANADA, MUSEO CASA DE LOS TIROS

Gallery of Art in Washington. It is worthwhile to cite the entire paragraph that is presented below the photographic reproduction of the work, however well-known it is and in spite of the countless publications and translations of which it has been the object:

> "L'œil existe à l'état sauvage. Les Merveilles de la terre à trente mètres de hauteur, les Merveilles de la mer à trente mètres de profondeur n'ont guère pour témoin que l'œil hagard qui, pour les couleurs, rapporte tout à l'arc-in-ciel. II préside à l'échange conventionnel de signaux qu'exige, parait-il, la navigation de l'esprit. Mais qui dressera l'échelle de la vision? II y a ce que j'ai déjà vu maintes fois, et ce que d'autres pareillement m'ont dit voir, ce que je crois pouvoir reconnaître, soit que je n'y tienne pas, soi que j'y tienne, par exemple la façade de l'Opéra de Paris ou bien un cheval, ou bien l'horizon; il y a ce que je n'ai vu que très rarement et que je n'ai pas toujours choisi d'oublier nu de ne pas oublier, selon le cas; il y a ce qu'ayant beau le regarder je n'ose jamais voir, qui est tout ce que j'aime (et je ne vois pas le reste non plus); il y a ce que d'autres ont vu, disent avoir vu, et que par suggestion ils parviennent ou ne parviennent pas à me faire voir; il y a aussi ce que je vois différemment de ce que le voient tons les autres, et même ce que je commence à voir *qui n'est pas visible*.
> Ce n'est pas tout."[25]

It is appropriate to read the text with the same spirit that it preaches. To begin to see what was not visible until the arrival of the Surreal considered the eye in the savage state. From the—appropriately named—formalist point of view, Picasso's *Harlequin* is a Late Cubist figure executed through the intersection of planes of colour, now structured with curved forms and with a space that, when it is expressed in abstract planes, regains clear senses of depth and perspective. The colouring is lively and intense, in contrast with the initial and founding Cubism. From a non-formalist point of view, enlivened by the new capacity of the eye that exists in a savage state and begins to see what was not visible before, the harlequin's face is a split, divided face, with all the psychological implications of this. One of his eyes may even be reminiscent of a vagina. This visual association is not unusual in Picasso. Being seated in an armchair, the figure occupies the place that female figures of an erotic nature habitually occupy in Picasso. The curved forms, more than a mere stylistic expedient, call to mind the synaesthesic qualities of the melted and the amorphous or the *formless*.

I would like to propose the relationship between this Picasso *Harlequin*

25. André Breton, "Le Surréalisme et la Peinture", in *La Révolution Surréaliste*, Year I, issue 4, Paris 15 July 1925, p. 26.

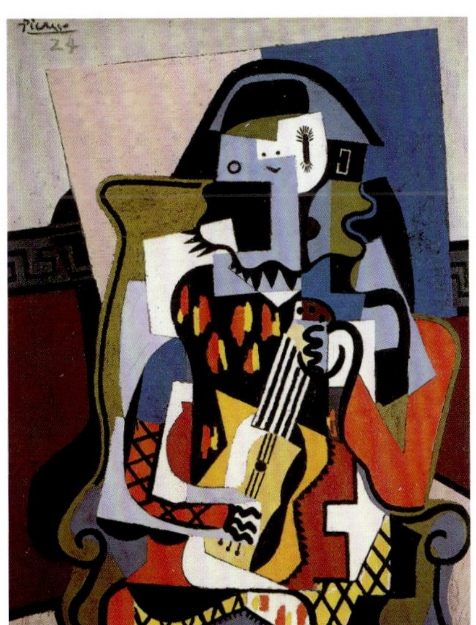

Pablo Picasso
Harlequin Musician, 1924
WASHINGTON, NATIONAL GALLERY OF ART
DONATION BY MRS. RITA SCHREIBER
IN MEMORY OF MR. TAFT SCHREIBER

and the *Harlequin* that Dalí painted in 1926—even though he put on his signature the date "1927"—which is conserved among the resources of the Museo Reina Sofía in Madrid. It is a figure with an almost monumental character. Does this size have any relationship with the megalomania described so powerfully by Freud as the quality of some extremely repressed neurotic characters such as narcissists and egocentrics? We deduce that it is a Harlequin on account of the rhomboidal grid on a segment of the lower part of the painting and of the title given to the work, because none of the harlequin's attributes is present. We think it represents a face, but we find none of the features characteristic of a face represented. We see what we cannot see. We notice a frown, a sign of anger. But neither eyes nor eyebrows are painted. We think it is a figure in a decidedly three-dimensional relief, but a black outline warns us that this relief does not exist. It is a figure of a certain thickness, but flat, with an edge—with an outline—that is precise, like a key or a coin. Everything in it is duality, polarity. Yellow and red. What Catalan or Spaniard could look at the association of these colours with indifference? The smooth and the abrupt. The abrupt thing because the piece coloured gray is soft, to the viewer's right, or is rough, to the left, as the paint is mixed with sand. The smooth and the crumpled. The smooth, in the face that is not a face is greenish blue. A marine colour. The rough side has the qualities of paper. Of the paper that has been crumpled with a hand and thrown into the waste paper bin or on the floor and has then been opened again, showing us all its creases. It is the wrinkled paper on which something has been written or drawn that is not satisfactory and has been sadly or violently rejected, and then the desire has been to recover it again typically prompted by regret. So we are faced with a painting that takes up the inheritance of Picasso's *Harlequin* stylistically, but that is developed in a key of necessary psychological interpretation, which is perhaps not even strictly Surrealist or does not keep to Freudian orthodoxy, but does not fail to evoke both.

In my opinion, this *Harlequin* of 1926 (1927) is the condensation of the *iconotema*, or of the iconographic concretion that Dalí took from Picasso's painting. In it the shaping of the evident has been suppressed by means of a sophisticated purification process.

But before returning to this *iconotema* I would like to relate this *Harlequin* of 1926 (1927) with *Pierrot Playing the Guitar* that Dalí painted in 1925. The Cubist world swapped the figures of *Harlequin* and *Pierrot*. Both appear playing the guitar in works by Picasso and Juan Gris. It has been affirmed that this painting by Dalí is the last in the *Cubist* series of his youth. But the Cubism of the piece is very relative. It is almost non-existent. We only find it in the linear and geometric delimitation of Pierrot's body. The rest of the work shows a space that is projected and contradictory in its directionality, just as it appears in some interior scenes in the work of Giorgio de Chirico and in Metaphysical painting. In the open window, the clouds are *Mantegna-style clouds* like those that appear in *Portrait of Luis Buñuel* from 1924. Although it is true that it was Juan Gris who painted *Pierrots* before the open window, Gris' open window was a window open to the moonlight, as the iconography of Pierrot demands. Dalí's Pierrot is peculiar and plays the instrument on the mid-morning of a bright summer day. So, if for some this *Pierrot Playing the Guitar* is reminiscent of Cubism, it is not only on account of the drawing of the character, since his sinewy face, seen from the front, recalls some compositions by Picasso from the years

1913 and 1914, compositions that, incidentally, have been taken as Surrealist compositions *avant-la-lettre*; but, also or mainly, because the sinewy face of Pierrot is superimposed on a profile in shadow, while, in turn, the front shadow of the figure is projected onto the wall. The front-view circular face of Pierrot has been identified by Rafael Santos Torroella (who has made such a wide-ranging and high-quality contribution to the knowledge of Dalí) with the poet Federico García Lorca, while Dalí, the profile in shadow, would be Harlequin. But perhaps Santos Torroella does not offer sufficient arguments to convince us that García Lorca is present in any of the figures of *Pierrot Playing the Guitar*. Santos Torroella is thinking of some compositions from 1926 in which Dalí represents the moonlight[26]. He affirms that García Lorca is represented in some of these compositions. He claims that the circular face of Pierrot is at the same time a schematic recreation of the circumference of the moon and of the face of García Lorca himself. But no clear resemblance exists between the face of *Pierrot Playing the Guitar* and the face of García Lorca. We find the face of Pierrot playing the guitar in Dalí's painting, as has already been anticipated, in some of Picasso's characters from 1913 and 1914 in the faces of some of the *putrefied things* that Santos Torroella himself has studied[27]. Although the concept is hard to define, Dalí, Lorca, Moreno Villa and many other personalities from the Students' Residence and from the Generation of '27 used the term *putrefied* to designate, revile and insult certain characters from Spanish and Catalan social and cultural life that were especially backward or pathetically paralysed in *over-sentimental*, crudely bourgeois or obsolete aesthetic personal formulas. Was Dalí already calling Lorca (even if lovingly) in 1925? It does not seem likely. The Pierrot painted by Dalí is smoking a pipe. García Lorca did not smoke in pipe. Dalí used to represent his plastic *alter ego* smoking a pipe. The profile in the shadow with which the circular face of Pierrot merges has been related, or is relatable, with drawings in which Dalí has represented himself or with drawings in which the artist represents another type of *putrefied thing*. Did Dalí call himself *putrefied* in 1925? It does not seem likely. A well-known picture of the *Order of Toledo*[28], in which some personalities from the Students' Residence and some of their relatives appear disguised, shows Dalí with a facial expression, clothing, a hat and pipe that could be related both to the figure of Pierrot in the painting and with the black shadow projected on the wall. There are almost more arguments to affirm that in *Pierrot Playing the Guitar* Dalí represented himself than to affirm that he was representing García Lorca. And it is worthwhile recalling now that Félix Fanés[29] and other authors have outlined the importance of self-representation in Dalí's plastic imagery.

But there is above all something that very soon began in Dalí: indeterminate meaning, open iconological meanings. There are also multiple meanings. And to use words from the rhetorical terminology, even if they are not very habitually applied: amphibology, paronomasia. That is to say, to a large extent, icons that—as Juan Antonio Ramírez has reminded us[30]—slide, condense and transform their meaning and grab meanings in their circulation from one work to another. There is also something else. There is a whole critical current that claims the presence of García Lorca in Dalí's work as an absolute certainty[31]. This critical current, which is very lucid and well informed as regards other aspects, supported by recognised institutions, has become paradigmatic when outlining the view of the young Dalí, but it has perhaps not contributed sufficiently convincing data for

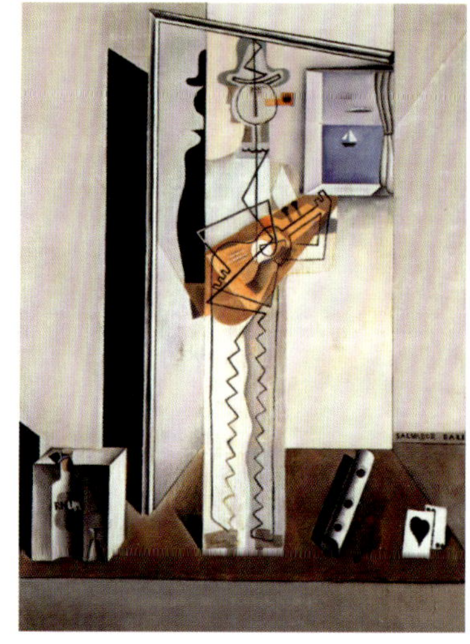

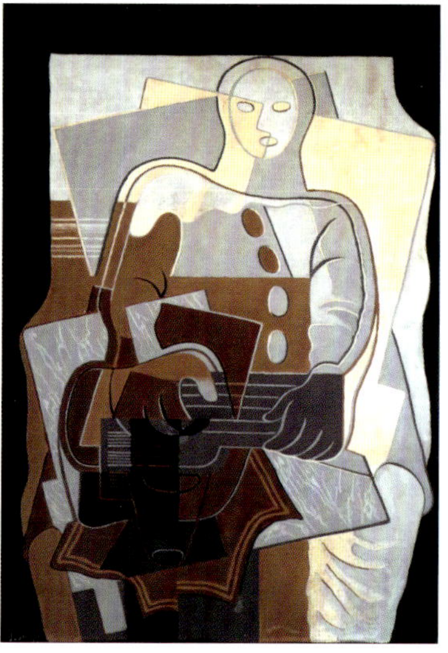

Salvador Dalí
Pierrot Playing the Guitar (Cubist Painting), 1925
MADRID, MUSEO NACIONAL CENTRO DE ARTE REINA SOFÍA

Juan Gris
Pierrot with Guitar, 1922
PRIVATE COLLECTION

26. See: Rafael Santos Torroella, *El primer Dalí. 1918-1929*, Students' Residence and Instituto Valenciano de Arte Moderno, with the collaboration of Telefónica and the Fundación Gala-Salvador Dalí, Madrid 2005, pp. 250 *et seq*.

27. Rafael Santos Torroella, *"Los putrefactos" de Dalí y Lorca - Historia y antología de un libro que no pudo ser*, Publications of the Students' Residence, High Council for Scientific Research, Madrid 1995.

28. Gathered under this name, coined by Luis Buñuel, are the comic acts and travels of a group of member of the Students' Residence. The centre of the acts and movements was the city of Toledo. Some photographs and documents of the members of the *Order of Toledo*, normally dressed up, have been ▶

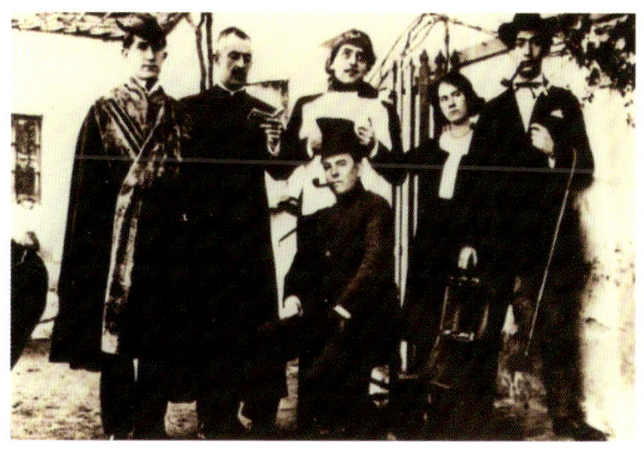

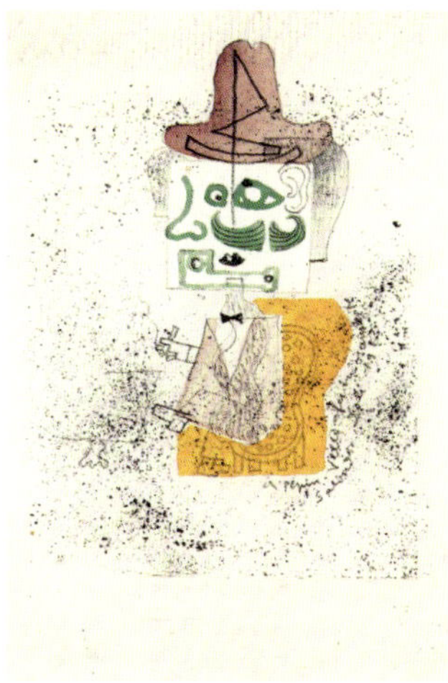

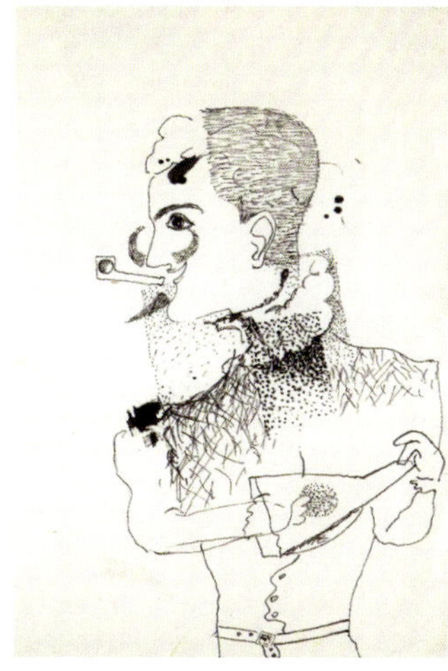

Salvador Dalí (first on the right) with Pepin Bello, Moreno Villa, José María Hinojosa and other companions attending a ceremony of the Order of Toledo, 1925
MADRID, ARCHIVO DE LA RESIDENCIA DE ESTUDIANTES

Salvador Dalí
Putrefaction (*to Pepín Bello*), 1923
MADRID, MUSEO NACIONAL CENTRO DE ARTE REINA SOFÍA

Salvador Dalí
Self Portrait, 1926
MADRID, MUSEO NACIONAL CENTRO DE ARTE REINA SOFÍA

all those interested in the painter's work. Nobody doubts the special intensity of the relationship between García Lorca and Dalí. Dalí himself stressed this in his *Secret Life*. The aesthetic diatribe between the two is one of the most important chapters in Spanish cultural history of the 20th century. But the derivations of the private relationship between the two are another matter. A certain presence of García Lorca exists in a certain space of the artwork of the young Dalí. But to consider this presence decisive is, perhaps, to project a fantasy or the desire of the critic who raises it. The interests and the references of the young Dalí were manifold and diverse. They were so many that, since Pierre Loeb commented on it in 1928, the main reproach that the international critics have made on the young Dalí has been precisely his extensive and voracious imitation of other people's formulas. It is true that Dalí transformed them, but it is also true that today they are easily readable by the contemporary viewer. Few experts have failed to notice, for example, that the decisive importance of shadow in *Pierrot Playing the Guitar* relates to the importance of shadow in the painting of Giorgio de Chirico and in the Picasso of *The Dance*, which Dalí was able to be perfectly acquainted with through the reproductions of *La Révolution Surréaliste* or by other means.

The critical divergence concerning Dalí revolves particularly around the analysis of the *iconotema* that Dalí took from Picasso in 1926. There are some who insist on seeing the fusion of the faces of García Lorca and Dalí in this iconographic concretion. The existence of drawings by García Lorca, such as the one entitled *The Kiss*, executed in 1927, where he repeats the shadow of the *iconotema* of Picasso that so obsessed Dalí, made some think that it is a shared theme and that both creators were *complicit* in its use. Although we may also think that the Lorca drawing is a response to the Dalí drawing, with a dimension of content that it never had in Dalí. There are those who, therefore, argue soundly that the iconotype that Dalí takes from Picasso is repeated in his painting as a recurrent or obsessive approach of self-representation. Perhaps it is appropriate to see that the iconotype used by Dalí does not always reveal itself as the same thing: it could be a plaster bust of academic reference, it could be a cut head, it could be a fragment, it could be the syntax of psychic splitting or it could be the motive for creating images of disturbing sexual ambiguity. And it could also be—and this is important, and the painter records it explicitly in a drawing signed in 1926—self-portrait. Also—and this too is important—Dalí did not express the psychic splitting through the icon taken from Picasso. Other

◀ conserved. Dalí, together with Buñuel, Moreno Villa, Pepín Bello, Alfonso Reyes and José María Hinojosa, participated in the actions of the *Order of Toledo*. As far as we know, García Lorca did not take part in the group's actions, which took place between 1921 and 1923.

29. In this regard, see *Fèlix Fanés, Salvador Dalí. La construcción de la imagen. 1925–1930*, Electa, Madrid 1999.

30. Juan Antonio Ramírez, *Dalí: lo crudo y lo podrido*, Antonio Machado Libros, Colección La balsa de la Medusa, Madrid 2002.

31. This *absolute* is encountered particularly in the publications of Santos Torroella, many of which have already been cited, but which have their origins in the monograph: *La miel es más dulce que la sangra. Las épocas lorquiana y freudiana de Salvador Dalí*, Seix Barral, Barcelona 1984. Ian Gibson, in his biography of Dalí, follows Santos Torroella's approaches, statements and evaluations to the letter. It is for this reason that Santos Torroella's points of view have been disseminated even further, together with the fact that most of the publications by this author are endorsed by the publisher of the Students' Residence, still prestigious today. The admirable human talent and great cultural breadth that Santos Torroella had mean that his contribution goes beyond this concrete point and his contributions and those of Gibson are of obligatory reference. But this should never conceal the opinions that, when considering the issue of the Lorca-Dalí relationship or Dalí's work in those years, are in the other corner. I wish to mention the valuable contributions by Fèlix Fanés and by Agustín Sánchez Vidal, even if it does not seem to me to be appropriate to show my greater proximity to these authors. All these issues have recently been revisited by Juan José Lahuerta in *Dalí, Lorca y la Residencia de Estudiantes*, Fundación La Caixa, Madrid 2010.

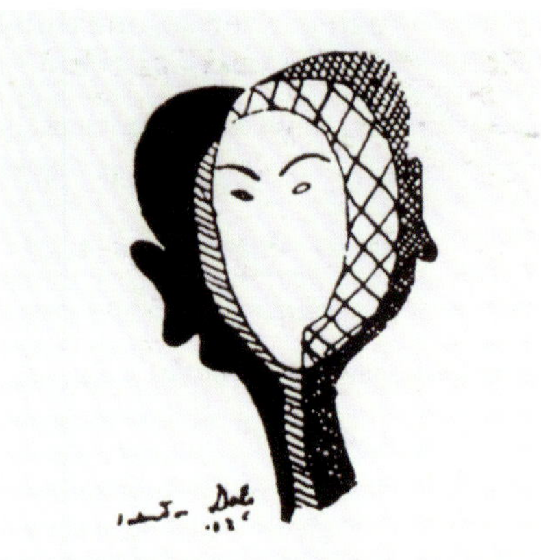

Salvador Dalí
Self Portrait, 1926
Published in L'*Amic de les Arts*, Sitges, 1927

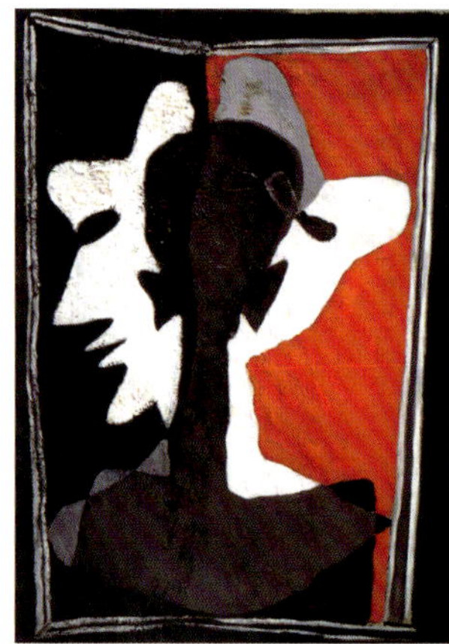

Salvador Dalí
Self Portrait Split into Three, 1926-27
FIGUERES, FUNDACIÓN GALA-SALVADOR DALÍ

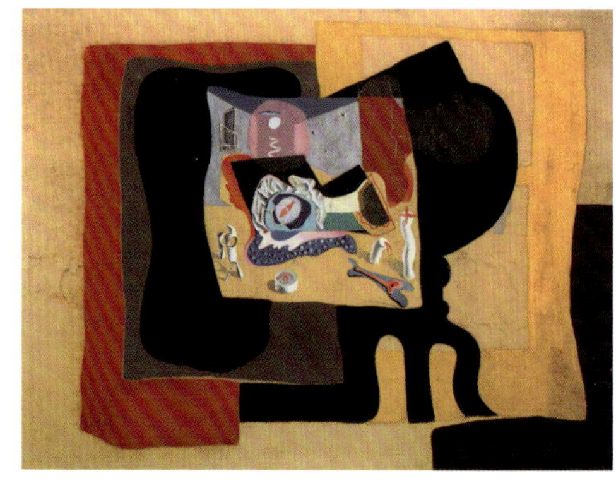

Salvador Dalí
Still Life and Mauve Moonlight, 1926
FIGUERES, FUNDACIÓN GALA-SALVADOR DALÍ

works by artists in these years, darker, less attractive, were also projected from this suggestion. In Picasso the possible reading from the *savage eye* of the inheritance of Cubist faceting also did not only occur in *Workshop with Plaster Head*. Although it is true that Dalí was obsessed with the black shadow of a head with rounded features and prominent lobed ear that appeared in the works, other compositions by Picasso, also reproduced in *Cahiers d'Art*, showed the slide from Cubist faceting towards psychological splitting or the quality of Cubist faceting for creating bicephalic or tricephalic heads or busts. And some of these images already have Marie-Thérèse Walter as their model, which is extremely important in suggesting that these icons were also created in Picasso not from a merely formalist viewpoint but through a certain emotional tension.

With the latter being true, what is clear is that the extent of *debt* that Dalí's work owes to that of Picasso, after the possible viewing in 1926, needs to be elucidated in all its complexity. Also needing to be elucidated is the *reading* (or the *readings*) that Dalí made of Picasso's work. Some *readings* did not begin in 1926 but at least two years earlier, and have not always been sufficiently reported, since it is necessary to find the *obvious* side and the *non-obvious* side in them, with the latter possibility perhaps being much more interesting.

Let us set another starting point in the interpretations that Dalí makes of Picasso.

In 1924, Dalí was thinking about the encounter with Classicism. Thus Josep Subías presented him on the pages of *Alfar*, a very influential magazine at the time in the environments of *new art*. Dalí intended to surprise his friends. In his brief text, Subías says many things. He says that Dalí's current moment, in May of 1924, is that of "precise vision" and of "heroic learning, of something exempt from lyricism", and cites the painters that the young artist from Cadaqués admired at that moment: Raphael, Poussin and Ingres, no less. Subías also cites Matisse, Goncharova and Larinov, Marc Chagall and Juan Gris. He does not mention Picasso and most of the works reproduced in the article have to do with *Noucentisme* and not so much with Classicism proper. Are we dealing with yet another of Dalí's *tricks*? At least we cannot think that Dalí was unaware to Subías' text and that Subías' text was innocent. Strictly speaking, Dalí's move towards Classicism went via another path.

The young Dalí was always, stylistically, a nomadic, multiple Dalí. We know the order in which his works were exhibited, but we do not know the

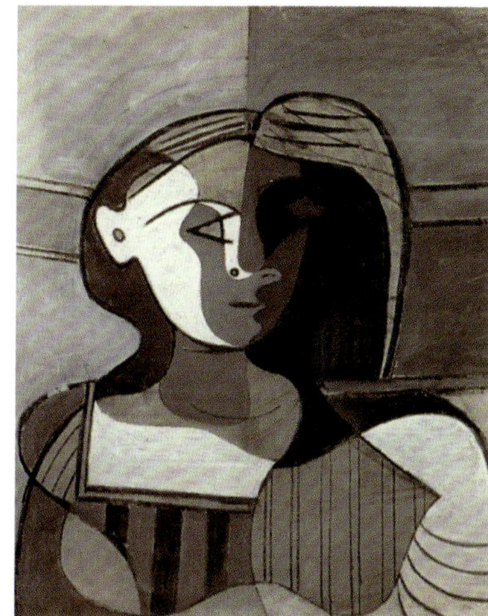

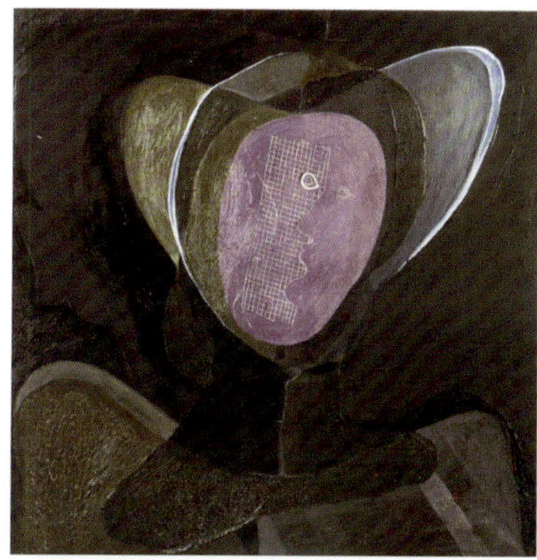

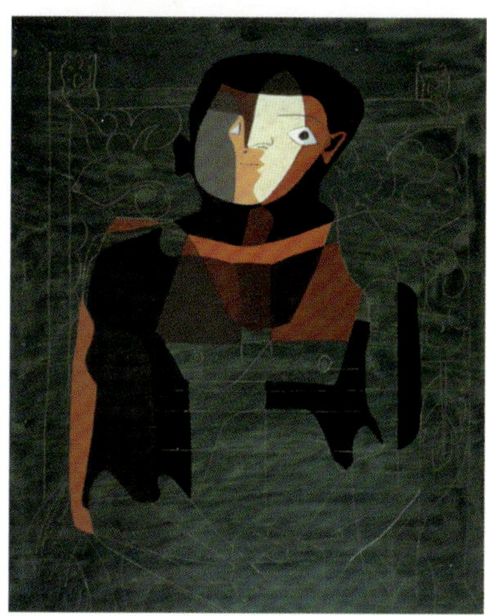

Pablo Picasso
Bust of Young Woman (*Marie-Thérèse Walter*), 1926
STRASBOURG, MUSÉE DES BEAUX-ARTS

Pablo Picasso
Head, 1926
FIGUERES, FUNDACIÓN GALA-SALVADOR DALÍ

Pablo Picasso
Man Seated in an Armchair, 1925
ARTIST'S HEIRS

order in which those with a similar chronology were created. Even so, one thing appears clear. With a view to reaching maturity, Dalí began his links with a new Classicism through two works, two oil paintings on cardboard, currently conserved in the collection of Museo Reina Sofía: *Nude in the Water* and *Nude*. Both pieces can be considered among Dalí's most significant realisations, even if they are usually disregarded somewhat, considered as *exercises* performed by Dalí in his brief period in the studio of academic painter Julio Moisés. But in around the year 1924, some of the most outstanding representatives in plastic renovation in Madrid would meet up in Julio Moisés' studio and nothing that these young proponents of *new art* executed there was banal or incidental. If these works, for some critics, are strange in the young Dalí, it is because they present unusual approaches in the painter: the aesthetic premises of the fragment and of the *unfinished*. And they also mark the arrival, clearly of another register that Dalí never wanted to make evident: that of eroticism. The value of these pieces is therefore double, one that they possess intrinsically and the other that of indicating that when Dalí chose the path of *another* Classicism he did so in a deliberate and conscious way, without allowing himself to be swayed, as is said so many times, by any *fashion* in the sphere of the *new*. Rather, if those in favour of *new art* sought the formula of Modern Classicism, it was to a large extent Dalí who showed the way to go.

The *other* Classicism towards which Dalí decided to guide his work was no novelty, since it was Picasso's Classicism. In 1924, when he decided to adopt the register of the Classical Picasso, Dalí was aged 20. Indeed, he was still very young and it could well be thought that the desire to emulate that is typical of his age was in play in him. But Dalí had already given sufficient proof that, as Moreno Villa said, in everything concerning the -isms, he almost knew too much. In 1924 Picasso's Classicism was already practically no more. In Barcelona and in Madrid, as we have already seen, the existence of the Classical Picasso was *detected* and publicised from 1916 and 1918. It is true that in their chronicles from Paris, Josep de Togores, who followed Dalí closely, still spoke of the move of Cubists towards Classicism[32]. It is also true that, in 1924, the monograph on Picasso published by Waldemar George in the Editions of *Valori Plastici*, the writings of Maurice Raynal in *L'Art d'Aujourd'hui*, those of Cocteau in *Art & Decoration* or the reproductions of the artist's works in *La Nouvelle Revue Française* could have encouraged a reconsideration of the Classical Picasso. Even so, and even if this was considerable, it was not sufficient. Dalí deliberately made a choice that was against the trend. Already at the age of 20 the painter was able to make the choice that most suited both his strategy and his character, irrespective of what the historical situation might favour or demand.

Twenty years after his choice, on the pages of *Secret Life*, as we have already commented, Dalí remembered the importance of his choice:

> "On my arrival in Figueres I found my father thunderstruck by the catastrophe of my expulsion, which had shattered all his hopes that I might succeed in an official career. With my sister, he posed for a pencil drawing which was one of my successful of this period. In the expression of my father's face can be seen the mark of the pathetic bitterness which my expulsion from the Academy had produced on him.

> At the same time that I was doing these more and more rigorous drawings, I executed a series of mythological paintings in which I tried to draw positive conclusions from my Cubist experience by linking its lessons on geometric order to the eternal principles of the tradition"[33].

If in the Academy of San Fernando the idea that modernity was Impressionism was defended, Dalí, in his confrontation with it, would decide to stand against that supposed modernity by laying claim to its opposite: Classicism. And later on, if the *sensitive connoisseurs* of art that for Dalí were *putrefied* found in Impressionism and its inheritance the essence of the painterly, the response could not be other than that of being anti-art, fostering a Classicist and Objectivist register. The move from Cubism to the new Classicism was at the basis of what Dalí was developing, but it was not his only motivation.

In the drawings with his father and his sister as models or in the study for the *Portrait of María Carbona*, Dalí reissued the *Ingresco* Picasso that the magazine *Vell i Nou* had published years previously. But, by taking compositional precision to the extreme and by eliminating any Expressionist temptation, always present in Picasso, Dalí erased the dividing line existing between new Classicism and Modern Realism. This was something that happened in a certain number of European painters and that Hartlaub and Franz Roh have outlined in their writings. From this premise certain important works by Dalí emerged, such as *Portrait of Luis Buñuel*, most of the portraits and compositions with figures in which Anna María Dalí was used as the model, and the small yet significant oil *The Girl of Figueres*.

However, in 1925, in a work such as *Venus and Cupid* Dalí's assumption of Classicism was to experience a turning point. Santos Torroella has shown how Dalí worked using a strict geometrical structuring of the volumes of the painting; this was something that the painter was to develop in other works and that made reference both to the writings of Severini and to the unexpected recovery of principles of geometry applied to painting in the Renaissance. Even so, in this painting Dalí offers for view, albeit in embryonic form, the first formulations of a perceptive and cognitive principle that would end up obsessing him and would appear in his youthful writings through a citing of Breton: the possibility that it is reality, outlined in its concise character of presentation, that contains the principles of sur-reality.

In *Venus and Cupid*, the Mediterranean landscape shows its intrinsic qualities in extreme form—uninhabitable rocky profiles, mouths of caves, strangely-shaped clouds, the still of the sea—creating in the spectator a sensation poised between the real and the imaginary. From this characteristic, which modifies the supposed neutral space of the view, the relationship between *Venus and Cupid*—which does not have the gestural language that the history of art has allocated to this topic—mimics, in its ambiguity, the relationship between mother and son. And, in doing so, he opens up the contemplation of the painting, unconsciously for the uninformed viewer and consciously for the experienced viewer, to the *gaze*, to the *vision* that psychoanalytical theory establishes. It is curious. We know, thanks to Moreno Villa and to other data recently found that, in his years at the Students' Residence, Dalí was an avid reader of Freud. But it was not until his return to Figueras that Dalí began to outline a subtle effect

32. Today the place occupied by Josep de Togores in the European art between the wars is not totally recognised. His work was commented on by Franz Roh and by the French critics and his production was managed for some years by Kahnweiler. On arriving in Paris, in 1919, he sent articles and texts to the periodicals and magazines of Barcelona, in which he theorised, based on his own media, on the passage from Cubism to the new Classicism. His influence was very great, and even decisive, on the young Miró and Dalí. On the writings of Togores in those years, consult: Eugenio Carmona, "Josep de Togores y la belleza impasible", in *Josep de Togores. Clasicismo y renovación. (Obra de 1914 a 1931)*, edited by Josep Casamartina and Marta González, Museo Nacional Centro de Arte Reina Sofía, Madrid 1997, pp. 14–25.

33. Dalí, *The Secret Life*, *cit.*, p. 204.

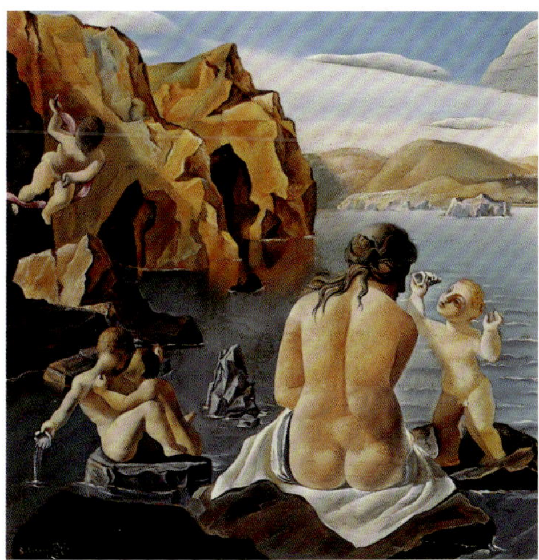

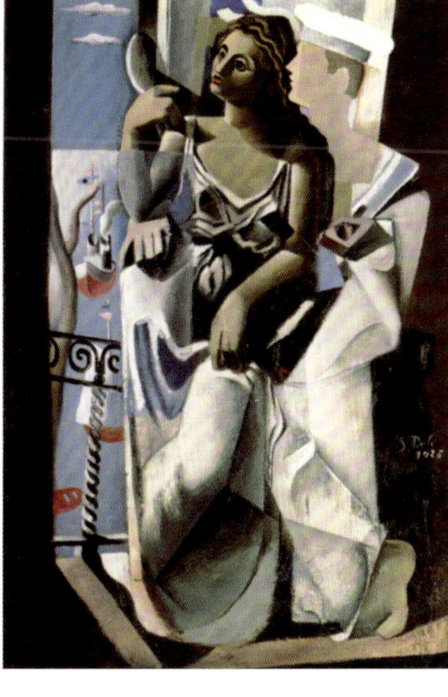

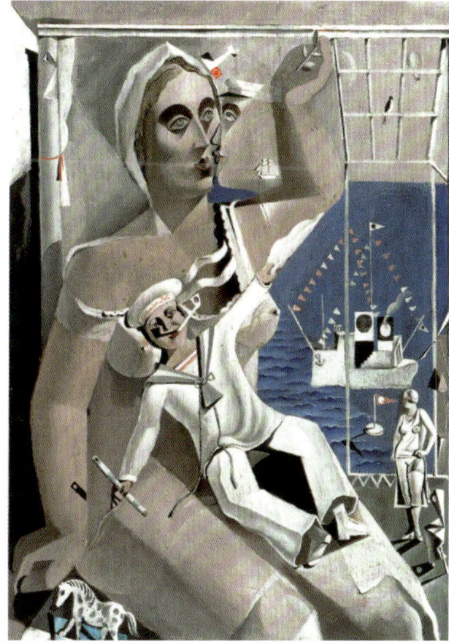

Salvador Dalí
Venus and Cupids, 1925
PRIVATE COLLECTION

Salvador Dalí
Venus and a Sailor. Homage to Salvat-Papasseit, 1925
SHIZOUKA-KEN, IKEDA MUSEUM OF 20TH CENTURY ART

Salvador Dalí
Departure. Homage to the Noticiario Fox, 1926
PRIVATE COLLECTION

of amphibology in his works. It was in this sense that Dalí himself called these paintings *mythological*[34].

The process followed by Dalí extended to the number of compositions in which the artist proposed the iconographic articulation of a female figure and a sailor. The sailor, a recurring theme in the spheres of *new art* and in the poetry of the Generation of '27[35], connoted the principles of free love and without obstacles in sexual definition. But he sometimes becomes a shadow, as in *Venus and Sailor. Homage to Salvat-Papasseit*, and he ends up becoming a boy, as in the work from 1926, *Departure. Homage to the Noticiario Fox*. That is to say, childish eroticism contains mature eroticism, as Dalí would say to us, echoing Freud. And this statement would be completed with the process of *displacement* in the iconological meaning of the female figure. The female figure—within a stylistic configuration typical of the Classical Picasso—is several things in one: she is a girl who expresses her sex, she is a prostitute, she is a mother, she is a goddess. Her clothing is also an amphibological iconography, because it wavers between intimate feminine nightwear and the Doric tunic. The female figure of these works by Dalí is located in the collective imagination of typical male neurosis, while the figure of the sailor extends the image of the development of the perverse polymorph into man's adulthood.

All this baggage, complex, latent, non-evident even though existing, was taken up and reconfigured by Dalí in the work that is the masterly culmination of this series and that, as the culmination, delves into other meanings. I am referring to *Composition with Three Figures. Neocubist Academy* (a work that is also known by another, less common title, *The Sailor. Neocubist Academy*.

The painting, large in size, 190 x 200 cm, was present in the exhibition that Dalí held in Dalmau between December 1926 and January 1927 and *L'Amic de les Arts* readily reproduced it on the first page of its first issue for the year 1927, publishing in this same issue an article by Foix on the painter, and announcing articles by Gasch and Cassanyes for the February issue. The piece therefore aroused as much expectation as the exhibition and the painter.

We are presented with a work with a peculiar path. I would like to have said: *presented with a mysterious work*. The painting was quickly bought by some relatives of Dalí's father, remaining in private hands for a long time. The

---

34. I therefore believe that there is a translation of certain Freudian principles into Dalí's work. But I do not believe there is a Freudian Dalí as Santos Torroella proposes.

35. I am thinking of the work by Maruja Mallo, that by Gregorio Prieto and the drawings of Lorca. I am thinking of some poems by Alberti and some of the work of Chilean poet Pablo Neruda collected in *Veinte poemas de amor y una canción desesperada*.

painting could practically not be seen until it was donated to the Museum of the Monastery of Montserrat. For a long time, even in important publications on the artist it had to appear reproduced in black and white and with rather unacceptable quality, which gave the impression that the reproduction reproduced in turn the photograph published in *L'Amic de les Arts*.

This circumstance has rather delayed the knowledge of the painting, and the difficulties in knowing the piece have perhaps influenced its interpretation[36]. First there is the title, which for some reason has never been particularly taken into account. The fact that the work is entitled *Composition with Three Figures* or that it is entitled *The Sailor* is not trivial: it is an invitation to begin to decode it. In the painting there are many more than three figures. One could say that the work is populated, almost *improperly*, with iconographic elements. But if we highlight a certain number we are led, perhaps, to the relationship between the three figures with the most presence as articulators of possible meanings. We will return to these three figures later. On the other hand, the fact that the work is entitled *The Sailor* indicates a main figure, a *protagonist*, that makes us start out with an initial identification that does not move us away from others, but rather locates these other interpretations of the male figure in the painting in the terrain of the indeterminate. If we place the emphasis in *The Sailor* as the title we are immediately relating this work with other previous ones, in which the figure of the sailor—whether adult or boy, corporeal or almost ghostly—serves to allude to love free of commitment or, in the case of the sailor boy, to establish peculiar suggestions on the relationship between mother and son in the broader sphere of the reception of some topics of original psychoanalysis.

On the other hand, it is well known that Dalí sent a photograph to García Lorca specifying to him that the work was entitled *Neocubist Academy*. This other title is also undoubtedly intended to conceal more complex meanings. But at the same time, it is a name that seems to be dedicated to the artistic circles of Madrid and Catalonia. The influence of Classical Picasso is evident in the three main figures on the canvas. But it is a Classical Picasso whose *page has been amended*. Dalí makes *a* Classical Picasso that is even more Classical than the Classical Picasso himself. The figures are more structured, solid and architectural; the Expressionist accent, the distortions and the unfinished elements that Picasso used to execute have been eliminated from them; and much clearer geometrical and simplifying facetings have been deposited in them than those that Picasso used at any time. And these geometrical facetings are perhaps what Dalí calls *Neocubism*. That is to say, for Dalí, *Neocubism* was the step from Cubism to Classicism, to Classicism structured soberly and *skilfully* by geometry. Dalí calls Neocubism what it would be better to denominate New Classicism. The painter performs a concealment by naming his own style. In 1924 he wanted to be recognised as *Classical*. In 1926 no longer. Although it is true that it was not only his Picassian Classicism that could be referred to as *Neocubist*. The bust deposited in the foreground, in the centre of the composition, is a recreation of the iconotype that we have converted, *almost*, into the protagonist of the *interpretation* that Dalí made of Picasso. *Neocubism* was also, therefore, tending his Cubist drawing towards the curved form and the versatile arabesque to create a complex form, articulated in facets. This is true, but no less true than the fact that, wherever it came from and whoever welcomed it, in 1926, Dalí's Neocubism was already, in the general context of

---

36. I would like to comment that I had the opportunity to present a detailed analysis of this work in the seminar, conducted by Joan Minguet Batllorí, *Dalí, art, anti-art y surrealisme* held at the Fundaciò Miró in Barcelona in 2004, in conjunction with the exhibition dedicated to the *Manifest Groc*; unfortunately the conclusions presented there have not been published to date.

37. See: Letter XVI in *Salvador Dalí escribe a Federico García Lorca, 1925-1936*, in *Poesía*, issue 27-28, Madrid, 1978, p. 42, Presentation, notes and chronology by Rafael Santos Torroella. The letter is a fragment and is not dated. The dating is by Santos Torroella. It is very significant that Dalí is already showing his rejection of nature and his liking for the Charleston and for elements of so-called *modern living*.

38. *San Sebastián* is undoubtedly a key text in the evolution of the young Dalí towards Surrealism and the formulation of the paranoiac-critical. The text is dedicated to García Lorca. "San Sebastià" was published for the first time, in the original Catalan, in *L'Amic de les Arts*, Year II, issue 16, Sitges 31 July 1927, pp. 52–4. It was translated into Spanish for the first time in García Lorca's magazine, *Gallo*, Granada, Year I, issue 1, February 1928, pp. 9–12. The notes by Juan José Lahuerta are very interesting in the edition of the text in Salvador Dalí, *Obra completa. Volumen IV. Ensayos 1. Artículos, 1919-1986*, Ediciones Destino, Fundación Gala-Salvador Dalí and Sociedad Estatal de Conmemoraciones Culturales, Barcelona 2005, pp. 912 *et seq*. For my part, I commented on this text by Dalí in "Ironía. Instinto", *cit*.

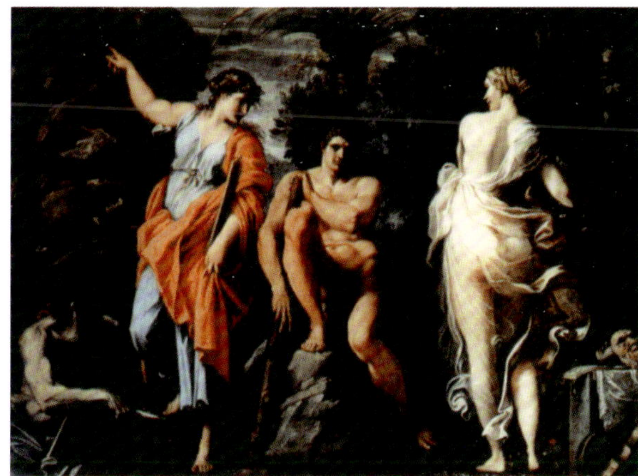

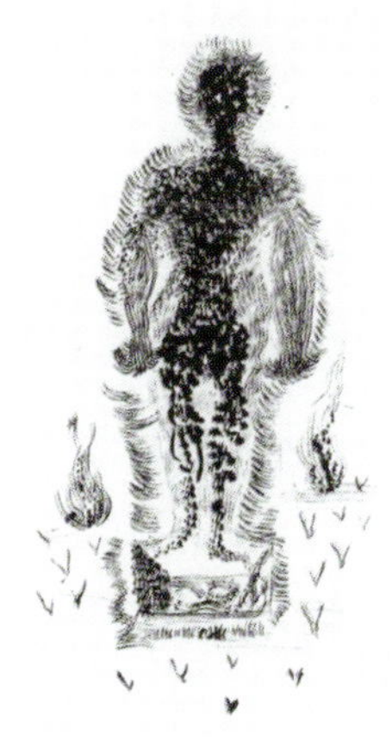

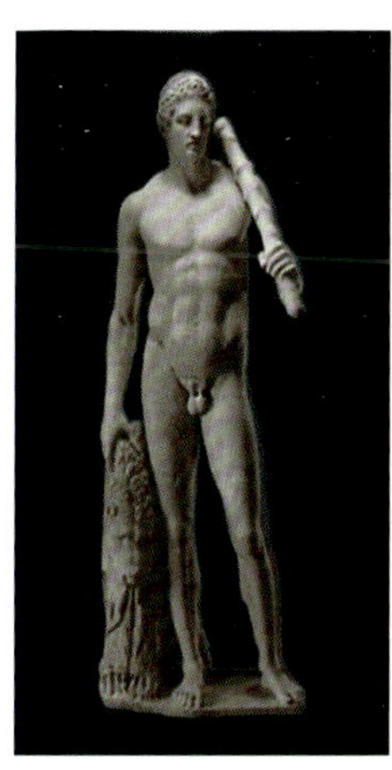

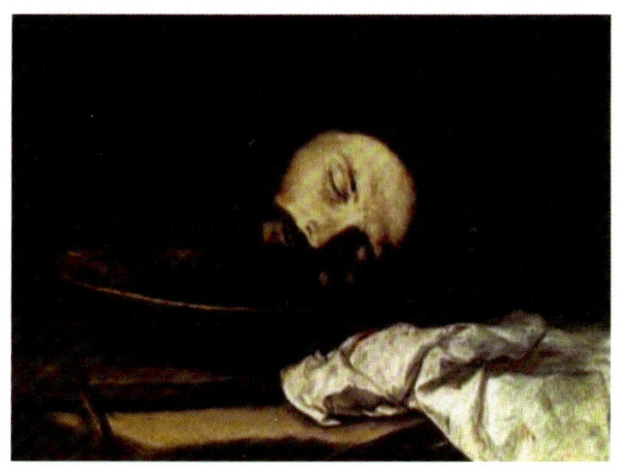

Annibale Carracci
Choice of Hercules
c. 1595–96
NAPLES, MUSEO NAZIONALE DI CAPODIMONTE

Salvador Dalí
Figure on Fire
c. 1927
ST. PETERSBURG, FLORIDA, THE SALVADOR DALÍ MUSEUM

Young Hercules, 125 AD
LOS ANGELES, CALIFORNIA, J. PAUL GETTY MUSEUM

José de Ribera
The Baptist's Head, 1644
NAPLES, MUSEO CIVICO GAETANO BANGIERI

the Modern Movement, and the wordplay is a valid one, *Postcubism*. And in Dalí this late Cubism, and its assumption of Modern Classicism, was used from 1925, as we have seen, to provide cover for complex symbolic, iconographic and psychological approaches. Therefore, to entitle the work *Necubist Academy* was to perform a task of concealment, but also to note—and this is important—that the entire Neocubist and Neo-Classicist sequence of the Spanish renewers had its effect in transforming the Modern into an *academy*. A contradiction. A paradox. Also a disqualification. Dalí disqualified the Neocubist and Neo-Classicist efforts of his *friends* of *new art*, and he also disqualified himself. Dalí liked the irony. And it is undoubtedly necessary to understand his painting from 1926 from the position of paradox and irony. And in particular it is necessary to understand that we are referring to his painting from 1926 in terms of plastic language and for him it was not this. As we will see.

In short, between the names and the languages: irony and paradox. Games too. As soon as we stand before this painting by Dalí, the rhetoric of "*the painting within the painting*" becomes powerful. To Neocubism and Neo-Classicism, Dalí adds a *Baroque* sleight of hand. Deception of vision, duality between appearance and reality, lucubration above all; Dalí is telling us that we are not contemplating one work, but several, and that, therefore, any unitary or univocal reading that we make is destined to fail or only to survive in its own partiality. But few Dalinian commentators (including the undersigned) have the capacity to articulate the holed sponge of *points of view*.

Some scholars of the artist and of *Neocubist Academy* have immediately associated the male figure that dominates the work with the image of Saint Sebastian. This is due to the fact that a reference to Saint Sebastian—together with the citing of the aesthetics of *Holy Objectivity*—is already made in a letter from Dalí to Lorca that could be dated at the beginning of the summer of 1926[37]. According to this, in Dalí's thought, the drafting of the essay entitled, in fact, *Saint Sebastian*[38], which he was to complete almost a year later, and the creation of *Neocubist Academy* shared a chronology for a few months. From the point of view of these scholars and commentators, the *Neocubist Academy* was supposedly a step further in all that is related with *Saint Sebastian* as prevalent myth in the context of Dalí's special relationship with the poet García Lorca. The pose of the right arm of the figure is reminiscent of the pose of the Saint Sebastians in Renaissance and Baroque paintings. Behind the figure, but visible to the spectator, is a strange space that is not well identified, but that could be a tree trunk. There is all this, but strictly speaking there is nothing more. Nothing further in the painting makes reference to the iconography of the saint in his martyrdom.

However, the work, when contemplated as such, perhaps as Dalí would want, namely without passion, with distance, with *lyrical objectivity,* has another *stamp.* If we contemplate the group of three figures referred to in the title of the painting, any scholar of the iconographies of the paintings of the Age of Humanism may detect the possibility—or the *motivated* intuition—of relating this triad with the one that is offered habitually when representing *The Choice of Hercules,* that is, *Hercules between Vice and Virtue,* the so-called *psychomachia.* What is more, the trio in Dalí's work brings to mind the well-known composition that Annibale Caracci was to devote to the theme, in around 1596, which is conserved today in the Museo Nazionale di Capodimonte in Naples, while the male figure in the painting by the artist from Cadaqués reminds us of the well-known sculpture representing young Hercules in the Paul Getty Collection.

In the *Neocubist Academy,* the female figure on the spectator's left, reclining in this potent foreshortening, is clinging to the rock, to the earth, she is telluric. The profile in shadow, almost masculine, like the profile in shadow painted by Picasso in *La Dance,* endows her with mystery and yet makes us understand that one of the essential meanings of shadow in Dalí could not be otherness, but sameness[39]. This figure shows her sexual area uncovered, but she does so chastely, without displaying her vagina: everything in her is *concept.* Her breasts, extremely turgid, are solid as mountains and a whitish halo connects her body with the face of the male figure. She is, in the roles of the *psychomachia,* the equivalent of *vice,* this is, attachment to earthly pleasures and the search for happiness in them. In the Dalinian imagination she is not vice, but *nature,* what the artist wants to avoid, although it attracts him: the sentimental feature, the epiphany of the sensorial, amorous *disorder.*

On the other side, the female figure on the spectator's right is, initially, ambiguous: she seems to be a goddess or a mythological being, but she is wearing not exactly a *peplos* but something similar to silk or satin nightwear. The same thing happens in other of Dalí's previous female figures. The artist always provoked this ambiguity. It was a calculated ambiguity: the image of the woman mother/lover, goddess/prostitute; these were *hesitancies* that in Freudian literature mark the tortuous, unresolved step of the perverse polymorph through the structures of the Oedipus Complex. But in the space of the *psychomachia,* she is *virtue.* And this is because she is erect and has fingers. She is the measurable, *what can be counted*[40]. Her profile in shadow—again Picasso[41]—makes her as mysterious as her antagonist. But on her head, barely distinguishable in photographic reproductions, particularly in the photographic reproductions in black and white, Dalí painted some geometrical figures: a circle, a prism with an engraved cylinder; there even appears the prefiguring of one of the Dalinian *apparatuses.* She is, therefore, the calculation, the mathematical, *astronomy*: the *lyricism* that arises, according to Dalí, from the containing of the primary human passions.

Due to its well-built form, the physique of the male figure is more relatable to that of a young Hercules (Hercules appeared in the *psychomachia* in his youth) than to the Apollonian and slender tone of the Saint Sebastians. On his back, this Hercules has the tunic of Nessers with the blood of the centaur, in the form of a spider, mixed with poison from the Hydra. It is the tunic on

39. He endows her with mystery and relates her to the true meaning of shadow in Dalí.

40. This phrase, which appears in Dalí's text *San Sebastián,* is very important within this text, attributed to the fisherman Enriquet, since it indicates the supremacy of Rational art in Dalí over any form of sentimentalism, biologism or surrender to nature.

41. Of course, the profile in shadow of this figure does not refer so much to her but is a copy of the profiles in shadow developed by Picasso in *La Dance* and in works immediately prior to and following this piece from 1925. The profiles in shadow by Picasso developed starting from 1917 are different, particularly from the disappearance of the marked angularity of the shadow of the nose.

This circumstance has rather his back that identifies Hercules in his final moment: that of his material disintegration that completed the heating of the waters that came to be named, for it same, starting from then, *Thermopylae*. On the same dates of the realization of the painting, or a little later, Dalí drew figures disintegrating[42]. And it is curious that Dalí, cancelling out the narrative conventions in the temporary development, joins together two different moments from the life of Hercules (or Heracles), that of the *psychomachia* and that of his earthly disappearance.

But the male figure in the painting is further complicated by several elements. One of these is by absence. Dalí has avoided representing the genitals of the protagonist of his painting. The shadow emerges of emasculation. Or at least it is made clear that the painter does not want his figure to have a sexual role. With it the artist, we would say, is simply expressing his *symptom* and his need to escape from nature. But the polysemy becomes even more complex when this male figure appears with sailor's cap, and this sailor's cap is combined with another element of the figure that, although attached to his body, seems extraneous to him: a forearm with marks blue veins and with a closed fist pressing on a perforated small cane. Apparently alien to its own body, this fragment of a figure need to be related to the icon of the cut-off hand that was so powerful in the Dalí of those years. Initially this icon was taken, again, from various of Picasso's still lifes from the second half of the 1920s. Still lifes by Picasso in which, surprisingly, the artist from Malaga evokes the academic representations of Hercules made in his childhood. This motif, separated from the body, is taken up again in drawings and photographs by Dalí himself and by García Lorca in these years, and I would like to bring up the fact that Freud, in his well-known text on *The Uncanny* (*Das Unheimliche*), cites the stories of Hauff. Among Hauff's short stories there is one devoted to a severed hand. Hauff was translated into Spanish by Calpe in 1920 and surprisingly the emblem of the publisher's Calpe is the demigod Hercules performing one of his labours. On the other hand, the perforated cane that holds down the sailor in *Neocubist Academy* is the same one that holds down the boy dressed as a sailor of another painting by Dalí from 1926, a crucial painting in his career path and in those years: *Departure. Homage to the Noticiario Fox*. In this painting, on the boy's sailor's cap, which is identical to the sailor's cap of the figure that we are commenting on in *Neocubist Academy*, Dalí inscribed his name. Is Dalí himself the boy dressed as a sailor, the emasculated Hercules in the heart of the *psychomachia*, the final Hercules about to disintegrate, the vagrant echo of a Saint Sebastian? The iconographic repetition of *Departure. Homage to the Noticiario Fox* is one of the few paintings by Dalí in which allusions appear to *modern life*, which the painter denominated *anti-art*, at the same time that the double role of the sailors and the identity of the female figure in connection with them demand an in-depth psychological approach from him. We have already seen this previously. But the painting becomes even more complex by the introduction into it of an element that is stylistically heterogeneous with respect to the whole. I am referring to the bust already mentioned, which, evidently, is a severed head, and which harkens back to other previous paintings by Dalí, but which opens up an iconographic sphere that is not only different to that of Hercules but even to that of Saint Sebastian, because it refers to the decapitated head of Saint John the Baptist. Another myth, like Saint Sebastian, that through religious iconography is transmuted

42. No precise catalogue of these figures exists, but the majority are conserved at the Fundación Gala-Salvador Dalí.

to the plane of the relations between sexual possession and violence; violence that leads, in any case, to the destruction of the beloved[43]. In *Neocubist Academy* Dalí traced an entire complex, polysemic and amphibological iconographic programme. Stylistically, the work participated in the same principles. The commentators of the time did not say anything regarding both parameters. How was Dalí able to keep all his codes so secret? Why did he not want to unveil them? Normally painters of Dalí's type do not reveal either their sources or their intentions. Or else they give false clues. Picasso always did both. But, in this case, Dalí had additional reasons.

When beginning to speak about *Neocubist Academy* I commented on the reception of the painting by the group of editors of the magazine *L'Amic de les Arts*. In his commentary, Sebastià Gasch dwells on the geometrical structuring that governs the composition of the work, but before explaining it he affirms that the canvas "has the appearance of a cinema overprint, because of the simultaneous representation of an interior and an exterior"[44]. Later on Gasch would reproach Dalí in a friendly way for imitating Picasso so much. But the fact that Dalí, through the mouth of Gasch, related his work to a film technique came to mean that the artist had begun his anti-art broadside in favour of mass culture, a moment that marks the passage of his work to his period of maturity. The iconographic complexity of *Neocubist Academy* was admirable, but in early 1927 Dalí no longer wanted to remember that. He was going to another place. Perhaps he had realised that the stage of his youth was over. ■

43. Could these Dalinian decapitated heads not be related to the description of the head of Saint Sebastian that Dalí gave in his text with the saint's name? If this is the case, the reference to Saint Sebastian would not be in the male figure in the painting but, paradoxically, in the bust with the form of a decapitated head.

44. Sebastià Gasch, "Les arts. Salvador Dalí", in *L'Amic de les Arts*, issue 11, Sitges February 1927.

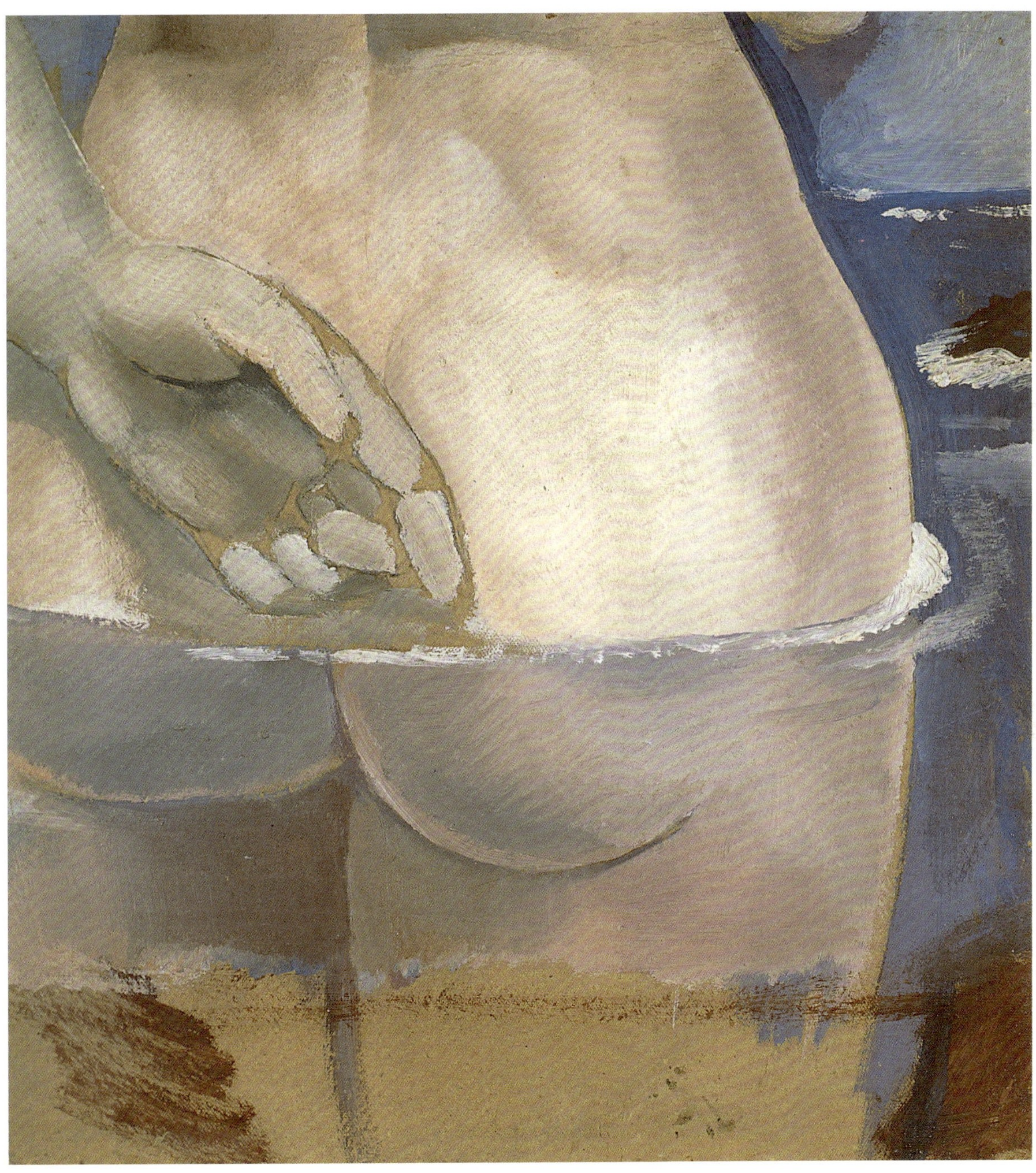

1.1 Salvador Dalí
Nude in the Water
[Nu a l'aigua / Desnudo en el agua]
c. 1924
MADRID, MUSEO NACIONAL CENTRO DE ARTE REINA SOFÍA. DE01567

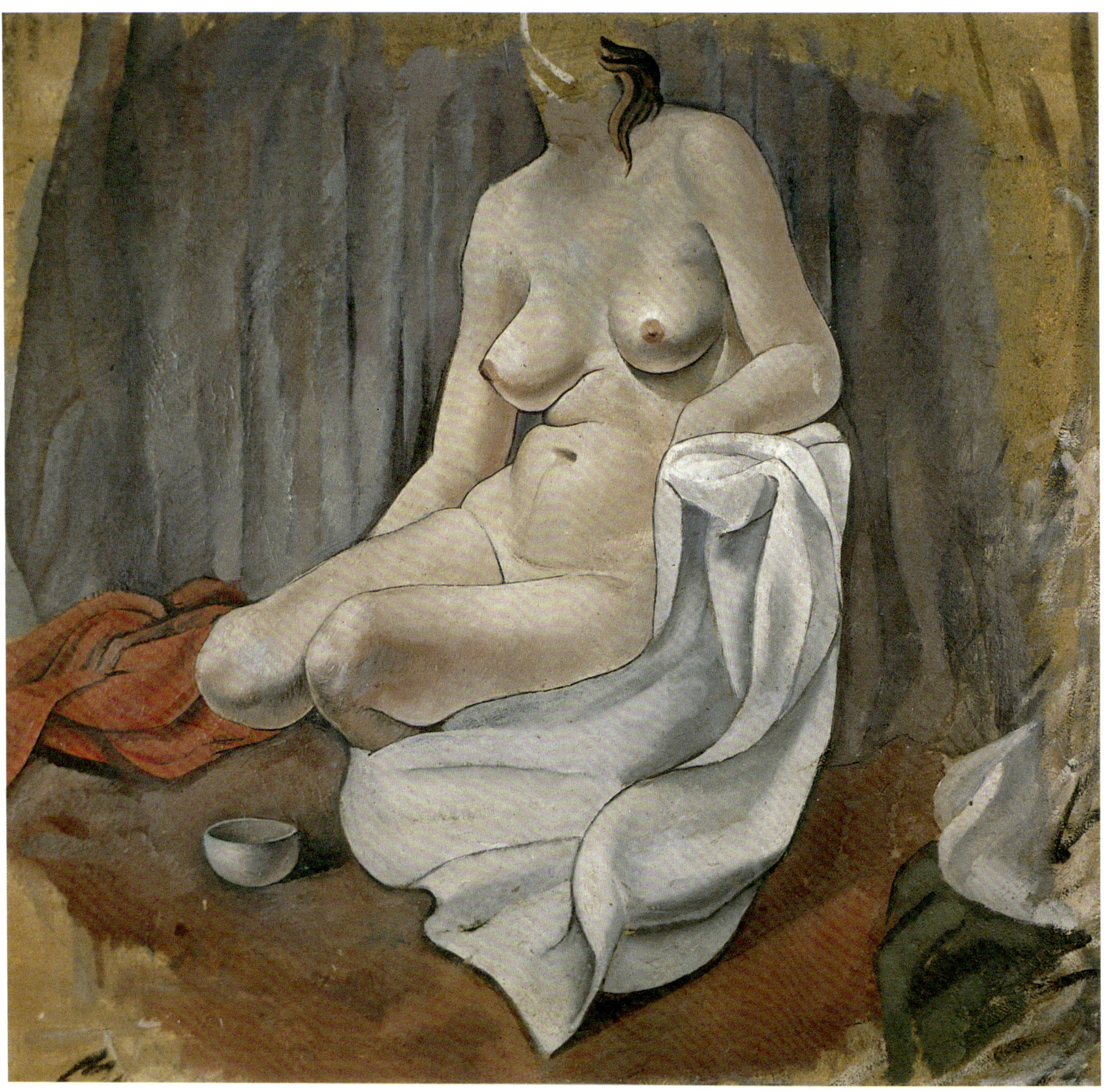

1.2 Salvador Dalí
Nude
[Nu / Desnudo]
1924
MADRID, MUSEO NACIONAL CENTRO DE ARTE REINA SOFÍA. DE01566

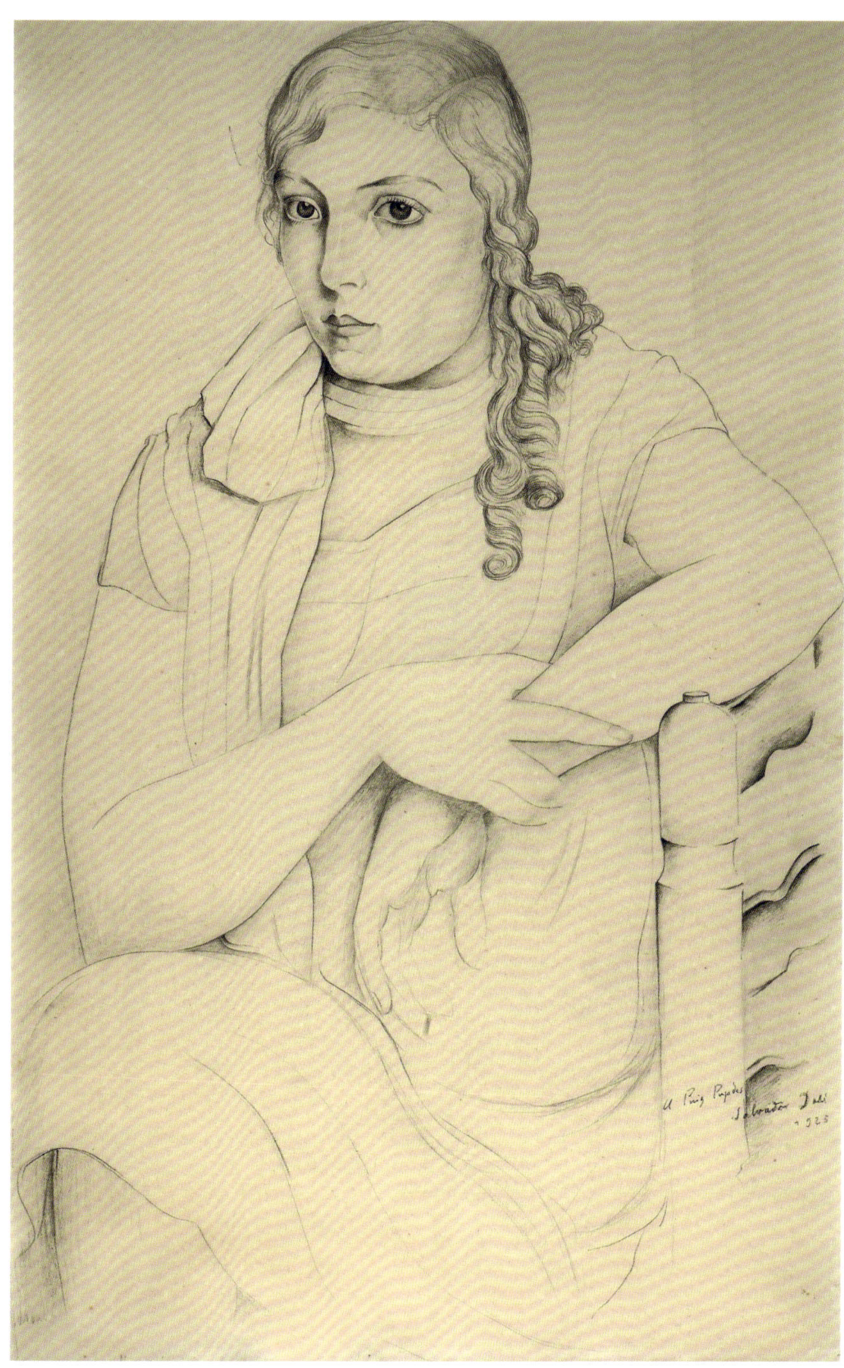

1.3 Salvador Dalí
Previous Sketch for "Portrait of Maria Carbona"
[Estudi per el "Retrat de María Carbona"]
1925
MUSEU DE MONTSERRAT. DONATED BY J. SALA ARDIZ. R.N. 200.413

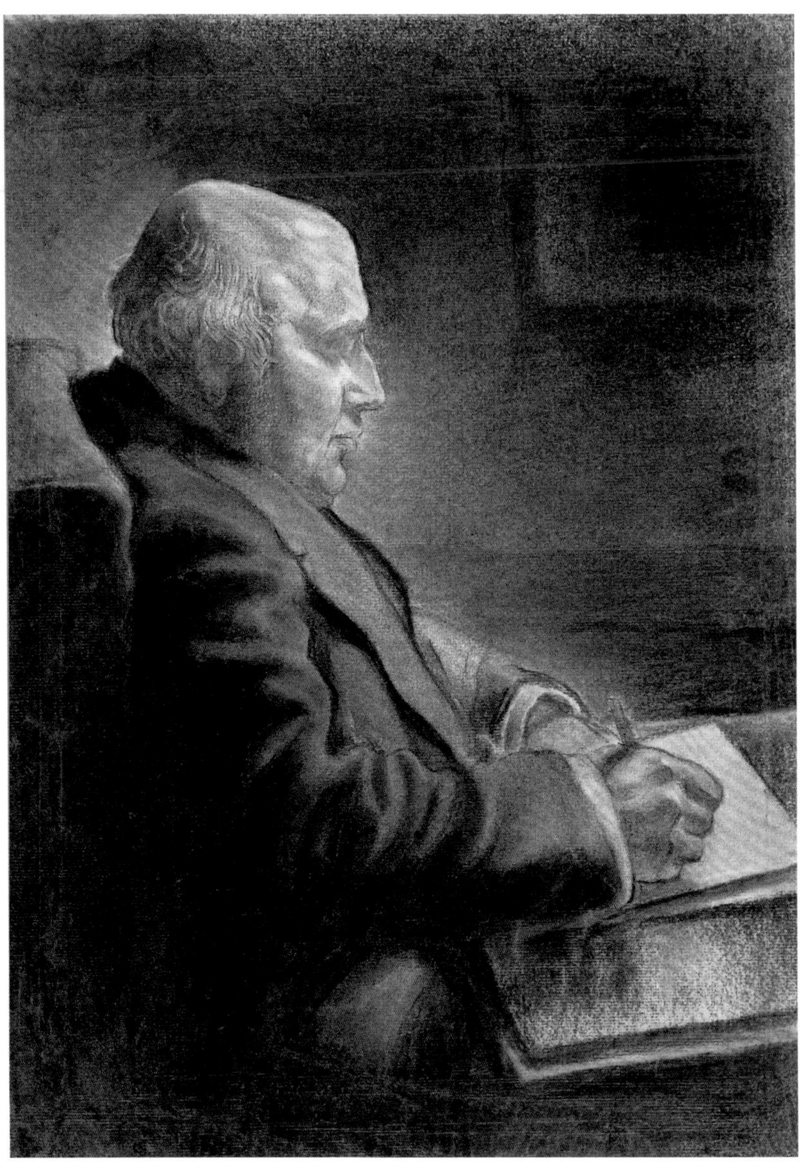

1.4 Salvador Dalí
Portrait of Artist's Father
[Retrat del pare de l'artista / Retrato del padre del artista]
c. 1925
MUSEU DE MONTSERRAT. DONATED BY J. SALA ARDIZ. R.N. 200.575

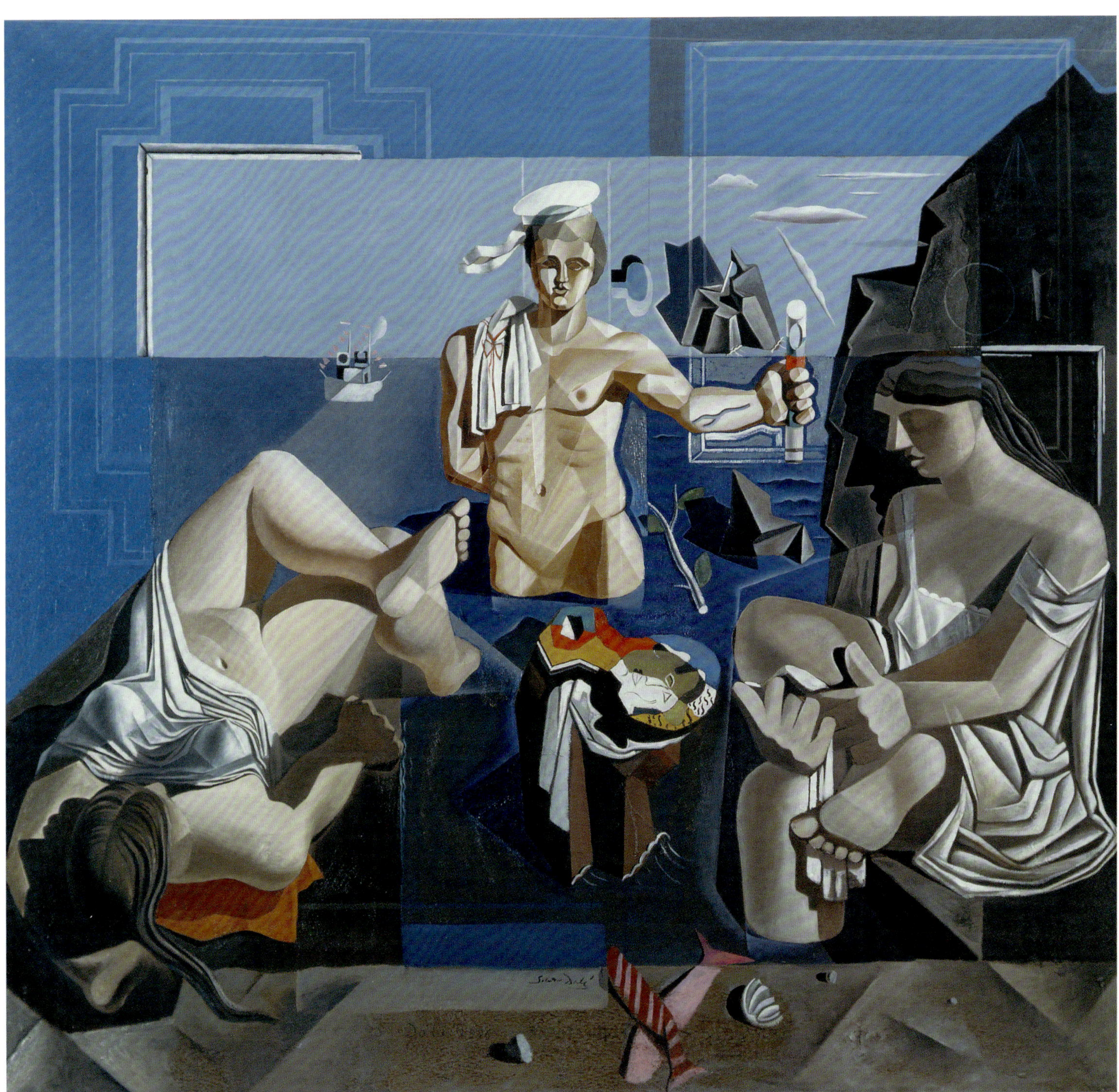

1.5 Salvador Dalí
Composition with Three Figures. Neocubist Academy (The Sailor. Neocubist Academy)
[Composició amb tres figures. Acadèmia neocubista (El mariner. Acadèmia neocubista) / Composición con tres figuras. Academia neocubista (El marinero. Academia neocubista)]
1926
MUSEU DE MONTSERRAT. DONATED BY JOSEFINA CUS. R.N. 201.390

1.6 Salvador Dalí
Harlequin
[Arlequí / Arlequín]
1926 (although dated 1927 by the artist)
MADRID, MUSEO NACIONAL CENTRO DE ARTE REINA SOFÍA. AS07488

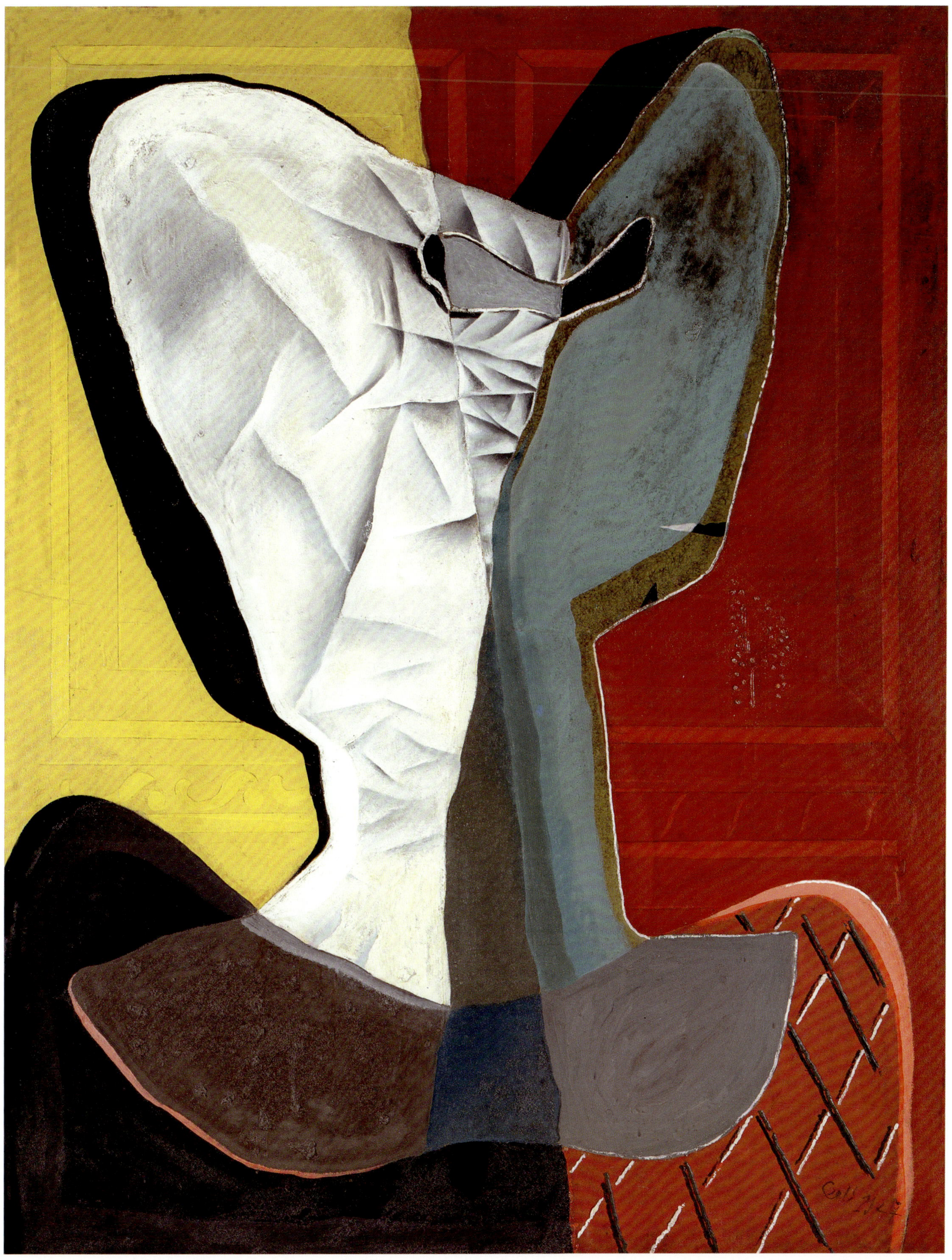

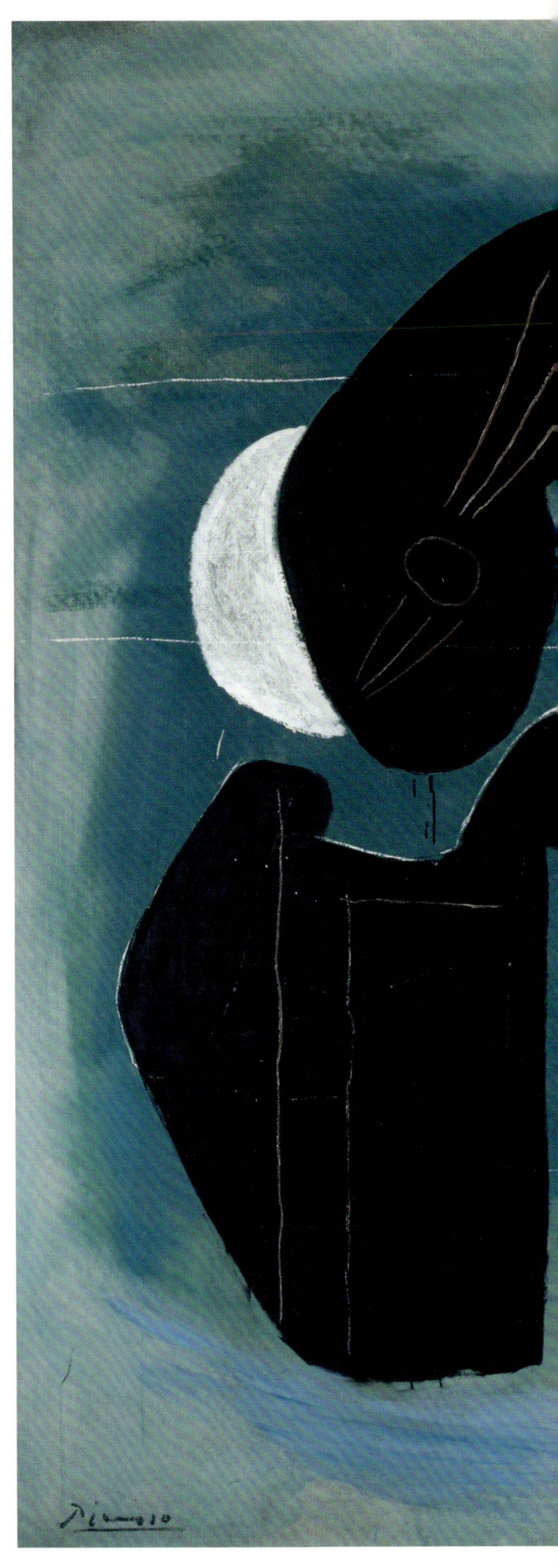

1.7 Pablo Picasso
Musical Instruments on a Table
[Instruments de musique sur une table]
1925–6
MADRID, MUSEO NACIONAL CENTRO DE ARTE REINA SOFÍA. AS10615

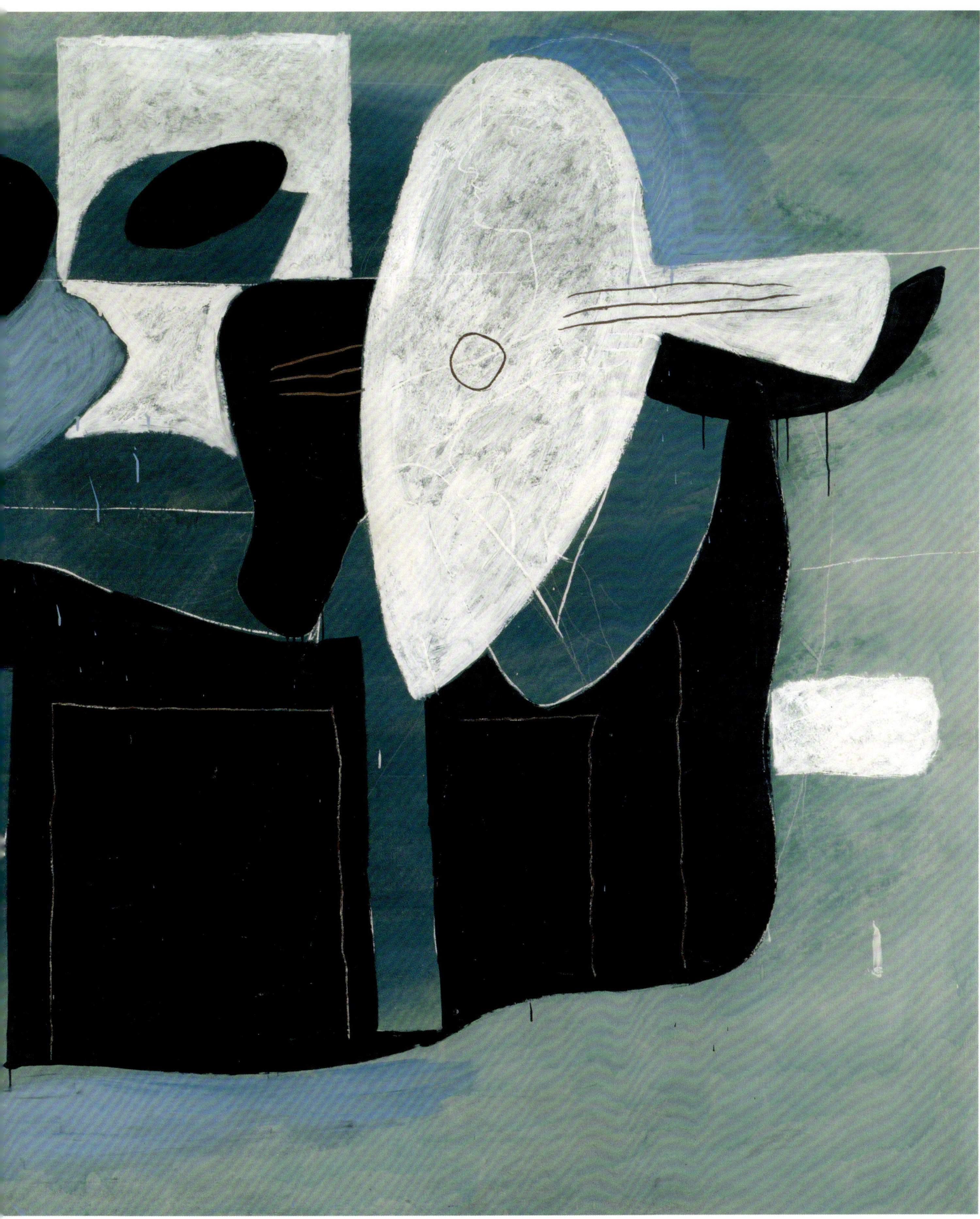

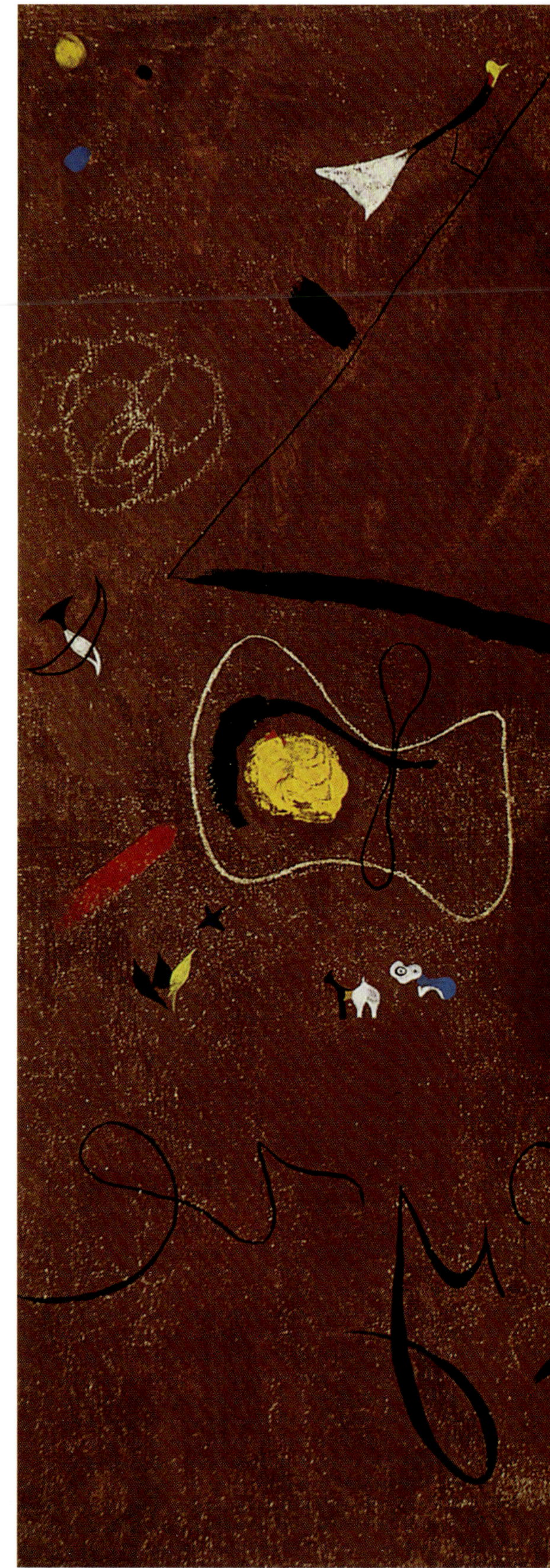

1.8 Joan Miró
Composition
[Composition]
1926
THYSSEN-BORNEMISZA COLLECTIONS. 1975.38

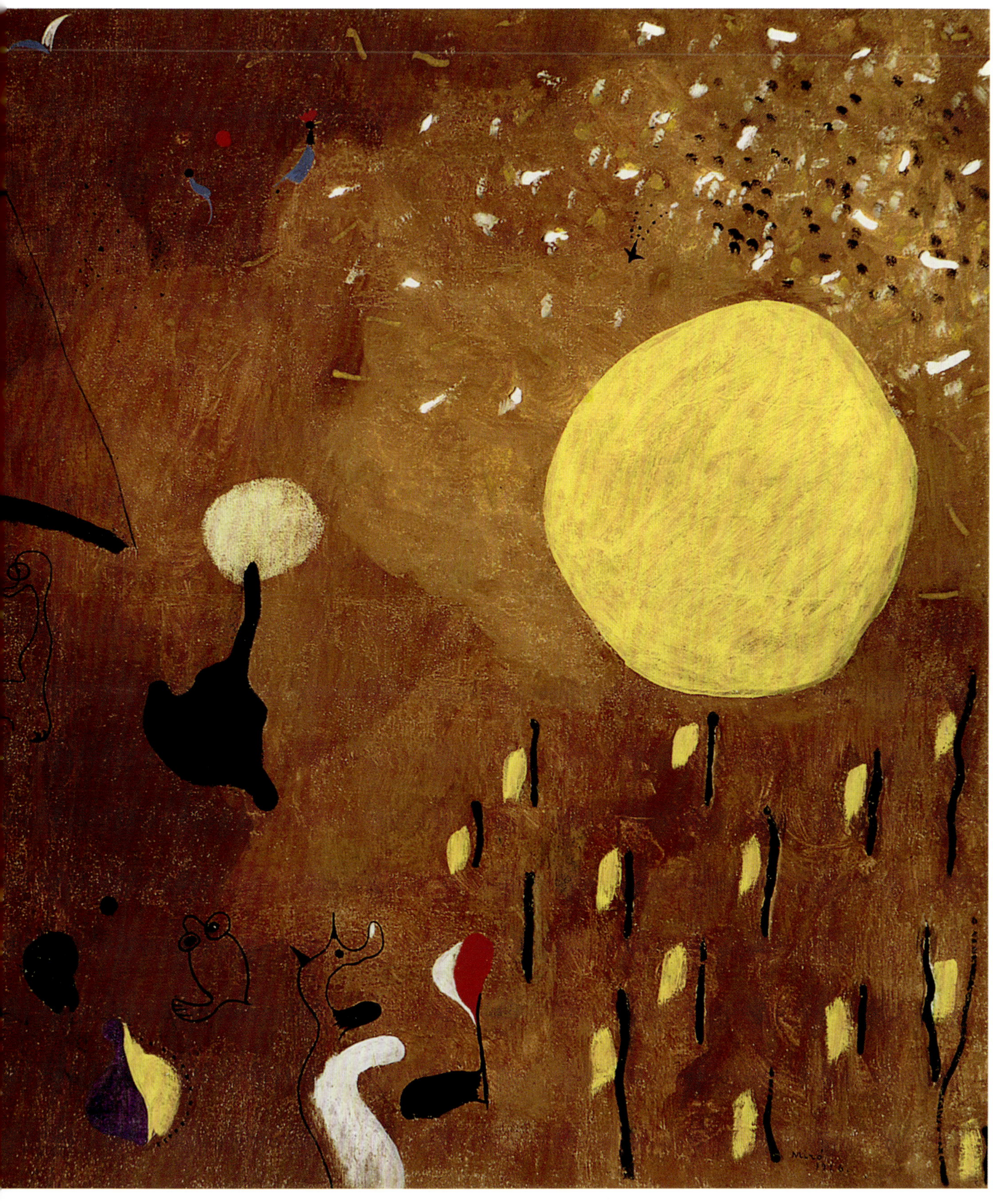

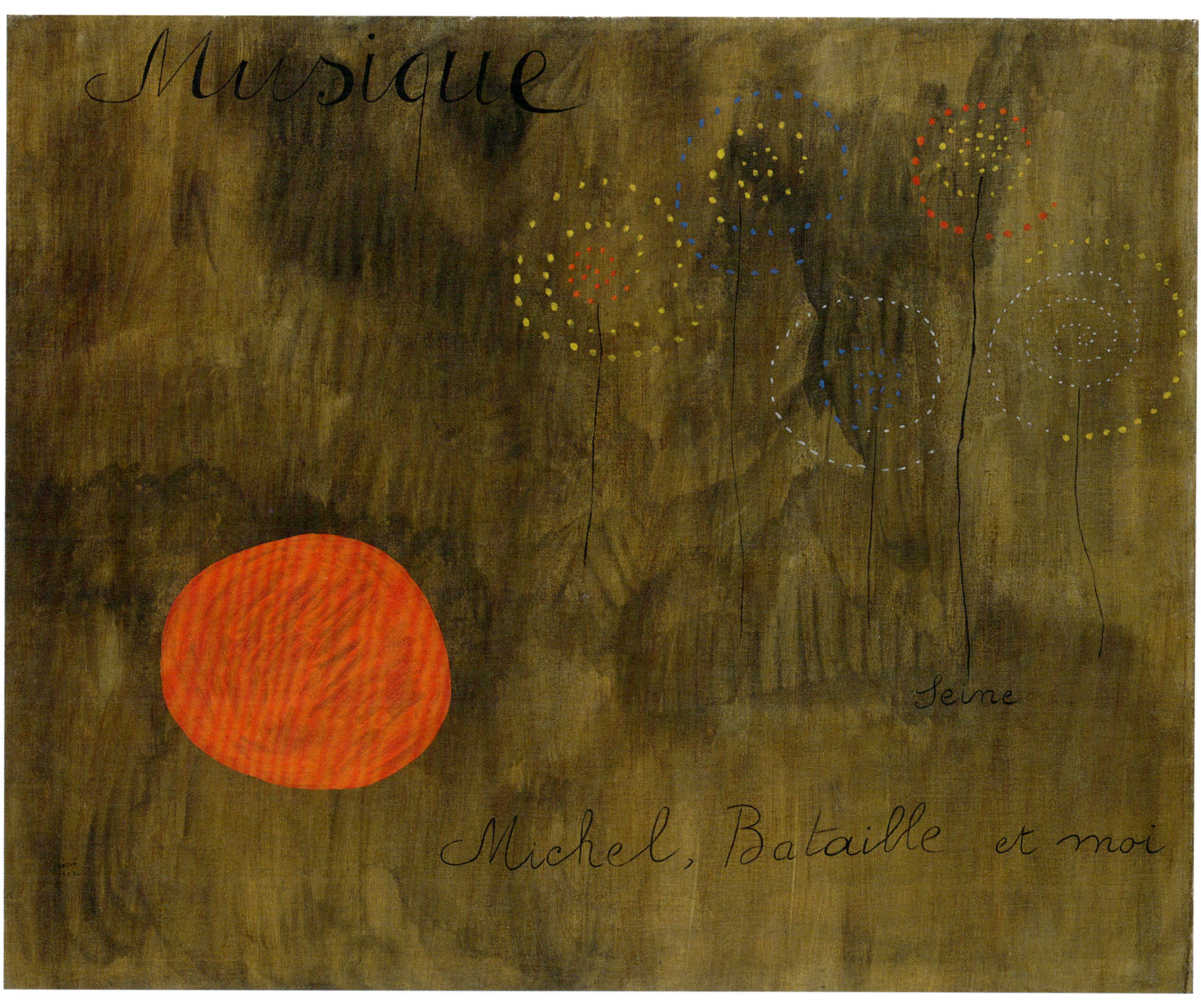

1.9 Joan Miró
Painting-Poem (Music, Seine, Michel, Bataille and I)
[Peinture-poème (Musique, Seine, Michel, Bataille et moi)]
1927
SWITZERLAND, VOLKART FOUNDATION

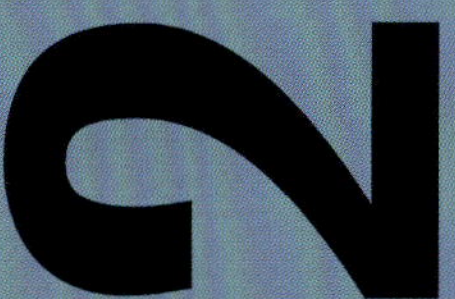

THE SECOND CONSIDERATION

GENIUS LOCI – MIRÓ. DALÍ.

MADRID/CATALONIA/PARIS, 1915–25

GENIUS LOCI

In 1926, when Dalí supposedly visited Picasso in Paris, Miró, who, despite spending long periods in Catalonia, was already well integrated in the French capital, was thirty-five years old. According to the criteria of that time, he was still a young adult. However, he had ceased to be a *young artist*. As is known, starting from 1923, when painting *Tilled Field, Pastoral or Catalan Landscape (The Hunter)*, Miró began to develop a system of painting that was crucial for Modern art, differing from any other plastic solution not contributed by the man himself. Starting from the following year, the reproductions of his works in *La Révolution Surréaliste* transformed him into an international reference for an entire new art. And it is curious, Picasso prior to 1924 was reinterpreted by Breton and the Surrealists, Miró prior to 1924 was not.

The frontier of the *young Miró* is usually established when the artist turned thirty-two. In Picasso's case, it is considered that he left his formative stage behind in 1907, at the age of twenty-six; and in Dalí's, in 1927, aged twenty-one. The first conclusion that these data seem to reveal is that of making us presume that Miró needed more time to find his own *manner*. But it would be a false conclusion. The young Picasso, and particularly the young Dalí, was much more indebted to other artists than the young Miró was. From the start, Miró showed a peculiar synthesis of language. The three artists coincided, in their youthful periods, in following paths full of difficult terrain—and steps backwards—that were not the paths or routes that were expected for young artists at the origins of the Modern Movement. And the three also coincided in possessing, in their youthful phases, a strong sense of the iconic. This developed in an unequal way with the evolution of each of them. A certain debate has existed among the critics regarding the sense of the iconic in the mature Miró[1]. It seems logical that those authors or art critics that were close to the development of Informalism or Post-Painterly Abstraction saw Miró as a preferably aniconic painter. It also seems logical that the critics and historians that were not in the orbit of these types of values (or that were historically witnessing their collapse) preferred a Miró as an unveiler of the world of signs. Miró, like Picasso, always denied that his painting was abstract, just as he denied—and it has subsequently been demonstrated—that he practised Surrealist automatism[2].

However, with all this we wish to arrive at a point. The Picasso of *Workshop with Plaster Head*, in 1925, and the Dalí of *Composition with Three Figures. Neocubist Academy* not only are, and continue to be, decidedly iconic painters, they are painters, furthermore, who develop an entire scaffolding and a rhetoric of representation and the symbolic that connect them with the great tradition of what we could call the *painting of museums*. The Miró of *Composition* (1926, in the Thyssen-Bornemisza Collections) and of the *painting-poem* with the inscription *Musique, Seine, Michel, Bataille et moi*, is elsewhere. There are several interpretations that have been proposed to elucidate critically the singular chromatic backgrounds that Miró develops in this series of works. Some of these interpretations are truly enriching[3]. Much has been said—and wisely—of Miró's painting of signs[4]. But the fact is that the Miró of these works, which are so often entitled *Composition*, is no longer exactly in *painting* as it had been understood since the Renaissance. A work of Cubism called *hermetic*, in spite of its

1. I refer the reader to the well-known text by Rosalind Krauss, "Magnetic Fields: The structure", in *Magnetic Fields*, The Salomon R. Guggenheim Foundation, New York 1972; and to Remi Labrusse, *Miró: un feu dans les ruines*, Hazan, Paris 2004. In any case, the theme of iconicity in Miró's work, or that of Miró's relationship with Abstraction recurs throughout the artist's historiography.

2. In this regard, see Rosa María Malet, *Joan Miró*, Ediciones Polígrafa, Barcelona 1983.

3. In this regard, as well as remembering the cited text by Krauss, we must mention two texts by Agnès de la Beaumelle, the first, "Joan Miró, l'invention du fond", in *Miró. La Collection du Centre Georges Pompidou, Musée National d'Art Moderne*, Editions du Centre Georges Pompidou/RMN, Paris 1999, pp. 16–23, and the second, *Note sur les fonds colorés de Miró (1925–1927)*, in *Joan Miró. 1917–1934. La Naissance du monde*, Centre Pompidou, Paris 2005, pp. 70–6. Likewise, meditations and especially excellent comments on the backgrounds in the paintings of Miró have been made by Jacques Dupin, Victoria Combalía and Tomàs Llorens.

4. Regarding this theme, see Sidra Stich, *The development of a sign language*, Washington University Gallery of Art, Saint Louis 1980.

radicalism in *less is more*, in spite of its derision of Renaissance plastic language, still continues to be related with a certain inheritance of plastic values. A *collage* no longer is, but it is not painting. And these *paintings* by Miró are painted surfaces in which signs have been deposited, but the way of approaching them can no longer be that of the *plastic values* inherited from the past. Today, at the beginning of the 21st century, and with the complex and varied trajectory of the Modern, it is possible to understand Miró from the *expanded field* of the painterly or from a concept of the painterly that is constantly *redefined*.

At that time, Miró caused a major impact among some experts on Modernism, but the critics did not know what to say of him. Waldemar George saw the basis of the issue clearly when he stated, albeit in 1928, that these paintings by Miró "liquidated the classical capital of the West" and supposed "the end of a civilisation", although he affirmed, hopefully, that they were also, at the same time, "the birth of a world"[5]. But other commentators, such as Leiris, present as *Michel* in the painting of 1927 that we have taken as reference, had recourse to *ekphrasis*; or others, such as Sebastià Gasch, who had known Miró for a decade, had recourse to stating the ineffable. And even if it is true that all painterly art is untranslatable and ineffable, to put aside his comments only reveals the failure of the critics' efforts. When presented with these paintings by Miró, the easiest thing was to evoke prehistory and cave art. But when doing this perhaps the critics were aware that, if this comment was right, it was not a matter of a mere return or a revival, but a full-blown attempt at refoundation. And the evocation of the prehistoric is possible, perhaps, in a work such as the *Composition* in the Thyssen-Bornemisza Collections, but it is more difficult in *Musique, Michel, Bataille et moi*. In this work, the reference has been replaced with his name (or by his pronoun) in calligraphic writing. In what we call *painting* either there is no reference and there is just painting, or the reference, transformed into an image to be able to understand it, it is replaced by an equivalent image. In other words, the decontextualisation of writing leads—and of the words that writing involves—is, as Jacobson says, in the hand, *poetry*. The poetry is the painting itself. But it is so as though it were so in its absence. The words had already existed *freely*. Words had been introduced in Cubist painting. But *words in freedom* did not abandon the frame of the sheet of paper. And the words in Cubist painting were invited signs, which created a link in hypertext, it is true, but which inhabited a surface defined by the painterly. Now, in these compositions by Miró, what was previously painterly is merged with the background of the canvas and is neither generous nor eloquent in its manner of being shown. The painterly in the background of the canvas is separated from the creation of form and of the sensation of space. It is separated from the skill of being painting or, rather, it conceals the skill of being painting, and it is then when writing ceases to be invited and becomes what we go to visit. The Western *logos* was constructed, until then, in reference to the plastic arts, in another way. Miró began an approach without a path of return.

We have spoken of *psychomachia* with regard to the Picasso and the Dalí of the years 1925, 1926 and 1927. In those years, Miró was also living his own *psychomachia*. But his psychic battle was that of the definition of the means and scope of *painting* as system. For this reason it is strange or surprising that when Dalí, in 1928, in one of his most important proclamations: *Catalan Art related with the most recent of young intellectuality*[6], when wondering if a Catalan *racial*

5. Waldemar George, "Las exposiciones. Joan Miró (galería Georges Bernheim)", in *Presse*, 16 May 1928, cited by Victoria Combalía in *El descubrimiento de Miró. Miró y sus críticos, 1918–1929*, Ediciones Destino, Barcelona 1990, p. 195.

art exists, instead of avoiding the topic, instead of going beyond it critically, instead of discrediting it as inappropriate, as someone such as him should have done, ends up answering his question by telling us that:

> "at the margin of all ruralism, of all anecdote, and precisely by cultivating the most living art of our time, Miró re-encounters, on the only path possible, that of spiritual intimacy, the very essence of our raciality"[7].

Of Catalan raciality, Dalí means. And he then complains about the false Catalanness "of some painters of gnarled trees" who call themselves Catalanist, with all this being interwoven in a text in which Dalí eulogises the art of the primitives and of children, talks to us of the Picassian revolution, of how Miró has come to change the history of art, or eulogises *Machinism* and Freudian theory as he offers us some recurrent examples of what soon afterwards he would call *paranoiac-critical.*

Dalí's reference to Catalan *raciality* is surprising, particularly in the example he chooses. But I believe that these types of questions, in the Spain of the 1920s, are to be found in its context. In the very month of October 1928 in which Dalí published the text to which we have referred, Federico García Lorca, in Granada, gave a lecture devoted to publicising Modern art, entitled *Sketch of the New Painting*[8].

The poet presented his own ideas, although also, as every artistic commentator does, he used others' opinions to support his own point of view; in this case, the opinions of the well-known critic of *Cahiers d'Art*, Tériade, and those of the editor of *L'Amic de les Arts* and *La Gaceta Literaria*, and the critic who introduced Dalí and Miró, Sebastià Gasch. But, in any case, García Lorca demonstrated his profound knowledge of the subject, making reference to artists and movements that very few, in Spain, could have known at that time. In fact his text is one of the most important *narrations* on the Modern movement in the plastic arts offered in the context of *new art* in Spain.

However, during his speech, García Lorca stated powerfully and in plain language:

> "We Spanish have the glory of having produced the three great revolutionaries of today's world. The father of all existing painters, who is the Andalusian Pablo Picasso; the man who made the theology and the academy of Cubism, Juan Gris from Madrid, and the divine poet and painter Joan Miró, a son of Catalonia. Note the race in the three. Picasso is the inspired Andalusian, of the miraculous inventions and the most surprising insight. Juan Gris is Castile, the reason and the burning faith [...] Joan Miró is more European and his art is now absolutely unclassifiable, because he has too many astronomical elements to attach him to a typical nationality"[9].

A reader today might perhaps be surprised by the *casualness* with which García Lorca uses the term *race*. Perhaps it is also surprising that García Lorca implies the possibility of the character of an Andalusian or a Castilian art compared with an international art. Furthermore, García Lorca hypothesises the existence of an Andalusian Cubism and a Castilian Cubism. The former is described—as might

---

6. It appeared in the newspaper *La Publicitat*, 17 October 1928. It is included in: Salvador Dalí, *Obra Completa. Volumen IV, Ensayos 1, Artículos 1919–1986*, edited and notes by Juan José Lahuerta, Ediciones Destino, Fundación Gala-Salvador Dalí and the Sociedad Estatal de Conmemoraciones Culturales, Barcelona 2005, pp. 118–32.

7. *Ibidem*, pp. 131–2.

8. I quote from the edition of Federico García Lorca, *Sketch de la nueva pintura,* included in Francisco García Lorca, *Federico y su mundo*, edited and prologue by Mario Hernández, Alianza Editorial, Madrid 1980, pp. 457–67.

9. *Ibidem*, p. 466.

be expected—among other things, in terms of its inventiveness and spontaneity. The latter—also as might be expected—in terms of its austerity and desire for standards. And finally, in contrast, in the Miró of 1928 we find, and I repeat the quotation, a creator who is more European and his art is now absolutely unclassifiable, because he has too many astronomical elements to attach him to a typical nationality. And all these statements are made by the poet who is *up-to-date* with the situation of the Modern, supporting his *discourse* with notions taken from the art critics who are truly opinion-makers.

Years earlier, almost a decade before García Lorca gave his lecture and Dalí published the text we have commented on, in 1919, *La trama del arte vasco* [*The Plot of Basque art*], a well-known essay by Juan de la Encina, a pseudonym, as is known, of Ricardo Gutiérrez Abascal[10], was published in Bilbao. In the beautiful book that left the press (and was soon reissued) the essay by Juan de la Encina was preceded by a preface in which the editors commented on his intentions. These intentions were overturned with the contemporary identification of *Euzkadi* through its new art. And Juan de la Encina has no doubt in his text in affirming the *ethnic* roots of Basque art, the close relationship between the idiosyncrasy and collective character of the Basques and their painting, reiterating the presence of *race* in the work of some leading artists. The positions of Juan de la Encina and the editors of his book seemed to coincide. But, it is worth saying now, Juan de la Encina was never to become a Basque nationalist, while the editors of his book were indeed militant nationalists.

The terms and conceptualisations used by Dalí, by García Lorca or by Juan de la Encina, have very *special* resonances today, to our ears. But the fact is, I fear, that these terms and conceptualisations, in their current quality as echoes or resonances that in printed letter, without the timbre or tone of voice of those who uttered them, without the expressions of those who spoke them, without the ears of those who received them and without the vital medium in which they were destined to flow, have ended up having a different meaning from the one they had. Currently we tend to give these terms and concepts a single meaning, when originally perhaps the meaning they had was multiple. Not all those who used them were saying the same thing with them. Many of the terms and expressions that we gather today and use in our interpretation were signs of a rhetoric of the time. On a structural plane it is possible, or likely, that this rhetoric served as a vehicle to express a common ideology in the painter, the poet and the art critic we mentioned. It is possible that through this rhetoric the three projected a similar vision of the world. For example, in all three culture appears to be something *superior* and classless. With their positions the three obviate the way in which the artistic production of the time in which they lived arises and is mingled in a society beset by social tensions. But on the plane of what today we call concrete ideological positions, the painter, the poet and the art critic sustained very different positions. The issue is complex. It is not trivial, but quite the opposite, in fact, but to dwell on it would take us away from where we want to arrive. Because what really interests us now is to show how another issue is latent in the rhetoric that articulates the opinions commented upon. It is something that has to do with the social psychology of art, which was lived with a particular intensity in Spain. It is this: the polarity between the need to have a positive living relationship with the vernacular and the need to also propose a positive, even if transforming, assumption of artistic or aesthetic

10. I cite from Juan de la Encina, *La trama del arte vasco. Primer volumen de la serie Pintores y Escultores Vascos*, Editorial Vasca, Bilbao 1920 (1919), facsimile edition of Museo de Bellas Artes de Bilbao, with the patronage of Iberdrola, Introduction by Miriam Alzuri, Bilbao 1998.

Modernity, especially on the terrain of the plastic arts[11]. We have always thought that the Modern meant the creation of a universalist aesthetic statute, in which there was no room for the encounter with the vernacular. The idea was around among some defenders of Abstract art, but it was mainly located on the terrain of architecture in the years of the so-called *International Style*. On certain occasions and in certain places, the *purity* of *International Style* was altered with *spurious* ornamentations that were stereotypical in their traditionalism and in their capacity for reference to the cultural tradition with which they wished to relate, or with the cultural reference they wished to impose. The sensation then arose, which ended up becoming an affirmation, that a conflict existed between the Modern and the culturally rooted or referenced. It was thought that the genuinely Modern should not possess any local accent. And it was also believed that any aesthetic affirmation of what today we call *identity* could not be realised from the premises of the Modern Movement. These were evidently false positions based on debatable extreme solutions.

Any informed reader today knows, for example, the implications in certain cultural traditions of the various -isms in the context of the first avant-gardes. In this regard much has been written and said about the *German-ness* of *German* Expressionism or about the *Dutch* quality of Neo-Plasticism. And the discoveries regarding this aspect that have been made in the Cubist environment would cause a certain surprise, since Cubism has always been thought of as the most founding Modern option and the one least involved in resonances or debts of a vernacular nature[12]. But in reality the issue is far from being resolved. The relations between the Modern and the vernacular are like the *Moebius strip* that flows on itself and shows one side or the other depending on the circumstances or the point at which we stop it.

The problem, as has already been anticipated, arises when the demand for identity or the need to give prominence to vernacular features are considered antagonistic, on the terrain of the plastic arts, to the encounter with the dynamics of the Modern and its new conceptions of artistic languages and the meaning of the artistic. The problem in reverse also arises. But in Spain, and probably in Catalonia, in the historical space that concerns us here, the former case occurred. However, perhaps there has not been an insistence on the mythical component of the constant appeal to the iconography of the vernacular, nor on the polarity between the static and the dynamic of the developments of identity. Neither has there been comment on the fact that, in a spontaneous or non-premeditated way, the artists, when they are aware of acting in a given environment, seek elements of cohesion in which to recognise themselves. And neither has there been comment, ultimately, on how these appeals to the vernacular may be a rhetoric capable of locating value judgement at a time of change in aesthetic criteria.

But even taking all this into account, I think it is necessary to add another perspective. The creators who founded Modern art were the first who worked with an idea and some stories of the *History of Art* that were already fully effective behind them. From the turn of the century, the so-called *Vienna School* had already given a certain profile to this possibility; from the end of the 18th century, the accumulation of studies by local scholars had fostered the notion of belonging and concatenation with respect to an accumulated historical-artistic inheritance. And the development of the *museum*, even in its most primary no-

---

11. I transfer the meaning of the term *vernacular* from architectural criticism to that of the theory of the plastic arts. The term *vernacular* does not exist in the [Spanish] dictionary. *Vernáculo* and *vernácula* exist to refer in particular to what is considered genuine or exclusively *domestic, native, of our house or of our country*. *Vernacular* would therefore be what conveys or possesses the quality of the *vernáculo*. For a current reflection on these issues, see: Bernd Hüppauf and Maiken Umbach (eds.), *Vernacular Modernism. Heimat, Globalization and Built Environment*, Stanford University Press, 2005. *Vernacular Modernism* is the title of a well-known film by Mike Hammond. On the other hand, Miriam Bratu Hansen applies the term and the general concept to film criticism and Keith Byerman to literary criticism.

12. Regarding these new aspects of Cubism, consult: Mark Antliff and Patricia Leighten, *Cubism and culture*, Thames and Hudson, London 2001. See also Eugenio Carmona, "São Paulo, O Cubismo e seus entornos", in *O cubismo e seus entornos*, Pinacoteca de São Paulo and Ediciones Expomus, São Paulo 2009.

tion, only served to strengthen what the history of art and learning on the cultural heritage registered in the spaces of memory awaiting continuity; a *continuity* that, as we know, was calculated not as the mere perpetuation of the existent but as the achievement of a change resembling a historical chain. Precisely in the framework of the so-called *Vienna School*—as is known and I believe it is a good idea to remember now—Alois Riegl related the notion of *Volkgeist*—the spirit of a people—with the History of Art. But even this link was not necessary. The idea that artistic creations are linked to geographical invariants, to the customs and the material culture of a given place, or the idea that these invariants configure a given taste and condition some given aesthetic parameters, is located in the foundational *episteme* of the History of Art, and very soon came to form important features of its rhetoric of explanation and its narrative resources.

Already Vasari, at the end of the 16th century, in his key work *Le Vite*, proposed a relationship between the *fame* of a city or country and the qualities of its artists, establishing that *manner* was not only a kind of anticipation of what would later be called *style*, but also the concrete expression of certain collective idiosyncrasies. And that is why Vasari talks of a *Tuscan manner* or a *German manner*. By the middle of the 18th century, two other *founders* of the History of Art moved, albeit in a different way, in the same direction. Lanzi did so in calling for the notion of a *school* that linked a shared space of creations—a city or a region—with certain common *characteristics*, while Winckelmann seemed to be convinced that the superiority of Greek art of the Classical age was due to the climate, the landscape, the customs, the diet, the sexuality and the political system of the Athenians of the time. There exists, therefore, a certain link between Winckelmann's criteria and Herder's *Volkgeist*. But it so happens that the influence of both was not only deposited in the first Romantics, but in Hegel, and the Hegelianism of the founders of the History of Art as a discipline is already known. And also, from another angle, the theory of the *milieu* of 19th-century Positivist Empiricism comes to have an impact on the same issue. The idea, therefore, that artistic production is interlinked with the geographical-cultural physiognomy of the space or place where this artistic production is performed is one of the *topoi* of the History of Art and is one of the characteristic elements of the narrative rhetoric in historical-artistic understandings or evaluations. At the beginning of the 20th century, and irrespective of the culture or formation of each of them, the artists knew this. Art historians extracted a register of rhetorical articulation from early art that returned with time, once the History of Art and the Museum had been formed, as a principle for the validation of their creations.

In any event, in Spain and Catalonia, the relations between Modernity and the vernacular can also be proposed over short and specific distances. And I will cite references that do not necessarily have anything to do with each other nor necessarily, do they have to converge on the same plane, but that undoubtedly interact in the relations between the ascent of artistic Modernity and rooting in the vernacular. A taste for the pure was especially important in the Spain of the 18th century. In the 19th century Mannerist and regionalist aesthetic registers were much valued by a rather unevolved bourgeoisie. Catalan painting was not exempt from Mannerist registers, but the so-called Renaixença modified the meaning of the poetics of Romanticism and Realism, through the demand for the natural and official use of the Catalan language and, in general terms, for the empathic claiming of everything it identified for Catalonia as culture that could recognise itself and be recognised from the outside. Although logically, as happens in so many cases of national self-recognition, the Renaixença was favoured by the cultured *petit bourgeoisie,* a view of the *popular* was decisive when it came to establishing themes and approaches.

At the end of the 19th century, before the *differential development* of the Spanish economy and society and that of the more advanced European spaces, Spanish culture in the Castilian language posed, through the so-called Generation of '98, the question of identity as a problem. But rather than reacting through an encouraging modernisation project, some important intellectuals of the Generation of '98, although not exempt from critical capacity and self-criticism, became entangled in searches of a metaphysical character, such as that for the *Spanish soul* and in thinking, like Unamuno, that there existed an *abyssal level* where the *pure* survived unaltered and decidedly authentic[13]. The influence of this type of thought was enormous. It would have been possible to respond to Unamuno and the intellectuals who used this type of analysis that at the abyssal level where everything remains unaltered, light does not reach and the cold makes life impossible. *Regeneracionismo* and the so-called Generation of 1914, even in its connection with certain aspects of the Generation of '98, came to represent the ascent of a reformist and pro-European spirit, but also in both ideological registers the prevalence of popular culture and the vernacular, even if reinterpreted, was decisive. So it was that the Generation of '27, that of García Lorca, who lived with Dalí in the Students' Residence, took up this determination and had to implement its relationship with popular culture and the vernacular in the context of an artistic Modernity that was already fully expanded in Europe and America.

In Catalonia things were different. Catalan culture was not totally extraneous to the intellectual atmosphere created by the Generation of '98. Neither was it totally extraneous to what the Regeneracionista spirit implied. But, above all, the dynamics of Catalan culture were its own dynamics. The fluid essence of the Renaixença, which in an accent characteristic of Romanticism favoured certain Gothic historicist revivalisms, slid towards what we know as *Modernisme*[14], that is, the Catalan version of European symbolism. In *Modernisme* the figure of Gaudí appears today as dominant, perhaps due to the transcendent originality of his proposal. The painting of *Modernisme* included some key names in the evolution of peninsular painting. But *Modernisme* in painting tended, even in some of its admirable creations, towards eclecticism and the diversity of plastic registers. The young Picasso was educated in the later environment of *Modernisme* that propitiated what for some is already *Postmodernisme*[15]. And it is undoubtedly significant that when Picasso passed through Barcelona, in 1906, on the way to Gósol, endowed with a spirit of research poised between Classicism and Primitivism, Eugeni d'Ors' notes were already being published in *La Veu de Catalunya* and the poet Josep Carner had given his book *Els fruits sabrosos* to the printers. Both references are the point of departure of a new situation for Catalan culture, that of the emergence of what we know as *Noucentisme*.

In recent decades much has been said and written on *Noucentisme*. On few occasions have the historians of art and culture seen, in reference to the past, how a cultural register was created that seemed not to have existed before. In reality, if we leave aside the contributions of Alexandre Cirici and Enric

13. I do not wish to leave aside the Modernist current of the Generation of '98.

14. The meaning of *castizo* in Unamuno is therefore not conventional according to the usual meaning of the term. But I pass on the meaning that the term and the concept possess in his work. The article by Miguel de Unamuno *En torno al casticismo* was first published in 1895; it appeared in book form in 1902. Contemporary editions exist.

15. See: Francesc Fontbona, *La crisi del Modernisme artístic*, Curial, Barcelona 1975.

Jardí, few spoke of *Noucentisme* until Jaime Brihuega placed it on the horizon of his studies of the artistic avant-gardes in Spain in 1981[16]. And it would seem that it is still necessary to explain what *Noucentisme* is, since it would seem that it is an exclusively Catalan cultural phenomenon, although, in a certain sense, it is not or it is not completely. In any event, there is no doubt that what *Noucentisme* meant is fully present, in one way or another, in the cultural and artistic spaces associated with the youthful works of Picasso, Miró and Dalí.

Today *Noucentisme* is a historiographical construction. At the time it was something similar to a *Kunstwollen*. Gaudí continued to raise some of his most important buildings in Barcelona until the 1920s, but around the middle of the decade of 1910 on *Modernisme* he began to show certain signs of exhaustion. *Modernisme* ceased in its own entropy, in its own capacity to develop. *Modernisme* had arisen in relation to the development of an upwardly mobile and opulent society, although it soon took its place, as we have indicated, between the bohemian and the marginal world. In any event, it was the Symbolist aesthetic that changed. Jean Moréas himself, the author of the *Manifesto of Symbolism*, moved towards Classicism at the beginning of the 20th century[17]. And it was Catalan society that changed. The upwardly mobile society, confident in itself, saw the emergence of the wounds of very serious and violent social conflicts. In this climate, and at a time in which Symbolism moved towards Classicism, many Catalan intellectuals, writers, poets, painters, sculptors and architects began to aspire towards an art of Classical spirit and cultural vocation together with the mythical notion of the Mediterranean entity. And it is worthwhile to remember now the pre-eminent place in the development of *Noucentisme* occupied by the opinions and approaches of Eugeni d'Ors, without detriment to the contributions of Josep María Junoy and Josep María Folch i Torres.

In the *Noucentista* plastic arts, and in the very definition of *Noucentisme*, a paradigmatic place was occupied by Joaquim Sunyer, Joaquín Torres-García and Enric Casanovas or, in the distance, Manolo Hugué. The plastic registers of *Noucentisme* were various: from the Classicist revival proper to the invention of a new Classicism through the Structuralism of Torres-García or the synthesis purified of Post-Impressionist elements, as was the case of Sunyer. Torres-García perhaps failed in his attempts to promote a new art through this approach. His place of reference in Modern art would be forged later, although it is related to the other Catalan moment of his work. In contrast, Sunyer's art would become a model of what *Noucentisme* involved, even though Sunyer cannot be gauged nor understood through the theories of d'Ors and Junoy, since the language of his painting is independent from the postulates of those who were his initial mentors.

Noucentisme, as is known, ended up uniting its destiny with Catalan political nationalism. From the early 20th century, a coalition of Catalanist and Republican parties won the elections for the Office of Mayor of Barcelona first, and the Provincial Government (the *Diputación*) later. As this victory extended throughout Catalonia, and taking advantage of and transforming the possibilities of a *Diputaciones* Law from Central Government, the Commonwealth (*Mancomunidad*) of Catalonia was created, formulated in 1911 and approved in 1914, which, *de facto*, and even without legislative capacity, was the first Catalan autonomous government of the 20th century. The first President of the *Mancomunidad* was the experienced and popular politician Enric Prat de la Riba.

16. It would be possible to break down a detailed bibliography of *Noucentisme*, but, generally, for a detailed consultation of all the components of *Noucentisme*, see: Martí Perán, Alicia Suàrez, Alicia and Mercè Vidal (eds.), *El Noucentisme un proyecte de modernitat*, Centre de Cultura Contemporània, Barcelona 1994, texts by the editors and by Jaume Vallcorba, Francesc Fontbona, Manuel de Torres i Capell, Manuel Rivas i Piera, Josep M. Ainaud de Lasarte, Norbert Bilbeny, Narcís Comadira, Joan Tarrús, Miquel Molins, Robert S. Lubar, Mercè Doñate and Vinyet Panyella. The reference to Jaime Brihuega is from the book *Las vanguardias artísticas en España*, Istmo, Madrid 1981.

17. On the passage from Symbolism to Classicism and on the penetration of Classicism into the art of the 20th century, see: Elena Pontiggia (ed.), *L'idea del classico, 1916–1932*, Fabbri Editori, Milano 1992, texts by Elena Pontiggia, Mario Quesada, Paolo Baldacci, Luigi Cavallo and Giovanni Muzio.

Being President of the *Diputación* of Barcelona, Prat had created the Institut d'Estudis Catalans, naming Eugeni d'Ors as its director in 1911. D'Ors' influence proposed the possibility of a relationship between *Noucentisme,* Catalanism and government itself. This possibility grew with the appointment of Torres-García, d'Ors' favourite painter, in 1912, to paint the frescoes of the Saló de Sant Jordi, which would become the Palau de la Mancomunitad. But the idyll only lasted until 1917, when Prat died. His successor, Puig i Cadafalch, a recognised architect linked to *Modernisme,* despite the evolution of his artistic personality, had a different sensibility.

In any event, the aesthetic ideas of *Noucentisme* pervaded Catalan artistic environments until at least the 1930s. Conceived, from its Classicist and Mediterraneanist ambitions, as an art opposed to Impressionism, Symbolism and *fin-de-siècle, Noucentisme,* justifying itself as an experience located in accordance with *the palpitations of the times,* became the backbone of Catalan art, and to a certain degree came to modify the orientation of the reception of the first avant-gardes in Catalonia[18]. But above all, and this is what most interests us now, *Noucentisme* propitiated a new sense of the relationship between the plastic arts and the grasping of the vernacular. This new sense was deposited, for example, in the work of Manolo Hugué, but above all in that of Joaquim Sunyer. And in that of Joaquim Sunyer especially through landscape painting. The term Classicism is relatively well suited to Sunyer's work. It is possible to relate it to his work inasmuch as Sunyer, in some of his more important compositions, linked the female nude with the landscape, with the allegorical character and manner of the Classical tradition. Sunyer also always favoured the balanced tone and the eurhythmy of forms and colours. But the term *Classical* is not applicable to him as, in his brushstrokes and in his application of colour, he never abandoned the subtle touch and velatures inherited from the Impressionists and, for some, also from Cézanne. Sunyer's topics were always, very preferably, *Mediterranean,* and Sunyer's painting came to be identified with the prototype of *Catalan painting.*

Other painters also aspired to claim this title in their inheritance from the 19th century. Dalí names some of them in his writing. Miró, therefore, was harassed or questioned on several fronts. The most unexpected front was his own home front: García Lorca, when considering the Cubism of Picasso as *Andalusian* and that of Gris as *Castilian,* and when saying that Miró's art was more international than Catalan, was not doing him any favour, from the point of view we are considering. So important was the dialogue or the permanence of the dialogue with the vernacular in most sectors of Spanish culture that this premise, this demand, the demand for the capturing of the *genius loci* acted as a lens that filtered the vision or as an index finger that pointed out or denied the validity of an artistic product.

The issue was not a *minor* one, in fact. In principle Miró should have been surprised, since until the end of the 1920s the artist continued to return to Mont-roig: that is to say, to the refuge, to the *Heimat* (homeland), which he considered the very being of his identity. But the others might not perceive this. And in truth Miró was already aware of the risk of this split between the internationalist requirements of the Modern and the mental paradigm of the vernacular when he embarked upon the transformation of his painting in the winter of 1922 and 1923. In relation to this, Miró wrote to Ràfols:

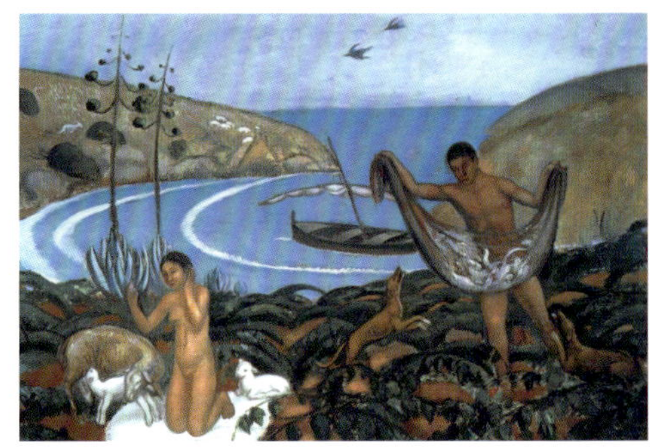

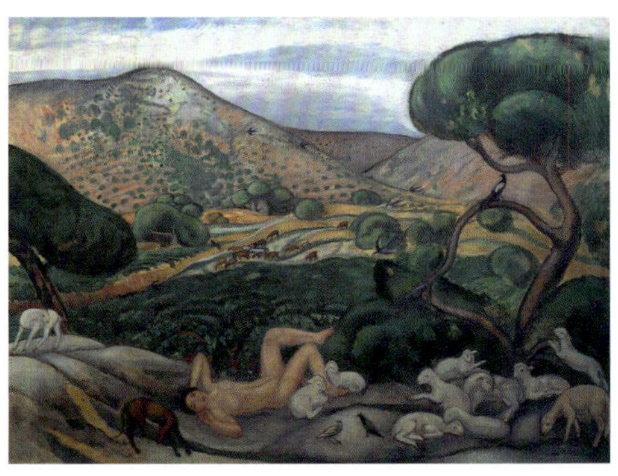

Joaquim Sunyer
Mediterranean, 1910–1
COLLECTION CARMEN THYSSEN-BORNEMISZA

Joaquim Sunyer
Pastoral, 1910–1
GENERALITAT DE CATALUNYA
ARCHIVO JOAN MARAGALL

18. This opinion that I express is not wholly shared by the specialists and scholars of this period of Catalan art. For my part, I have expressed it in *Picasso, Miró Dalí y los orígenes del arte contemporáneo en España, 1900–1936,* Shirn Kunsthalle and Museo Nacional Centro de Arte Reina Sofía, Frankfurt and Madrid 1991, and in *La generación del 14 entre el novecentismo y la vanguardia (1906–1926),* Instituto MAPFRE de Cultura, Madrid 2002.

> "I have already been able to release myself completely from the natural and landscapes have nothing to do with external reality. They are, however, more from Mont-roig than *après nature*. I always work at home, and I only have the natural to consult. Interference of figures (some of them large in size) and beasts. In the still lifes I capture objects that are despicably ugly. I know that I am going down some very dangerous paths and I confess that sometimes I feel the panic typical of the walker who has unexplored paths before him; I react quickly, thanks to the discipline and seriousness with which I work and, at the moment, faith and optimism cheer me again. Interference in the current painting of things extraneous to painting to give a greater emotive force to the work"[19].

Miró knows he is approaching an unexplored painting terrain. He knows that what he is creating has at its centre the very heart of the Modern Movement. He knows that they are works that, if they are successful, will make him an interlocutor *without geography* of the international avant-garde. And it is for this reason that, together with the risk, although assumed, there arises the fear of loss: the loss of what unites him psychological and culturally with being in the world, and it is for this reason that the artist affirms plainly that his transforming works, *La tierra labrada*, *Pastorale* and *El Paisaje catalán (El cazador)*, are pieces totally of Mont-roig: they belong above all, to Mont-roig, they belong to the talisman-place, to the place that condenses in him the essence of his personal way of understanding the vernacular.

In fact Miró already had this concern from the summer of 1920, a few months after arriving in Paris. Picasso writes this on his return to Mont-roig:

> "I agree with you that it is necessary to stay in Paris to be a painter. It may be that here they call us poor patriots! Europe and the countryside. Two things exciting our sensibilities and brains. Our work abroad is more *patriotic* than those who work at home, without seeing the world. I have just arrived in the countryside and prepared to begin to work fiercely. Some months here and then once again to Paris!"[20]

With the same problem in his head, the painter writes to both Ràfols and Ricart, his two early companions on the Barcelona scene, within the space of just a week. He tells Ricart:

> "I don't know what makes those who lose contact with the brain of the world fall asleep and mummify. In Catalonia no painter has reached his fullness. Let us see, then, whether Sunyer decides to spend some seasons in Paris; he will fall asleep forever! The fact that the locusts of our home worked the miracle of waking him up goes very well for the intellectuals of the Lliga, so they say it[21]. It is necessary to be an international Catalan, a homely Catalan does not have nor will he have any value in the world"[22].

And he says to Ràfols, in passing, but making a self-affirmation, beginning a letter:

---

19. Letter from Miró to Ràfols included in *Joan Miró. Escritos y conversaciones*, edited by Marguit Rowell, Institut Valencià d'Art Modern, Colegio Oficial de Aparejadores y Arquitectos Ténicos de la Región de Murcia, Valencia and Murcia 2002, p. 136, Republishing of the UK edition *Joan Miró: Selected Writings and Interviews*, Thames and Hudson, London 1986. For the correspondence between Miró and Ràfols, see also: *Joan Miró Ferra. Cartes a J. F. Ràfols*, Editorial Mediterrania and Biblioteca de Catalunya, Barcelona 1993.

20. Rowell (ed.), *Joan Miró, cit.*, p. 123.

> "Dear Ràfols: already outside of all the spiritual fermentation of Paris, so necessary and fundamental, and now calm in the countryside of Catalonia, also necessary and fundamental, I write to you"[23].

Miró's great effort, the great psychological synthesis that helps him make a transforming step forward consists in tracing a unitary map with two different geographies, of different density and different quality: Paris and the countryside. By Paris he does not mean "the French capital". Neither does he mean the city of society life. Miró, who needed to tell everything about himself through his letters to his friends, had already made statements against French *good taste* and had affirmed that he worked in solitude and with effort. *Paris* is the *place* where the authenticity of living art exists, as though this living art existed outside of the concrete realities of French culture and society. *Mont-roig* as the place—in the most complex sense of the term—of the vernacular. But the vernacular not understood as what can be stereotyped into concrete formulas or what corresponds to a catalogue of material culture of a given political-administrative area. Nor as something that responds to the desire of an ideological research. The vernacular as something that claims a root further on, or on another side, of the will of the conscious self. Both when speaking about *Paris* and about *Mont-roig*, Miró is moving on the existential plane, it is true, but also on a referential plane on which both places belong, also, to what, from a psychological point of view, we could call his *imago mundi*, his *imagination*.

The *determination of place* repeatedly invoked by Miró with regard to Mont-roig has been interpreted as the taking of a political position in favour of Catalanism, of politically militant Catalanism. Miró is as Catalanist as the sea is marine[24]. In his letters he is in favour of and against political Catalanism. Above we have remarked on one in which Miró does not show some politicians of the Lliga Regionalista, the party of Prats de la Riba and Puig i Cadafalch, in a very good light; the party that, in coalition with others, began to govern Catalonia politically based on Catalanist emancipatory prerequisites. But be that as it may, this is not the issue. Or rather, it does not seem to be very appropriate to relate Miró's relationship with the vernacular in this way. Those who know the young Miró and know his intensity as a creator know that Miró is not moving in strictly political terms, unless—and this is not the case—we consider any human action as political. This is not the path. Tomàs Llorens has recently focused on the issue in different terms. He has considered it in terms that have to do with the logic of things in Catalan culture. He has considered these, so to speak, in terms that have to do with social mentalities and the sociology of customs. Miró's parents were wealthy merchants. Success in business provided them with sufficient capital to buy a piece of land in the countryside. This form of property was a sign of prosperity. This was so in Catalonia and equally so in Spain, especially in Andalusia. The countryside—and this was very important—was also associated with a healthy lifestyle. The young Miró cured his health problems in the countryside. And, starting from here, later, when establishing his relationship with the countryside from an aesthetic experience, he developed an entire principle of living. I also believe that Miró's action before nature should be considered in the light of the contribution of John Dewey in *Art as Experience*. To this could be added all the revisions of the vernacular brought

21. He is referring to the Lliga Regionalista, a Catalán party founded in 1901, which held power in Catalonia between 1907 and 1923.

22. Rowell (ed.), *Joan Miró, cit.*, pp. 123 and 124.

23. *Ibidem*, p. 124.

24. Irrespective of the meaning that this phrase may contain, I would like to cite the book by Joan Minguet Batllorí, *Joan Miró. L'artista i el seu entorn cultural (1918-1983)*, Publicacions de l'Abadia de Montserrat, Barcelona 2000.

into the historical time of the young Miró by the Catalanist yearnings or by the Regenerationist aspirations that saw in the rural environment the uncorrupted authenticity of *being Catalan*.

And I believe that to these points of view we should add the possible conception of Miró's relations with Mont-roig and Camp de Tarragona from the point of view of the psychological school of *object relations*. Miró's relation with Mont-roig is a space of transition between his self and the world and, ultimately, it is an adopted, non-native relationship, deriving from a positive affective displacement.

But we have arrived at this point in Miró through Dalí. And Dalí? It would seem that the issue did not affect Dalí. But it undoubtedly must have affected him, because if not, it would not have provoked him in his writing. In 1927 Dalí began an entire publicity campaign in favour of the new sensibility that, in his view, involved pushing the functional, mass, machine-society, able to create an entire new popular culture, which Dalí considered *anti-art*[25]. The Dalí who is the apologist for this *new sensibility* is the one who argues against a García Lorca devoted to traditional, folkloric or anthropological popular culture. In the quarrel between the two creators, the scholars closest in sensibility to García Lorca have always considered Dalí's posture as a sham and snobbish. The concept of *anti-art* in Dalí could be the object of a long investigation. But what I am interested in outlining now is that perhaps Dalí, evidently, did not *only* want to be snobbish. Likewise, in his praise of the new popular culture Dalí not only wanted to find a sound justification for his highly figurative painting, which he considered *anti-art*, but, as a good laboratory paranoiac, Dalí was proposing an entire rhetorical battery against something that at times caused him as much phobia as lobsters: the deterministic weight of the vernacular. And Dalí was contradictory, because at the same time as he was eschewing the deterministic weight of the vernacular, he praised Figueres and Cadaqués, one of the strong points of his youthful work, praise that would later be recurrent in his old age. Curiously, the very young Dalí—although nobody identifies him with this—supposedly had Leftist leanings and sympathised with Catalanist and Federalist groups[26], attitudes that would never be traceable in the young Miró. But, in any event, Figueres and Cadaqués would come, as *determination of place*, to have a similar importance in Dalí to that of Mont-roig in Miró. And in both cases, Mont-roig, on one hand, and Figueres and Cadaqués on the other, were, let us not forget it, *the father's house*.

The chronology means that Miró and Dalí share a short number of years in what we consider to be their *youthful stages*. 1920, 1921, 1922 and the beginning of 1923 are those years. We could also venture to consider the year 1919. Dalí was then just a boy aged between sixteen and nineteen. Miró was a young man aged between twenty-six and thirty. Dalí was approaching the completion of his initial studies and his encounter with the Students' Residence and with the Academy of San Fernando. Miró was in a very different situation, not only because of his age; he had just made a public appearance on the Barcelona scene, and he had held his first one-man show in Dalmau. Furthermore—and this is substantially different—these were the years when Miró arrived in Paris. His first visit to the French capital occurred in March 1920. And we already know of his comings and goings between Paris and Mont-roig. We also know that the encounter with Paris, in principle, upset him. Dalí, although for other reasons, was also changed by his encounter with Madrid. And it was in fact in those years and

25. This name anti-art applied by Dalí is very important in a key moment of his production and requires a monographic treatment. In principle, to learn about some of its aspects, I believe it is a good idea to refer to the books already cited by Félix Fanés (1999 and 2004) and by Joan Minguet Batllorí, *El 'Manifiesto Amarillo': Dalí, Gasch, Montanyà y el antiarte*, Departament de Cultura, Generalitat de Catalunya, Círculo de Lectores and Fundació Joan Miró, Barcelona 2004.

26. Surprisingly, at the start of the dictatorship of Rivera, Dalí and his father were harassed by the police, and the young Dalí even went to jail, under the suspicion of having separatist ideas. These biographical aspects are shown in: Rafael Santos Torroella, *El primer Dalí, 1918–1929. Catálogo Razonado*, Institut Valencià d'Art Modern and Publiciones de la Residencia de Estudiantes, Valencia and Madrid 2005.

in those circumstances that the relationship or the conflict between the vernacular and Modernity were expressed with greater intensity in both. Significantly, this happened when they had to face this *outside* their native environments. The responses would not be univocal and this was not the only aesthetic problem to which they had to respond, and what also attracts the attention is the root in both artists of the codes of so-called *genre painting*. Miró and Dalí expressed themselves in those years, preferably, through works representing landscapes, still lifes and figures. Neither of the two was reduced, however, to the anecdote, quite the opposite.

We know of an early letter from Miró to Ricart, sent in 1917, in which the young artist describes to him his state before his encounter with nature:

> "Solitary life in Ciurana (*sic*), the primitivism[27] of those admirable people, my intense work, and more than anything my spiritual withdrawal, living in a world a child of my spirit and my soul, far removed, like Dante, from reality (do you understand?) have confined me inside myself. And as I have become more sceptical about everything surrounding me, I have ended up moving closer to God, to the Trees and Mountains, and to Friendship. A primitive like the people from Ciurana and a lover like Dante"[28].

Miró was not a philosopher. Neither was he a specialist in aesthetic theory. Miró's words need not be taken with the meaning of someone who chooses them meticulously or conscientiously to establish a *discourse*. Miró was a passionate young man. Miró sought places, such as Siurana, that were difficult to reach, located in natural environments so sublime, even virginal, but modified and reconsidered through the lengthy hard work and cultural action, in the broadest sense of the term, of the human presence. Miró feels the emotion of someone who absorbs with the senses *places* that possess the absolute of authenticity and that harken back to their origin: *origo rerum*, yes, but also *origin* in an almost Blochtian sense of the term. There has been a desire to see in Miró's words the realisation of a change or a return to the *Romantic idealism of the nature*[29]. But, as I say, Miró was not a philosopher. Miró thought and felt in other terms. Miró did not feel he was the maieutic, the intellectual midwife, who had to interpret what appears as mysterious or unfathomable. His encounter with the natural environment was not the encounter with Nature as an absolute, but an encounter with concrete fact of rural nature, of the countryside, with nature reworked by human action in tune with it. A similar feeling and a demand were experienced, more than a decade later, and in tune with the surreal, by the creators of the Castilian *Vallecas School*.

It is not coarse geography that is painted by Miró. Although his themes were many, in his work there predominates a correlation between architecture and nature, although what we call nature is always the countryside of farmland, crops, agriculture.

Starting from 1914 and until early 1917, when he was aged between twenty-one and almost twenty-four, Miró began to approach landscape painting in Post-Impressionist terms. His use of colour was so intense and plethoric, and even bold, that some of these paintings, together with some contemporary still lifes, led to this moment in his work being called *Catalan Fauvism*. And, although

27. The concept of *primitivism* in Miró has been considered when examining the relationship between the artist and the *genius loci*. In is undoubtedly a substantial concept in this phase of Miró's work and in the formation of his creative personality, but, apart from this mention, the author does not offer others to help us form an in-depth reflection on the matter. The topic is postponed, therefore, even though it has been analysed by some authors. In short, in this letter, the reference to the primitivism of Siurana has been interpreted in various ways, but I think it advisable to take into consideration that proposed by Maria Josep Balsach in *Joan Miró. Cosmogonías de un mundo originario (1918–1939) [Joan Miró. Cosmogonies d'un mon originari (1918–1939)]*, Galaxia Gutenberg, Círculo de Lectores, Barcelona 2007, translation by María José Viejo.

28. Rowell (ed.), *Joan Miró, cit.*, pp. 84 and 85.

29. To rebut these theses, see that expressed by Valeriano Bozal in *Miró. Càntic del sol*, Museo Patio Herreriano, Valladolid 2003. And, by the same author, *Pintura y escultura españolas del Siglo XX*, Volume I, (1900–1939), Espasa Calpe, Madrid 1999.

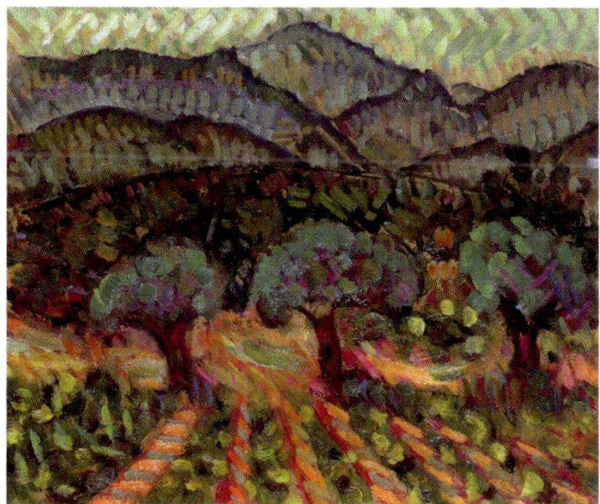

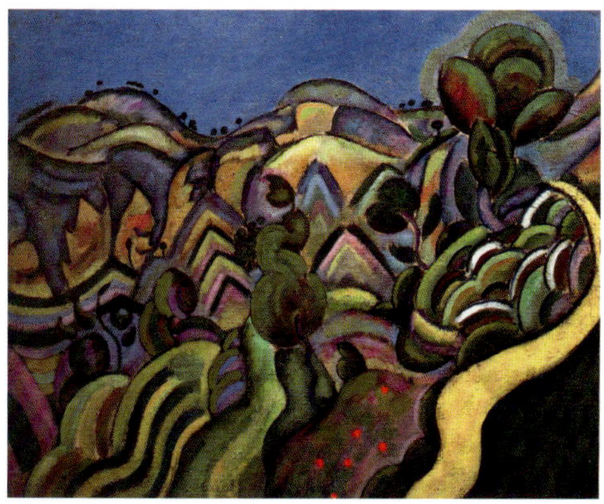

Joan Miró
Landscape of Mont-roig, 1914
PRIVATE COLLECTION

Joan Miró
Siurana, the Path, 1917
MADRID, MUSEO NACIONAL CENTRO DE ARTE REINA SOFÍA

the consequences of this register remain in important works from 1918, such as *Threshing*, in early 1917 Miró changed. This can be called *logical* personal evolution. We may also talk of the non-topicality of Fauvism—something I do not believe Miró cared about very much—and the desire for assimilation of other -isms. Both things are true, to a large extent. But perhaps it is worthwhile to meditate on the fact that Post-Impressionist-Fauvist language did not enable Miró to show on the surface of the canvas the plastic equivalent of the vernacular features of the geography that he had chosen as his subject. The introduction of stylemes taken from Simultaneism and from some derivations of Cubism and, to a lesser extent, in my opinion, of Futurism, produced truly singular compositions with Prades and Siurana as the motif. But this formula, in Miró almost always intensely colourful, lasted but an instant and may be boiled down to in a limited number of works. In my opinion, the vernacular demanded even more. And this demand occurred at a time when the figurative claims of the new Classicism (or Modern Classicism) became intense[30]. In his writings published in the creative magazines and in the Catalan press, the painter Josep de Togores, so important for Miró and so influential on Dalí, speculated and commented upon this evolution of the Modern[31]. In his letters, Miró began to use the terms *Classical* and *Classicism*, although it will be worthwhile, as we will see, to discern the scope or the definition of what Miró wished to express with these words. But even so, I consider that Miró's encounter with representative objectivity was motivated more by his desire for empathy with the topics he tackled than by the taking of a position on the artistic scene, even though some of the exponents on the artistic scene favoured him. Thus there arose the stage of his painting that has been called, not very successfully in terminological terms, *Detailistic*. It is true that Miró tends to be meticulous, neat, even painstaking. But this is not due to merely artisan taste or mere virtuosity. It is due to his empathy with what he takes as his model, something that Franz Roh identified and which justified Miró's presence in the book that was central in the Spanish culture of the moment, *Magic Realism: Post-Expressionism*. Now, this encounter of Miró with objective reality, achieved along his own path, did not lead him to a mere representative Verism, even if this Verism was *Modern*. And this was the case because, firstly, the plastic desire of the young Miró was always that for synthesis and because, secondly, Miró developed a distinctive conception or a peculiar slant on the term *calligraphy*. The concept of *calligraphy* in the young Miró would require detailed study in itself. In principle, and following the indications of Margit Rowell when annotating Miró's correspondence, the artist would use the term to refer to works as different as *Tile Factory in Mont-roig* and *Threshing*, both from 1918. With regard to the former, the following paragraph may be enlightening:

> "No simplifications nor abstractions. For now what interests me most is the calligraphy of a tree or a roof, leaf by leaf, twig by twig, grass by grass and tile by tile. This does not mean that these landscapes do not end up being Cubist or furiously Synthetic"[32].

It is curious because in an important work such as *Mont-roig, Vineyards and Olive Trees*, from 1919, currently in the Metropolitan Museum of New York, we see Miró reconcile the Objectivism in the description of the vines with abstractised and colouristic angular planes to allude to spaces or fringes of cultivated land.

30. Robert Lubar maintains the theory that the passage of Miró to the *Detailist* landscape or close to *Magic Realism* is determined by the rising up of his Catalanist or nationalist spirit, in the opposite way to *Noucentisme*. What I wish to affirm here, even taking account of what Lubar claims, is something different, because I believe that the theme in itself, and the need to outline a vernacular accent in it is what ends up gradually modifying the plastic language used by Miró. See: Robert Lubar, "Miró Before 'The Farm'. A Cultural Perspective", in *Joan Miró. A Retrospective*, The Salomon R. Guggenheim Foundation and Yale University Press, New York 1987, pp. 10–28.

31. See, on this regard, Eugenio Carmona, "Josep de Togores y la Belleza Impasible", in *Togores, clasicismo y renovación (obra de 1914 a 1931)*, Museo Nacional Centro de Arte Reina Sofía and Museu Nacional d'Art de Catalunya, Madrid and Barcelona1997, pp. 14–21.

But in any event, this other passage could be related to the second work cited above, *Threshing*:

> "I continue working. I have not yet been able to finish any canvas (with the exception of a sketch on threshing and some drawings). This calligraphy making is very entertaining"[33].

We have previously located this second work in the context of the Post-Impressionist- Fauvist inheritance. It is a completed painting, the painter himself tells us it is a canvas, but at the same time he calls it a *sketch*. This name, *sketch*, seems to allude, therefore, to a denomination of a style[34]. The other painting, *Tile Factory*, is one of Miró's works that puts us on the path towards the artist's relationship with one of the variables of Modern Realism, although the Neo-Objective formula is not even condensed in the piece. If we have, therefore, to join together two pieces so different under the concept of *calligraphy*, then *calligraphy* in Miró must be, firstly, a way of relating the icon with its quality as a sign. And this would be enormously important in the artist's work as far as *The Farmhouse* and, subsequently, the new type of painting that begins in 1923. It is as though Miró, before each icon, proceeded as though he has to execute a logogram. And it would show how his conception of painting as pictographic writing was very early. Yet, at the same time, the idea of calligraphy harkens back to school and learning to write and the moral and social conventions that are derived from *good handwriting*. Old school calligraphy (and perhaps modern too) required considerable effort in training the hand. Old-fashioned calligraphy forced the scholar to trace arabesques, some of them gratuitous having to follow a precise rhythm of execution that was not natural, but that ended up achieving the peculiar shape of each letter. Perhaps Miró thought this. Perhaps he thought that each iconic element required its own formalisation on the basis of small details and lines. One needed to make an effort and be meticulous to achieve this and, above all, it was not necessary to simplify the letter to the writer's will, or rather the writer had to submit accurately to the particularities of the pattern of the letter to be written. In third place, each pattern of letter and each hand ended up defining a *ductus*[35]. Miró would tell us that each iconic element observed required its own *ductus* to be painted, and the sum of *ducti* would end up endowing the painter's hand with its own personal *ductus*. This is what Miró is encountering in works such as *Tile Factory*, his own gesture, his own hand. And perhaps the artist himself never thought that through conceptions linked to notions of writing and calligraphy his work would advance towards iconic densification, to then, at another moment after his youthful stage, depart from it.

On the other hand, this work, *Tile Factory*. It is a simple, even humble place. When Miró painted a landscape with the presence of rural Gothic architecture, it seemed that the sensation of monumentality could declare its presence. But Miró almost always chose as his theme settings and places that might seem anecdotic. In *Tile Factory*, as in so many of his landscapes, Miró even chose to show a sky thick with clouds, clouds with almost whimsical shapes and potent in their density, which is quite the opposite of what could be expected from the meridian and the clear Mediterranean sky. It is Miró's *paintwork*, therefore, that elevates the painting to its exemplary quality and not the motifs chosen. And it is the young artist's synthetic plastic language that endows the

---

32. Rowell (ed.), *Joan Miró*, *cit.*, p. 92.

33. *Ibidem*, p. 95.

34. Unless it is indeed the allusion to a sketch of the painting, currently in the Foundation Francisco Godía. Although in his letter Miró speaks of a *canvas*.

35. The term *ductus* is frequent in treatises on calligraphy and writing, but it is not frequent in dictionaries. Although here I use it in an *open* meaning, in writing, in calligraphy and in typography, the form of the letters depends on their structure as such, and this depends on how the line is executed. These movements of the fingers and the arm that define the form of the letters is called *ductus*.

compositions with singularity when viewed. Miró's procedure is the opposite of Sunyer's. When choosing a location as a theme or a motif of his painting, Sunyer ended up distilling an emblem of *Mediterranean-ness*. But it is an emblem that, in its apparent simplicity, is in fact sophisticated. The abrupt or primary character of the Mediterranean geography is softened with his Post-Impressionist technique and its calm desire to make us feel subtly faced with a new Arcadia. Sunyer's landscapes have the hallmark of a significant artist and have behind them the emergence of an entire cultural will, but they also have a mystifying aspect. The effort of the young Miró is quite the opposite, in my view to Sunyer's. In Miró "Mediterranean-ness" is an anthropological question and not so much a cultural *desideratum*. Miró's Mediterranean is abrupt and difficult, but irresistibly intense and genuine. Miró's Mediterranean geography does not aspire to be mythical, nor to be beyond time: it is concrete in its rural design and, more than mythical, it is ancestral.

Current critics tend to want to reconcile, as we will see, the contributions of Miró and Sunyer, but in addition to the generational difference between the two, as Robert Lubar has already pointed out[36] and as may be supported now, their proposals belong to different aesthetic categories and different intellectual positions. What perhaps, at the end of the decade of 1910, neither Sunyer nor the *Noucentistas* expected was for a young painter to wait for the moment to bear witness. Or Dalí, perhaps, simply, was merely waiting to cite them.

Knowledge of the young Dalí and the recovery of *Noucentisme* have run in parallel. Both are relatively recent facts, but from the first moment it was noted that Dalí made Sunyer one of his references. Although perhaps these types of paragons and relations are made on occasions without developing a prior reflection. Santos Torroella has proposed a meeting point, for example, between Sunyer's *Pastoral*, from 1910 or 1911, and Dalí's *The Smiling Venus*, executed in 1921, when the painter was 17 years old[37]. In *Pastoral* the female nude body and the orography of the hilly landscape merge and an entire concept is expressed through the union between woman and nature. In its simplicity, *Pastoral* is a symbolic painting. *The Smiling Venus* is a frivolous painting. It does not have any stylistic relationship with *Pastoral* and the iconographic relationship is very superficial. The two female figures only coincide slightly in posture, a posture that, on the other hand, is conventional in reclining nudes. The smiling Venus in Dalí's painting does not symbolise anything. She is a girl enjoying a beautiful summer's day by the sea, although the very young Dalí plays evoking ironically, almost in caricature, some well known masterpieces of the History of Art from Giorgione to Manet.

This adolescent Dalí, a painter so advanced that, in the photographs conserved, already appears so different in his appearance from his fellow students, is suffering the loss of his mother, and has already decided upon his vocation as a painter. This is the moment in which his father decides to send him to the Academy of San Fernando in Madrid. At this time, in 1920 or 1921, the very young Dalí is a painter in the trail of Impressionism. Cadaqués and its surrounding area, pure Mediterranean, of glowing, glimmering dawns and evenings, serve as his passionate motif. Dalí knew, undoubtedly thanks to Pitxot, his father's friend and a talented painter himself, about the Mediterranean painterly Luminism of the turn of the 19th and 20th centuries, so important for the Catalan school. And he did so with intensity and effectiveness. The two landscapes of

36. Lubar, "Miró Before 'The Farm'...", *cit.* Also of the same opinion is Tomàs Llorens, 2008, in *op. cit.*

37. In *El primer Dalí...*, *cit.*, p. 116.

1920 or 1921 conserved in the Kunstmuseum in Bern are evidence of this. This intense encounter with his own origin has the power of a moment of initiation. It is a pulse of recognition and acceptance of himself, and perhaps for this reason Dalí leaves us two magnificent self-portraits by the sea and—why not?—in a psychic drive that was to grow, several portraits of his father. But also early masterpieces such as that in the Masaveu Collection in which Cadaqués, bathed in the reddish light of dawn, already appears as an effigy, as does the well-known *Cadaqués visto de espaldas* belonging to the Fundación Gala-Salvador Dalí.

But these wonderful paintings that Dalí executed at the age of just 16 or 17, to what extent they are imbued with the demands of *genius loci*? It was at this time of adolescence when Dalí felt the most temptation from left-wing political militancy and when he contributed to the magazine *Empordà Federal*. However, his works seem to have arisen more from the desire to be in line with the Luminist and Colourist current of Catalan painting and with the virtuous and plethoric development of the application of colour. Living in the Mediterranean, what creative and lively teenager has not suddenly *discovered* the sparkling sea and the light, in their own environment, in the happy days of summer or in the subtly coloured atmospheres of a clear, temperate winter day?

Curiously, this was to be the type of painting that was heir to the Impressionism that Dalí would hate as soon as he arrived in Madrid, at the Academy of San Fernando and the Students' Residence. And it must be taken into account that Dalí was to exhibit some of these paintings in January 1922 and that in September of the same year he was already living in Madrid. But it was Impressionism that the professors at the Academy wanted to teach him. That is to say, the painters of the Academy wanted to teach him what he already knew. And it was another type of painting, the most similar to that of the *Noucentisme* applied to the graphic arts, that was praised in the exhibition that we have just commented upon. Furthermore, in 1922 we witness what we could call a *hidden transformation* in Dalí's work. His fellow students at the Students' Residence were surprised to discover, unexpectedly, his *Cubist* paintings. But before arriving in Madrid Dalí had not yet shown any connection with the languages of the avant-garde.

Be that as it may, the fact is that, again—and suddenly—Cadaqués and landscape painting make an appearance in Dalí's work. Cadaqués was also to be present in another type of composition. But we find exactly eight landscape paintings of this type, between 1923 and 1924.

1923 was an important year in Dalí's life. The poets of the Generation of '27 accepted the arrival of Rivera's dictatorship *without comment*. For Dalí, however, the loss of democratic freedoms had other consequences. They closed *Empordà Federal* magazine to which he had continued to contribute, even while in Madrid. The dictatorship closed the Figueres Nationalist Centre. Dalí's father was detained, accused of being a *separatist*. And Dalí himself was imprisoned as a reprisal against his father. Does the resurgence of Cadaqués as a topic in Dalí's work, in 1923, have any relationship with all these facts? We are not accustomed to considering Dalí's work in these terms, but perhaps it would be appropriate to begin to do so. Another important fact happened in Dalí's life. On 22 October the Disciplinary Council of the Academy of San Fernando temporarily excluded him, for one year, for demonstrating against the staff of professors, as they refused to give a professorship in painting to Daniel Vázquez

Díaz. Dalí then began, together with some painters from the Generation of '27, to frequent the studio of Julio Moisés.

It was at this time, in these landscape of 1923, when Sunyer's influence is identified in Dalí's work. Did the circumstances of that year make a re-encounter with the *genius loci* formed through unexpectedly being in tune with *Noucentisme* arise in Dalí? I will answer this question as follows: yes and no. I believe that, on one hand, Dalí retrieved Cadaqués with all that this implies. But on the other it is clear that Dalí was painting *in the manner of* and that these paintings are exercises in which Dalí wished to face and transcend some references that acted as paradigms in his plastic imagination. It may be, therefore, that Dalí is recreating the *genius loci* of Cadaqués. But it may also be that these works were *painting on painting*. Dalí knew how to play with double meaning with *dejà vu*. Dalí knew about the power of the citation. This must be clearly understood. We are not, as Loeb has already said, dealing with a youngster who does not have his own manner. We are dealing with a young painter who sees the construction of his own *manner* in the *appropriation* and *rectification* of the *manner* of others.

Perhaps it is in *The Jorneta Stream* that Sunyer's influence on Dalí is considered most evident. Or it could be said in another way. Perhaps it is in this work that Dalí *cites* Sunyer most clearly. The olive trees that Dalí paints are undoubtedly an icon-sign of Sunyer's painting. But Sunyer would never have painted a scene in an unstable imbalance as Dalí does. Dalí's forms are much more *concrete* than Sunyer's forms. Dalí moves away from all Impressionist inheritance while Sunyer attempts to conserve it. Dalí's Mediterranean is rugged, Sunyer's is tranquil. Dalí sets the female nude against the landscape. Sunyer would also do this, but in a very different way. After a brief initial period, Sunyer's nudes would quickly harken back to the nude of the Classical tradition. Dalí's nudes clearly reference Cézanne and Derain. I believe that Dalí is "doing a Sunyer", *amending Sunyer's page* and establishing a powerful standard principle that Sunyer lacked. In other words, Dalí cites Sunyer, but works the citation and transforms it into text; in text that is more in contrast with the citation than it initially appeared.

It has also been affirmed that in *Cadaqués seen from the Tower of Creus*, Dalí is following Sunyer's steps. I do not know of any painting by Sunyer in which the atmosphere is so limpid and the masses and volumes are so solid. In my opinion, these Dalinian concretions are closer to Togores than to Sunyer. And as in Togores, Dalí knows about Cubism and knows about the passage from Cubism to Modern Classicism. When painting the village of Cadaqués, both in this work and in the well-known *Port Alguer*, Dalí was not engaging in *Cubism*, as has been affirmed. Dalí had Derain in mind, who knew the Cubists. And Dalí, above all, also had Vázquez Díaz in mind, whom he had defended so much, who had also known the Cubists, and who between 1918 and 1923 executed a whole series of landscapes in which the Impressionist inheritance is modified by the desire for constructed form. In creating his landscapes, Vázquez Díaz always took the Basque Country as his motif. Dalí is transferring Vázquez Díaz' formula to the Mediterranean context. That is to say, in these landscapes Dalí seems caught by the capacity of seduction of the *genius loci*, and it may be that to a degree he is, but he is also applying *a formula*. Dalí's simplifications are not Cubism. They are simplifications demanded by the motif chosen to paint. They are the simplifications that someone who has seen and dealt with Cubism and knows that, on some occasions, *less is more*, is able to perform.

These landscapes by Dalí are not only reminiscent of those of Vázquez Díaz; they are also reminiscent of those that Benjamín Palencia was to paint years later. Dalí's landscapes are therefore in some ways in a double tradition: the *Noucentista* and that of Basque-Castilian Novecentismo; neither would it be extraneous to the development of landscape painting in the context of the Generation of '27, although perhaps it was Dalí, at this point, who would show the way to his artist friends of the Residence and those of García Lorca. And there is something more. It has been pointed out that in paintings such as *Cadaqués seen from the Tower of Creus* or in *Portodogué* or *Port Alguer*, the presence of girls carrying *Dolls*, a typical ceramic pitcher, is evidence of Dalí's relationship with the vernacular. It is worthwhile saying that these figures are not found in Sunyer but in Togores. And it is also worthwhile saying that these presences of the *topical* are only possible in someone whose gaze is distanced from what he represents. Beyond the vernacular, beyond his love for the *genius loci*, would the intellectualised Dalí be beginning to contemplate his own native space from the perspective of the *exotic*?

Let this question remain in the air. And so it should, because it is worthwhile to comment that the place where Dalí expressed his relationship with the vernacular best was in some paintings in which the female figure is the protagonist. The year is 1925 and Dalí has begun his *interpretation* of Picasso.

In a work such as *Figure at a Table*, Dalí proposes a new theme: that of the psychological interpenetration with the female figure. The pensive figure seems not to be thinking of anything concrete: she is attempting to cope with her inner flow. It is significant that in the context of the Generation of '27, or of *new art*, other creators of the age of Dalí, such as Ángeles Santos or Mariano de Cossío, proposed compositions with the same appearance. In *Portrait of my Sister*, the reference in the title to the family environment does not conceal, if one wishes to see it, the claiming of another scope. The physical behaviour of Anna María, Dalí's sister, and her capacity to occupy the foreground of the composition, make her appear as a concrete woman, but at the same time as an allegory. This allegory is deduced or is projected from the landscape in the background. What is revealed is a maritime accent intimately linked with an architecture. The architecture seems to be the spontaneous popular architecture of some Mediterranean coastal areas. As it is. But Dalí has modified it. Dalí has adapted it even more in its cubic form and has purified it in its volumes and adornments. Dalí has brought Mediterranean vernacular architecture closer, on one hand, to the purified architectures of Metaphysical Painting and, on the other, to the incipient Rationalistic architecture. Dalí does not understand the relationship with the vernacular unless it is in its adaptation to Modernity. That is to say, Dalí does accept the vernacular only if the vernacular can be reabsorbed by Modernity. It is the eyes of the Modern that make us look at the identity again. Keeping this in mind, Dalí's proposal is very different from that of *Noucentisme*. Dalí's relations with *Noucentisme* and with Sunyer that have been mentioned are, therefore, apparent. Dalí plays with *Noucentisme* to amend its page. Eugeni d'Ors symbolised the *Noucentista* aesthetic in *Teresa, la bien plantada*. Now Anna María is the new Teresa. But her image is not composed from the forms of a Symbolism that is fleeing from itself, but from the adaptation of resources to a Classical Picasso who has been robbed of all his Expressionist tensions. In *Figura de espaldas* we have the same transcription.

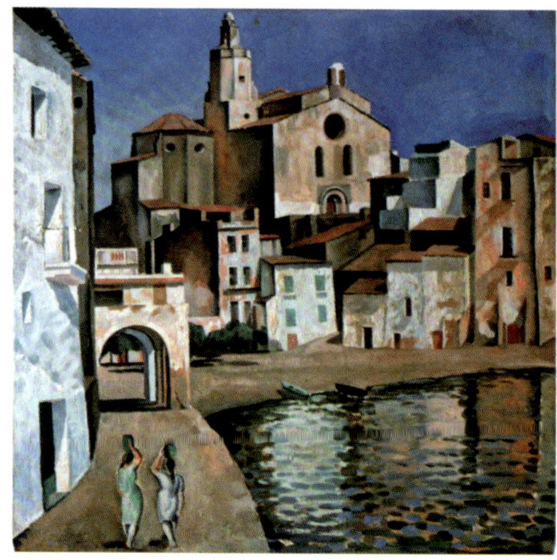

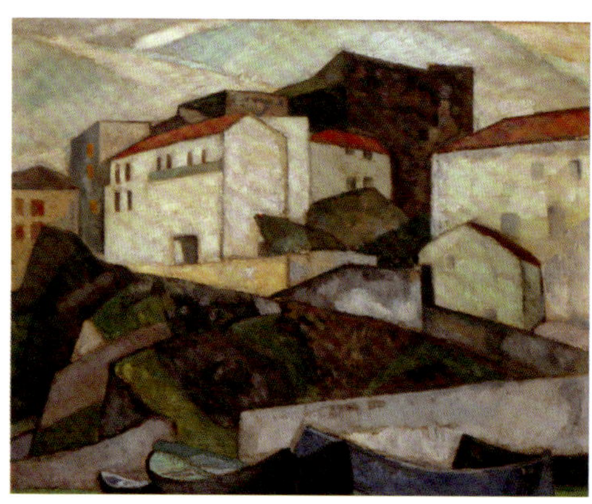

Salvador Dalí
Port Alguer, 1924
FIGUERES, FUNDACIÓN GALA-SALVADOR DALÍ

Daniel Vázquez Díaz
Boats on the Ramp, 1919
BILBAO, MUSEO DE BELLAS ARTES
BILBOKO ARTE EDERREN MUSEO

Mariano de Cossío
The Painter's Woman, 1927
PRIVATE COLLECTION

Ángeles Santos
Pensive, 1929
PRIVATE COLLECTION

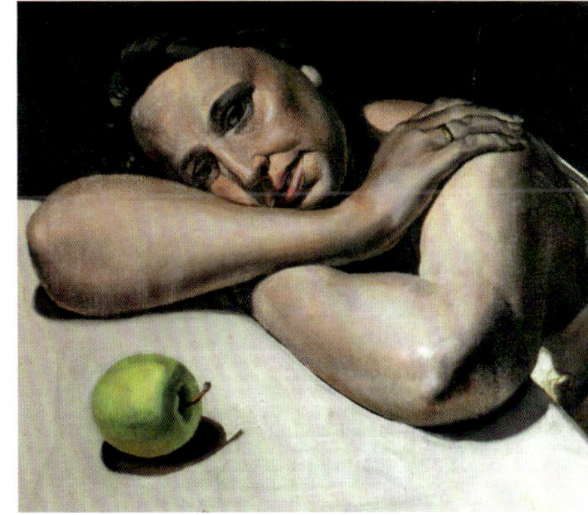

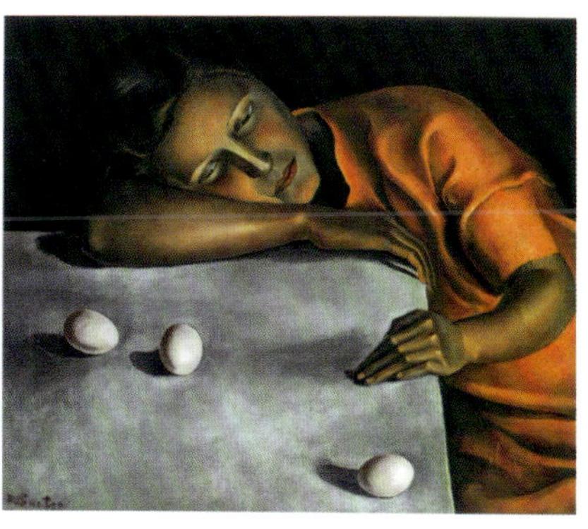

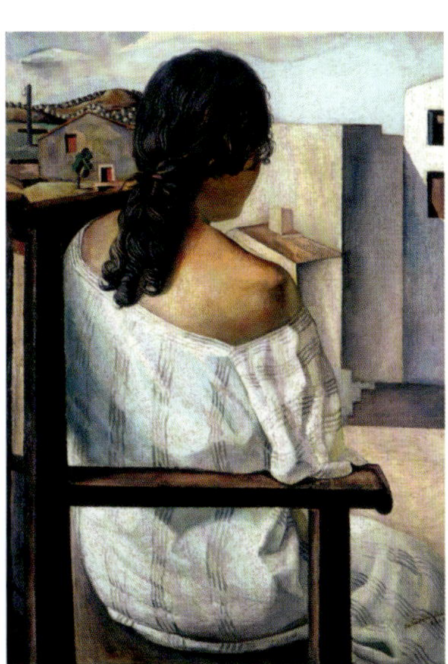

The maritime and fishing space has been replaced by the rural space. By a farmhouse with small hills in the background, beside which there is—and this is no mere chance in Dalinian thought—by a telephone pole: the reference to the rural in Dalí is not a reference to the ancestral, here it is a reference to the here and now: the vernacular does not exist if it is not in dialogue with the present. But, why in the painting with a maritime theme does the female figure look at the spectator and in the one with a rural theme she turns her back and looks towards the house? Was it only because Dalí wanted to show his virtuosity by painting her wavy hair? In any event, the equivalent of the portrait of Anna María may have nothing to do with García Lorca, but with *Portrait of Luis Buñuel*. The Rationalist architecture of the square in the background, the University City under construction, is intended to possess the same meaning as the popular architecture in the portrait of Anna María. The maritime citation in the *Portrait of Anna María* is here the sky of Madrid, with its clouds like lips, *à la* Mantegna. It is one for the other. The vernacular for the Modern and the Modern for the vernacular. ■

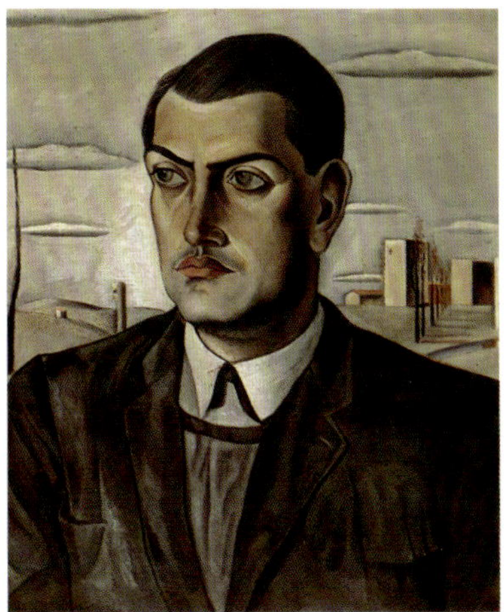

Salvador Dalí
Figure from Behind, 1925
MADRID, MUSEO NACIONAL CENTRO DE ARTE REINA SOFÍA

Salvador Dalí
Portrait of Luis Buñuel, 1924
MADRID, MUSEO NACIONAL CENTRO DE ARTE REINA SOFÍA

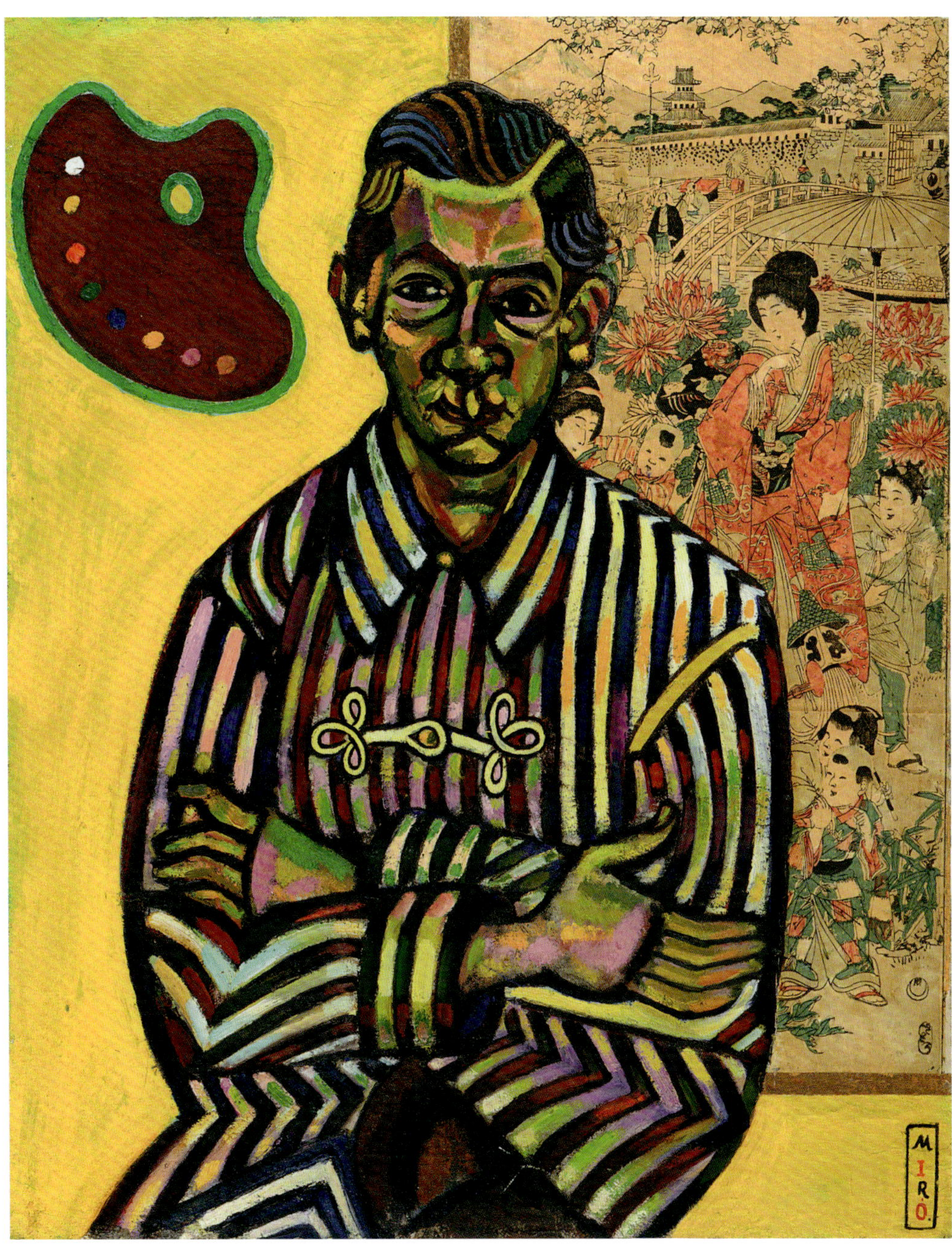

2.1 Joan Miró
Portrait of Enric Cristòfol Ricart
[Retrat d'Enric Cristòfol Ricart]
Winter 1916 or early spring 1917
NEW YORK, THE MUSEUM OF MODERN ART, FLORENE MAY SCHOENBORN BEQUEST. 822.1996

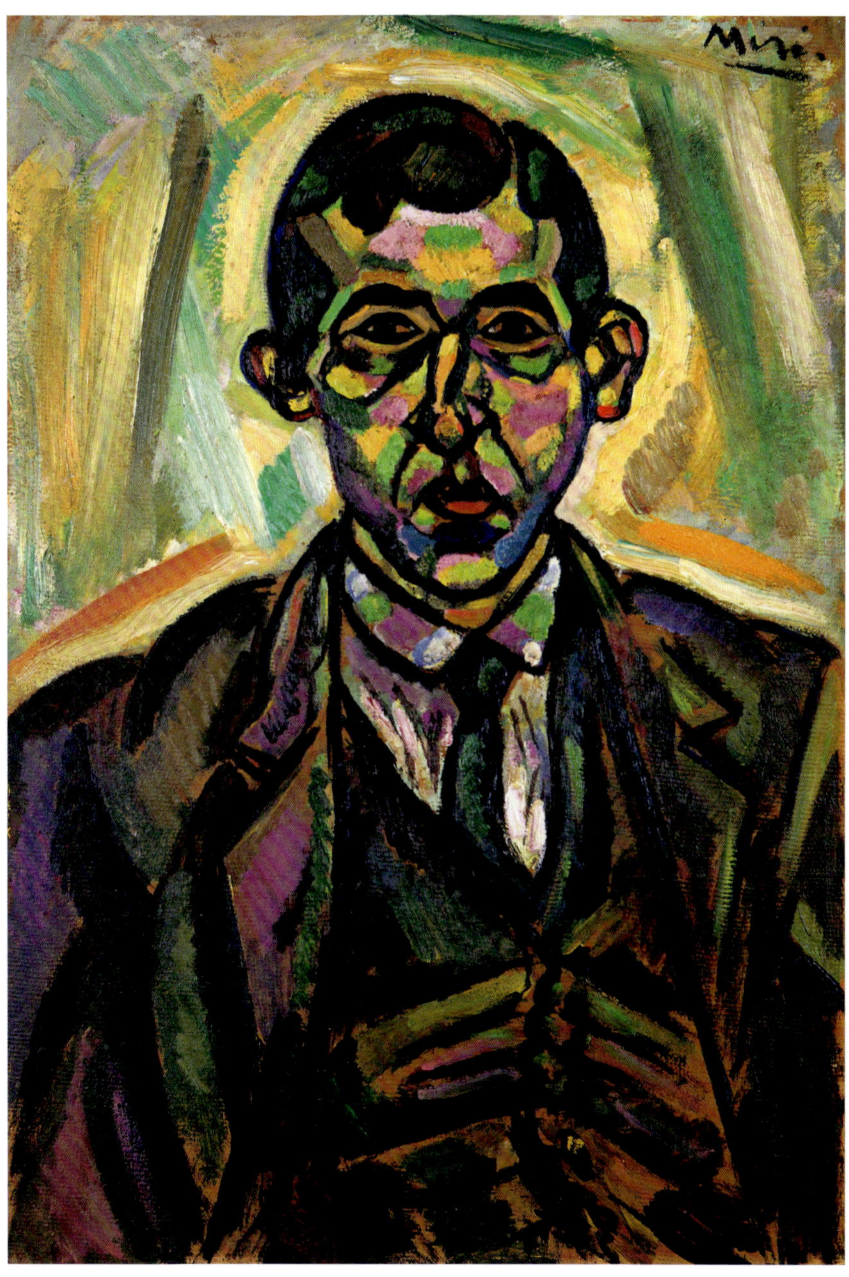

2.2 Joan Miró
Portrait of Josep F. Ràfols
[Retrat de Josep F. Ràfols]
1917

ST. LOUIS, MILDRED LANE KEMPER ART MUSEUM, WASHINGTON UNIVERSITY IN ST. LOUIS
GIFT OF MR. AND MRS. SYDNEY M. SHOENBERG, JR., 1961

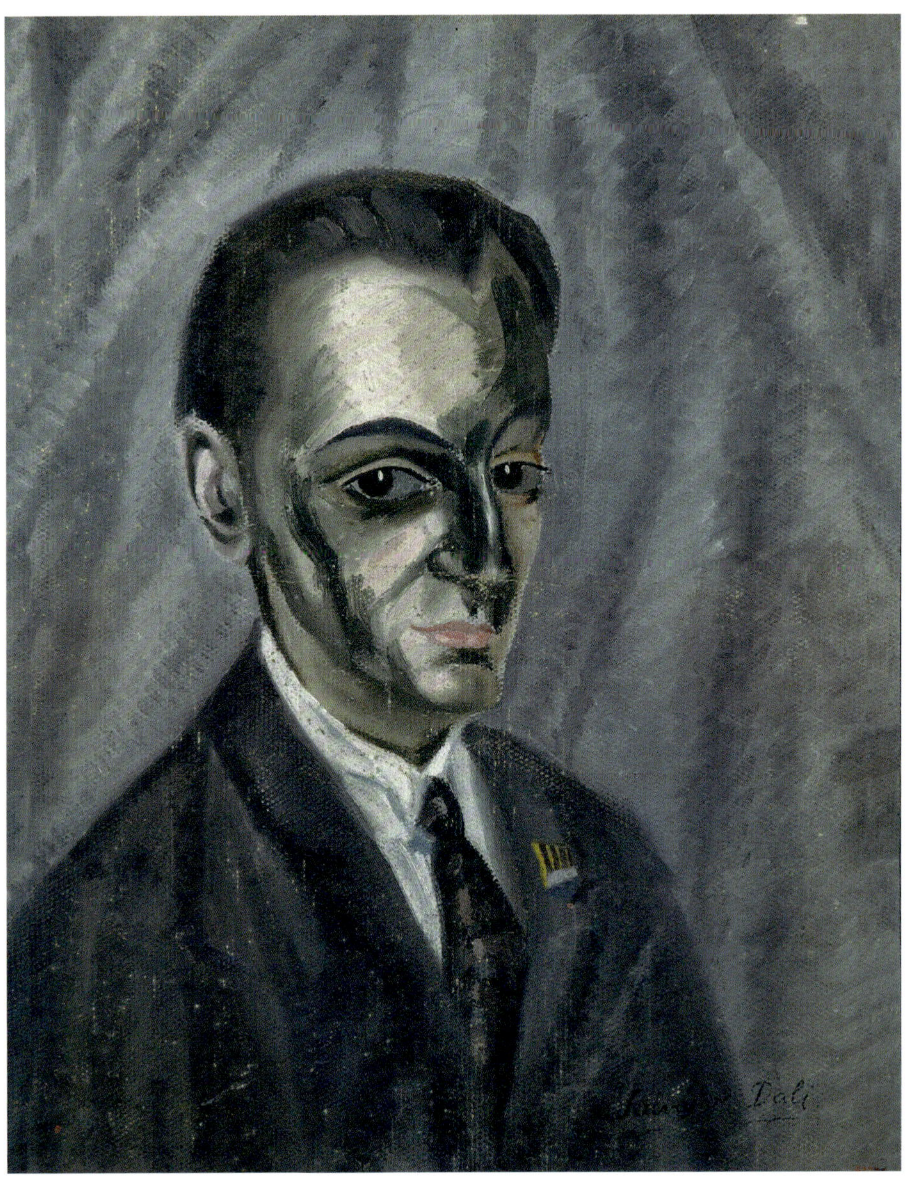

2.3 Salvador Dalí
Portrait of Joan Torres i Darnis
[Retrat de Joan Torres i Darnis]
c. 1922
BARCELONA, MNAC - MUSEU NACIONAL D'ART DE CATALUNYA. 043720-000

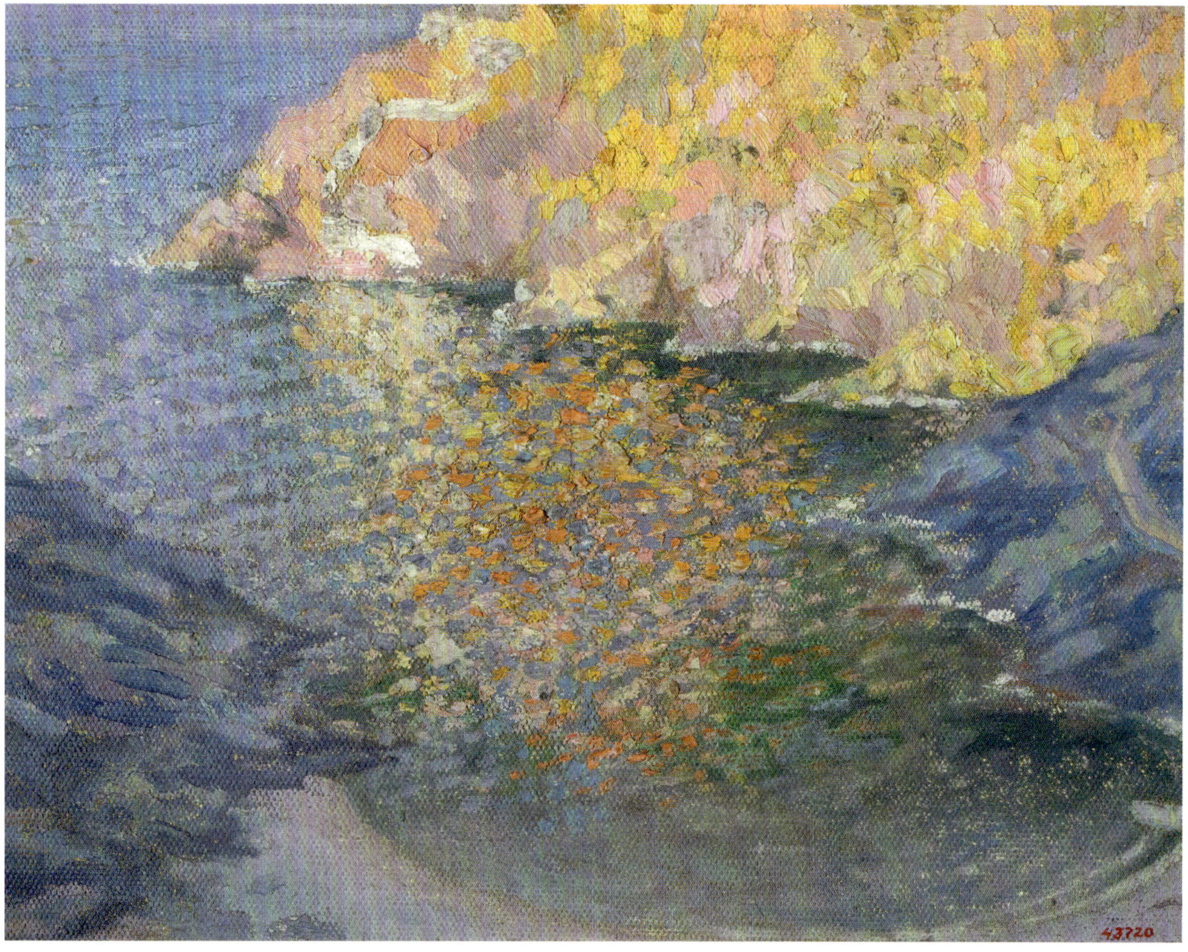

2.3 verso
Nans Cove. Cadaqués
[Cala Nans. Cadaqués]
c. 1920

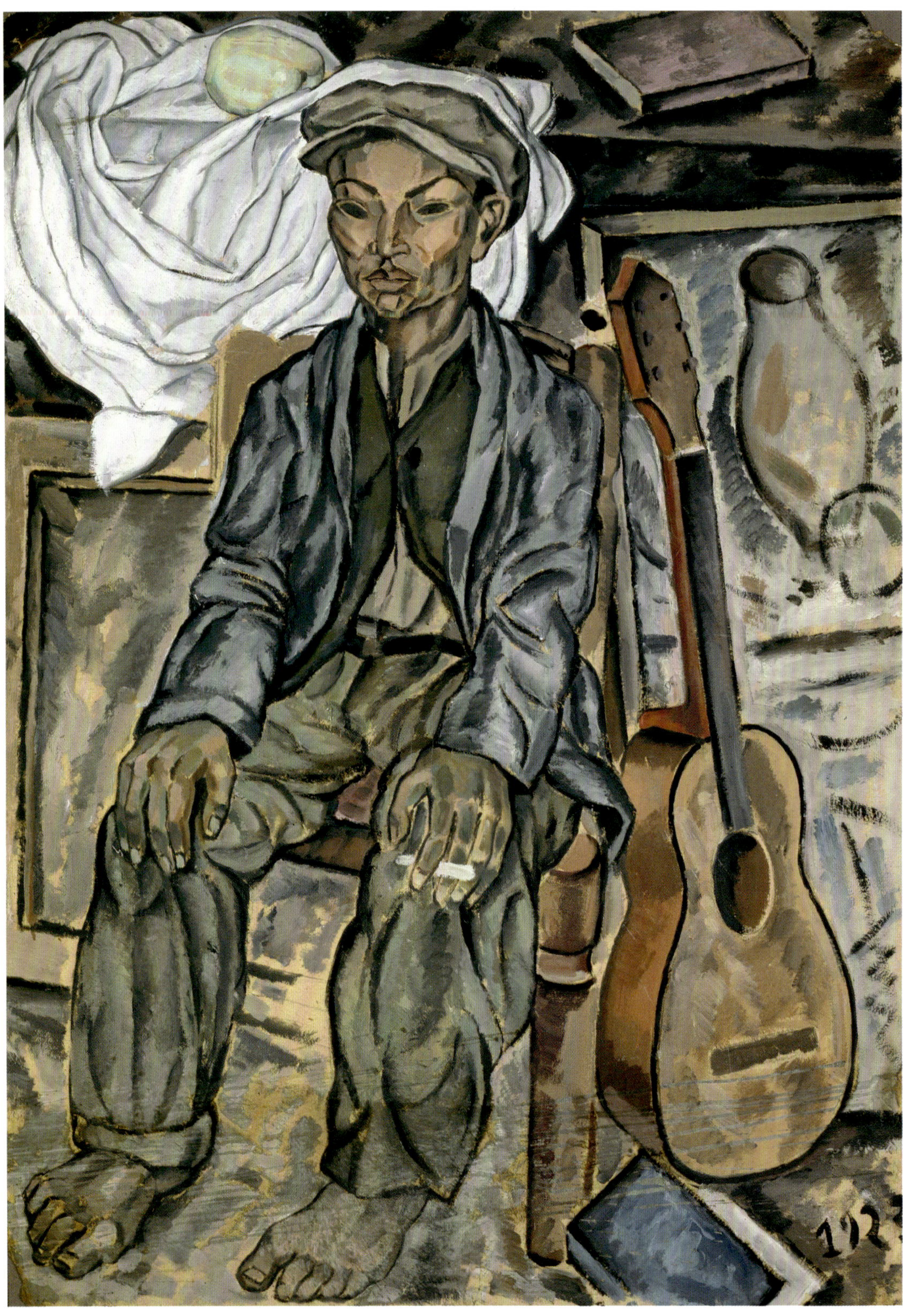

2.4 Salvador Dalí
Figueres Gypsy
[Gitano de Figueres]
1923
MADRID, MUSEO NACIONAL CENTRO DE ARTE REINA SOFÍA. AS11129

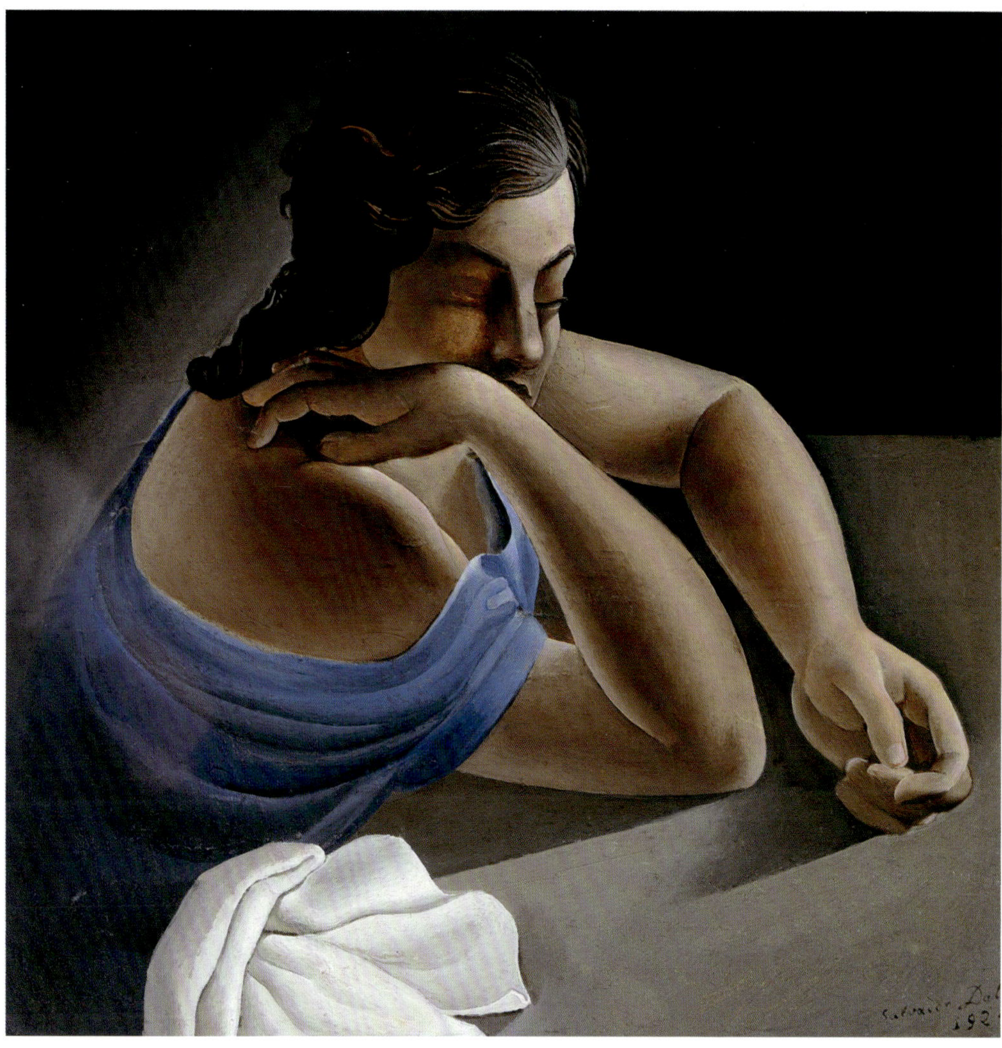

2.5 Salvador Dalí
Figure at a Table (Anna María Dalí)
[Figura en una taula (Figura en una mesa. Anna María Dalí)]
1925
MILAN, PRIVATE COLLECTION

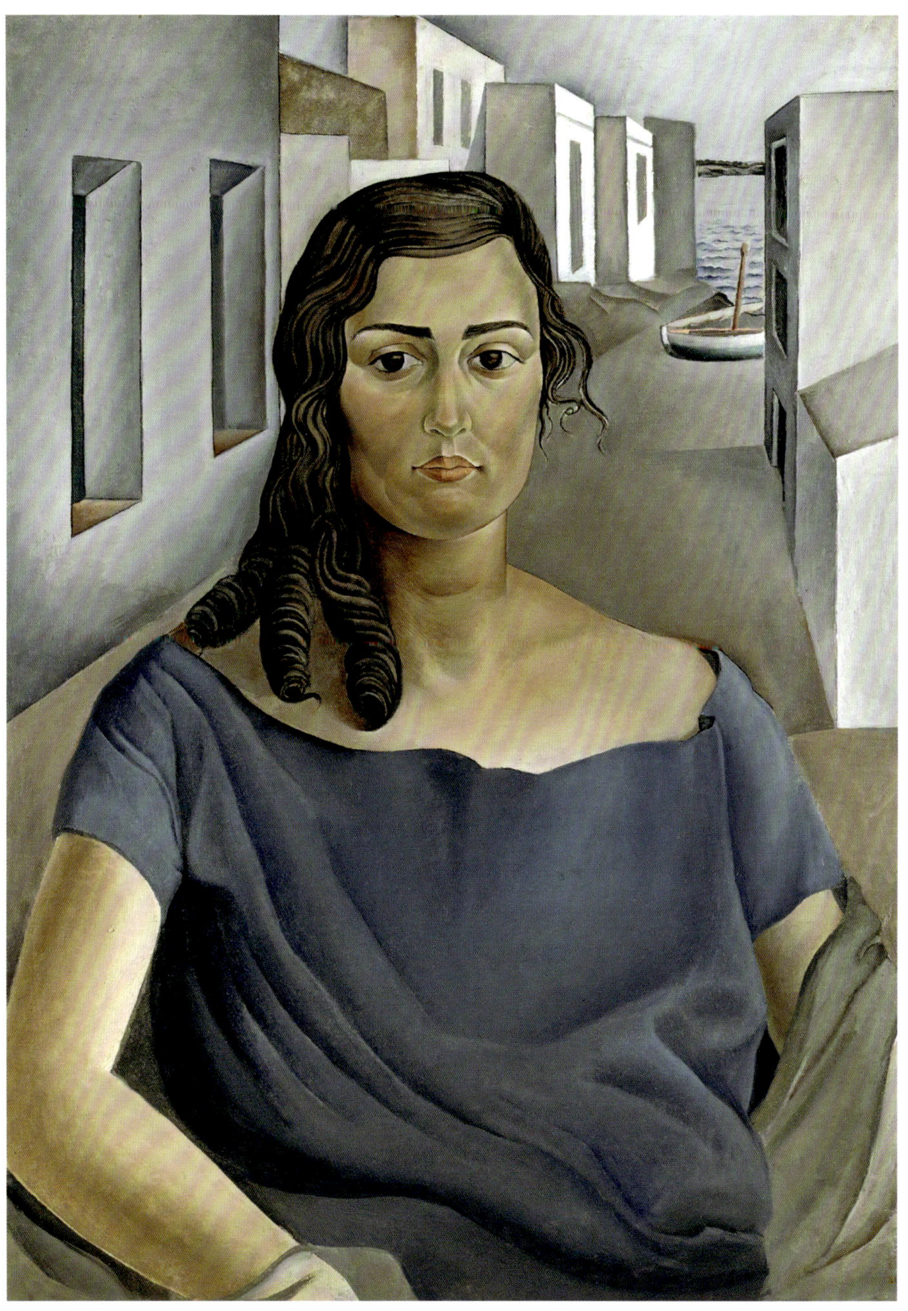

2.6 Salvador Dalí
Portrait of my Sister
[Retrat de la meva germana / Retrato de mi hermana]
1925
FIGUERES, FUNDACIÓ GALA-SALVADOR DALÍ

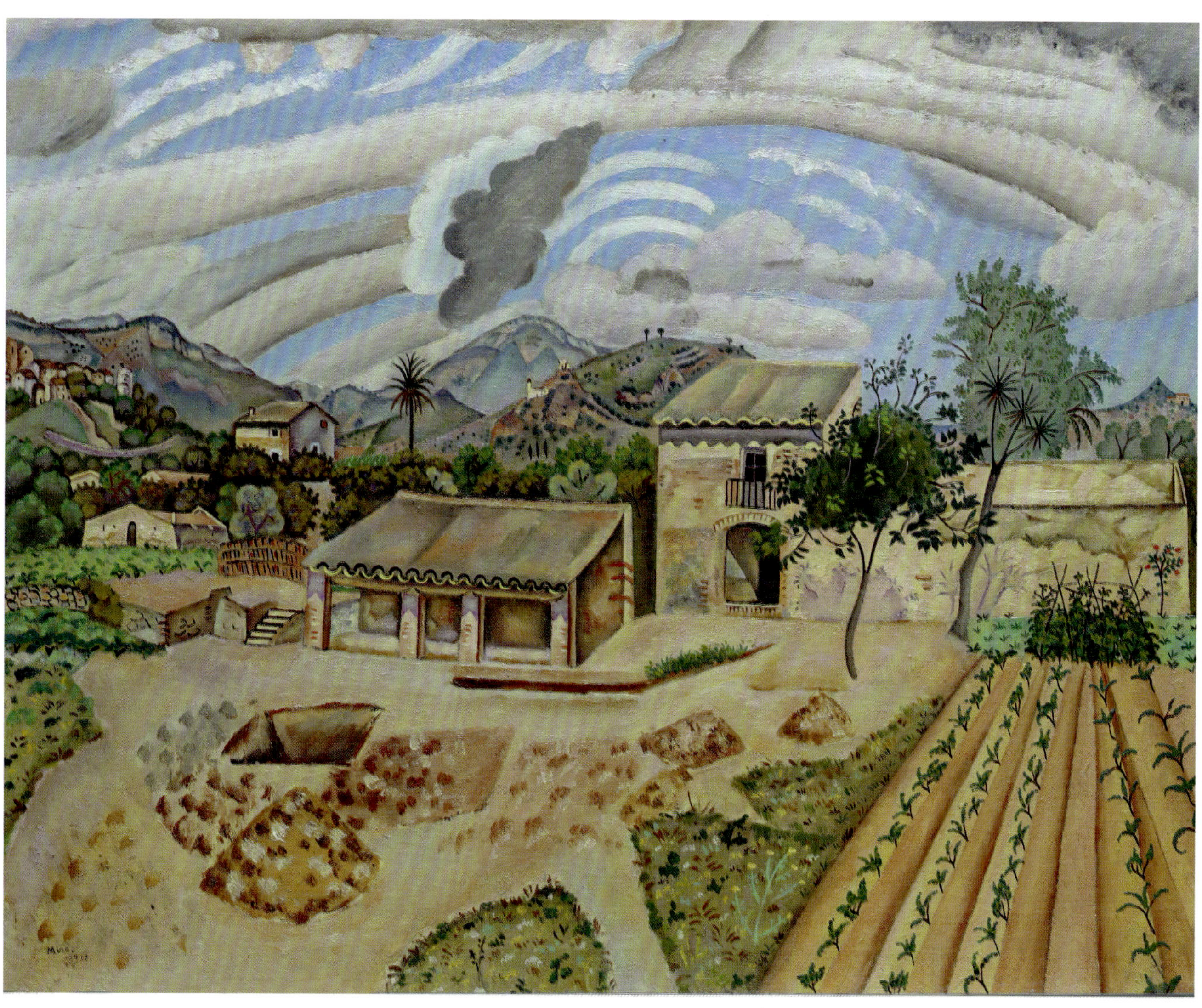

2.7 Joan Miró
Tile Factory in Mont-roig
[Tuilerie à Mont-roig]
1918
NEW YORK, PRIVATE COLLECTION. COURTESY OF MDP & ASSOCIATI, LUGANO

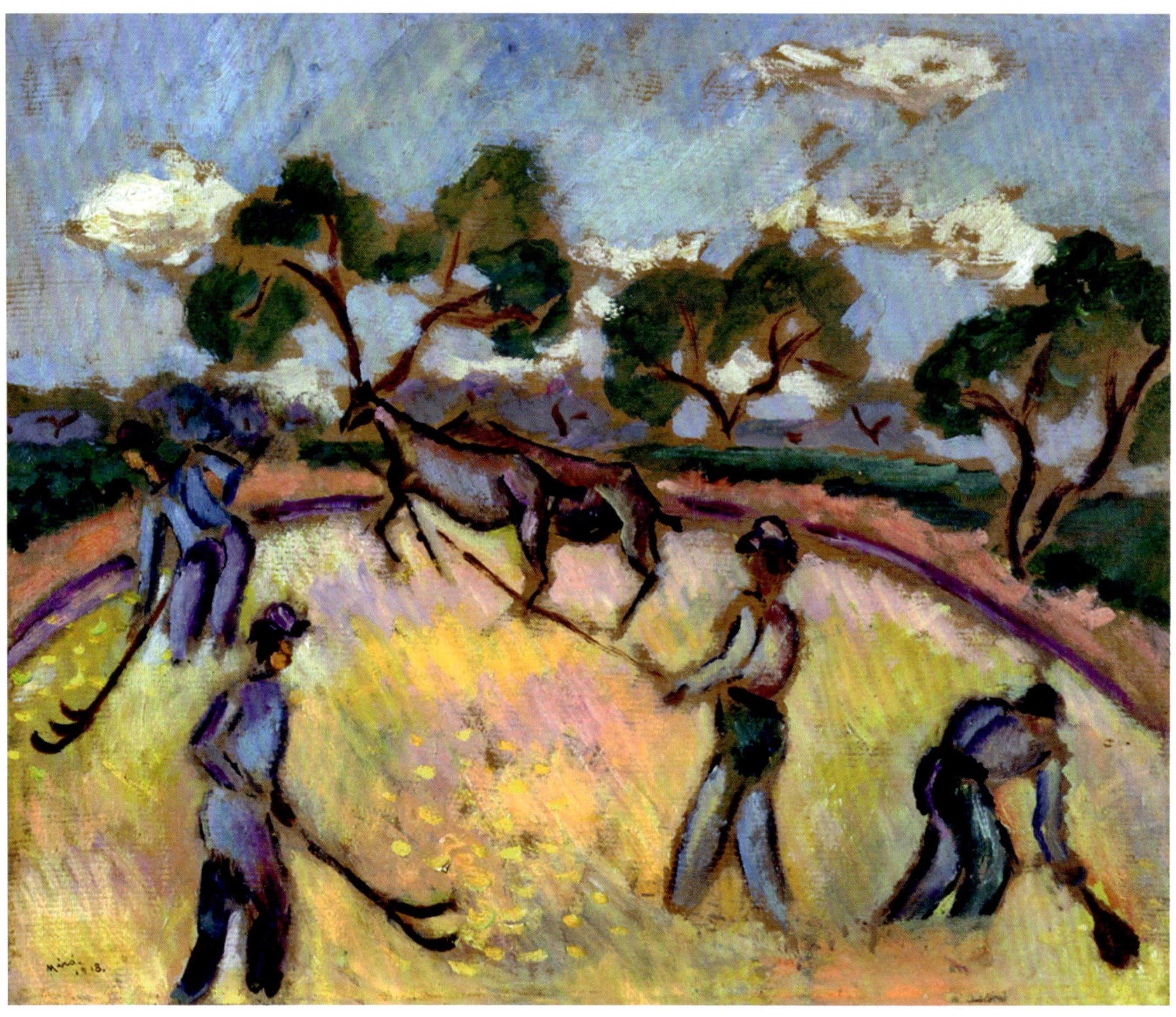

2.8 Joan Miró
Threshing
[Battage du blé]
1918
PARIS, COLLECTION MAEGHT. BAC 2242

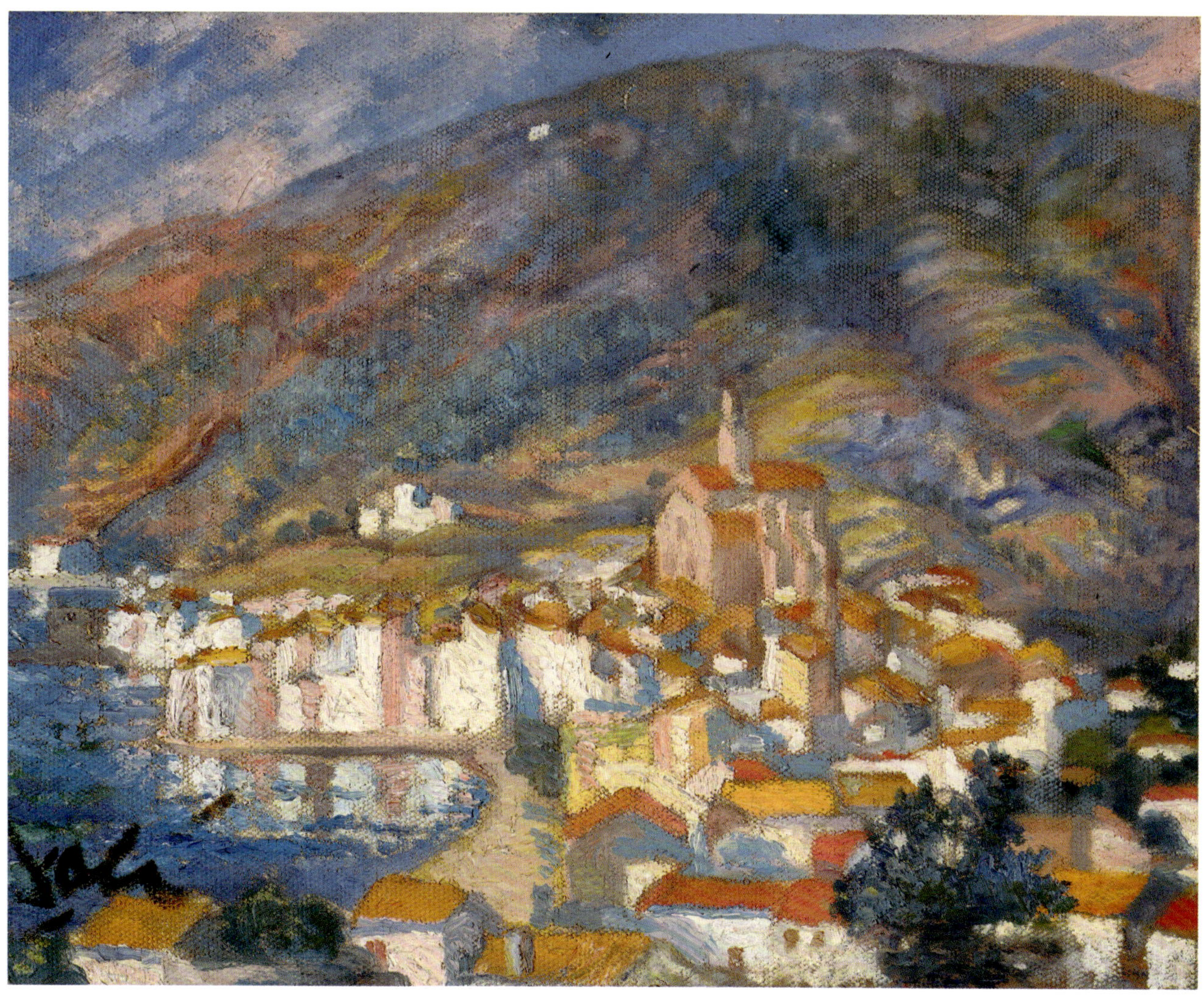

2.9 Salvador Dalí
Landscape of Cadaqués
[Paisatge de Cadaqués / Paisaje de Cadaqués]
1920–1
OVIEDO, COLLECCION MASAVEU. C/TV.136

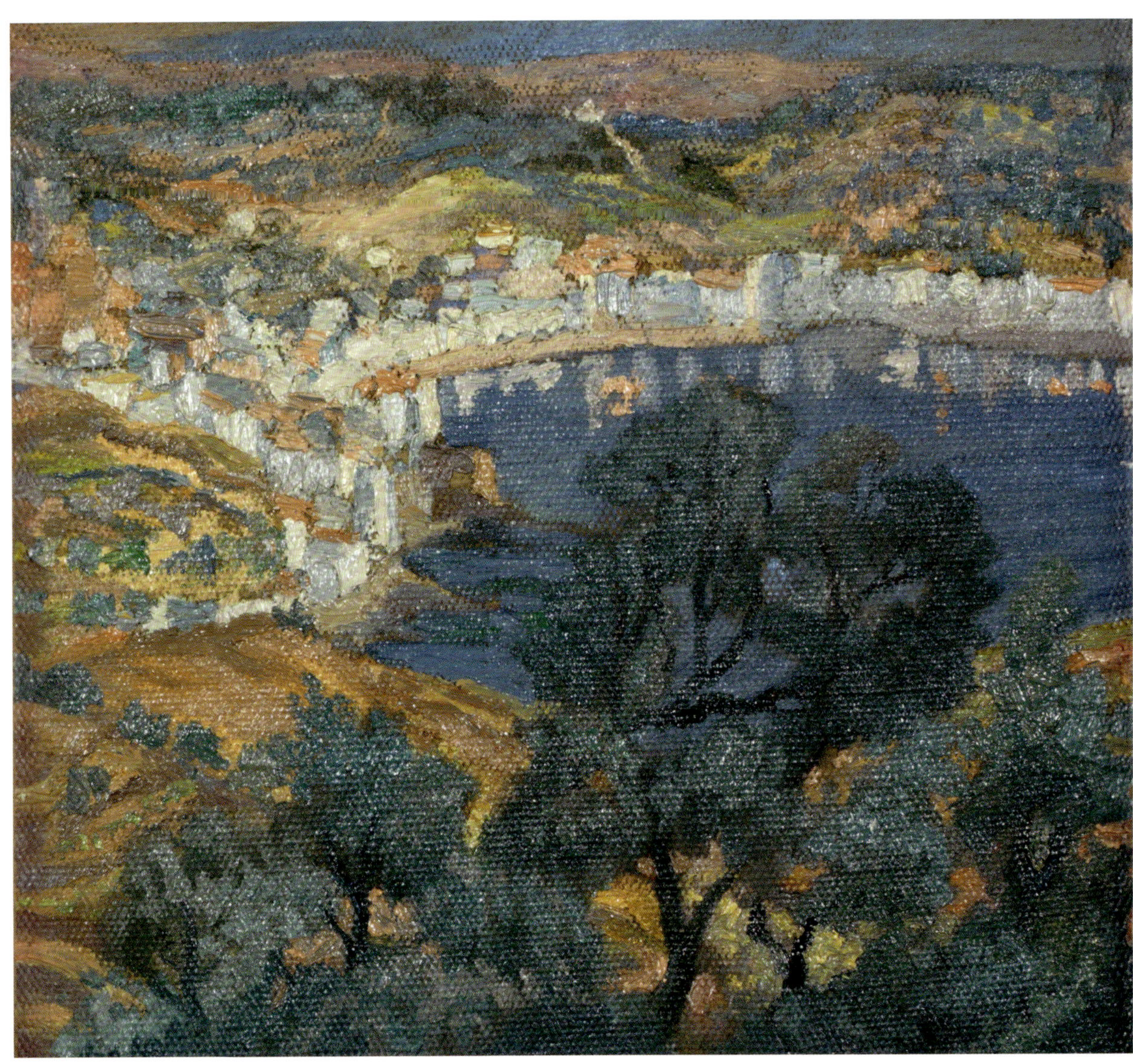

2.10 Salvador Dalí
Landscape of Cadaqués
[Paisatge de Cadaqués / Paisaje de Cadaqués]
c. 1921
BERN, KUNSTMUSEUM BERN, BEQUEST OF GEORGES F. KELLER 1981

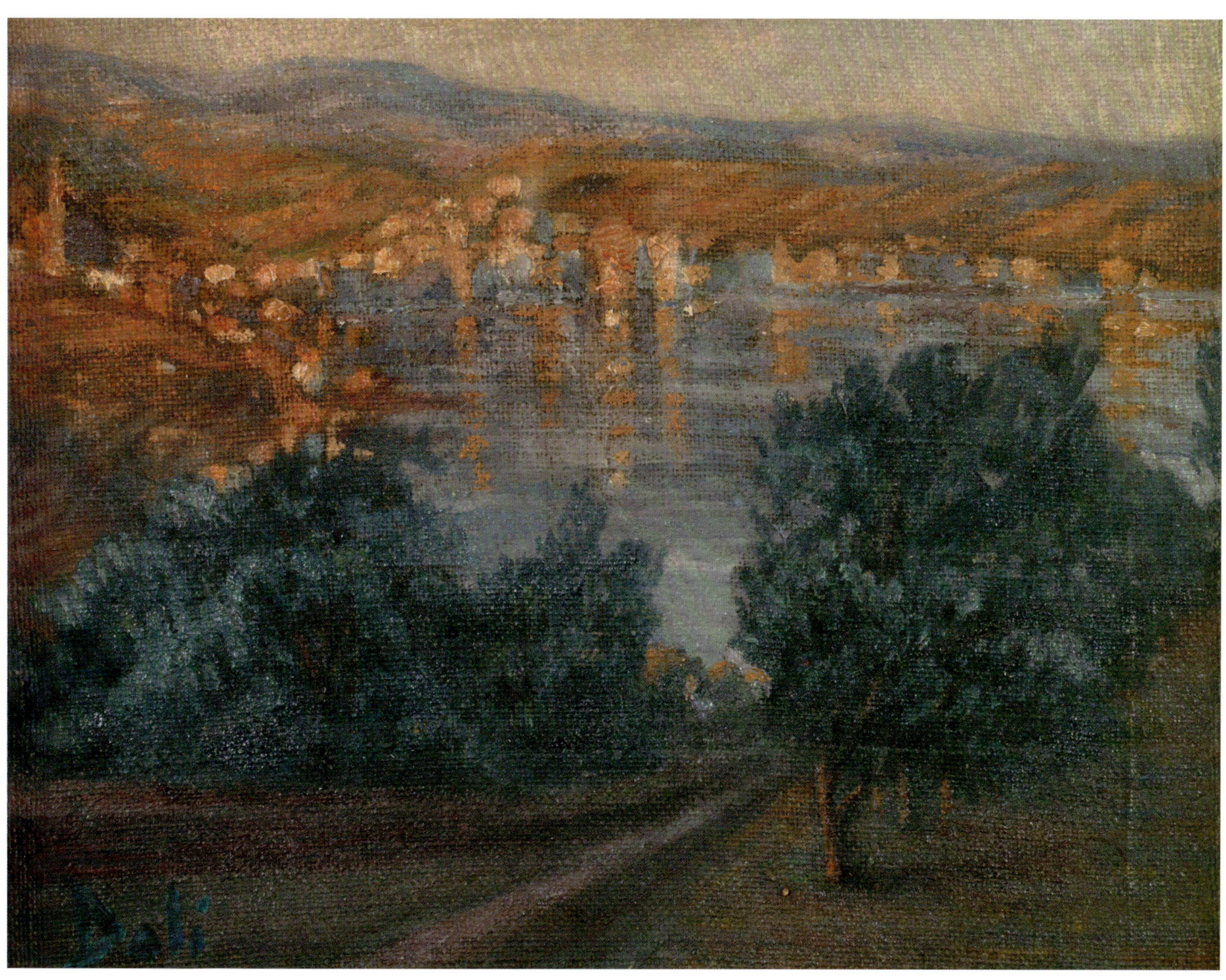

2.11 Salvador Dalí
Landscape of Cadaqués
[Paisatge de Cadaqués]
c. 1921
BERN, KUNSTMUSEUM BERN, BEQUEST OF GEORGES F. KELLER 1981

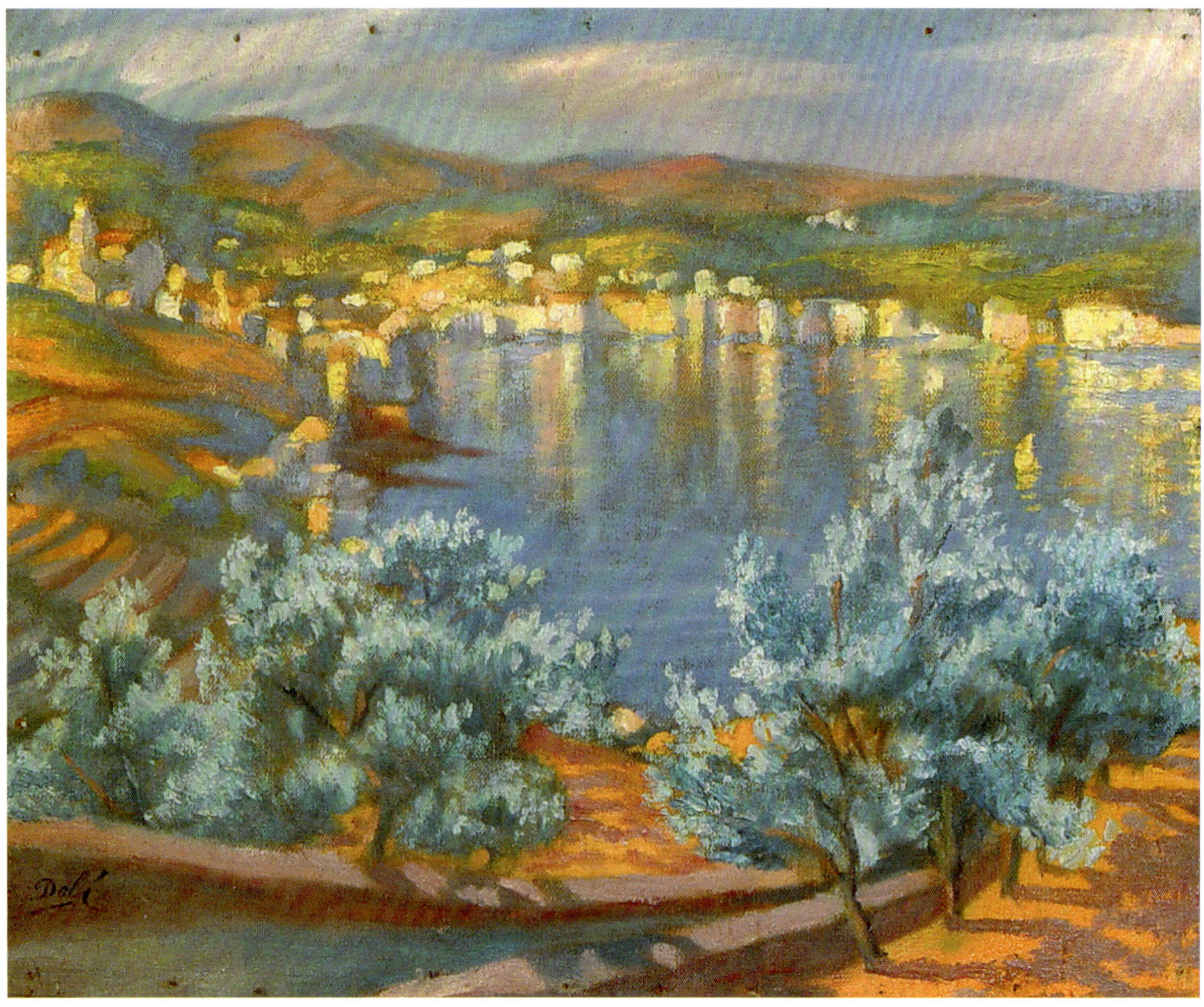

2.12 Salvador Dalí
Landscape of Cadaqués
[Paisatge de Cadaqués / Paisaje de Cadaqués]
c. 1921
PRIVATE COLLECTION

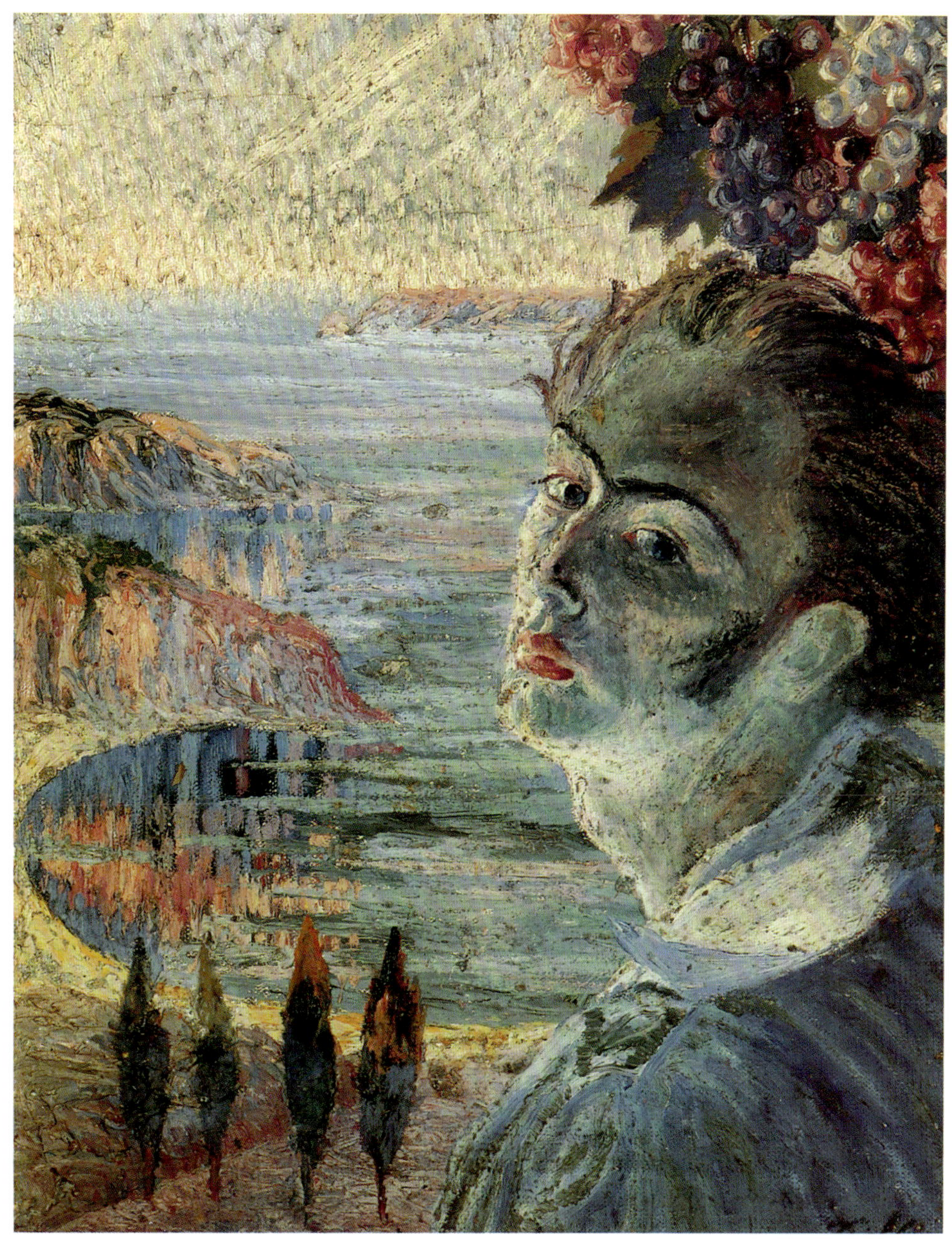

2.12 verso
Self Portrait
[Autoretrat / Autoretrato]
c. 1920

2.13 Salvador Dalí
The Jorneta Stream
[El torrent de la Jorneta / El torente de la Jorneta]
c. 1923

DEPOSIT OF PRIVATE COLLECTION, TENERIFE
CABILDO INSULAR DE TENERIFE, TEA TENERIFE ESPACIO DE LAS ARTES. DG2010-01

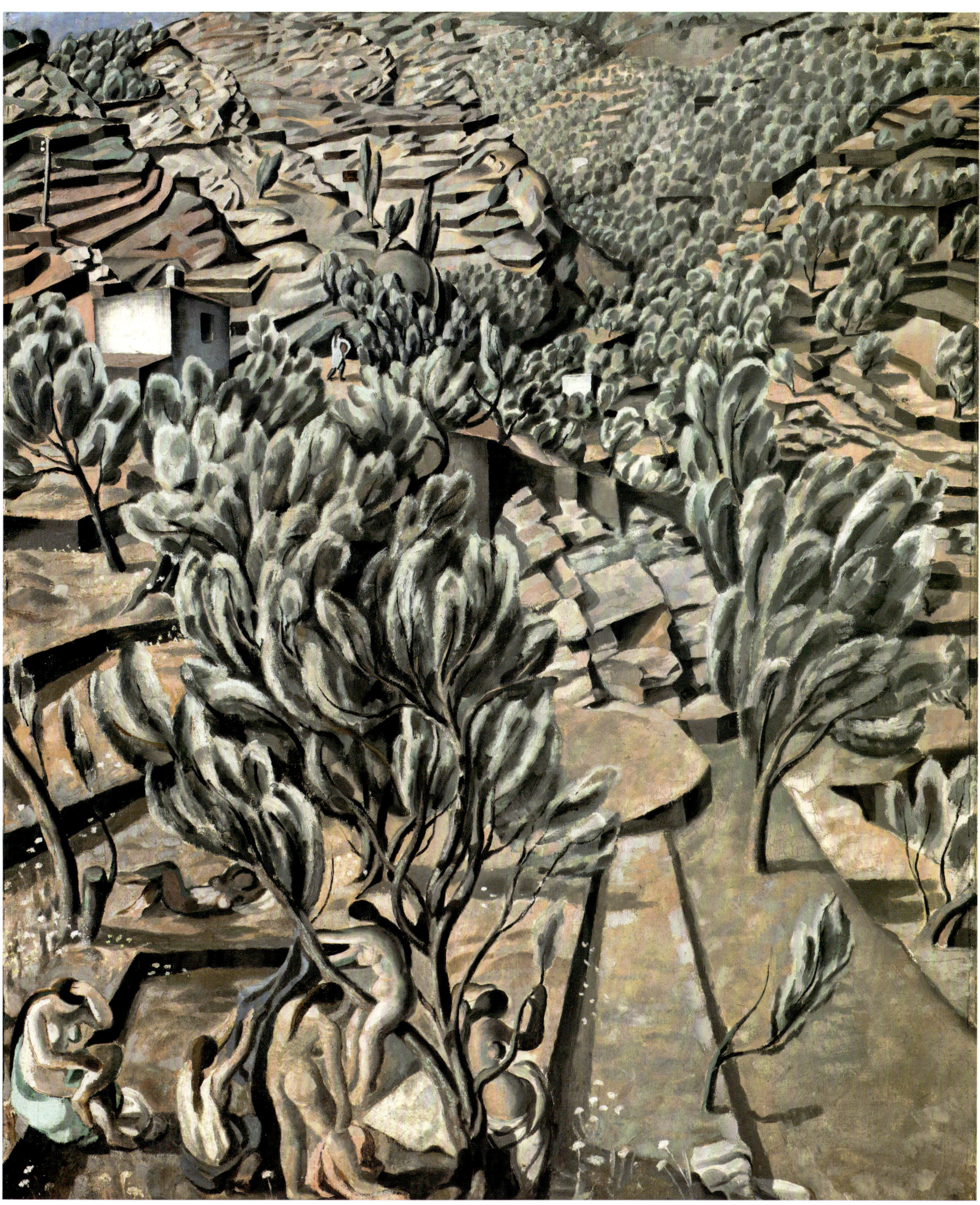

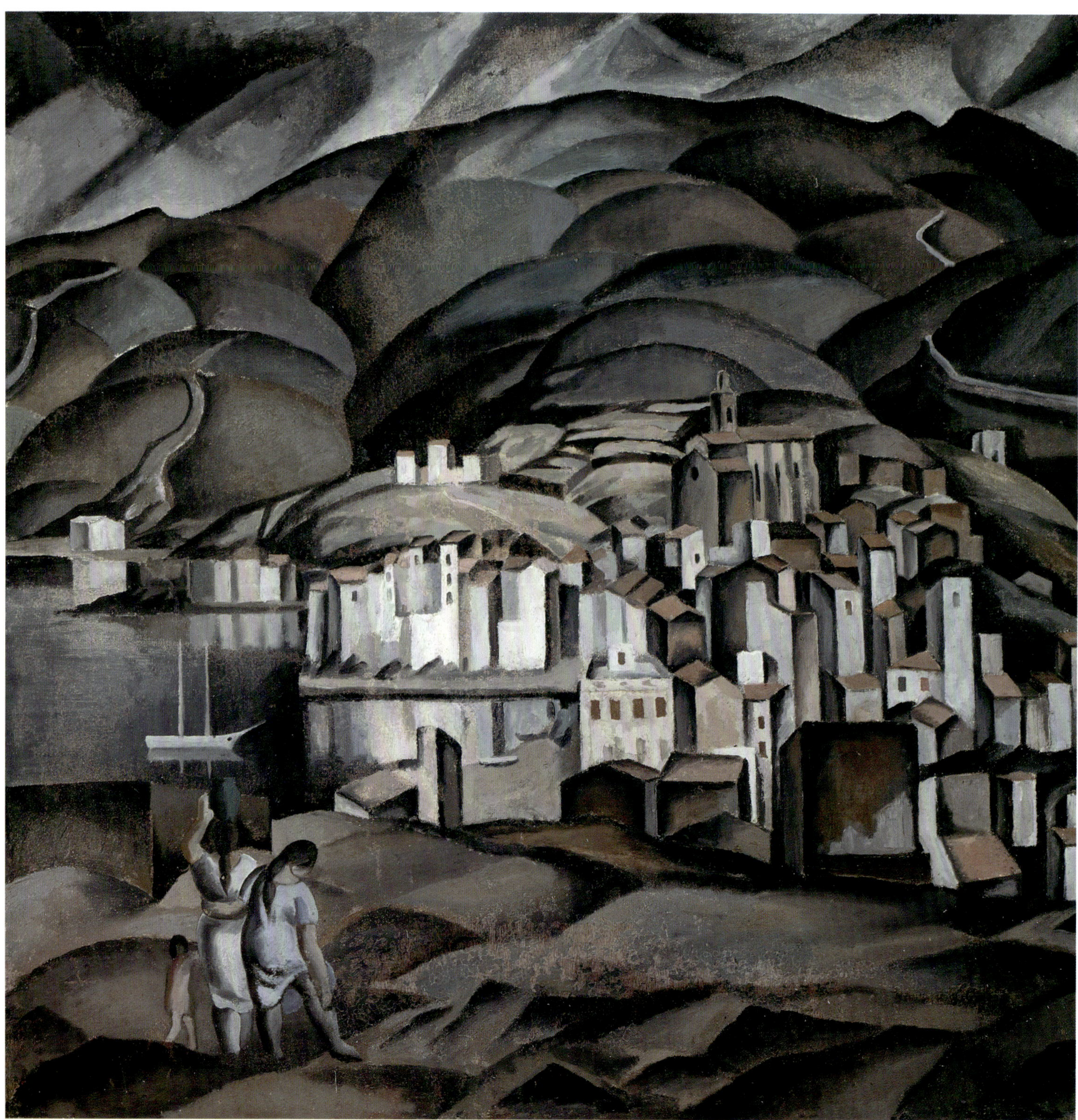

2.14 Salvador Dalí
Cadaqués Seen from the Tower of Creus
[Cadaqués vist des de la Torre de Les Creus /
Cadaqués visto desde de la Torre de los Creus]
c. 1923
FIGUERES, FUNDACIÓ GALA-SALVADOR DALÍ

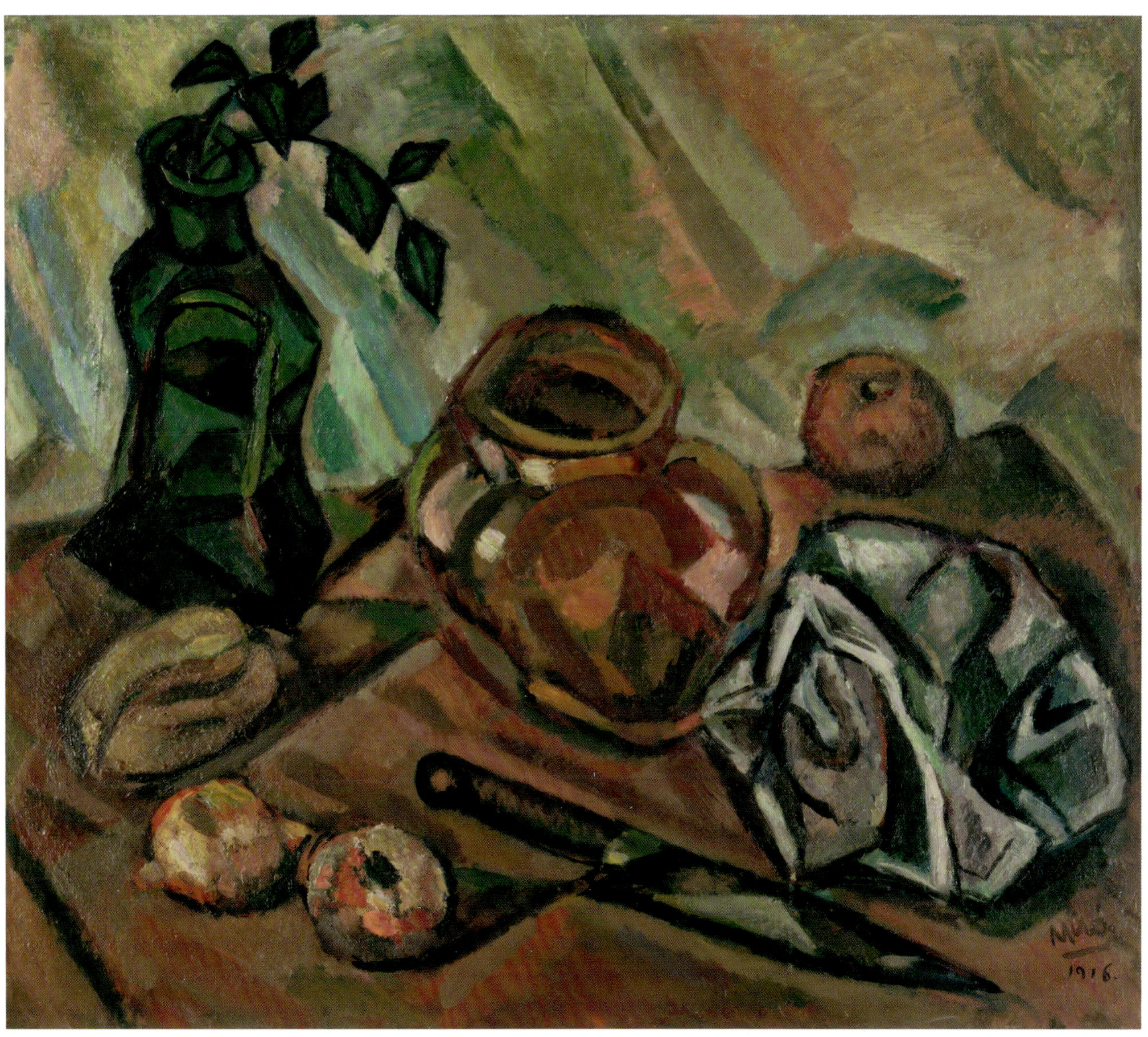

2.15 Joan Miró
Still Life with Knife
[Nature morte au couteau]
1916
SWITZERLAND, NAHMAD COLLECTION

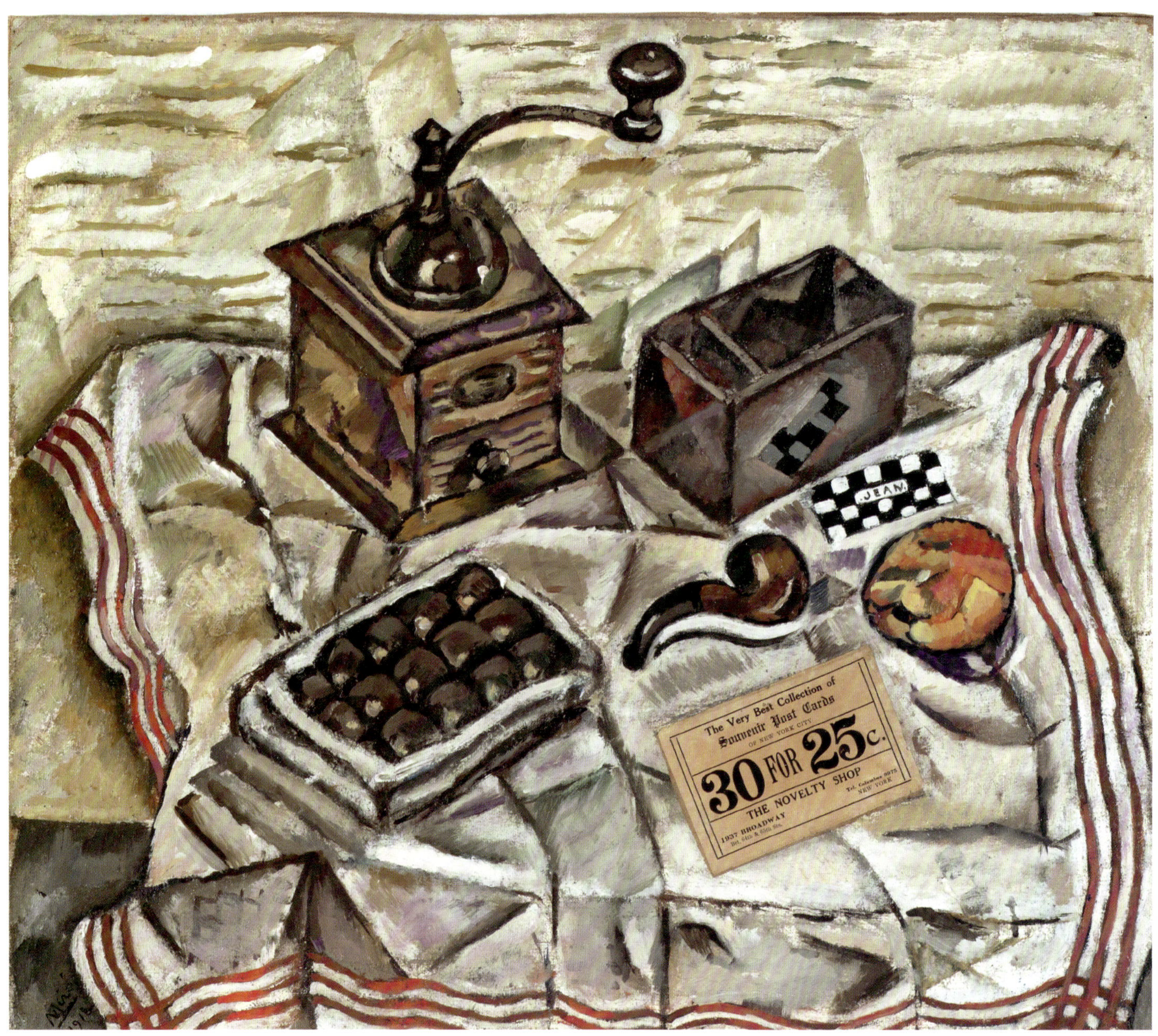

2.16 Joan Miró
The Coffee Mill
[Le Moulin à café]
1918
NEW YORK, PRIVATE COLLECTION. COURTESY OF MDP & ASSOCIATI, LUGANO

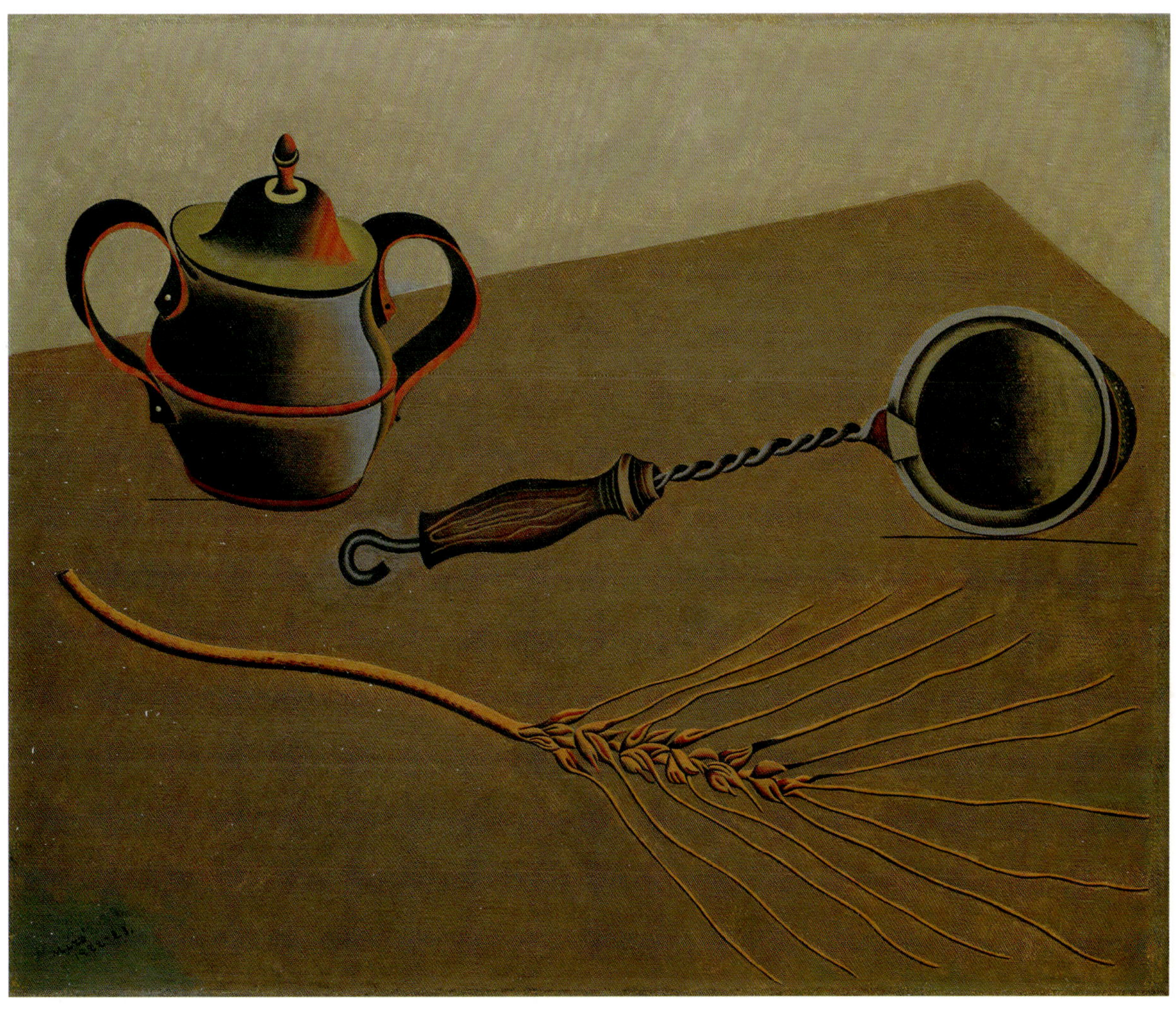

2.17 Joan Miró
Still Life I (The Ear of Corn)
[Nature morte I. (L'Épi de blé)]
1922–3
NEW YORK, THE MUSEUM OF MODERN ART. PURCHASE, 12.1939

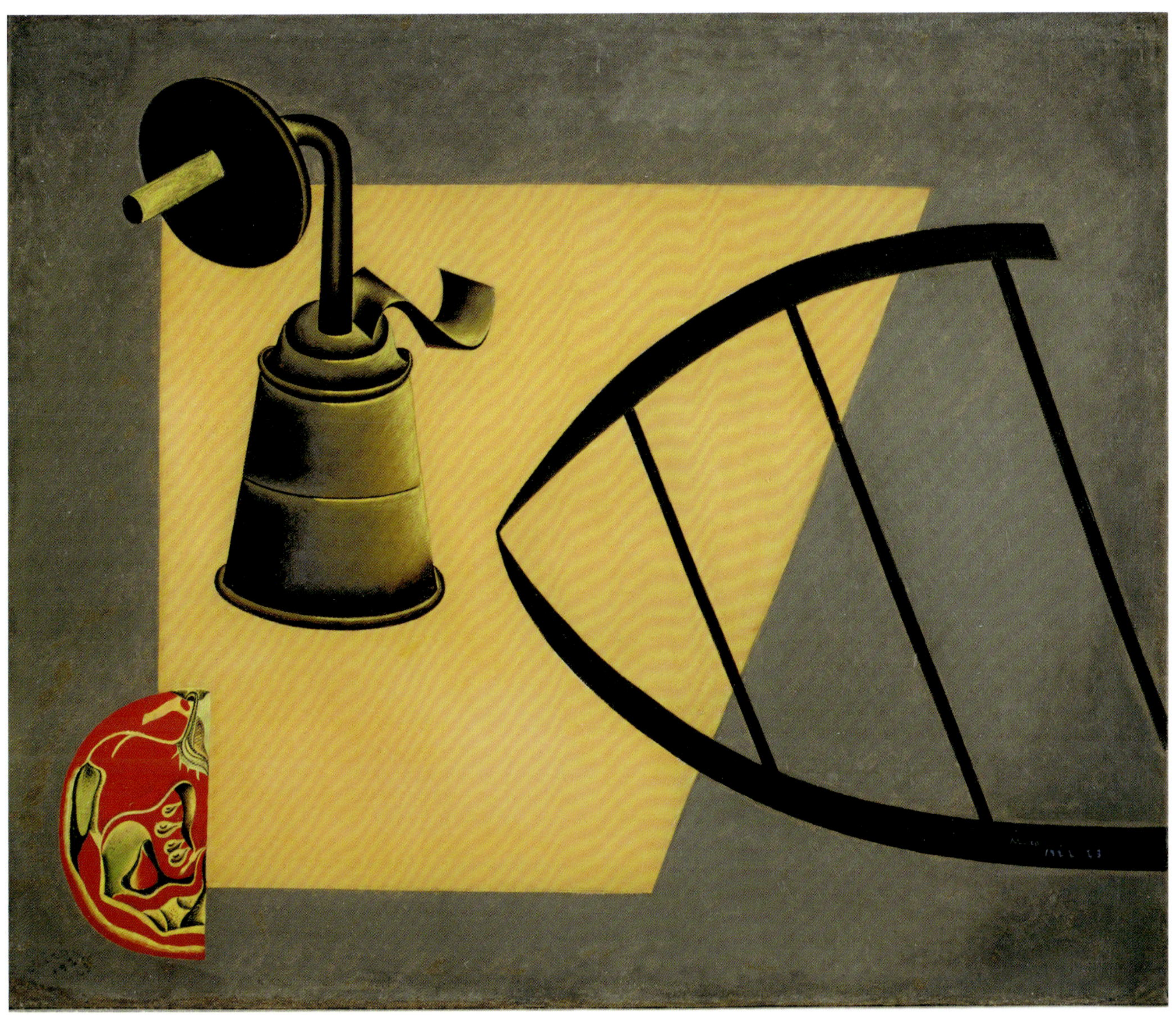

2.18 Joan Miró
Still Life II (The Carbide Lamp)
[Nature morte II. (La Lampe à carbure)]
Mont-roig and Paris 1922–3
NEW YORK, THE MUSEUM OF MODERN ART. PURCHASE, 11.1939

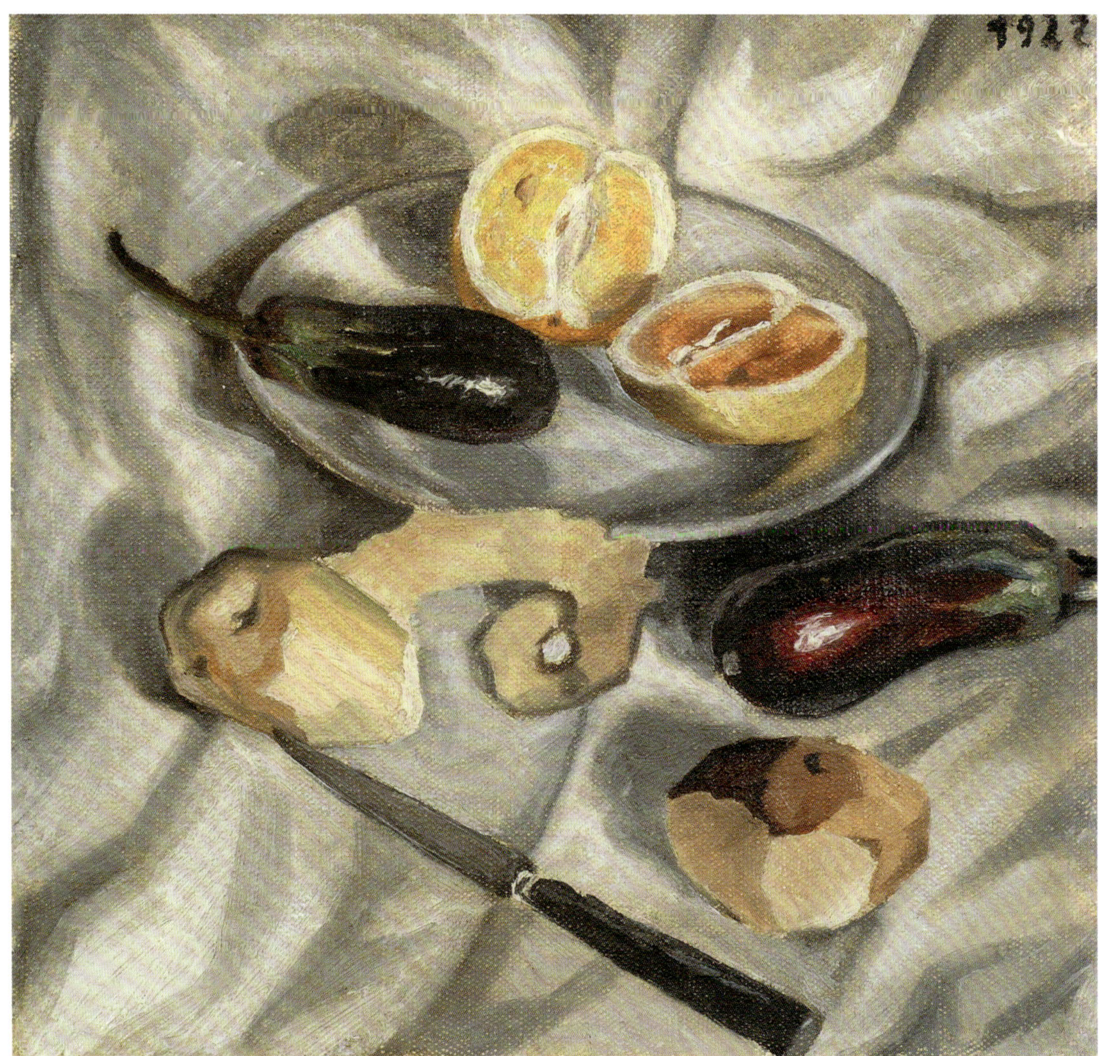

2.19 Salvador Dalí
Still Life with Aubergines
[Natura morta emb albergines / Bodegón con berenjenas]
1922 (reverse *c.* 1919)
BERN, KUNSTMUSEUM BERN, LEGAT GEORGES F. KELLER 1981

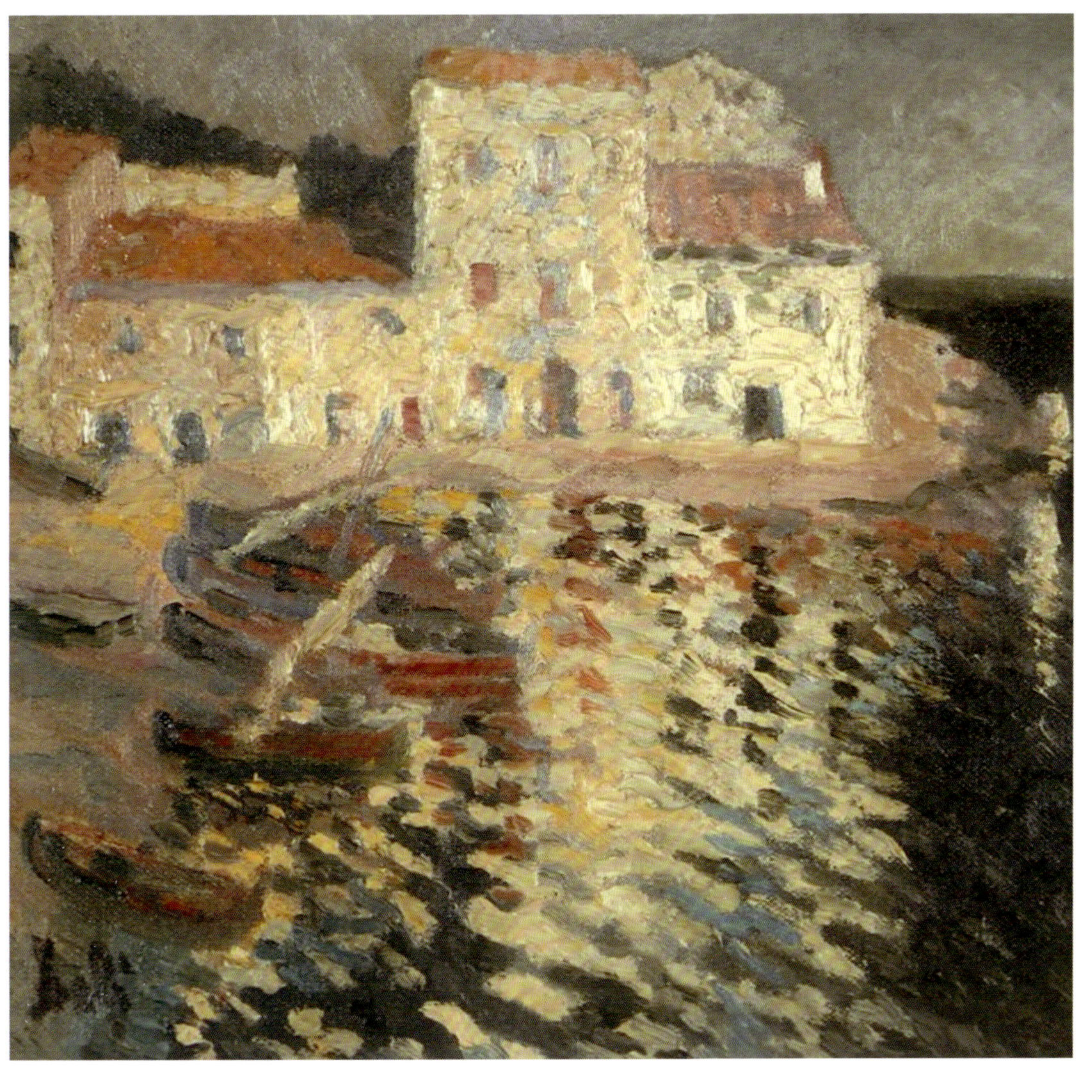

2.19 verso
Cadaqués
c. 1919

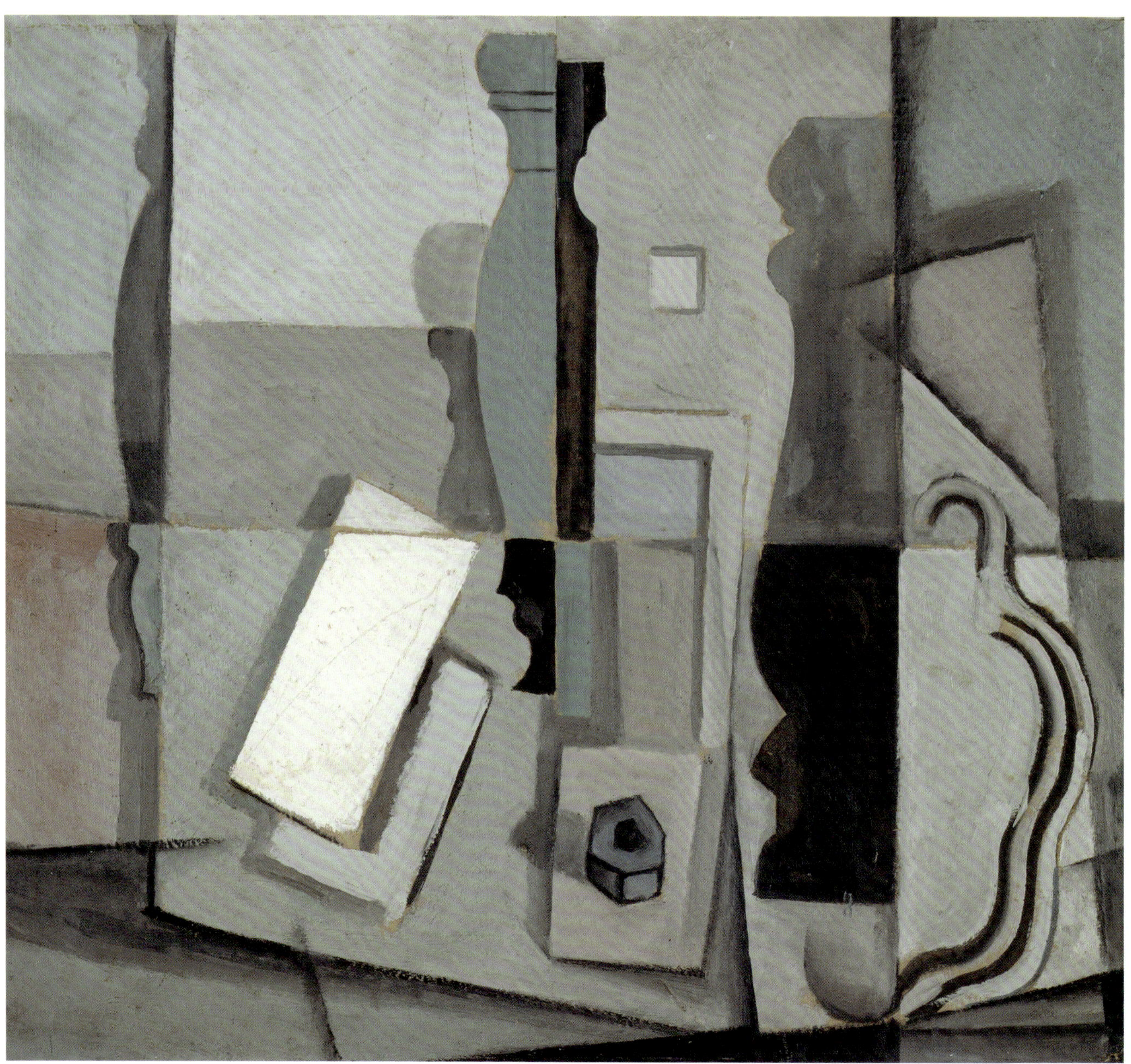

2.20 Salvador Dalí
Still Life
[Natura morta / Naturaleza muerta / Bodegón]
1923
MADRID, MUSEO NACIONAL CENTRO DE ARTE REINA SOFÍA. AS11132

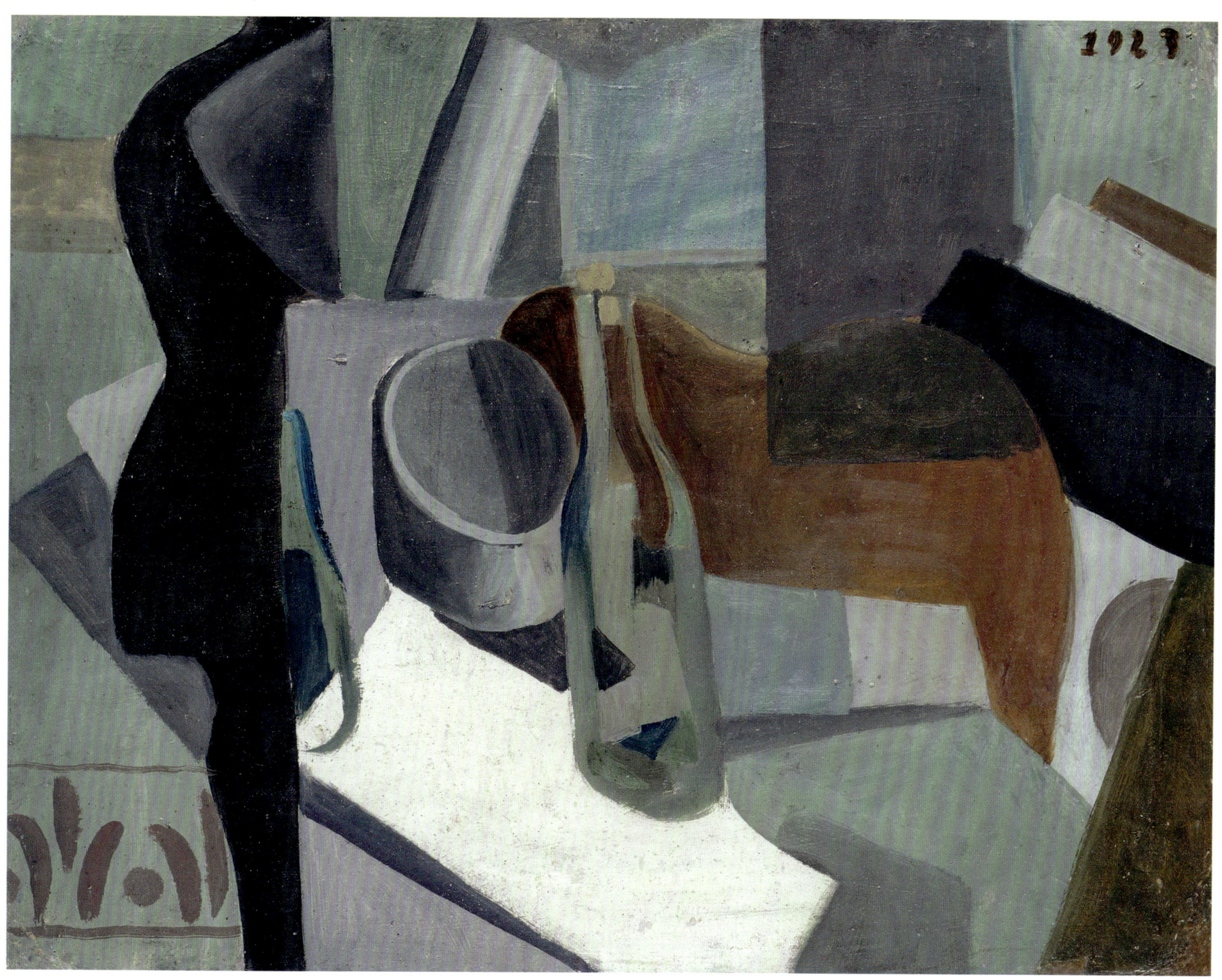

2.21 Salvador Dalí
Still Life
[Natura morta / Naturaleza muerta]
1923
MADRID, MUSEO NACIONAL CENTRO DE ARTE REINA SOFÍA. AS11130

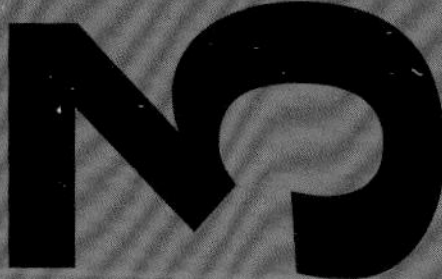

THE THIRD CONSIDERATION

WHEN MIRÓ ALMOST MET PICASSO

Barcelona, 1917 and more besides

WHEN MIRÓ ALMOST MET PICASSO

The female figure is powerful. The architecture contained in the painting is evocative and revealing, but by entitling his work *Portrait of my Sister* Dalí, in his painting executed between 1924 and 1925, shifted the interest of spectators, and of most of the critics and commentators, towards the private and autobiographical space, diverting the essential questions on the painting: the development of his plastic language and the wager regarding the relationship with the vernacular. This was a form of *concealment* that was habitual in Dalí, but this concealment perhaps hid another issue: to outline the decisive presence of the vernacular myths in his painting, Dalí had had to formulate a plastic language that, although renovated, although filtered through the new Classicism, although akin to the new Realisms, returned Modern art to the *legibility* of museum paintings. This being the case, perhaps the encounter between Modernity and the vernacular did not emerge in a wholly good light, or remained on the terrain of a certain ambiguity.

This ambiguity is also related to another. Dalí had approached the Neo-Classicist register in 1924, after having undertaken an entire cycle of paintings the previous year with figures, especially self-portraits, with an *experimental* character. Dalí, especially in two significant works, *evoked* Cubism, the initial Cubism, the Cubism prior to 1914 and even, if we study the dates, the Cubism prior to 1912. These two works were in fact called *Cubist Self Portrait* and *Cubist Composition*, considered by some experts as a *Portrait of Federico García Lorca*. It is right to call these works *Cubist* if we keep in mind that what we know as *Cubism* today marks a very broad register of related or interlinked possibilities. Despite what is commonly thought, in 1923 Cubism had not yet disappeared. In 1923, Juan Gris, cited in this year by Dalí in one of his declarations to Josep Subías, when exhibiting at the Galería Simón, resuscitated the presence of Cubism, although not without some polemic. But also in around 1923 Cubism was *resuscitated* in the environments of *new art* and of the painters of the Generation of '27. It has always been thought that Dalí took Cubism to the Students' Residence. His *resident* friends *discovered* him as a Cubist painter in his room. This is what Dalí tells us in the *Vida secreta*; it is what Dalí wanted us to know. But the painters of the Generation of '27, who were five or six years older than Dalí, had already begun a *re-encounter* with Cubism with the scene of Manuel Ángeles Ortiz, Ismael de la Serna[1] and Pancho Cossío in Paris.

But the issue is not who was first. The issue is the emphasis that Dalí places on reviving the Cubist cause. An emphasis that reaches until 1926, that is expressed in *Composition with Three Figures. Neocubist Academy* and that, therefore, goes back over the same *corpus* as his youthful stage. There is something, therefore, that, irrespective of the context, although without excluding it totally, takes Dalí to Cubism from a purely personal impulse. I fear that the reasons for this impulse will always be undecipherable. We will only outline some approximate insights regarding the issue. We have already seen the importance of the year 1923 in the biography of the young Dalí, and perhaps his move towards Cubism is not extraneous to everything that happened then. It is said that it was in this year that Dalí began to read *Valori Plastici* and *L'Esprit Nouveau*[2]. The Italian magazine had disappeared in 1922, while the French one continued to run. Cubism was supremely important in both. We need only remem-

1. Curiously, Ismael de la Serna, or Ismael González de la Serna, would be referred to by Dalí in some of his texts, particularly in *Nuevos límites de la pintura*.

2. This fact is reiterated by all the experts on the life and work of Dalí. Santos Torroella transforms it into a recurring theme in his annotated catalogue of the young Dalí, but recently all these aspects of Dalí's activity have been successfully reviewed by Juan José Lahuerta in *Dalí, Lorca y la Residencia de Estudiantes*, Fundación La Caixa, Madrid 2010.

ber the special issue devoted to Cubism in *Valori Plastici* and the importance of Cubism in the poetics of Le Corbusier and in the entire spirit of his magazine. Both publications treat Cubism as a primordial referent and the true generator of the Modern. But neither of the publications proposes, exactly, the validity of Cubism as such, if not in some of its historically located derivations. Dalí seems to have wanted to take possession of Cubism not so much as the actuality of the artistic scene as the foundation or power that it was necessary to possess to be truly Modern. Such an ambition could not occur in him without an emotional shock or without an important psychic impact. And let us remember, furthermore, that Dalí was then nineteen years old. On arriving at the Academy of San Fernando he found that the Impressionist inheritance that he had cherished in his adolescence had become a scholarly and academic proposal. So, what to do?

Outside of the Academy and outside of the Residence, Dalí discovered something: the work of Rafael Barradas. And undoubtedly someone too: Barradas himself. The relationship of some of Dalí's works with Barradas is very well known today. What is not given to this relationship is its special significance. In my opinion, Barradas came to refract the trajectory of the young Dalí. Barradas was a personality who was to a certain extent obsolete. Or rather, he was like a kind of *Bambocciante* of the daily life of Madrid, transformed into a specific *modern life*, in the neighbourhood of Atocha. But Barradas was also contagious vitality. He was the development of the language of the first -isms understood as such. And he was—and this is important—somebody extraneous to the Students' Residence and to the environment of the Generation of '27. García Lorca had rejected Barradas' figurines for his first work performed in public. In the first prints in which he imitates Barradas, as is known, Dalí represents himself and has himself accompanied by Maruja Mallo and Luis Buñuel, not by García Lorca. These prints are night-time scenes. The nocturnal was something alien, if not contrary, to the day-time spirit of the Residence. Dalí did a self-portrait in the *clownista* style of Barradas with the newspaper *La Humanité*. Evidently Dalí, in the 1923 of the dictatorship of Rivera in which he was imprisoned, associated—albeit for an instant—the taste for -isms of Barradas with sympathy for the Left. This association and this situation lasted a moment, but they were sufficient for Dalí to take up Cubism as a transformative element.

It has always been taken for granted that Dalí took to Cubism almost as a simple game, as a mere *sport* of the Modern, just as Ortega, the philosopher in fashion at the Residence, preached in *La deshumanización del arte*. I believe that Dalí's Cubist promotion had motivations of major importance: the importance of the separation of everything that, in principle, was his own. And, by virtue of this, Dalí's Cubist research is surprisingly, but dialectically, combined with his reflections on the vernacular. Dalí's new Classicism appears and is effective to the extent that it is a derivation of Cubism. And Dalí was familiar with the theories of Severini and Togores in this regard. And it is for this reason that, in addition to this route between Cubism and new Classicism, Dalí had recourse to other possibilities. We have already outlined his re-reading of Cubism prior to 1914 in *Cubist Self Portrait* and *Portrait of Federico García Lorca*. The *Still Life* (FGSD122)[3], from 1923, in the Museum Reina Sofía, with the allusion to an interior and the arrangement of objects merged together in front of an open window, evokes, possibly, Juan Gris, the Juan Gris who exhibited these types of compositions, especially *Open Window with Hills* in the Galerie Simon, in Paris,

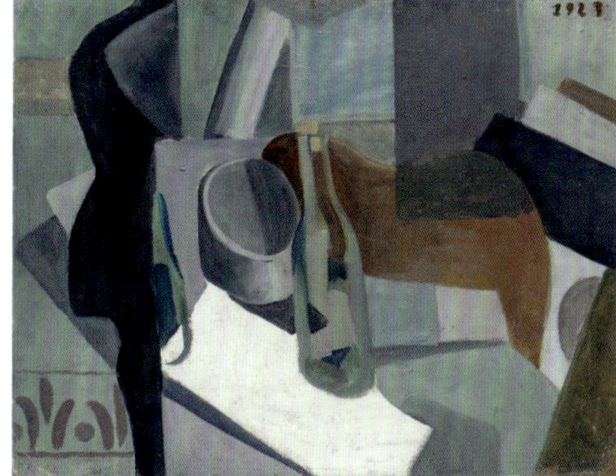

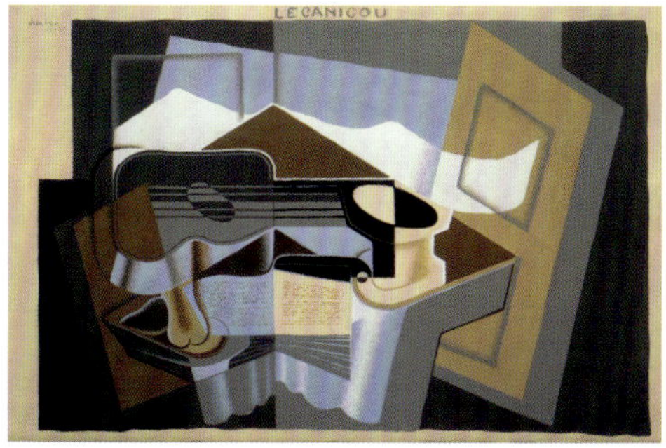

Salvador Dalí
Still Life, 1923
MADRID, MUSEO NACIONAL CENTRO DE ARTE REINA SOFÍA

Juan Gris
The Canigou, 1921
BUFFALO, NEW YORK, ALBRIGHT-KNOX ART GALLERY
ROOM OF CONTEMPORARY FUND

as has already been indicated, in 1923. Another *Still Life* (FGSD123), also from 1923 and also in the Museum Reina Sofía, has been related to a work by Giorgio Morandi[4]. The relationship is based on the use of a wooden balustrade as a motif and in the effects of estrangement caused by painting the shadow of this balustrade, which appears as though suspended in the air inside an urn. Dalí creates the same effect of *metaphysical* estrangement by painting the shadow in his work, although he repeats it three times and the motif chosen is not the same. Iconographically Dalí ratchets things up. Iconographically the work, with this presence, becomes hard to translate or interpret. Stylistically, on the other hand, I believe one can say that it is not very close to the technique used by Morandi. Dalí also proceeds by vertical and horizontal secant planes, resources that we do not find in Metaphysical Painting and that, nevertheless, is a recognisable styleme in the work of Juan Gris between 1912 and 1914.

Other still lifes (FGSD146 and FGSD132) executed in 1924 have been related to the purism of Ozenfant and Jeanneret. In the former, the relationship established is surprising since the still lifes of Ozenfant and Jeanneret are flat and in this piece the volumes and the overlapping of planes in perspective stand out. In the latter, the relationship with Purism is more evident or more verifiable, but it also has volume effects that are extraneous to this Post-Cubist tendency, while the grid composition, although it was used by the Purists, comes, once again, as is known, from Juan Gris. When he exhibited it in Dalmau, in 1925, Dalí called another work, *Siphon and Bottle of Rum* (FGSD136), *Cubist Painting* as is subtitle, while today we would relate it better with the environment or the consequences of Metaphysical Painting, just as we relate with this tendency or with this sensibility the *Still Life* (FGSD135) that belonged to Federico García Lorca, and the painting also called *Still Life* (FGSD134), which today has definitively disappeared, because it is known that it was split up and painted on the reverse. And, in this almost exhaustive journey, different from what has been noted so far are *Pierrot and Guitar*, from 1924, in the Thyssen-Bornemisza Collections, and *Still Life* (*The Watermelon*), also from 1924, in The Salvador Dalí Museum in St. Petersburg, in Florida. This second piece relates to the type of Cubism executed by the painters of the Generation of '27 resident in Paris, which makes it a strange piece, almost excursive, in the catalogue of Dalí, while the previous one also expresses its singularity, being a *collage*. Intended as a gift for his cousin, Montserrat Dalí, the painting has a small cutlery toy made of brass added. In contrast to what it may seem, collage was not such a strange technique for Dalí, but it was absent from his relationship with the *painting* format. And yet, in spite of the singularity of this addition, the most prominent in the painterly part of the work is its construction by concurrent planes recreating a sensation of space, as we find, once again, in Juan Gris and in the Cubist school starting from 1917.

Dalí recreates Cubist possibilities, in around 1924, at the same time when he begins to be cited with the new Classicism and when he extends Sunyer's *Noucentista* tendency. Dalí calls a piece that we might consider Metaphysical Painting *Cubist*, just as two years later he was to call *Neocubist* a piece that we might better consider Modern Classicism. I believe we can deduce, even with all the possible reservation, that Dalí is calling a concept *Cubist*, rather than a type of language, however broad the linguistic register that we call Cubism is. I believe also that Dalí in this case does not *usurp* the plastic register of other art-

3. Since the names of some of Dalí's compositions of those years are similar, I use the cataloguing carried out by the Fundación Gala-Salvador Dalí on the institution's website.

4. See: Santos Torroella, *El primer Dalí. 1918-1929*, Students' Residence and Instituto Valenciano de Arte Moderno, with the collaboration of Telefónica and the Fundación Gala-Salvador Dalí, Madrid 2005, p. 208.

ists in such an evident way. Picasso is absent from Dalí's Cubist references, and it is Juan Gris who appears as a vestige, as a shadow. When Josep Subías, as we have already commented, wrote on Dalí in 1924, he affirmed that his most recent influence was Juan Gris. Very few have repeated this or have related Juan Gris's influence to the works we have commented on. What can we do with all this?

It is truly difficult to reconstruct the meaning of Dalí's Cubist experience of the year 1924. There is a factor of *period* or *moment* already indicated: the pro-Cubist revival of the painters of the Generation of '27. But those who know Dalí know that this must not have influenced him *decisively*. The success of Gris in 1923 could well have attracted him. But perhaps the issue begins to be revealed if we consider that Dalí *exercised* in Cubism. Dalí did Cubism to train a Cubist hand. A hand and a head, a mind. A hand and a mind that after Cubist painting could approach Classicist painting without the risk that the resulting Classicism or Realism would be antiquated or old-fashioned, but fully Modern. It is for this reason, among others, that Dalí makes Cubism coexist with Classicist and *Noucentista* registers. And Dalí himself even gave us a hint of this. Dalí admitted to Descharnes that his *Still Life* (FGSD132) of 1924 and the *Noucentista* landscape entitled *Port Alguer*, with the same date, were the same work in two different versions[5]. The relationship between the two works that Dalí established, in the late 1960s or early 1970s, was a hallucinatory vision based on the mechanisms of paranoiac-critical association. But this vision included a parameter of relationship in the Cubist *manners* of Dalí and his Classical *manners*, in which the Cubist serves as support or as a generating matrix, as teaching the hand that was to paint the Classical in the register of the Modern.

It is in this strange manner that Dalí's Cubist work is related to the *genius loci* and the attraction of the vernacular. Dalí, as Eugeni d'Ors said, always lit a candle to San Miguel and another to the devil, at the same time. After experiencing Cubism, Dalí trusted that the spectator, when presented with *Portrait of my Sister*, would not see a traditional painting but rather notice the hand of a Modern painter, as happened with the Classicist work of Picasso or that of many painters linked to the New Objectivity (*Neue Sachlichkeit*). And the fact is that Dalí attempted to offer a solution that related Modern language—clearly Modern language—and vernacular themes. In *Landscape of the Ampurdán with Figures* and in *Berceuse locale*, temperas on cardboard executed around 1923, and in other contemporary drawings, Dalí blended the reference to his native landscape with some figures, children and women whose physiognomy, particularly their heads, are realised by means of spherical forms with semicircular pronouncements for the nose and the arch of the eyebrows. The bodies also have circular and rectangular outlines. These forms are reminiscent of the solutions of Juan Gris and Léger in which the geometric principle of their construction is exaggerated. Theoretically, these works were the solution: they combined Cubism, the figurative evolution of Cubism and vernacular landscape elements. But whether for the paleness of the tempera or for the schematic nature of the figures, they were rather languid and dry compositions, barely comparable with the figurative force of the Dalí who used Classicism with the encouragement of Cubism.

In this context, with such extensive references, it is unusual for a work such as *Figueres Gypsy* to be, to a certain degree, isolated. Iconographically it is a less clear work than it first seems. The character, with naked feet and cigarette in hand, alongside a guitar without strings, is seated on a reed seat, but surrounded

5. The Fundación Gala-Salvador Dalí dates this composition (FGSD140) around 1923. Robert Descharnes reveals this confession by Dalí in *Dalí de Gala*, Edita Vilo, Lausanne 1962, p. 137.

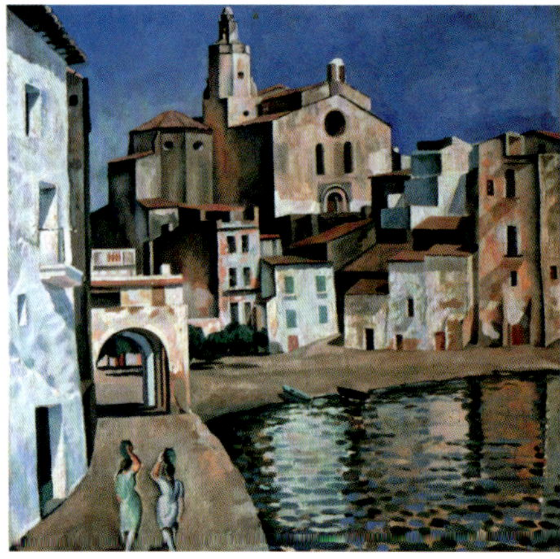

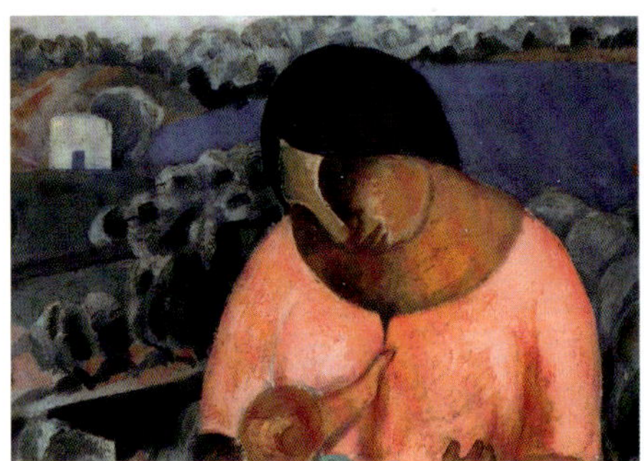

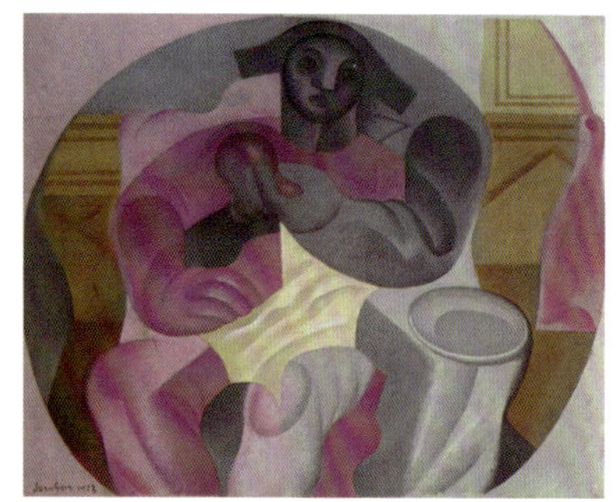

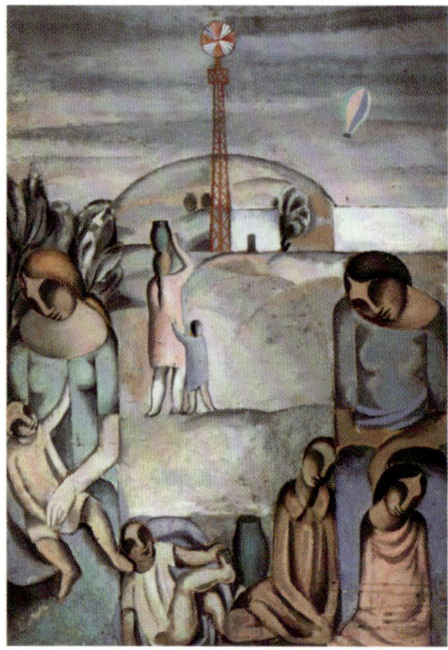

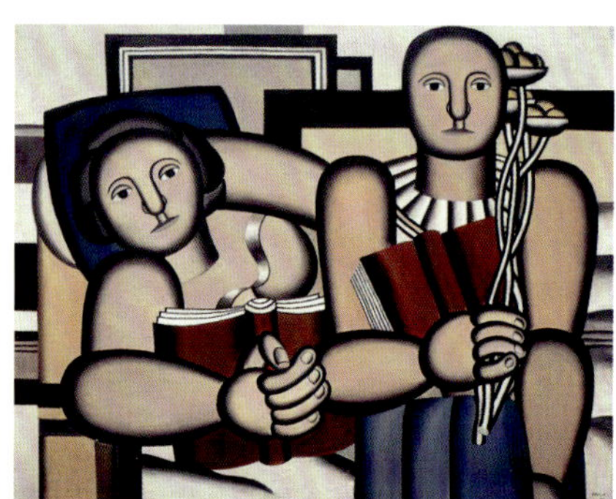

Salvador Dalí
Port Alguer, 1924
FIGUERES, FUNDACIÓN GALA-SALVADOR DALÍ

Salvador Dalí
Berceuse locale, *c.* 1923
FIGUERES, FUNDACIÓN GALA-SALVADOR DALÍ

Juan Gris
Harlequin Sitting, 1923
ANN ARBOR, MICHIGAN, THE UNIVERSITY OF MICHIGAN MUSEUM OF ART
GIFT OF THE CAREY WALKER FOUNDATION

Salvador Dalí
Figures in a Landscape at Ampurdán, *c.* 1923
FIGUERES, FUNDACIÓN GALA-SALVADOR DALÍ

Fernand Léger
Two Women in an Interior, 1922
PARIS, MNAM. CENTRE GEORGES POMPIDOU
DONATION ZOUBALOFF

by paintings, books and a beautiful white cloth on which fruit is laid like in some well-known still lifes by Cézanne. Is the character visiting a painter's studio or is he himself a kind of second-hand dealer? In either case, the relationship between the character of popular extraction and the world of art has been established in the painting. What did Dalí mean by it? Knowing Dalí, it was not very likely that such an association did not have some meaning to convey. But we will leave this aside for the time being. A paradox is outlined as regards the theme. Another paradox is the stylistic one. The character's clothes, their relief effects, similar to those of the face, are reminiscent of the forms of clothing in relief of some Classicist compositions by Picasso, or even of some compositions by Bores from the same period as Dalí. And yet, in spite of the fineness of some lines and of some of the symbols represented, the work conveys a strange sensation of coarseness.

Is this *coarse manner* related to that conveyed by some portraits by Miró, and those by Ràfols or of Ricart or his own *Self Portrait* executed in around 1917? It is hard to respond to this question. Dalí's tendency was always to move towards refinement. Only contact with the emerging mass media made him think otherwise. Miró's orientation was always the opposite. As soon as he arrived in Paris he found French *good taste* deplorable. He displayed this in many of his letters and repeated it on numerous occasions. Picasso had said the same thing and these types of statements have always been related to the intrinsic personalities of the two artists. But to speak out against *good taste* was easy in avant-garde environments. And what was deduced from this statement had something to do with their character, certainly, but also with strategy. In spite of his excellent education, Picasso always wanted to be recognised as a *primitive*, as a *primitive* who had more to do with the *savage*.

Miró, with a clearly urban origin, also always wanted to be recognised, as we have already mentioned, as a *primitive*. But as a *primitive* who wanted to be recognised, in the best sense of the word, as a *peasant*. The constant encounters with Mont-roig, and with Siurana, Prades and even Cambrils, made him identified with this state. In landscape painting Miró found the possibility of translating and recreation this *desideratum*, together with the immersion in the encounter with the *genius loci*. However, in the painting of figures and in the still lifes of those years it is not exactly the theme that conveys the encounter with the vernacular, it is the style. It would seem as though Miró, when painting landscapes, took on a register, according to his own terms, a *calligraphy*, that when transferred to other matters—especially to still lifes and paintings with figures—endowed them with the mark of the primitivism he wanted to achieve and, therefore, with a trace of the vernacular.

However, as happens in the painting of landscapes, Miró's primitivism and demand for the vernacular always had to do with the demands for -isms that the young Miró found indispensable. It is here, in this situation, that the young Miró and the young Dalí shared something in common. The young Dalí, although barely 20 or 21 years of age between 1924 and 1925, could have observed Miró's work published in *La Révolution Surréaliste* and could have taken another path. A path to absolute topicality in the dynamics of the Modern Movement. But this did not happen. The young Dalí closed a cycle. But he closed it because he refocused on an entire series of problems: the reading of Cubism as a paradigm of the Modern, the relationship with the other -isms, the meaning of the new Classicism, the probabilities of a Modern Realism, the iconological density of the represented and the topicality of the *genius loci*, the correlation between the vernacular and Modernity, which were problems or focuses of attention for a young creator that, on the Catalan scene, had already been outlined years earlier, in the second half of the previous decade.

They were outlined in the previous decade. They influenced and brought about an entire environment. The references were shared. But they were not taken up by the Catalan creators of the moment, with the exception of the young Miró. And, apart from his personal talent, this was what, in the long run, ended up differentiating Miró from the rest.

To investigate the Miró of the *genius loci*, it is therefore necessary to see his work and his social relationships as an artist from another side. And it is necessary to go back a little in time. Let us set a date: 1917. Why 1917? We could have chosen 1916, in which Miró got to know Dalmau and began to relate with the artistic environments of the Catalan capital. We could have chosen 1918, in which Miró, in Dalmau, had his first solo exhibition. But even so, the year 1917 has other resonances. In 1917 Picasso was in Barcelona. In 1917 Picasso's and Miró's paths crossed. Picasso would turn thirty-six during his stay in the Catalan capital, Miró twenty-four.

The *Ballets Russes* arrived in Barcelona from Madrid at the end of June. Picasso accompanied them and Olga Koklova. In the early summer the Ballets embarked upon a US tour. They returned in November, and it was then that *Parade* was performed. From June to late November Picasso remained in Barcelona[6]. At the beginning of December he was already with Olga in Montrouge. Picasso's brief stay in Madrid has been established by Ramón Gómez de la Serna[7]. The writer tells us that, except for the King, Alfonso XIII, some noble ladies and the writer himself, who paid homage to him at the Café Pombo, nobody knew anything about Picasso and almost nobody wanted to congratulate him. Did Gómez de la Serna exaggerate? In Barcelona things would have been otherwise. *Parade*, which did not figure as a special performance, had its detractors, some of them indignant, but it did gain a small crop of admirers, including Eugeni d'Ors. And among them, also, the young Miró. It has been doubted whether Miró met Picasso personally at this time, but in his conversations with Raillard, Miró remembered his encounter with Picasso at that time and how, initially, he hardly dared approach him[8].

Picasso received a much better welcome in Barcelona than in Madrid. The photograph of the homage that was paid to him at the Galeries Laietanes has become famous. But if we pay close attention to the photograph we can see that Picasso is the youngest of all those gathered there. Among those congregated there were Iturrino, Maeztu, Fernández Soto and Ricard Canals. All these belonged to the *fin-de-siècle* moment and none to the *Noucentista* or avant-garde environments. Related to *Noucentisme*, and present in the photo, we can recognise Xavier Nogués and Manuel Humbert. Feliu Elies was also there. But they were all critical of Modern art. Picasso was praised, but Picasso was not in the environments in which he should have been. But were there really advanced or innovative artistic environments in the social and politically conflictual Barcelona of 1917? Even without Picasso or Braque, the Cubism that arrived in Barcelona in 1912, thanks to Dalmau, was a pioneer of the international presence of the movement and shocked the artistic scene, but it did not have any repercussions or *visible* consequences. And a little later we will see why I say *visible*. The *Noucentisme* that was gestating from before Cubism arrived, was semi-official in 1914 and extended into the intellectual and creative consciousness. It favoured institutional performances, but did not forge an environment truly determined to take a risk on *the new*. The new avant-garde circles were in fact being born in 1917 and had no precedents. Some European avant-gardes, as is known, had taken refuge briefly in Barcelona during the war years: Robert and Sonia Delaunay, Albert Gleizes, Francis Picabia and others[9]. None of these was influenced by Picasso, in fact. In 1917 the pro-*Evolutionist* transformation of Torres-García occurred. In his powerful circle, Torres would not have had Picasso as a reference. In 1917 two key creators in the Spanish reception of avant-garde art were already in Barcelona: Celso Lagar and Rafael Barradas. Neither of them cited Picasso in their works. All this was the case and yet, in his letters of those years

6. I specify all these data because in some publications there is an insistence that Picasso was not in Barcelona at the time of the première of Parade. I believe that Josep Palau i Fabre has sufficiently clarified this stay by Picasso in the city. See: *Picasso. De los ballets al drama (1917–1926)*, Polígrafa, Barcelona 1999, pp. 53 *et seq*.

7. See: *Completa e veridica storia di Picasso e del cubismo*, Chiantore, Torino 1945.

8. In *Joan Miró. Ceci est la couler de mes rêves. Entretiens avec Georges Raillard*, Seuil, Paris 1977, p. 50.

Miró talks of Picasso as a legend but nobody discussed Picasso in Barcelona, nor his paternity or leadership of Modern art. A peculiar situation.

Another peculiar situation occurred. And this time it had to do with Picasso's own creations. *Parade* was received by the criticism, mainly by the antagonistic critics, as a *Cubist* ballet. In fact, as we know, aesthetically Picasso's contribution to the project was mixed. The opening curtain was not, strictly speaking, Classicist, but rather was reminiscent of a certain *naïf* tone, with certain aspects of the *pink* Picasso. The costumes of the Chinese magician, the American girl or the acrobats did not go beyond the recognisable for the audience. It was the stage, the French Manager, the American Manager and the horse's face that dominated the comments and their impact in Barcelona. Cubism returned to Barcelona through Picasso and this time it caused more scandal than in 1912. On the other hand, at the same time as Picasso was returning to Barcelona, the magazine *Vell i Nou*, very widespread in artistic circles, presented him as the reviver of Classicism, publishing some of his *Ingresian* drawings, including the portrait of Ambroise Vollard, executed in 1915. With this, *Vell i Nou* became the first publication that, internationally, was to speak of the Classical Picasso—Cubist Picasso and Classical Picasso, therefore. The Barcelona of 1917 got to know the artist in his duality. A duality that was not presented as antagonistic or as paradoxical. Evolved Cubism and New Classicism were the two sides of the same coin. Or better still, the New Classicism was considered the evolution of the very heart of the Cubist experience. Miró was of this view. It was to be through his own knowledge and through his friendship with Josep de Togores that he was to theorise on this issue, as we have already said, in his chronicles of Paris published by the Catalan press[10].

In his letters to Ràfols and Ricart, Miró would speak of Cubism and Classicism, while referring to Picasso, and he would propose the complicit mediation of Togores in this dichotomy. This occurred in his letters written between 1918 and 1920. Which means that the dialectical relationship between the inheritance of Cubism and New Classicism is something that Miró thought about following Picasso's visit to Barcelona. Undoubtedly it was something that he found difficult to meditate on and to assimilate. On the other hand, for the Catalan artistic scene, the relationship of kinship and identity between Cubism and New Classicism was not new. This relationship had already been proposed at the time of the Cubist exhibition in 1912 at the Dalmau gallery. Most of the commentators on the exhibition showed a hypostasis of concepts between Cubism and New Classicism[11], which in turn came from some early commentators on the Cubist experience, such as Roger Allard and Olivier Hourcade. But this also came from the theses of d'Ors and Junoy, almost strictly contemporary with those of Allard and Hourcade, and prior to the Cubist exhibition in Barcelona. This has perhaps not been very well understood by the current historians, but it is very important. Starting from the understanding of Cubism as Classicism in concept or in essence, *Noucentisme* was compared with it and given a similar trajectory to the Modern. And what is more, the hypostasis between Cubism and New Classicism that the critics dwelled on for some years became hypostasis between *Noucentisme* and avant-garde art, with the proposal that both were identical daughters of d'Ors' *palpitations of the times*. Initially, the comparison between Cubism, Classicism and *Noucentisme* implied criticism of Futurism and the work of Marcel Duchamp, since a version of *Nude Descending a*

---

9. There is an extensive bibliography commenting upon the European presence of the avant-garde in Barcelona. It is worthwhile to cite the already mentioned book by Brihuega (1981) and, for example, without neglecting other publications, I would like to cite *Las vanguardias en Cataluña. 1906–1939. Protagonistas. Tendencias. Acontecimientos*, Fundació Caixa de Catalunya, Olimpíada Cultural, Barcelona 1992, edited by Daniel Giralt-Miracle, texts by José Corredor-Matheos, Daniel Giralt-Miracle, Joaquim Molas, Joan M. Minguet Batllorí and Jaume Vidal i Oliveras.

10. In this regard, see: Carmona, "Josep de Togores y la belleza impasible", *cit*.

11. I believe that this theme of the relationship in hypostasis between Cubism and *Noucentisme* is central to understanding the Catalan artistic scene of the turn of the century. However, the view I express here is not particularly shared by the critics and the Catalan historiography. The arguments expressed are to a large extent similar to those outlined by Robert Lubar in "Miró before 'The Farm'. A Cultural Perspective", in *Joan Miró. A Retrospective*, The Salomon R. Guggenheim Foundation and Yale University Press, New York 1987, and were reconsidered in depth by Lubar himself in "Cubism, Classicism, and Ideology: The 1912 'Exposició d'Art Cubista' in Barcelona and French Cubism Criticism", in *On Classic Ground. Picasso, Léger, De Chirico and the new Classicism, 1910–1930*, Tate Gallery, London 1990, pp. 309–23. Likewise, see in this regard the clarifying contributions by Jaume Vallcorba-Plana in *Josep Maria Junoy. Obra poética*, Edicions Quaderns Crema, Barcelona 1984 and in *Noucentisme, Mediterraneisme i Classicisme. Apunts per a la història d'una estètica*, Quaderns Crema, Barcelona 1994, pp. 42–7. For my part, this theme was central in one of the chapters of my doctoral thesis, *La renovación plástica española del momento vanguardista al retorno al orden*, presented in 1989 and some of it is included in *icasso, Miró, Dalí y los orígenes del arte contemporáneo en España, 1900–1936*, Shrin Kunsthalle and Museo Nacional Centro de Arte Reina Sofía, Frankfurt and Madrid 1991, and on other publications. On the other hand, on the Cubist exhibition of 1912 see the monograph by Mercè Vidal, *L'Exposició d'Art Cubista de les Galeries Dalmau*, Universitat de Barcelona, Barcelona 1996.

Staircase was exhibited in Dalmau in 1912, and was rejected by d'Ors and Junoy when commenting on the exhibition for not being, in their view, pertinent to the normative and Structuralist spirit that Cubism involved. But later on, during the years of the First World War, such selective rigour diminished considerably, and the relationship of aesthetic comparison between *Noucentisme* and avant-garde perhaps became effective in the light of the progress of New Classicism in France and Italy. This is what was observed in the contents of the creative magazines. The magazines that were promoted, starting from 1917, with an avant-garde spirit, such as *Un enemic del poble* or *Troços/Trossos*, did not hesitate to publish contents with a *Noucentista* character. And it was not mere eclecticism or mere fellow-travelling, because *Noucentista* art was greeted as consistent with the spirits of both publications. Perhaps the issue was different in *Arc Voltaic*, the magazine in which Miró actively participated. But on the other hand, in publications such as *Revista Nova*, *La Revista*, *Themis*, *El Camí* or *L'Instant*, or even in *Terramar*, promoted by *Noucentista* intellectuals and creatives, the presence of avant-garde writers such as Pierre Reverdy, Pierre Albert-Birot, Tristan Tzara or Vicente Huidobro was systematic. And it was not mere eclecticism. The *coexistence* between *Noucentisme* and avant-garde appeared again on the levels of equity and aesthetic correlation[12].

I believe this situation marked the acceptance of artistic Modernity in Catalonia, even up to the arrival of Salvador Dalí. It also decisively marked the appearance of Miró on the scene. Although perhaps Miró did not feel very comfortable with it. As has been mentioned before, between 1918 and 1920 Miró talks, albeit briefly, of Cubism, Classicism and Picasso, with the mediation of Togores. For Miró, Picasso's Cubism is the *promise of a pure and simple art* and Picasso is the only realiser of a Classical art, not dead, as so many preach, in his view, but alive. For Miró Picasso is the *panther* who knows how to jump from Cubism to the rediscovered Classicism. Here is a long quote from a letter to Josep D. Ràfols, written in 1919:

> "It is necessary to go towards a Classicism, not to the dead thing that Junoy preaches, the cadaverous reversal to the Greeks and to David. It is necessary to escape from the sick preaching of Torres-García (art in relation to eternal man and passing man), leaving aside all of the past. These two things are characteristic of incomplete spirits. I always have in my memory my visit to Picasso's mother's house. Remember what Togores said, that Picasso was the precursor, that it was necessary to go to the discipline of David together with the freedom, the complete abstraction of his Cubist canvases. I feel very much akin to Togores; he remembers that I told him that it was necessary to go to a *Classicism passing through Cubism* and to a pure art (*le cubisme n'est que la promise d'un art pur et simple*, G. Apollinaire), totally free, but *Classical*. To dig, dig very deeply, as I always tell Ricart, and it is by digging very deep that there will appear, splendid, new problems to solve, that will take us away from the fatal *interesting, momentary*, and to do *good painting*"[13].

Indeed, Miró had gone with Togores to Picasso's mother's house and he had seen his canvases executed in Barcelona. Indeed, Miró talks of arriving at Classicism

12. For the academic theses that support this statement, see the previous note. In my doctoral thesis, presented in 1989, I specifically considered the coexistence between *Noucentisme* and avant-garde in the Catalan creative magazines.

passing through Cubism. Dalí would be onto this years later. Miró disowned the position, in 1919, of someone who had been his first protector, Josep María Junoy. And this was because Junoy, the first Catalan apologist of Cubism[14], had given a lecture in the Athenaeum of Barcelona in which he preached the return to traditional Classicism. Miró disowned Torres-García, formerly a master of *Noucentisme* who now, in full revelatory mode, preached a completely transformed art extraneous to the tradition. Miró did not want to take up either position. But let us not deceive ourselves: Miró was never exactly Cubist, nor was he ever tempted by the essentiality of a Classical art. Miró was attempting to dominate the rhetoric of the moment in which it was necessary for him to live and work. A rhetoric that justified the New Classicism, which even for him had other meanings[15], and that returned to Cubism as the origin of the Modern. But Miró was not Togores; he wanted to speak his friend's language, but he did not allow himself to be fully seduced by his position. What is more, Miró did not like everything he saw in Picasso's mother's house. Many years later—sixty years later, in 1977—speaking with Raillard, something he did not comment on at the time in his letters to his friends, and with Picasso already dead, Miró admitted that he found the famous *Harlequin* of Barcelona "horrible; no, not horrible; insignificant, empty, hollow..."[16]. Miró understood, as can be deduced from the above quotation, that the Cubism *in planes* that Picasso practised in Barcelona was, strictly speaking, an antechamber for a second Cubism that would be championed by Gris. Miró understood that this Cubism *in planes* favoured the entry of abstraction into painting without giving up figuration, and he also understood that this Cubism was different to that of the set and the managers of *Parade*, whose language was indebted to the Cubism practised by Picasso in 1914.

The comparison of three nudes by Miró helps us evaluate his process of compression of this whole sequence. In the first of them, executed in 1917 and entitled *Nude with Flower and Bird*, we find a Miró who is a Colourist with rounded ways, Primitivist in the shape of the figure and indebted in some ways to Simultaneism. No Cubist aspect can be discerned in the canvas. In *Nude Standing*, from 1918, Colourism is not part of the painting proper but is introduced with ornamental elements such as the carpet and the curtain. The body of the figure, on the other hand, has scant colour and appears broken up and segmented in volumes. Miró's reconsideration of Cubism is evident in it, in the body of the figure, although without giving in to the abstraction of the motif. And finally, in *Nude with Mirror*, from 1919, the chromatic condensation is inherited from Cubism and the articulation of some abstract planes to compose the body of the figure too. However, these abstractions are stylemes or partial features, they do not order the composition as a whole and are undoubtedly present to compensate for the treatment of the model going towards the terrain of Objectivist painting.

In short, Miró, through Picasso, wanted to understand the phenomenon that reigned supreme in artistic circles in 1917, which would have to remain alive until the arrival of Dalí: the drift of Cubism towards New Classicism. But Miró did not make a dogma of this situation, as Togores or as other Catalan painters of his generation did, nor did he want to justify the historical relevance of the *Noucentista* proposal in Modern Classicism. Miró took what interested him of this situation. And he took what interested him because, from 1917, Miró had his own plan, his own position about the identity of Modern art.

---

13. Letter from Miró to Ràfols included in *Joan Miró. Escritos y conversaciones*, edited by Marguit Rowell, Institut Valencià d'Art Modern, Colegio Oficial de Aparejadores y Arquitectos Ténicos de la Región de Murcia, Valencia and Murcia 2002, p. 136, Republishing of the UK edition Joan Miró: *Selected Writings and Interviews*, Thames and Hudson, London 1986, pp. 110 and 111

14. See the works of Jaume Vallcorba-Plana cited in previous notes.

15. From the letters to his friends we deduce that Miró also understood *Classicism* in Modern art both to arrive at a work with one's own defined personality and to establish a synthesis of the -isms that would arrive, in the way that Cézanne wanted with Impressionism, at an art *like that of the museums*. I believe that the detailed study of the terminology used by Miró in those years would clarify the understanding of his work a great deal. Miró did not use terms such as *Classicism* or *calligraphy* in a conventional manner.

16. Joan Miró. *Ceci est la couler de mes rêves...*, *cit.*, p. 235.

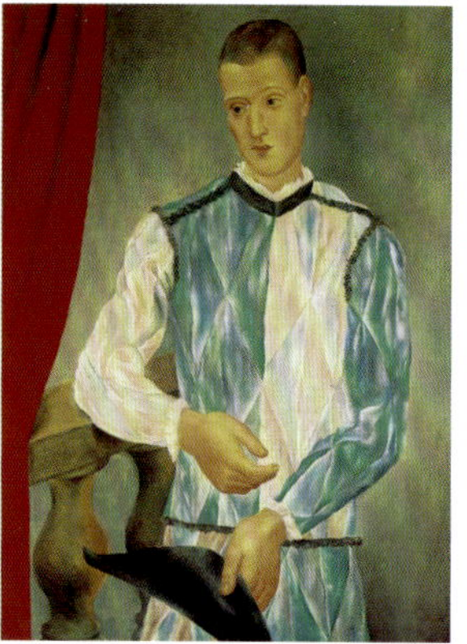
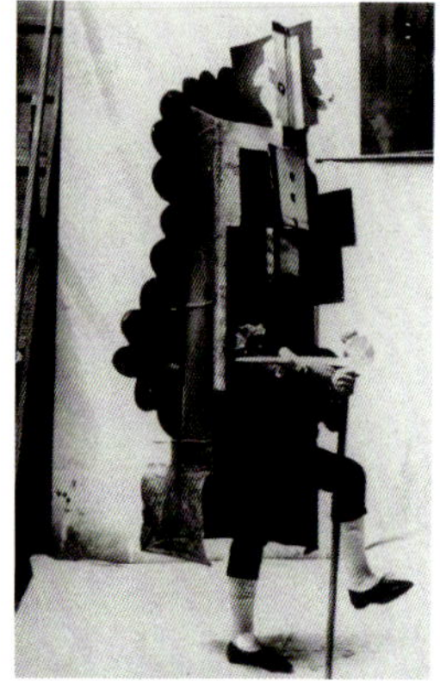
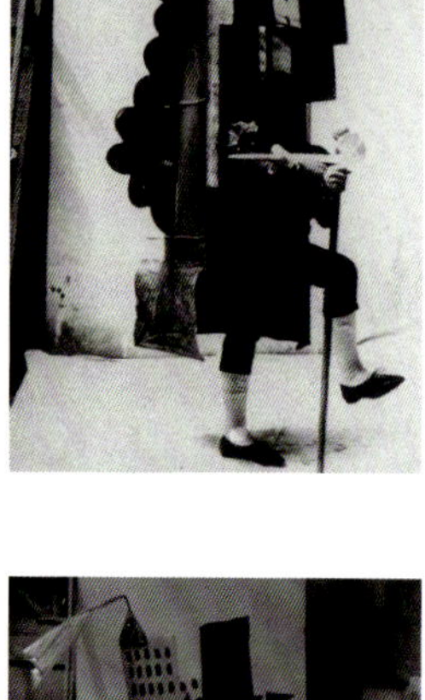
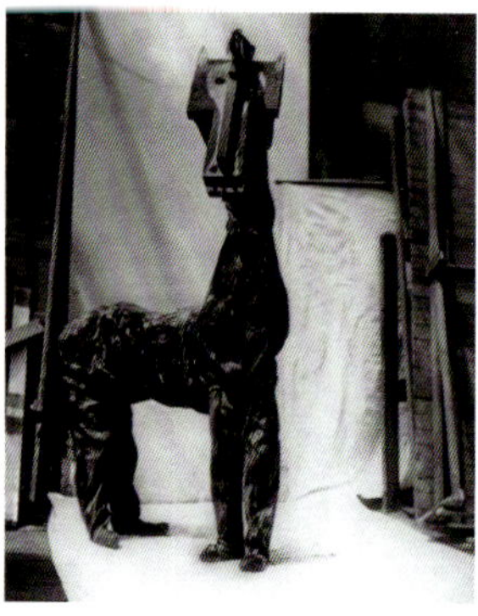
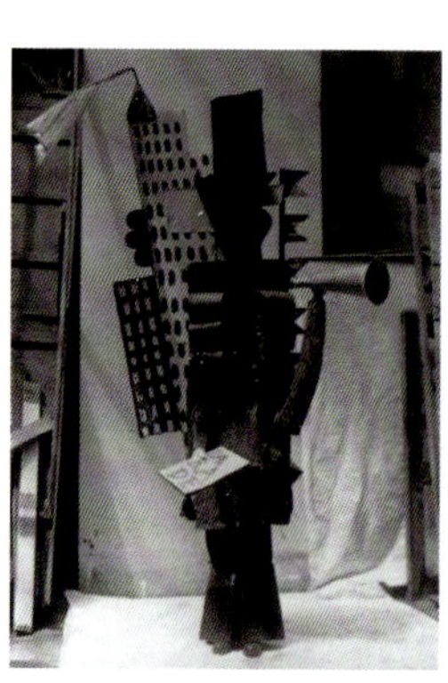

Pablo Picasso
Harlequin, 1917
BARCELONA, MUSEU PICASSO

French manager of *Parade* (1917)
design of clothing by Pablo Picasso
PARIS, BIBLIOTHÈQUE MUSÉE DE L'OPERA, ARCHIVES KOCHNO

Horse in *Parade* (1917)
design of clothing by Pablo Picasso
PARIS, BIBLIOTHÈQUE MUSÉE DE L'OPERA, ARCHIVES KOCHNO

US manager of *Parade* (1917)
design of clothing by Pablo Picasso
PARIS, BIBLIOTHÈQUE MUSÉE DE L'OPERA, ARCHIVES KOCHNO

On 13 September 1917, he wrote to Ràfols:

> "I always work from the beginning, as if we began to paint today.
>
> For me, the art that will come, after the grandiose French Impressionist movement and of the liberating movements of Post-Impressionist, Cubism, Futurism, Fauvism, tends in all to emancipate the artist's emotion and to give him absolute freedom.
>
> I believe that tomorrow we will have no school ending in '-ism' and we will see a canvas of a racing locomotive coloured in a totally opposite way to a landscape depicted at 12 noon. In the free spirit everything in life will produce its own different sensibility, and we will want to see, only, through the canvas, the vibration of a spirit, a very heterogeneous vibration. All the Modern schools have raised their own flags; Impressionism, *peindre n'importe quoi*, to paint light; Fauvism, to synthesise; Futurism, movement. To paint a street in a big city, with big houses, with the noise of car horns (does noise not contribute to the vision of things?), with people hurrying around like crazy and with trams and underground railways, the Impressionist currency is no use for this and this landscape that I see before me, where I am writing, olive trees, locusts and vines, and plenty of light, awakes an emotion that is completely different from that of a New York street. After the contemporary liberation of the arts we will see artists arise without any flags, with the strings of their spirit vibrating with different musics.
>
> We do not use Impressionism to paint a busy New York street, nor do we use Futurism put to paint a beautiful woman standing before us. Let our paintbrush mark our vibrations"[17].

The quotation is a long one, but it is justified by the intensity of what Miró says

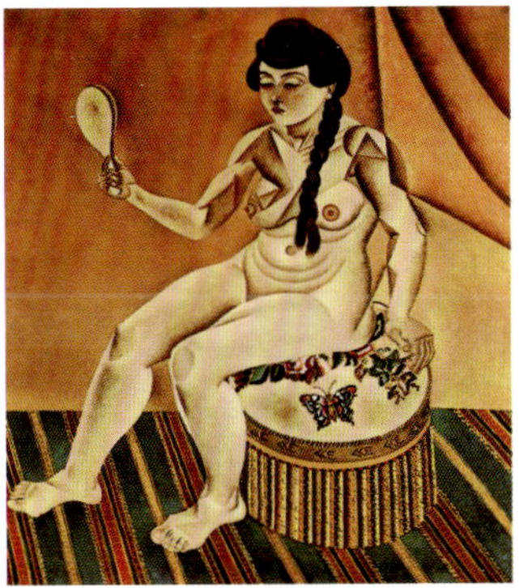
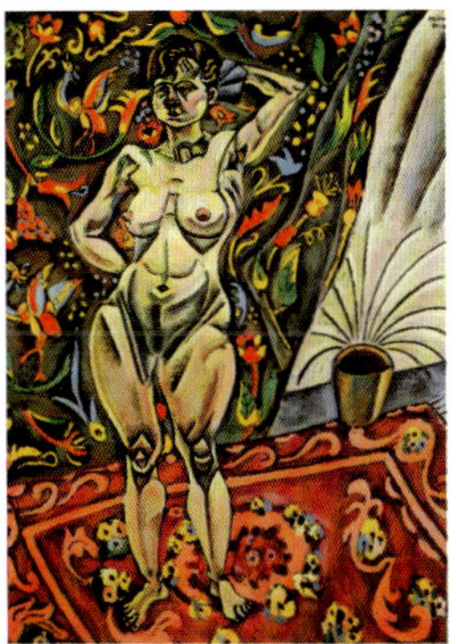
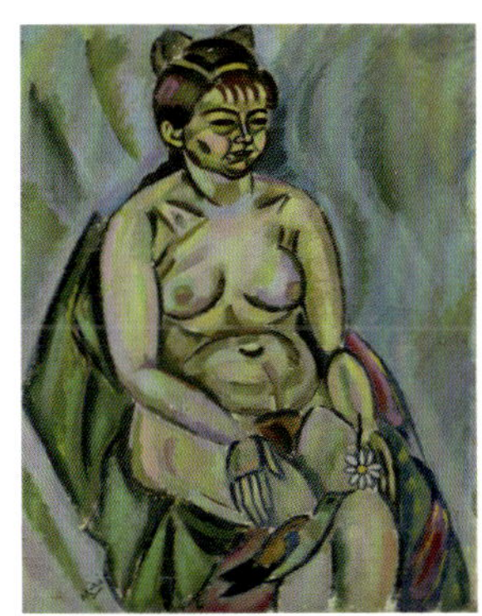

Joan Miró
Nude with Mirror, 1919
DÜSSELDORF, KUNSTSAMMLUNG NORDRHEIN-WESTFALEN

Joan Miró
Nude Standing, 1918
SAINT LOUIS, THE SAINT LOUIS ART MUSEUM, FRIENDS FUND

Joan Miró
Nude with Flower and Bird, 1917
SEATTLE, WASHINGTON, SEATTLE ART MUSEUM
THE JACQUES AND NATASHA GELMAN COLLECTION

and by what he reveals in the text. Miró does not mention Cubism; he evidently rediscovered it as such at the end of 1917, on seeing it in the figurines of *Parade* and in the paintings of Barcelona women by Picasso. But we will dwell on an early reference in the quotation: the term *vibration*, which Miró uses so much, is from Rafael Barradas.

What a strange fascination Barradas had. We saw how he fascinated Dalí. Now we see how, very early, in 1917, he had fascinated Miró. And he continued seducing so many others and converting them with conviction to the path of the -isms. Barradas was not very appreciated in Barcelona. His proposal, which followed the path of connection between Cubism and Futurism, did not find agreement with *Noucentista* tendency to consider Cubism as a *pro norma* and *pro forma* art. Barradas had to leave Madrid in March 1918. But his vitality was contagious, as was that of the poet Salvat-Papasseit. Both, together with the *evolved* Torres-García, promoted the appearance of the magazine already mentioned, *Un enemic del poble*. Miró was involved in it. But Miró cooperated with them of another ephemeral editorial project, *Arc Voltaic*, which appeared in 1918. Each of the promoters of the publication placed a motto on the cover: "Poems in Hertzian waves" was undoubtedly the motto of Salvat; "Vibrationism of ideas" that of Barradas and "Forms in emotion and evolution" was Torres-García's. Was the fourth motto, "Plasticity of the vortex", Miró's? We do not know with any certainty, but what there is no doubt about is that Miró, committed in the encounter with avant-garde art, would now never give up its premises no matter how much the so-called *return to order* and the New Classicism crossed has path. Miró published two drawings in the poor, brief publication that was *Arc Voltaic*, a nude and a rural street scene. Both compositions were resolutely -ismic, but the painter had not had to give up either his themes or his love for the vernacular. Barradas undoubtedly helped him to reinforce his positions and Miró made the term *vibration* his own, translating it into his own space.

Secondly, we may deduce something from the long quotation above: Miró was proposing a sum of the first -isms as the consolidated language of the Modern. This consolidation of the -isms was also called *Classicism* by Miró, in a single proposal. It was an idiosyncratic use of the term, but its meaning can be understood. And it was not a peripheral proposal. The sum and consolidation of the first -isms was something that Pierre Albert-Birot was proposing at the same time from the pages of the magazine *SIC*, through what he called *Nunism*. And the sum of the -isms also appeared on the pages of the magazine *Nord-Sud*, even though today we identify this publication more with the survival of Cubism. Miró, therefore, was up-to-date. I believe that all his work is to be under-

17. Rowell (ed.), *Joan Miró, cit.*, pp. 86 and 87.

stood from this desire for accumulation and condensation of the first -isms, at least starting from 1917. And I believe that to the -isms prior to the First World War it would be necessary to add two aspects always recognised in Miró: his notion of primitivism and how this notion of primitivism is bound to the need to shape the vernacular.

It is from these premises that it is necessary to understand the three magnificent portraits of three characters that we have been citing throughout this text: the portraits of Josep F. Ràfols and of Enric C. Ricart and Miró's own self-portrait. In the three, the *ductus* of Miró, the *calligraphy* of his drawing outlines the Primitivist writing of what we have called the *coarse manner* but which perhaps, due to its origin, it would be better suited to being called *rustic manner*. Miró consolidated his *rustic manner*, which did not eschew simplifications nor the deforming of conventional physiognomies in two works executed in Siurana in 1917, *Mary* and *Women Playing Cards*, but these are two works that we cannot identify well because they are not easily exhibited and they are only known through reproductions in black and white. In the portraits to which we are referring, Miró maintained the architecture of the features and the evidence of the resemblances and has recourse to formal simplifications that Cubism has not read yet, but which are in the proximity of it. This does not prevent his extreme freedom of colour and its arbitrary use. An arbitrary use of colour that, however, being related to the *rustic manner*, is not dissonant but rather achieves a high degree of internal cohesiveness in the composition. The background of the portrait of Ràfols is indebted to Fauvism. But that of Ricart has become famous for showing the meaning that Miró gave to the *collage*, showing with the glued print a reference to Japanese art that was to last and become key in his mature work. The evolution of the portrait in Miró, as we see in the well-known selfportrait from 1919, would go on, after assimilating what happened in 1917, to suppress the confusion of colour, to seek simplicity and austerity, to introduce slight Cubist faceting and to settle on the likeness of the model from a love of the concrete in his contemporary paintings of landscapes. The Objectivism of Miró would therefore not be an evolution of a New Classicism, which he never exercised, but of the love for small things that arose in his paintings of landscapes that he commented on so much in his letters and that led him to want to shape the capture of the specific.

In the still lifes the evolution is similar although the genre marks its specific circumstances. The first still lifes by Miró, those executed in around 1915, are difficult to associate. A major change took place in 1916. Works such as *Vase of Flowers with a Lemon* mark a particular point of encounter. Miró opted for a simple theme that, nevertheless, brought together objects whose relationship was, evidently, more sought after than random. But the whole painting is resolved by means of the articulation of brushstrokes that are reminiscent of the *steps* of Cézanne and by means of the concatenation of chromatic planes that possess the intensity of Fauvism together with the articulation of sharp angles characteristic of Futurism. The result successfully shows associations that could be paradoxical: that of Futurist dynamism with a theme in itself static and totally antagonistic to the springs of *Modern life*. This is the capacity for reconciliation of Miró, and it was unique. Miró added the -isms and assimilated them without feeling the need to militate for any of them. What was achieved in *Vase of Flowers with a Lemon* is in relation to works such as *The Rose* and *The*

Blue Bottle, and this principle that unites rustic primitivism and angularity of the *vortex* is made even more complex in *Portrait of Vicens Nubiola* which combines representation of figure and representation of still life. But another work from 1916, *Still Life with Knife*, in the Nahmad Collection, seems to mark the end of Miró's interest in dynamic surfaces and to begin something that was to be important in his work: the concentration on objects and on the physiognomic personality they possess. The background of this work outlines the line of relations between Cézanne—also cited in the apples—the Fauvists and the Orphism that so interested Miró. The jar and the bottle, on the other hand, seem to already denote some consequences of the faceting by planes of Cubism. Miró, therefore, reconciles what seemed irreconcilable and his desire for synthesis of the first -isms was not mere theory but something that was resolved in practice and which offered unique works.

Without completely giving up this synthesis and although situated in this context of the year 1917, such a representative work of Miró's as *North-South* is different; it seems even an *excursus* in relation to the rest. In principle, its general tone harkens back to the author's youthful taste for Fauvism, which, in contrast with the landscapes paintings, had not developed in his initial still lifes. Nevertheless, the chromatic circles of the piece reference Simultaneism and perhaps Miró is indicating to us how to his sensibility, the work of Delaunay, rather than being a derivation of Cubism, is from the Fauvist experience. But in any event, when presented with *North-South* it is very difficult not to want to investigate the possible symbolic meanings of the work. The overall setting is a mixture of referents: the earthenware pitcher, the cage with the bird and the pot refer us to the rural domestic scene, while the book by Goethe locates us on the intellectual plane, and the plate with the legend NORD-SUD, in capital letters, speaks to us of Paris, and of the avant-garde magazine promoted by Reverdy and Huidobro. The apple is almost impossible not to contemplate as an allusion to Cézanne, whom Miró cites so often in his letters. And, in short, these same referents could well contain metaphors or symbols. Joan Sureda has reminded us of the relationship of Torres-García and Eugeni d'Ors with Goethe[18]. We know of the impact of the translation of the German writer into Catalan, and it is tempting to think that Miró is alluding to the *Theory of Colours*. Miró comments by making two semiological noises: he does not represent the front part of the cage and he does not relate the flowers physically with the pot. But there is no doubt that he is proposing to us that if Goethe is the theoretical reflection on colour, that same colour, arbitrary and rich, occurs in nature in the plumage of the goldfinch and in the petals of the flowers, at the same time as form and colour are in the popular art represented in the earthenware pitcher and in the coloured bobbin.

Art, culture and nature. Also an anticipatory relationship between the written and the painted. These are the terms of the relationship established by Miró in *North-South*. Presented with this statement, presented with the intense colour of the piece and also presented with its metaphoric aspect, the contention, the sobriety and the representative character of the objects in *The Coffee Mill* demonstrate that Miró, in 1918, when dealing with the still life paintings, has reached a turning-point. Behind this turning-point is the understanding of the trajectory that leads from Cubism to the New Classicism. But this understanding was not possible in Miró without his own interpretation. From

18. Joan Sureda, *Torres-García, pasión clásica*, Akal, Barcelona 1998.

Cubism he took a different use of colour, more intoned in similar chromatic ranges, and a desire to delimit the objects in the receptacle of its own form. He also took the development of the unity of the painting by means of the subtle articulation of facetings in certain spaces on the surface of the canvas. From New Classicism Miró did not take anything that in principle we would relate to the restoration of the meaning of the Classical in the history of painting. Through reconsidered Cubism, Miró replaced the search for the Classical with the encounter with representative objectivity and certain absolute equivalences between the icon and its representation. All this is already formulated in *The Coffee Mill.* Although in this work Miró has added something more. He glued onto the canvas the wrapping of a packet of postcards with views of New York. At that time, a transformed Torres-García, associating with the Agrupació Courbet that was led by Miró, spoke a great deal about New York and was even to begin his experience of New York not long afterwards. Miró also talked in his letters, as we have seen, of the sensibilities of the -isms on the basis of contexts and the necessity to contrast the needs of the new artist, who should necessarily be a *primitive* one with the New York street as an emblem of a new urban way of life disconnected from the presence of History. Miró wishes to tell us, therefore, that he is very aware of the transformations of modern life, but that the *vibrations* of his paintbrush can only be with what the themes, from a Modern mentality, demand of him. And of Miró, starting from 1918, the move from Cubism to New Classicism demanded the encounter with the corporeal nature of objects and with the effect of their presence before the gaze. Starting from here the figurative space created by Miró was filled with icons that were expressed in densely conceived spaces. Miró found a sense of iconicity that related him with *Magic Realism.* We find it in meticulous works of figures such as *The Table* (or *Still Life with Rabbit*), *The Game of Spanish Cards* or *Horse, Pipe and Red Flower*. This world of icons as potent signs in their physical presence, crowded in a space that competes with them in the sense of plasticity, and in demanding the gaze, cites reality and transforms it. The spectator takes full account with his eyes of an objective world that, nevertheless, refuses to imitate things in their mere appearance and makes them pulsate and be deformed from themselves as though they had an intensity of life shaping their bodies and forms. Through this journey Miró arrived at *The Farmhouse* between the years 1921 and 1922. But before beginning the *great transformation* of his work, Miró offered, after *The Farmhouse,* a brilliant full stop to the youthful period of his work. We find it in paintings such as *Still Life I* (*The Ear of Corn*) and *Still Life II* (*The Carbide Lamp*). From intensity and meticulous attention, Miró has returned to concentration and a parsimony that contains something of lasting and decisive wisdom: the truth of things does not consist in saying much about them but in telling something revealing, precise and exact. The space already competes with the objects. It is different from them and aspires to be abstract. The objects float in the abstract without wanting to narrate their story to us but proposing their understanding through empathy with their presence. Never was *less* so clearly *more* as in these works by Miró. And as Miró himself explained the meaning of these works to Roland Tual:

"I work the figure and the still lifes and I do my 7 hours of daily labour. I do not do the things that I said in Paris; those to do with herbs and birds and snails. The effort of my last painting does not allow me to undertake such topics.

I dig around in the kitchen looking for humble objects, and any object, an ear of wheat spike and a cricket, I make a painting. To give a communicative emotion to these things we have to love them considerably, since you can be sure that if not, you will make a painting without any interest. I become more demanding with myself every day, a demand that makes me re-do a painting if one of the corners has a millimetre too much, to the right or the left. In the room that I use as my studio I always have books that I read when resting from my work. This demands a continuous spiritual vibration of me...

When I paint, I caress what I do, and the effort of giving them a communicative life tires me considerably. Sometimes, at the end of my work session, I fall in an armchair, exhausted, like after the sexual act of making love! Excuse, dear friend, the crudeness of language with which I express myself, but I cannot find other words"[19].

■

19. Rowell (ed.), *Joan Miró, cit.*, p. 132.

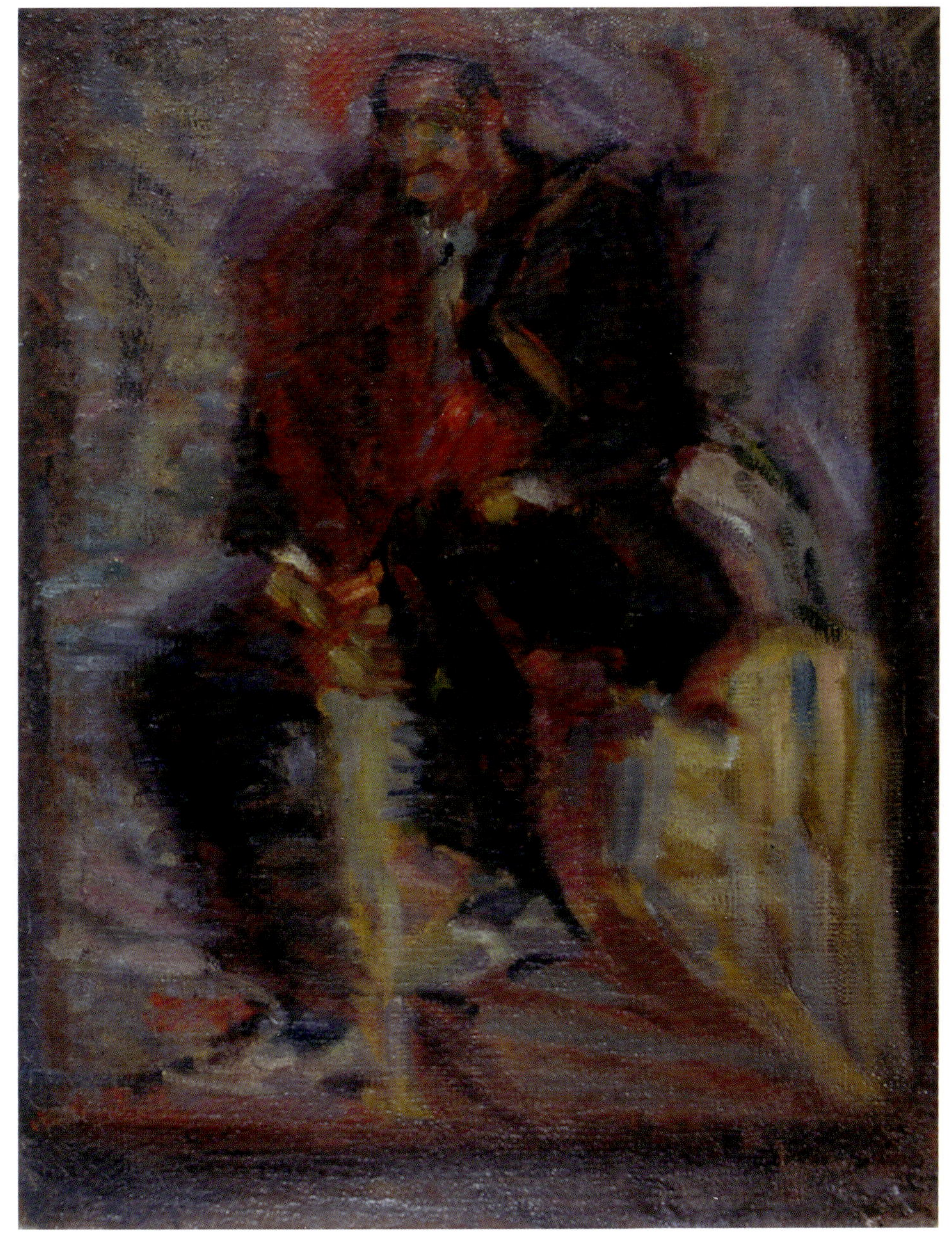

3.1 Joan Miró
The Peasant
[Le Paysan]
1915
PARIS, COLLECTION MAEGHT. BAC 4085

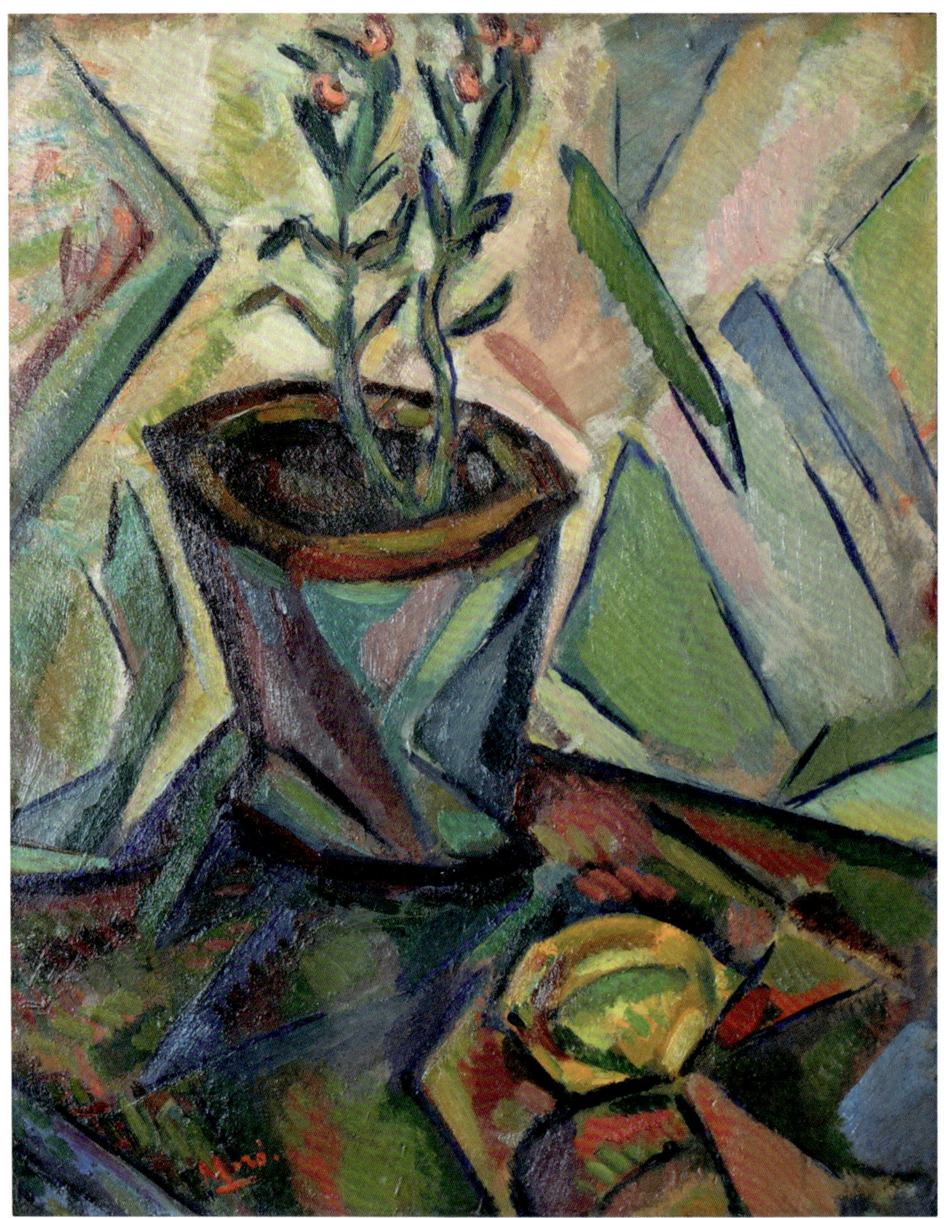

3.2 Joan Miró
Vase of Flowers with a Lemon
[Le Pot de fleurs et le citron]
1916
MADRID, JOSÉ LLADÓ

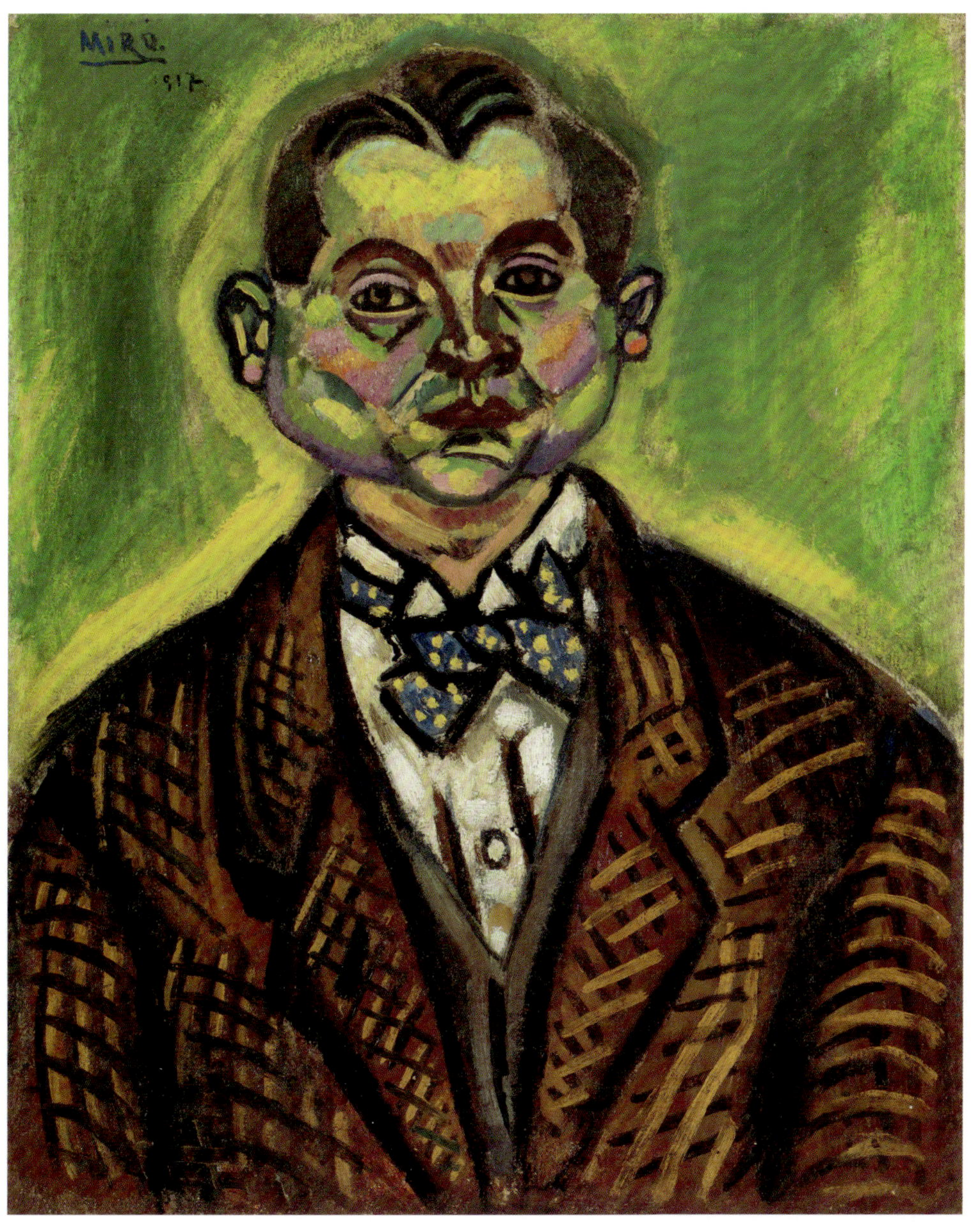

3.3 Joan Miró
Self Portrait
[Autoretrat / Autoretrato]
1917
NEW YORK, PRIVATE COLLECTION, COURTESY OF MDP & ASSOCIATI, LUGANO

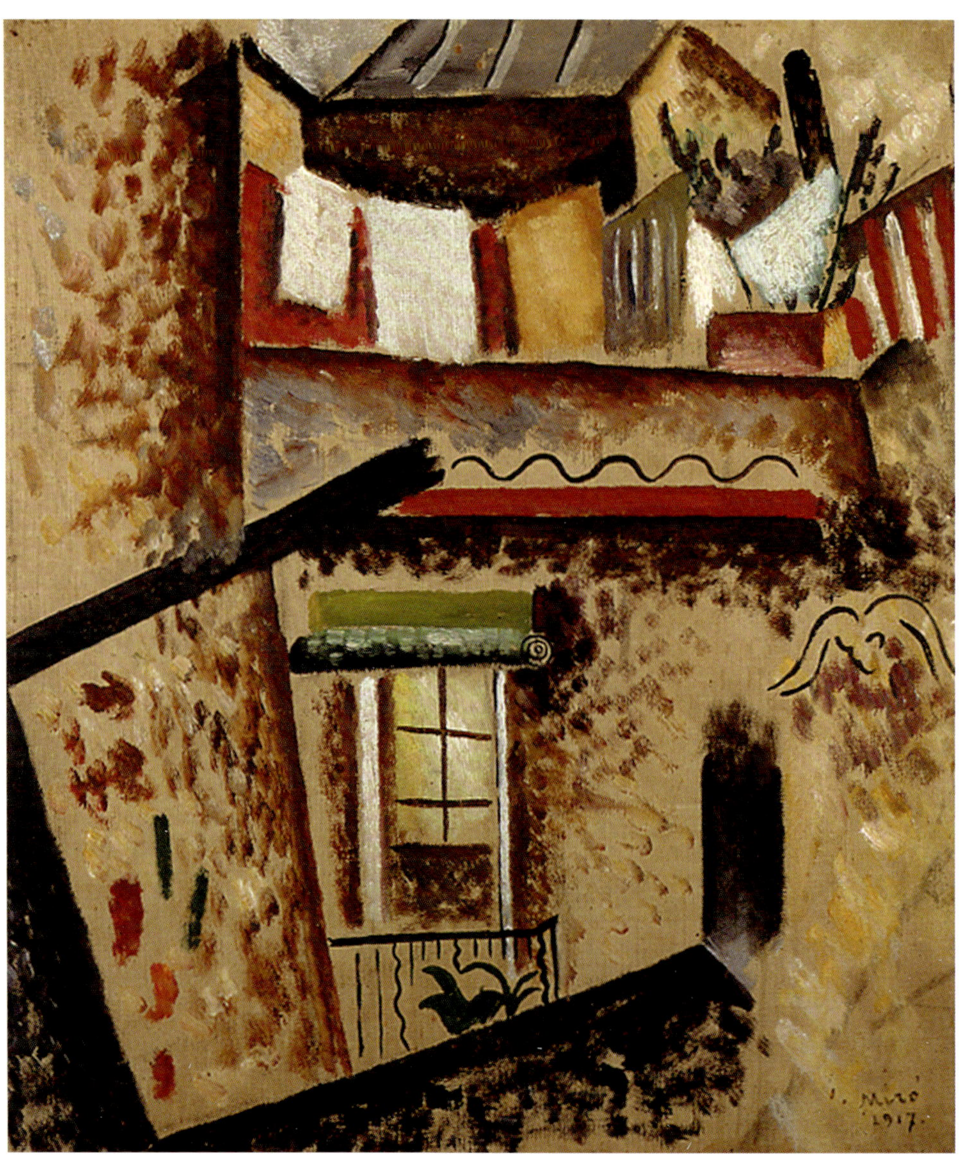

3.4 Joan Miró
The Balcony below Sant Pere
[El balcó, Baixa de Sant Pere]
1917
PARIS, COLLECTION MAEGHT. BAC 2241

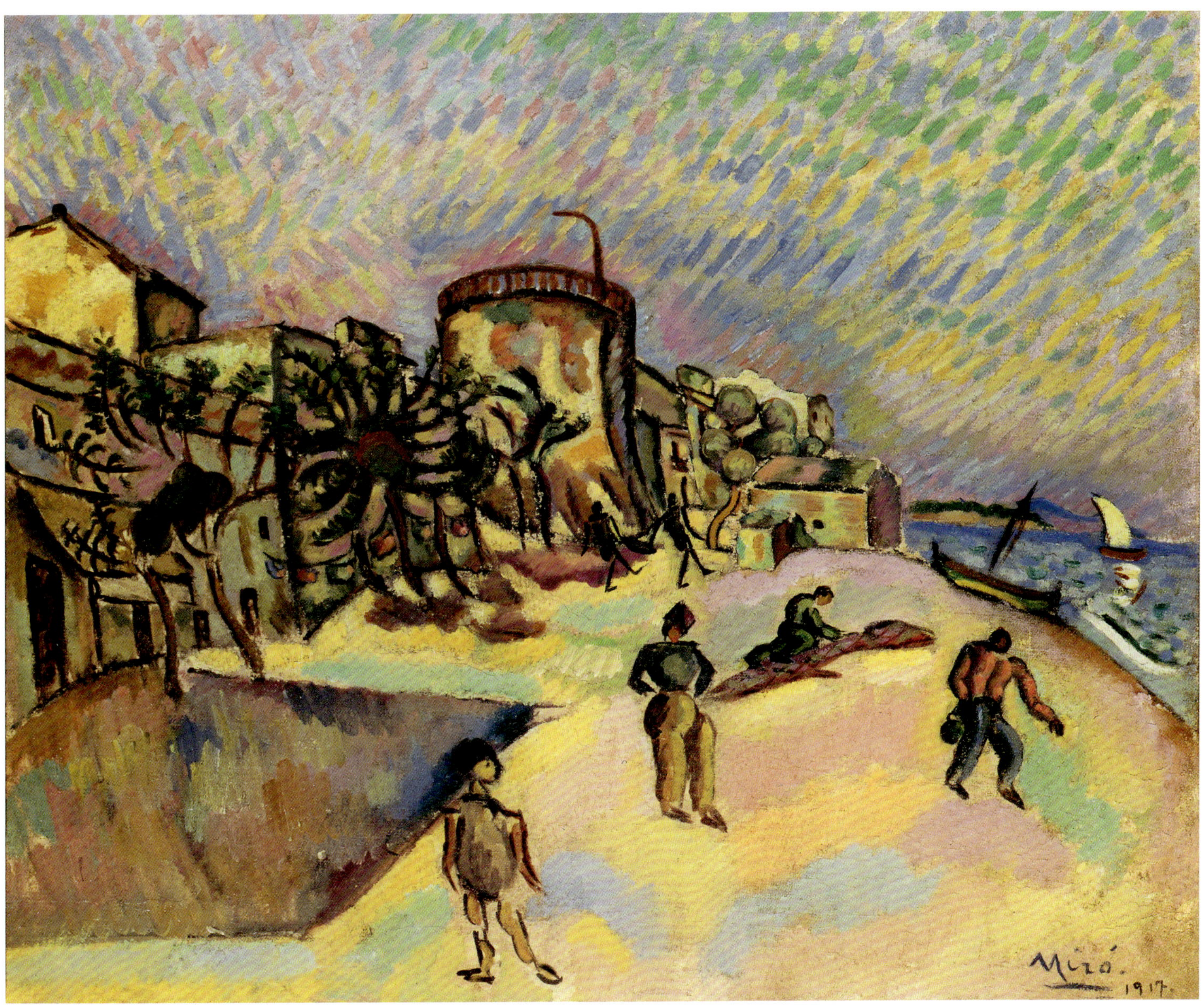

3.5 Joan Miró
The Beach at Cambrils
[La Plage à Cambrils]
1917
SWITZERLAND, NAHMAD COLLECTION

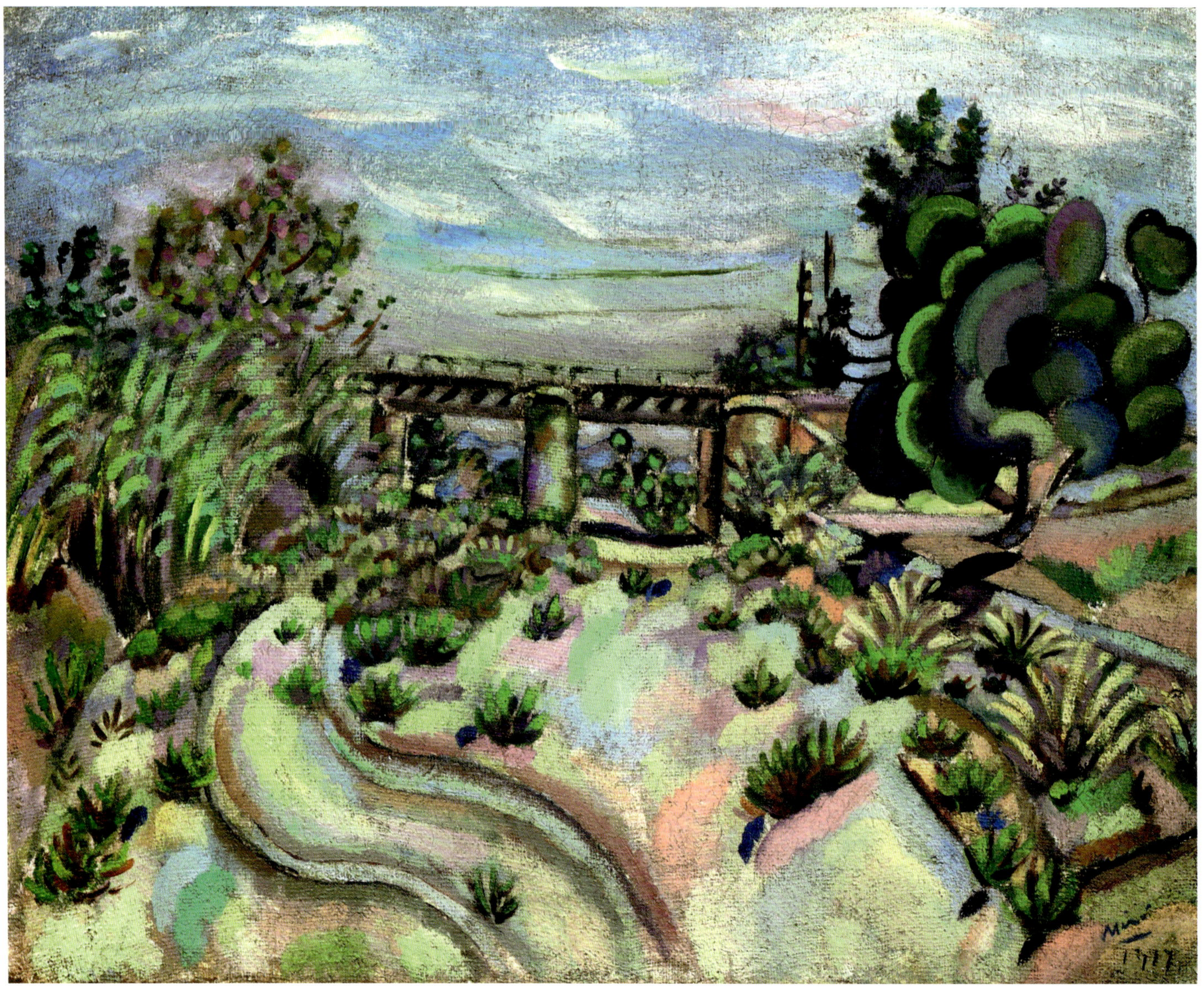

3.6 Joan Miró
Mont-roig: The Bridge
[Mont-roig: le pont]
1917
SWITZERLAND, NAHMAD COLLECTION

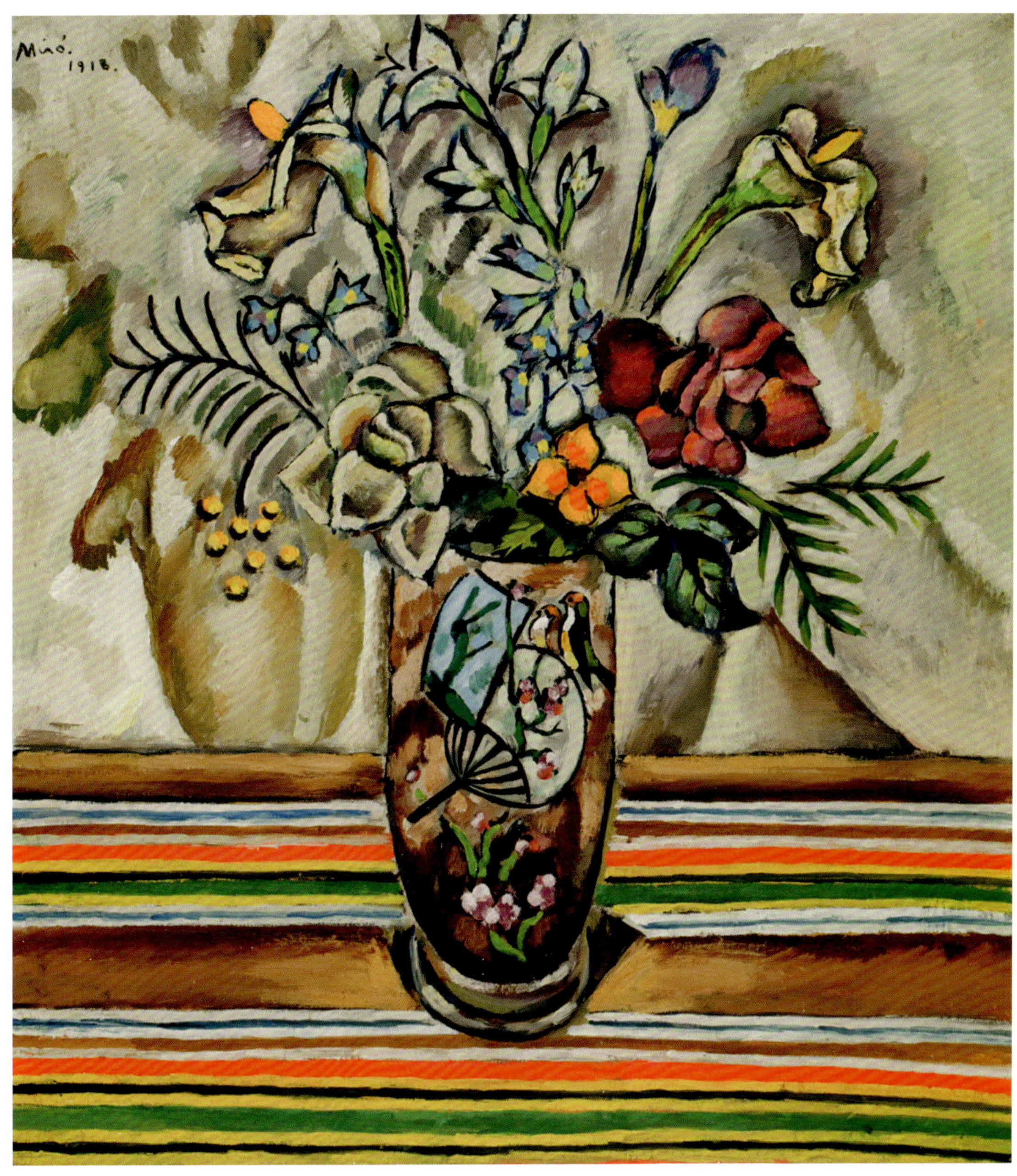

3.7 Joan Miró
Flowers
[Fleurs]
1918

MILWAUKEE, MILWAUKEE ART MUSEUM
GIFT OF MRS. HARRY LYNDE BRADLEY. M1977.124

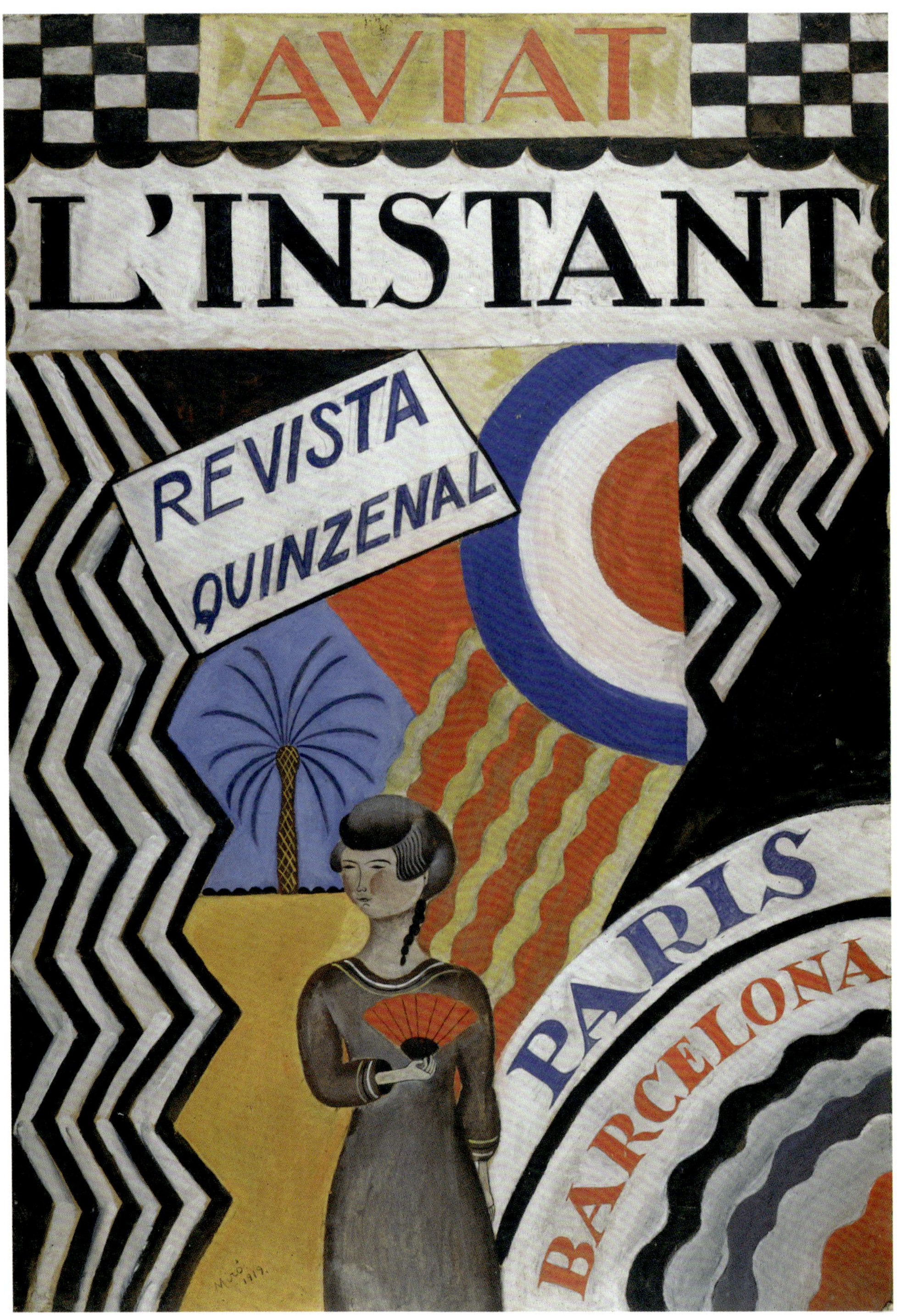

3.8 Joan Miró
Poster designed for "L'Instant" magazine
[Projet d'affiche pour la revue "L'Instant"]
1919
VALENCIA, IVAM - INSTITUT VALENCIÀ D'ART MODERN. 1996.019

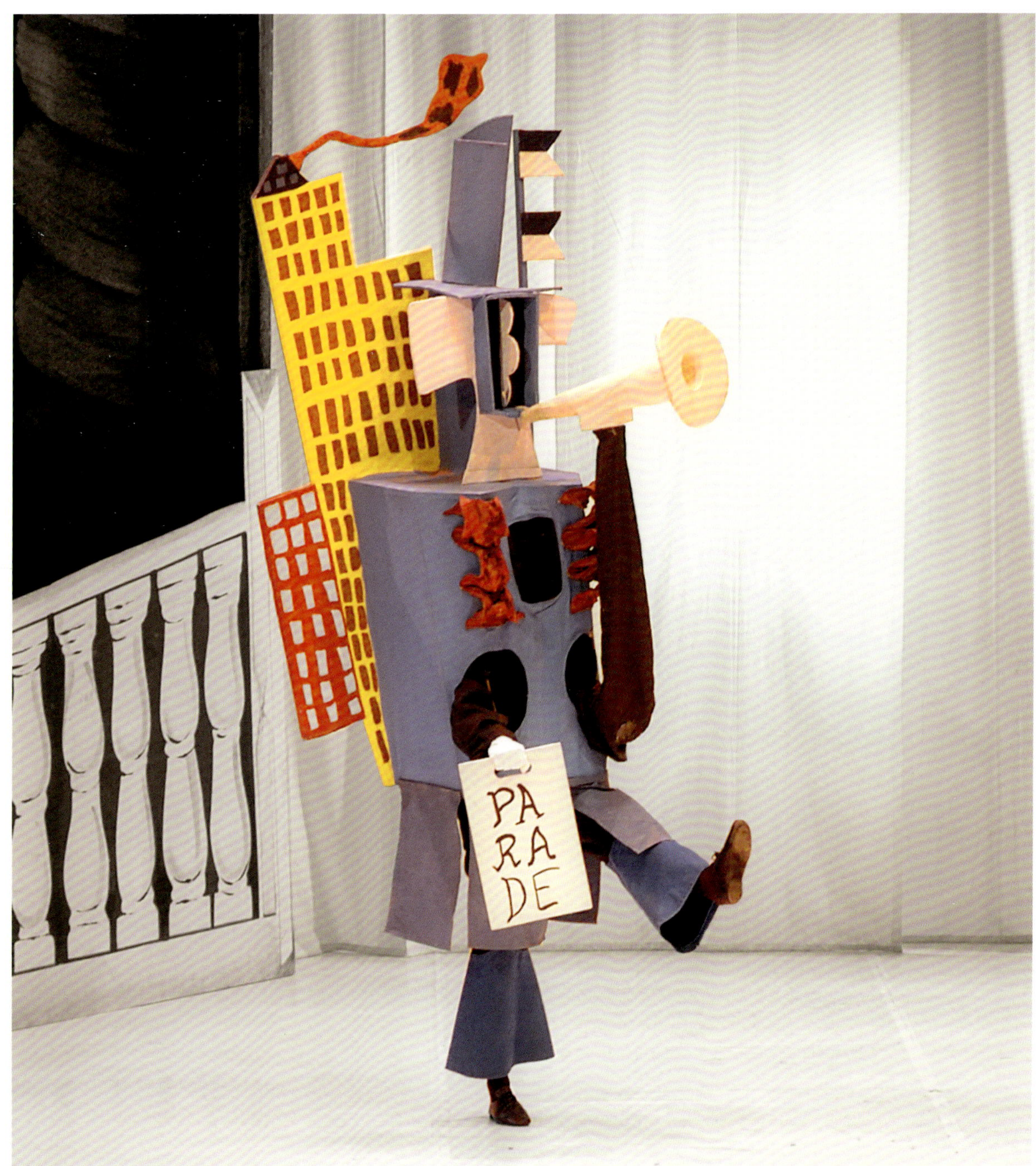

3.9
Parade: The American Manager
[Parade: costume de manager américain]
modern reproduction of the 1917
original to a drawing by Pablo Picasso
BORDEAUX, OPÉRA NATIONAL DE BORDEAUX

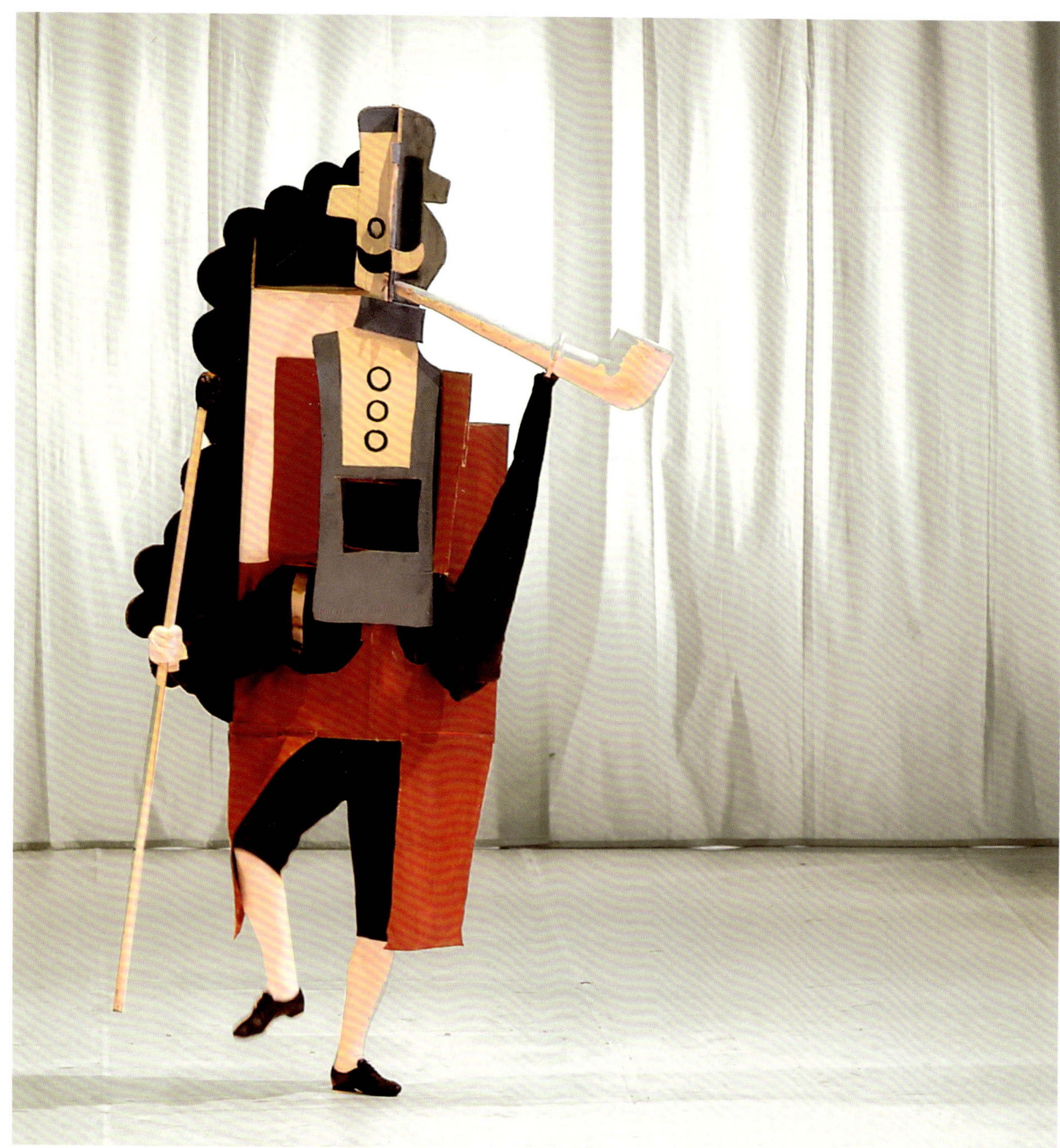

3.10
Parade: The French Manager
[Parade: costume de manager français]
modern reproduction of the 1917
original to a drawing by Pablo Picasso
BORDEAUX, OPÉRA NATIONAL DE BORDEAUX

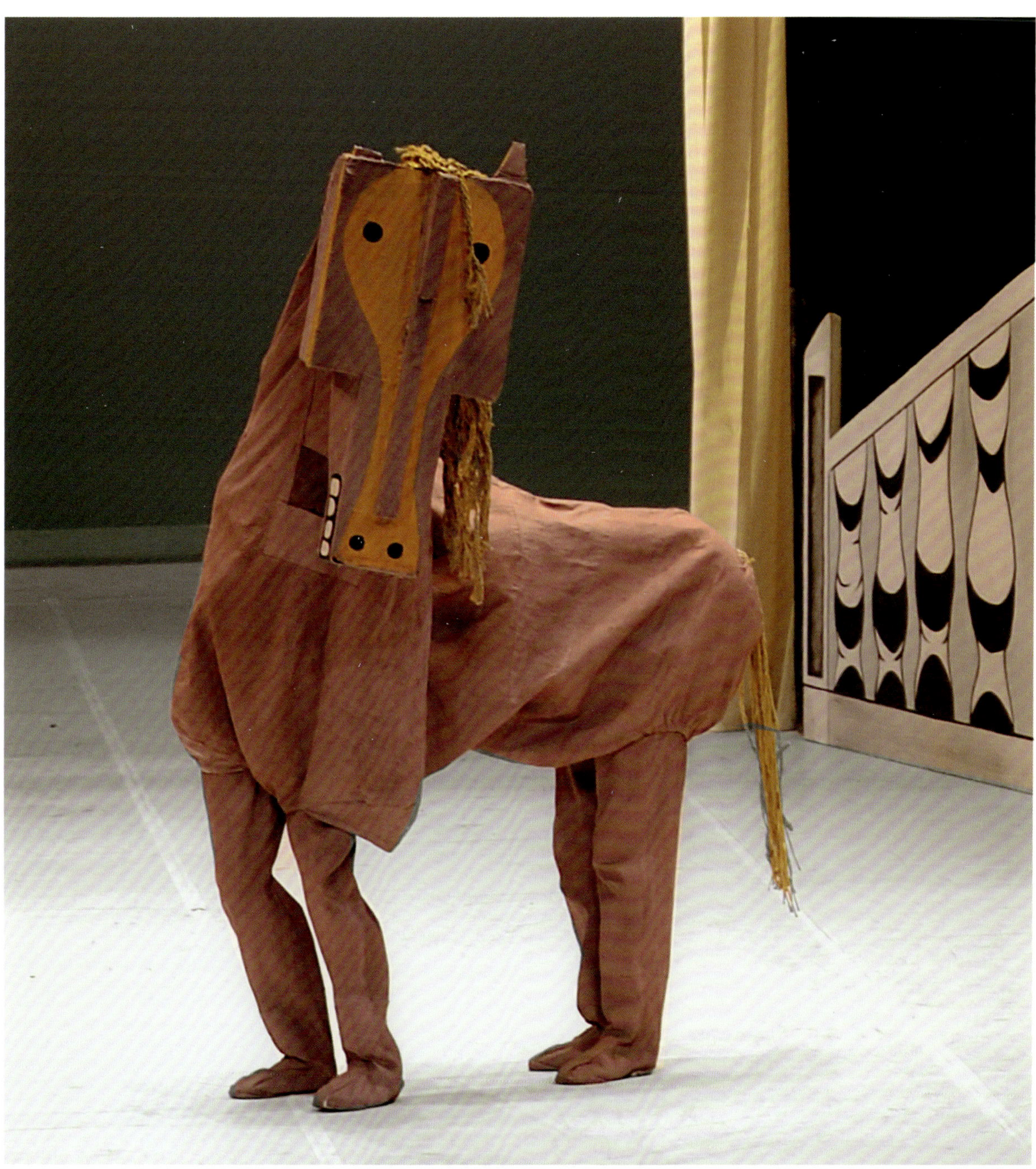

3.11
Parade: Horse
[Parade: costume du cheval]
modern reproduction of the 1917 original to a drawing by Pablo Picasso
BORDEAUX, OPÉRA NATIONAL DE BORDEAUX

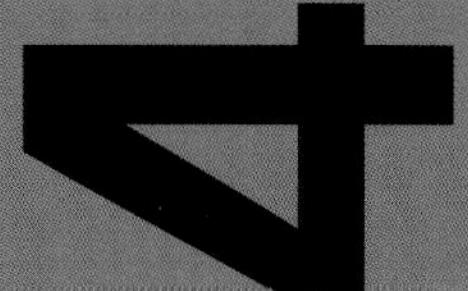

THE FOURTH CONSIDERATION

ON THE THRESHOLD OF MODERNITY PICASSO ORIGINS AND TRANSFORMATION

BARCELONA / MADRID / PARIS, 1895–1907

ON THE THRESHOLD OF MODERNITY

Cubism, Classicism, Primitivism, New Modern Classicism, the sum of all the -isms, love of the vernacular, dialectical relationship between Modernity and identity. All these references traverse the work of Miró and of Dalí in their formative stages as artists. In the background is Picasso. Always Picasso. As though naming Picasso were to put *the name of the father* on one's lips.

Picasso was in Barcelona in 1917. Ten years earlier he had also passed through the Catalan capital on the way to Gósol. He could not finish his summer stay there. He had to return to Paris urgently, and on returning, some months later, in the first half of 1907, a before and after was created for the History of Art. In *Les Demoiselles d'Avignon* there lies the origin of *the new*. In the creative process of *Les Demoiselles d'Avignon* there lies the threshold of Modernity. All we can say of the young Picasso, Miró and Dalí has its beginning here. But, today how do we approach the whole complex constellation of the work without being weighed down by the enormous amount of art literature it has generated and the variable points of view it has provoked? We have a path to avoid the sensation of loss. We have a notebook. A ten cent notebook. A hundred and twenty lined pages. They should be white. Today, due to aging, they have elegantly altered their tones towards sepia. The drawing of a bird as the frontispiece. A school handwriting that is not very airy and re-inked. A hand that is fake clumsy and fake forced, to place on record, on the cover, that the notebook contains drawings by Señor Picasso. Eighty-four drawings: nude female figures, still lifes, lines drawn quickly, sketches of *castellets* (traditional Catalan human towers or pyramids). And on the back cover multiplication tables. Has somebody who had a notebook like this studied the multiplication tables at some time?

This cheap school notebook worked on by Picasso, on the threshold of *Les Demoiselles d'Avignon*, is known today as *Cahier* no. 7. First in pencil and then in ink, the artist probably drew in it between May and June of 1907. If we dwell on this notebook we will find the keys we need. And we will find these keys if we dwell, in particular, on a certain female figure[1].

The importance of *Cahier* no. 7 has been attributed on the basis of the relations between *Les Demoiselles* and so-called *black art*[2]. Alfred J. Barr was the first to talk, explicitly, of the link between *Les Demoiselles* and so-called *black art*. And it was a *black art* that then included, both in 1939 (*Picasso, Forty Years of his Art*) and in 1946 (*Picasso, Fifty Years of his Art*) the African art of sub-Saharan peoples and the art of the aboriginals of Oceania and Melanesia. It was also—and it is necessary to point this out—a *black art* of which decidedly interesting aspects were intended to be underlined, but which was referred to with adjectives and terms that could prove ambiguous due to their possible pejorative character. And even so, all the *identity* of the complete project of *Les Demoiselles* is considered from the presence or the contingency of this relationship. After Barr's statement, the most extensively used and repeated opinion is that *black art* infused *Les Demoiselles* with its last and most *audacious* meaning. Nevertheless, Picasso himself explicitly denied that *black art* was the trigger of the last stage of *Les Demoiselles*. Must we believe Picasso when he speaks of Picasso? In principle, nobody echoed what the artist affirmed. Nobody except Christian Zervos and James Johnson Sweeney. Neither was echoed initially. After the holding, in

1. Many of the considerations given here on *Cahier* no. 7 can be found in Eugenio Carmona, "Cahier de dessins appartenant à Monsieur Picasso", in *Picasso y la escultura africana. Los orígenes de Las Señoritas de Avignon*, TEA and Fundación Picasso, Santa Cruz de Tenerife 2010, pp. 21–90.

1984, of the important exhibition *Primitivism in the 20th Century: Affinity of the Tribal and Modern*, in 1988 William Rubin began his extensive, elaborate and *peculiar* text on *Les Demoiselles* perhaps diminishing the importance of the *black art* or reducing it to very concrete aspects. Pierre Daix began by admitting the influence of *black art* in Picasso's painting, but the change of heart he had subsequently is well known. Where do we stand, therefore? Curiously, most of the post-colonial studies start in their analyses from the *admitted fact* of the decisive relationship between *Les Demoiselles* and *black art*. And if this relationship had been established in a different manner to how it has been supposed[3]?

The issue was to return again and again, but be that as it may, what we go to directly is *Cahier* no. 7, and *Cahier* no. 7 has just one *bibliography*: the commentary by Pierre Daix in the catalogue of the exhibition devoted to *Les Demoiselles* in 1988[4]. Pierre Daix estimates that *Cahier* no. 7 must be considered in connection with albums 8, 9 and 10. This group could be located at a precise juncture: the final stages in the preparation of *Les Demoiselles*, after the definitive abandonment of the work that Picasso supposedly entitled *The Brothel*, a work executed approximately between April and May of 1907, and on which the artist painted his well-known *Woman with Clasped Hands*, today in the Picasso Museum in Paris (MP16, DR 26). But this does not locate us, according to Daix, in the prologue of *Les Demoiselles* but in *excursive* developments related with *Nude with Drapery*. Although, Daix continues, in these notebooks there appears "an unprecedented figurative violence, truly savage, in the drawings of the faces" and "in the way of cutting male or female bodies". There is "an unrestrained primitivism, no longer solely formal but culturally barbarous", which is the very idea that the painting of *Les Demoiselles d'Avignon* will represent. These notebooks would denote how Picasso did not approach the work from the implications of the theme but from "figurative violence" and from "painterly violence". It gives us the sensation, Daix adds, that Picasso moved from "the violence of the motifs or the theme to the violence of the means of expression". And this second *brothel*, that is to say, *Les Demoiselles*, must therefore be an "avant-garde" work until it ended up becoming "a radical answer to previous painting from drawing and painting in themselves".

This last statement by Daix is both powerful and enlightening. Truly, the new art in the making would not end up being the same until the encounter with *painting in itself*. But it is inevitably curious how the term *violence*—repeated by Daix many times—is associated with the notion of *avant-garde* and the aesthetic identity of *Les Demoiselles*, without us knowing well whether this sensation of *violence* is associated more with today's spectator than to the very genesis of the work and its premeditation. Certainly, the comments on *Les Demoiselles* are beset with certain elements of rhetoric from which it is very difficult to detach ourselves, which have ended up being confused with the work itself.

In any event, according to Daix, when developing the elementary grammar of a new vision Picasso supposedly moved from a "conceptual Primitivism" to a "Primitivism of painterly language". A crucial situation, brilliantly considered by Daix who nevertheless—and here is the duality of evaluation—considers that even though it is manifested in *Cahier* no. 7, even though it is better outlined *as a problem* in *Cahier* no. 8. Could we maintain this same opinion today?

Daix states that the formal, geometrical and symmetrical stylisations that we *discern* in *Cahier* no. 7 seem to have been caused by reflections on the

2. I cite the catalogue of the 1988 exhibition through the following edition: *Les Demoiselles d'Avignon*, Barcelona, Ediciones Polígrafa, Museu Picasso, Ajuntament de Barcelona with the patronage of IBM, Caixa de Catalunya, Fundación para el Apoyo de la Cultura, edited by Hélène Seckel, texts by María Teresa Ocaña, Héléne Seckel, Briguitte Léal, Charles de Couësin Thierry Borel, Leo Steinberg, William Rubin, Pierre Daix and Judith Cousins, Editor-in-chief of the edition in Spanish Joaquim Horta of the Regidoria d'Edicions i Publicacions, translations by Tona Gustà, Marina Casariego and Marta Fontanals. From now on I cite this publication as "LDDA Barcelona".

3. Perhaps it would be interesting to have an exhaustive account of the relations established by the critics between the so-called *black art* and the work of *Les Demoiselles*. But it would perhaps exceed the framework of what is proposed here. In any event, Pierre Daix is extraordinarily sincere and effective when approaching the topic in his well-known *Dictionnaire Picasso*, Robert Laffont, Paris 1995, pp. 49–51, 52–8 and 246–54, in the entries devoted to *Iberian Art*, to *Black Art* and to *Les Demoiselles d'Avignon*. Although more than fifteen years have gone by since Daix made these reconsiderations and since then on the historiography has not stopped raising the issue.

pure plastic forms of certain sculptural pieces coming from so-called *black art*. This is the opinion of Daix in 1988 and at the time it was also the opinion of William Rubin, since Rubin even related figure 57r of the notebook with a Bambara character. And Daix even insists, when he tells us that "it is the first appearance of an unquestionably 'negro' influence in the albums" and that likewise "the fact is noteworthy that [this appearance] is not exercised in the sense of brutal or barbarous distortions or violence, but of a stylisation, rather, that is skilful and harmonious". Once again, as so many times in the comments on *Les Demoiselles*, *black* is considered *barbarous and brutal* and alien to the *skilful and harmonious*. Yet, in any event, for Daix, the stylisation with which Picasso worked as to be used for the expansion of the "violent" and "paroxystic" language characteristic of *Les Demoiselles*, even in the use of scribbles, but its *real* destiny lies in the "formal liberties" of *Nude with Drapery*. And, ultimately, in a certain way, "it is the end of the investigation of anti-Classical drawing coming from Matisse. Here, Picasso has not only assimilated it and appropriated it, but he has also begun a personal type of gestural, automatic investigation, that was to fertilise both his surrealism as his drawings of *War and Peace* or of his old age".

It is no small thing that in *Cahier* no. 7 Picasso evolved the starting point for the plastic language that was to develop during his maturity. The statement would have deserved a more exhaustive comment. In any event, ambivalences remain regarding the place of the notebook in itself and in its relationship with other albums and notebooks. Doubts remain regarding its links with the project of *Les Demoiselles d'Avignon*. The possibility remains that in this notebook Picasso's openness to the assimilation of so-called *black art* was established. Although the paradox traced by Daix almost without realising it also remains: if Picasso is *skilful and harmonious* in the *Western* sense of both terms and is extraneous to so-called *black art*, then why seek *black art* in the notebook? The Bambara sculpture mentioned by Rubin does not appear similar to us today to that traced in the notebook, nor to a large extent relatable to it. Daix also affirms that the scribbles that Picasso uses in the final canvas come from *black art*, but Rubin, in the same catalogue where both texts appeared, filled with mutual citations, in fact thought the opposite[5].

As we will see, there are sixteen albums of Picasso's drawings considered to be related to the work on *Les Demoiselles*. At the time they were diverse materials regarding which we do not know well whether Picasso adopted a different attitude. If we accept the established chronology for the albums, and if the so-called *Cahier* no. 7 is considered to have been worked on by the artist between May and June of 1907, this work came to *coincide* with albums 5, 6, 8, 9, 10, 11, 12 and 13, albums the chronology of which includes some of the months cited. That is to say, *Cahier* no. 7 was not alone. The chronology established for the albums, more than separating some files from others, tends to establish the harmony with them of a work in which correspondences are possible.

Even with respect to the relationship of *Cahier* no. 7 with other albums, something is intriguing or surprising. In the frontispiece of the cover, in black ink, Picasso drew the light outline of the figure of a bird. Inside, on the first page on the front side, this time with a paintbrush and in a rich reddish-coloured ink, Picasso repeated the figure, powerfully, although executed quickly in just two lines, and mysteriously superimposed on a scene in pencil, the content of which is hard to reveal. The beak, the claw and the posture are those of a bird of prey. It

4. See: Pierre Daix, "El álbum 7, dinamismo de las muchachas, rapidez gestual, formalismo 'negro', bodegones", in "El historial de Les Demoiselles d'Avignon revisado con ayuda de los álbumes de Picasso", in the volume of the 1988 exhibition catalogue, pp. 511–3, for the first subtext, and 490–545.

5. See, in this regard, William Rubin, "La génesis de Les demoiselles d'Avignon" in "LDDA Barcelona", pp. 368–487. Especially on pp. 474 *et seq.* Rubin says that the scribbling on the faces of the demoiselles considered in relation to the so-called *black art*, especially, "the one that is standing on the right", comes from the graphic and ornamental evolution in the use of Iberian Art. This conclusion is both important and commendable; but, for my part, I would like to outline that these scribbles are very similar to some that are on objects and statuettes of the so-called Narada II archaeological stage in Predynastic Ancient Egypt. And we already know about the importance of the lost Egyptian path associated with the painting. Rubin points out this last fact in particular.

has been thought that Picasso was drawing an eagle. But the pose of the eagles, even with wings furled, is more raised and its expression is more haughty. The profile is perhaps more reminiscent of that of a hawk. It is even reminiscent of certain representations of the god Horus as a hawk in Ancient Egypt, although with the significant absence of the snake. But the fact is that this same drawing, with similar characteristics, appears again in albums 12 and 14. The first situated chronologically between June and July of 1907, and the second in July of the same year. The date of the first album could coincide with *Cahier* no. 7, the second could not. Picasso's red bird seems to be an emblem or a *signature*. It is at the very least a *sign* that identifies the artist, but that is different from the aesthetic meaning of everything the albums contain. Is their coinciding presence in these three albums pure chance or does it have some meaning? Was Picasso simply playing with the same form in the three notebooks or, by repeating it, did he leave the trace that relates together these three containers of creations? Does this bird offer an *Egyptian route* in connection with the albums and the work of *Les Demoiselles*; an Egyptian route, forgotten today, but commented on or suggested at the time by some of the specialists on the issue?

Beyond the reasonable formal correspondences between the drawings that they contain, every relationship that may be established between albums 7, 12 and 14 is purely speculative or intuitive. But how do we resist the temptation to think that, close to taking the work on *Les Demoiselles as finished*, after developing the compositions we find in albums 12 and 14, Picasso might have opened *Cahier* no. 7 again to reconsider it? Perhaps it was then, and not before, that he traced the sign of the bird in red in the notebook, sealing it and giving it the standing of full relevancy with respect to the great painting with the five female nudes. In fact, as has already been anticipated on several occasions, *Cahier* no. 7 was first done in pencil and then gone over in ink in some compositions. The poor quality of the paper of the notebook, or the hurried realisations, have led to the presence of marks and tracings.

On the cover, *Cahier* no. 7 opens with its clumsy school handwriting already commented on. The very nature of the notebook as object prompts this game, this theatre. But, is there underlying in Picasso's comicality the fact that the artist, perhaps unconsciously, at that time was a beginner who had to face, with resignation and fear of tedium, learning a new calligraphy, that is, a new way of drawing? Does this farce of writing like a child not reveal the desire for ingenuousness, that is to say, the desire to be like a primitive? The intentionally not very skilful calligraphy and the disquieting outlined red bird, schematic, but ancient, is in contrast with the powerful ink drawing that, strictly speaking, opens *Cahier* no. 7. The work is on the front side of the third page (3r) and was entitled *Study for the Seated Girl: Nude with Drapery*.

The title was intended to be conventional, but nothing is innocent and it was quite the opposite. It is not neutral. It is a title that acts in favour of a given prior conception of this concrete composition and of the group in the creative process of *Les Demoiselles*. From what the drawing tells us today, we cannot agree with this title. In principle, drawing 3r is a more complete and secure work than the rest of the compositions. It is a female figure sitting in drapery. In drapery or in clothing? In drapery or in sheets? It could be said that it is a figure standing. But this would be falling into the same error as to consider it a seated figure. The position of the figure is in fact one of the issues that believe it is worthwhile to discuss or to reconsider[6].

In the critical *corpus* of *Les Demoiselles,* it is normally considered that a figure of this type is associated with all the preparations dealing with a *seated figure in an armchair* that appears in the first *versions* of the work. This *seated figure in an armchair* probably had its roots in drawings and compositions from the autumn and winter of 1906, and it is perhaps to be considered in connection with the second figure on the viewer's left in *Les Demoiselles*. But the confluence between the figure and the clothing or drapery has meant that its figurative outline has been placed more in relation with *Nude with Drapery* than with *Les Demoiselles*. Perhaps it is both and perhaps neither. In the figure in the notebook, the clothing, the diagonal inclination of the figure, the right arm raised over the head and the upper drapery are reminiscent of *Nude with Drapery*. But the outline of the body in tapered forms meeting at a sharp angle, the shape of the torso and hips and the hand on the thigh holding the cloth reference *Les Demoiselles*. The female figure of *Nude* rest a foot solidly on the ground and, despite its peculiar posture, appears to be taking a step or beginning a dance with eyes closed. The female figure in the notebook and the female figure of *Les Demoiselles* to which we have remitted it have an ambiguous state. Some specialists say that the strange way of being of this figure indicates that she is not sitting, but sitting down. Others see it, in the sketches, leaning on in the figure identified with the sailor. The figure in drawing 3r of *Cahier* no. 7 is neither sitting nor leaning, because it has neither where nor what to do so. And the same happens with the figure of *Les Demoiselles* we have mentioned. But neither is it standing, because it is not resting on the floor, unless it is performing some sophisticated and rather unnatural acrobatics. Are the withdrawn arm, the inclination of the head, the position of the torso and the hips, the way of bending the left leg and the way of picking up the cloth with the hand not postures characteristic of a reclining figure? Is the shape we find in drawing 3r so contradictory?

I believe that on very few occasions are Picasso's resources for the rhetoric of the image and the creation of icons taken into account. In this figure, particularly in that of the notebook, we are presented with a case of *amphibology* or of *dysemia*. And I beg forgiveness for using such terms. What I mean is that in this figure, as in so many others, Picasso is adding together different referents that, when put together, project a certain ambiguity of meaning, understanding this *ambiguity* as something positive and valuable, that is to say, as a consciously or unconsciously intentional *poetic* feature. One plane of the figure harkens back to the stereotype of the *Reclining Venus*. Another plane of the figure harkens back to the outline of the *Venus pudica*. The first, logically, is lying down. The second is usually standing. These types of Picasso's figures have also been associated with the iconographic outlines of the *Venus anadyomenes,* or rising from the water, which all art historians can undoubtedly perceive from the very first moment, the important thing is not to rule out this possibility or this reference *a priori*.

The figures of *Reclining Venus* have marked the history of painting erotic—and of the erotic—in Western art. The models that Picasso may have taken into account are extremely well known: Giorgione, Correggio, and, among the creators closest in time, it is worth remembering the key contributions of Bouguereau and Corot. The representations of *Venus pudica* were important in Antiquity. The Renaissance partially took them up, but they did not prosper either in the Baroque period or in the first half of the 17th century and, to a large

6. And this discussion on *Les Demoiselles*... would not be completely new. Leo Steinberg already took as a case study the problems that were derived from discerning the correct position for the second woman to the spectator's left in the oil on canvas of 1907. But Steinberg made a lucidly pertinent analysis, although it was not taken into account, when considering that this demoiselle was viewed from above. See the publication of "El burdel filosófico" in "LDDA Barcelona", pp. 328 *et seq*.

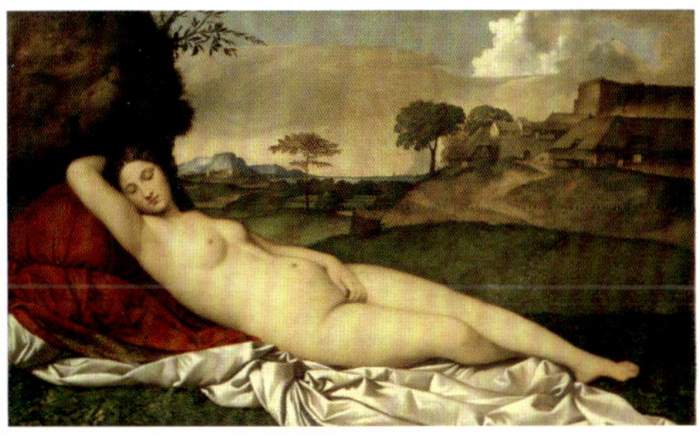

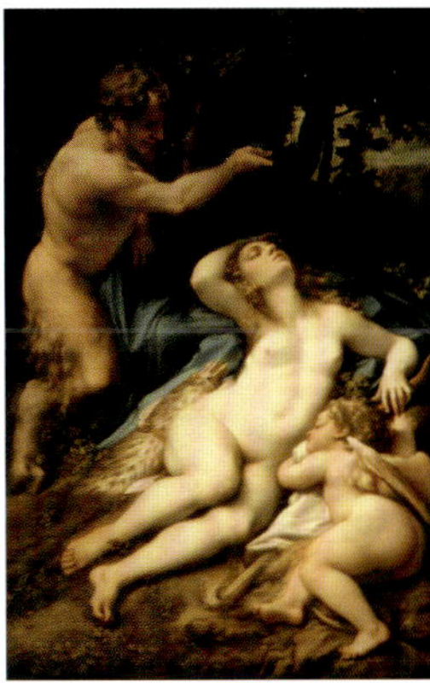

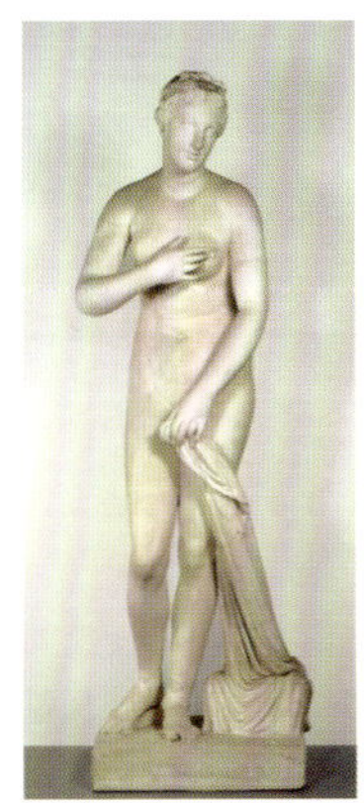

Giorgione
Venus sleeping, 1510

Correggio
Venus and Cupid with a Satyr, 1524–5
PARIS, MUSÉE DU LOUVRE

Menophantos
Venus pudica, 1st century BC
ROME, SAN GREGORIO AL CELIO

Apollo Lycaeus
Copy of Praxiteles or Euphranor
PARIS, MUSÉE DU LOUVE

Postcard from late 19th or early 20th century reproducing the *Apollo* of the Uffizi Gallery in Florence. Photograph by Giorgio Sommer

extent, they expressly *ceased to be of interest* during the 19th century. The most imitated model was undoubtedly Praxiteles, replicas of whose work spread all over the Hellenistic environment and entered the Roman world. Votive offerings and small statuettes for the home representing *Venus pudica* were common. Another issue, and an issue that may have affected Picasso, was to make the chastity of these figures a false chastity, and the wish to cover a motif more related to the incitement to desire than to chastity. From positions close to this possibility, Jean-Auguste Dominique Ingres, a constant referent for Picasso, as is known, transformed *Reclining Venus* into *odalisques* and *Venus anadyomenes* into fountains, while Alexandre Cabanel, in a genuine *tour de force*, merged the models of reclining Venus and Venus rising from the waters into a well-known painting. In all these references, especially in that of the *Reclining Venus*, the stereotype of the raised arm bending over the head is recurrent. It was no novelty that Picasso proposed it. But the semantic dysfunctions were not extraneous to his historical path and Picasso could have seen them close together, especially in the Museum of the Louvre and in publications that, although rather learned or academic, could have been within his reach.

The stereotype of the raised arm bending over the head perhaps arose in the figures of *Wounded Amazon* by Phidias and Kresilas. But centuries later the admirers of Praxiteles and his followers used it for the representation of Apollo Licio. The transfer between the iconographic models and the identities of male and female is surprising. This final complexity becomes even greater if we keep in mind that Antonio Canova used the model of *Reclining Venus* to represent *Endymion's Dream*. Curiously, some of Picasso's drawings in the albums or in sketches or preparatory work have drawn attention due to the corpulence of the female figures or to the presence of anatomical features that could conventionally be considered male. This *homogenisation* of the body in the preparations for a work that was considered to have a clear sexual component may be surprising. Such bodily *homogenisation* could have been derived from the nudes of El Greco or in those of Michelangelo, to which it is undoubtedly similar, but it could also have had as its basis the transfers of sexual genders in some iconographic proposals of Antiquity or faithfully imitating those of Antiquity.

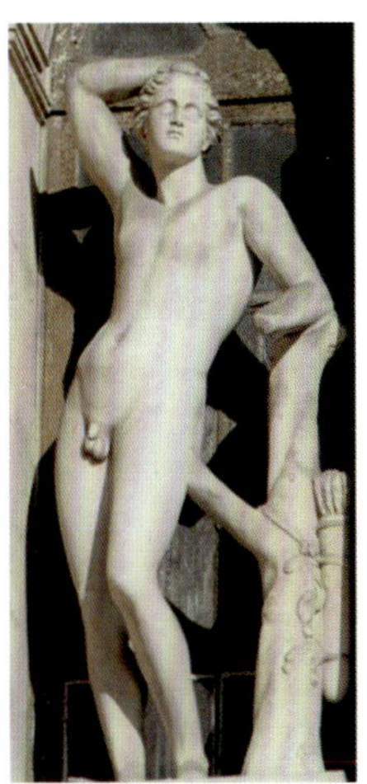

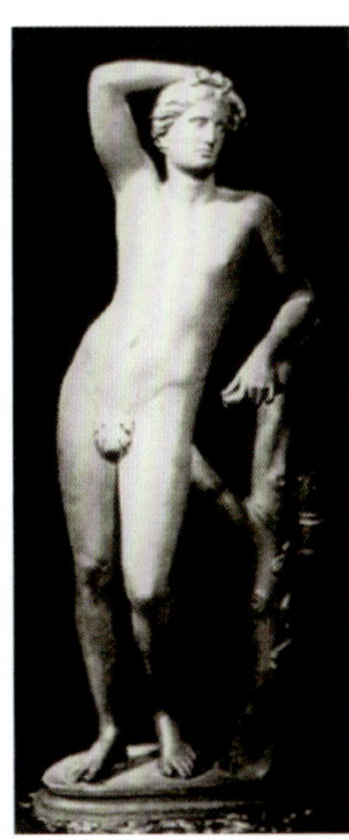

But, leaving this question simply outlined, and still in the psychological enigma that it raises, it is worthwhile to add, with the risk of being heavily exhaustive, that the model of *Reclining Venus* was anticipated in the early representations of *Ariadne's Dream* that had so much influence on Giorgio de Chirico. And, in short, Picasso's synthesis between the iconic outlines of *Reclin-*

ing Venus and *Venus pudica* would have had a singular precedent in the rather uncommon, little known figure of the so-called *Sleeping Bacchante* found in the Roman necropolis of Carmona[7]. Taking into account that female figures in works by Picasso, executed subsequently by the artist, have been identified with or related to bacchantes, could it be thought that in 1907 the artist was already clearly planning the representation of the sexuality of the brothel with the euphoria of the bacchic?

Up to the present day many reflections have been made on the *ideological* path that Picasso could have been following in his desire to shift the representations of Venus towards that of prostitutes or, conversely, on his intentions in representing some prostitutes as though they were Venus. It does not seem questionable that the artist was striking a powerful blow against the idealised hypocrisy of the nude in painting. From the psychological point of view, the *dysemia* (anxiety) promoted by Picasso seems to have a clear premeditation. The eye is always that of the painter or that of the spectator. The gaze is never the gaze of the figure depicted. The *Venus pudica* shows the instant in which the physical desire occurs on the part of the observer. The chastity accentuates this desire and even confirms it. The *Reclining Venus* shows the instant in which this desire could be consummated or has been consummated. Picasso merges both moments by suspending the rules of action and time. Yet, with this even being able to be the case, there has been little consideration of the meaning that the artist's iconographic *dysemia* incorporated in its plastic language. The figure that interests us, by mixing the references to the *Reclining Venus* and the *Venus pudica* in the same *format*, is proposing a notion of perceptive simultaneity that, in my opinion, is as important as all the references to the totality of *front* and *profile* views that, systematically, and with a transforming accent, have been commented upon for *Les Demoiselles*, and for Cubism as a whole, based on its alternative to the perceptive or visual order created in the Renaissance. In this image we may be witnessing the convergence of the *front view* and the *raised or aerial view*. Indeed, as Leo Steinberg has wisely suggested, it is as though we could see the figure, from above, reclining in a bed or couch, but to the viewer this figure is presented frontally: two different perspectives for a single surface. Picasso therefore discarded the foreshortened view or the projective trick of Manet's *Olympia* or, previously, of Giorgione, who offered us an optical contradiction between the position of the couch where the figure is resting and the position of the body of the figure itself. In Correggio, this contradiction achieves its maximum expression and the foreshortening of the figure is as evocative and skilful as it is forced. Picasso opted to link several visual dissonances, evocative and powerful, in his drawing, and with it he anticipated the epistemological fractures that critics of Picasso have stated as characteristic of *Les Demoiselles*.

In drawing 3r most of the *dysemia* used by Picasso comes from the fact of having made the triangular folds of a curtain converge towards the character. The spectator who wishes to understand the figure as a *reclining figure* finds nowhere to recline her. It has been considered that these folds succeed in relating the drawing more to *Nude with Drapery* than to *Les Demoiselles d'Avignon*. However, these same folds are in *Les Demoiselles*, although not associated with any specific figure, but as *characters* of the painting and blue in colour. I believe this comment removes some doubts on the relevance of *Cahier* no. 7 to the central axis of *Les Demoiselles*. Now, the issue does not finish here: the drawing opening the notebook continues it.

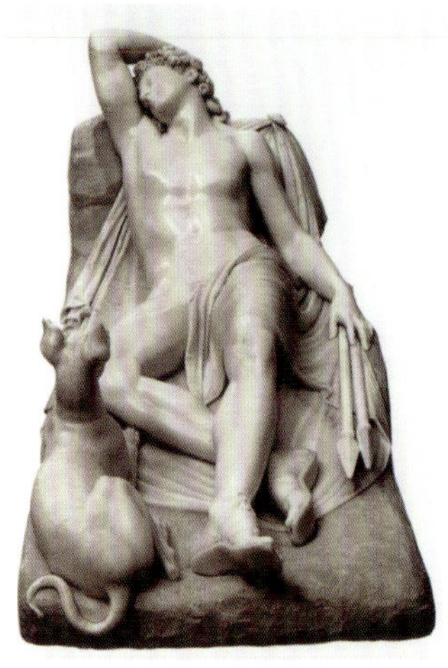

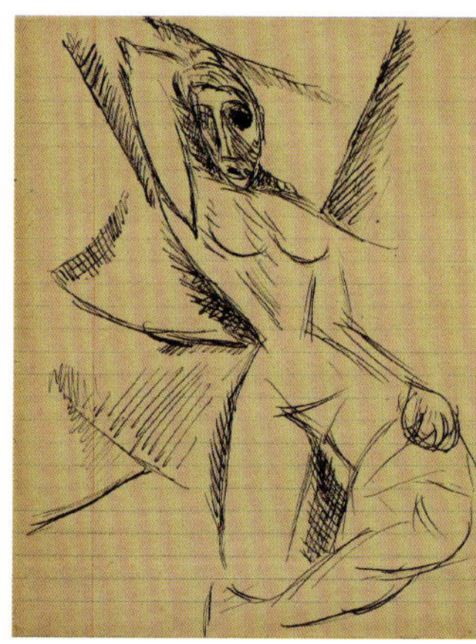

Antonio Canova
Endymion's Dream, 1819–22
POSSAGNO, GIPSOTECA ANTONIO CANOVA

Pablo Picasso
Cahier no. 7, c. 3r
MALAGA, COLLECTION OF THE PABLO RUIZ PICASSO FOUNDATION - BIRTHPLACE MUSEUM, FPCN: 2037

7. See: *Necrópolis de Carmona. Memoria escrita en virtud de acuerdo de las Reales Academias de la Historia y de Bellas Artes de San Fernando* by D. Juan de Dios de la Rada y Delgado, Imprenta de Manuel Tello, Madrid 1885.

Alongside the *double vision*, the relationship established between the character and the drapery already outlines, in advance, another of the paradigmatic registers of full-blown Cubism: that of the relationship between background and figure; rather, that of the new relationship, by means of spatial synthesis, between background and figure that is considered to achieve its greatest degree of realisation in Picasso's work in the summer of 1910, in Cadaqués, thanks to what Kahnweiler referred to as the *break with the homogeneous form*. And what this break with the homogeneous form permitted was that the iconic sign and the background on which it was placed merge, identifying the painting as a surface and not as a three-dimensional box.

Here, in the work we are commenting upon, drawing allows solutions and bold actions that initially were not permitted in painting, although Picasso was to work throughout 1907 to make this possible. In drawing 3r the background and the figure are related on a plane of equality because Picasso works both with the same graphic character and from a similar (and dominant) formal module. The graphic character makes it a purified abstraction that was not taken up by the artist until *Cahier* no. 7. The dominant formal module is a triangular form with sides that are sometimes concave and sometimes convex. A triangular form with concave/convex sides that is complemented with tapered forms. The concretion of the triangular form to which I refer is condensed in the pelvic space of the figure. Picasso creates a special pubic triangle, a special *delta of Venus*. This concrete form has its three convex sides, which accentuates its expressive and dynamic character, and is repeated in the triangular shape formed by the torso and in the shape formed by the combination of the narrow waist and the abundant thighs. But then it is repeated in each of the folds of the drapery, creating a succession of forms that themselves favour plastic movement and unify the way of understanding the relationship between background and figure. Picasso unified the psychological perception of the human and the object and this was to have a key influence on the aesthetic conceptions of the 20th century. As we see, with drawing 3r, despite the iconological power of their conception, we are in the antechamber of the most transformational principle proposed in *Les Demoiselles* and at the starting point of the Modern notion of *pure painting*.

Through the work that we see in the albums and in some contemporary works on paper, Picasso worked in several directions until he found the graphic synthesis and the modular meaning that was proposed in the composition of *Cahier* no. 7 on which we are commenting.

Before executing *Cahier* no. 7, in *Cahier* no. 4 Picasso was interested predominantly on the female figure with arms raised in a square form over the head, giving rise to an icon to which we will refer later. But Picasso was also interested in the art of Ancient Egypt[8] in this *Cahier* no. 4. And this is more important than people would like to accept. Picasso strengthened his Primitivist ambitions and had recourse to new registers. Ancient Greek, Pre-Classical Greek and Iberian art already existed. Now the attention to Ancient Egyptian Art, although existing in Picasso from 1902, added, in a different context, a new value to be borne in mind. However, in any event, alongside this attempt, another of greater importance had slipped through silently but powerfully.

Prior to *Cahier* no. 4, the sketch was a help for quick group compositions and for studies on some characters. The compositions destined for more important purposes continued to be done three-dimensionally, with effects of volume

8. Rubin already pointed this out with conviction. See the text by Rubin in"LDDA Barcelona", pp. 374 *et seq*. His quotation from André Salmon, in note 34, p. 471, is especially appropriate and revealing.

and of light and shadow. Now, the figure in the sketch, in outline, became a *major work,* and Primitivist assimilation was decisively allied into the enterprise. I am fully aware that what I have just stated supposes the introduction of an entire *thesis* on the formal or linguistic development of *Les Demoiselles d'Avignon*, but bringing back to the present the study of the albums and preparatory sketches for the work only demonstrates what I consider as evidence.

It was in *Cahier* no. 5 that Picasso rehearsed the possibilities of a new body canon. He also placed on record a new synthesis of the face as a schematic mask derived from Iberian Art. I believe Pierre Daix has evaluated this last issue very well, but originally, undoubtedly, in view of the vast amount of material to be taken into consideration, he did not take *Cahier* no. 7 into account.

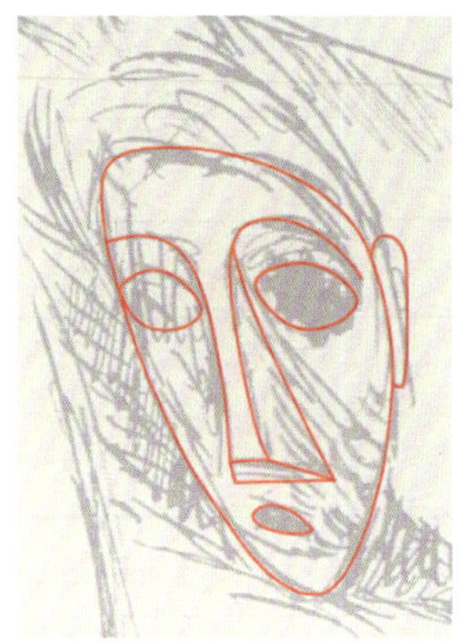

Summary line drawing on the face of figure c. 3r of *Cahier* no. 7

I will expound what I mean directly: the formal similarities between the face of figure 3r in *Cahier* no. 7 and that of the *demoiselle* that, in the background, on the spectator's right, enters in scene and draws the curtains, are more than evident. The colour modifies the perception initially, but what we could call the *drawing* or the *design* makes both faces similar. And this although the experts on *Les Demoiselles* know that Picasso *ultimately* modified this figure, together with two others. The hairstyle and the inclination of the head are different. Also, in the painting, Picasso eliminated the arch of the eyebrows, moving away both from the acquisitions from Iberian Art and from the facial models of so-called *black art*. But the oval of the face, the form of the nose, the sketch of the mouth, the arch of the eyebrows and the form of the eyes coincide. And how curious that where in drawing 3r an ink stain was formed accidentally (or so it seems) Picasso deposited a black stain in the effigy of the figure of the major oil painting; this black stain is repeated in all the works, paintings or drawings that are related to this head. The other four young women in the painting from 1907 have strong gazes, whereas this one, in contrast, expresses an inexplicable blindness. It is a blindness that perhaps, being inexplicable, has not been commented upon very much. And the mythology of the blind eye in Spanish culture is vast. Is this *demoiselle* blind like the *Celestina* painted by Picasso years earlier and later repeated in his old age?

Certain questions immediately arise regarding this similarity. The first is the one that reconsiders the relationship between *Cahier* no. 7 and the oil on canvas of *Les Demoiselles d'Avignon*. Evidently this relationship was closer than has been supposed. But how was this relationship formed? Did the notebook anticipate the painting, barely, although decisively by one or two months? Or, in the midst of executing the painting, did Picasso take up the notebook again? And, whatever the case, if this *young lady* has always been considered to be one of the paradigmatic *black* or *African* figures of the painting, is the figure in the notebook to be considered in the same way or is there another issue involved?

We find the maximum stylisation of a face or mask, formed by taking on certain plastic intensities of Iberian Art, in *Cahier* no. 5, in the drawing on the back of the third page (3r). It is considered as a *Study for the "Woman with Clenched Hands": Woman's Head* and is executed in pencil with touches of black ink. In fact, considered today, this drawing does not *necessarily* seem to be a sketch or a trial for another work. Neither does it appear that he face is that of a woman. I believe we are dealing with a proposal that is an end in itself and that takes up and *completes* that developed in other albums and drawings from the autumn of 1906. In my opinion, the importance of this drawing from *Cahier* no.

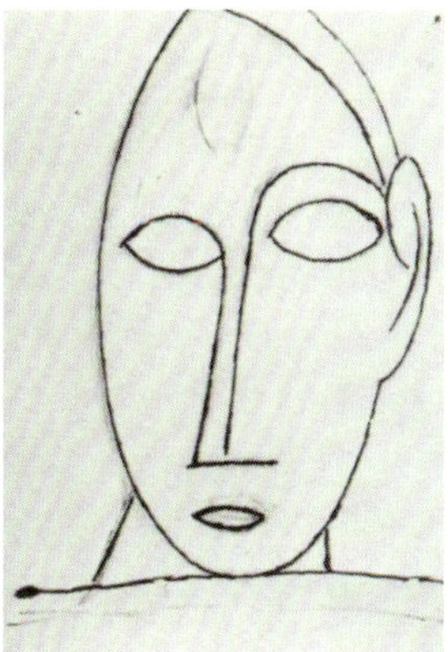

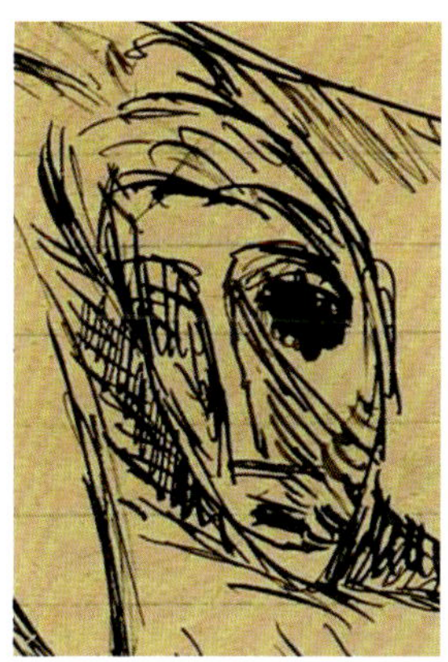

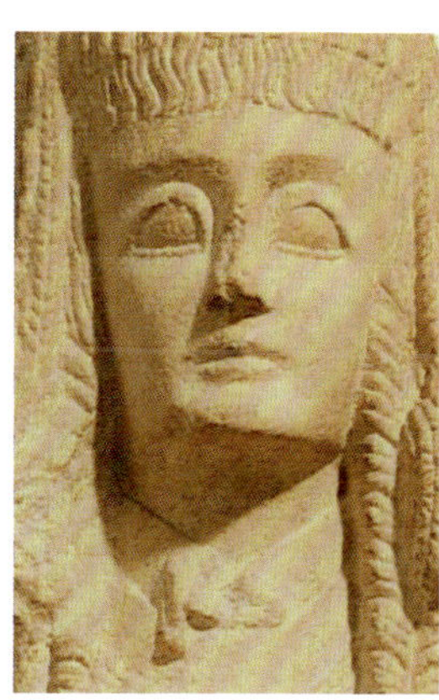

Pablo Picasso
Study for woman with hands clasped in *Cahier* no. 5, April-May 1907
PRIVATE COLLECTION

Pablo Picasso
Detail of drawing c. 3r in *Cahier* no. 7

Dama del Cerro de Los Santo statue (detail) between the 3rd and the 2nd century BC
MADRID, MUSEO ARQUEOLÓGICO NACIONAL

5 is enormous. Synthesised in it is one of the major stylistic *secrets* of *Les Demoiselles d'Avignon* and its link with the artist's graphic work on *Iberian Art* clarifies a question that is always latent in the comments on the painting that are always unexpectedly resolved in favour of so-called *black art*. If we keep in mind what this drawing reveals, we can appreciate to what extent some risky interpretations of *Les Demoiselles* are the critics' and commentators' projections rather than proven positions on Picasso's work.

As though it were a matter of applying Morelli's method, the bulky ear of the drawing of *Cahier* no. 5 is identified with the disproportionate ears of the Iberian sculptures of the sites in Osuna. But today's spectators can observe something that is interesting or important and that, to some degree, has already been anticipated. From the schematic head of *Cahier* no. 5, together with the oval form of the face, the eyes and the mouth, we can deduce both a nose of the prismatic type (the so-called *portion-of-brie nose*) and the graphic sign that combines nose and eyebrows. That is to say, both possibilities come from the same origin: they are not two different options, nor do they represent two different *styles* in the grasping or imitation of the language of the primitive. Although, clearly, in numerous manifestations of *primitive art* similar solutions can be found to those that Picasso now *finds* deriving formulas from Iberian Art.

But if in *Cahier* no. 5 we find this schematic face that clarifies so many things concerning *Cahier* no. 7 and the stylistic personality of *Les Demoiselles*, no less important are other drawings in this booklet, *Cahier* no. 5, that were *recycled* by Picasso. One of these, known as *Study of Foot with Joined Hands* (1v) on the back of the first page, is a *study of proportions*. It is undoubtedly a peculiar study of proportions. Picasso seems to be seeking to attain an *elongated canon* taking as his major module the overlapping of rhomboidal geometrical figures arranged at an acute angle and not on one side. Does a mysterious evocation of the golden proportion exist? We do not know, although, in any event, this has certainly not been the line of investigation recently promoted around Picasso's relationship with these topics. From a certain perspective linked to the new cultural sociology of art, there has been the intention to locate—as, for example, David Lomas has done—Picasso's attempts associated with certain anthropometric studies from the late 19th and early 20th century, but with anthropometric studies of a segregationist character destined to demonstrate the link between physical deformity and social marginalisation[9]. It is argued that although Picasso may well not have known these studies, he was indeed probably in tune with the age, in tune—*organic*, we would say—with these and that he developed an anthropometric canon in order to create figures marked by the *difference* and the *deformity* of being prostitutes, and prostitutes of *non-European* races. This position has been echoed to a certain extent[10]. But, despite this, it is a type of approach that does not take certain things into account. On one hand, it could be said that the statements that it contains are merely speculative, since they propose conclusions of great scope without providing specific conclusive evidence. What is proposed is a suggestion that involves Picasso, in a mechanical way, in some determinants of social psychology, filled with scientific spirit. On the other hand, one is not taken into account that the physical canon that Picasso seems to want to develop is *elongated* and *stylised*, while the main anthropometric feature of the degraded beings is the reduction of stature and the reformulation of the external limbs and factions. In the well-known treatise by Carl Heinrich Stratz, *Human Figure in Art*, where the bodily canon of so-called *black art* is taken in consideration for the first time, we can verify this fact[11].

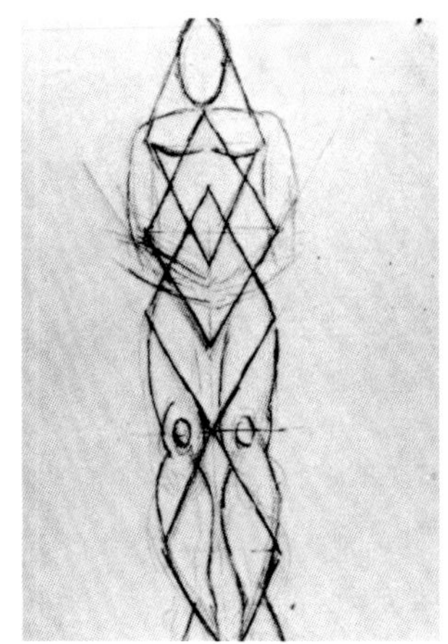

In *Les Demoiselles*, Picasso moved away from the aesthetic category of the *beautiful*. An aesthetic category of the beautiful in which Matisse, Derain or Braque were *still* to be found. Perhaps Picasso wanted, intuitively, to be located in the aesthetic category of the *ugly*, for the moment not so much of the *monstrous*, if the *ugly* could, strictly speaking, be an aesthetic category. And this change by Picasso, which has antecedents in Spanish Baroque and in Goya, was once again not well understood and associated with the reception of the ominous and the abject as *presumable* forms of transgression. The term *deformity* is explosive in its polysemy and has negative resonances, being associated with socially *differentiated* attitudes. And, in any event, why was Picasso, when developing his small and slight drawings of human proportions, also on paper of poor quality, going to be more in tune culturally with anthropometric studies with a racist and supremacist substratum than with positions on the human proportions that were so habitual in the artistic studies of an academic nature? It is not logical to think that Picasso, when developing a new type of graphic synthesis, thought about how to apply this graphic synthesis to the human figure as a whole? And do we not know very well, and without any debate, that although Picasso appears as the quintessential anti-academic artist, that throughout his life, and in different ways, he used the academic formation he had received?

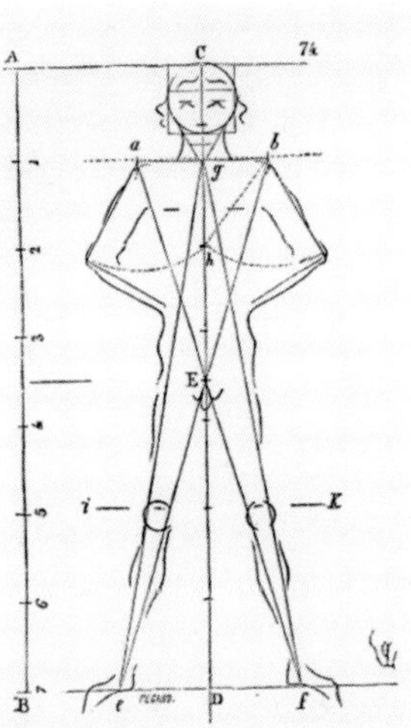

The elongated canon on which Picasso speculated is reminiscent of the elongated canon of the figures of El Greco. But other antecedents to that developed by Picasso can also be indicated. The Gothic canon was also elongated. Some drawings contained in the *Livre de portrature* by Villard de Honnecourt, created in the first half of the 13th century, shows figures composed through triangles, in a way that could basically be related with that of Picasso. In 1521, the *Vitruvian Man* by Cesare Cesariano is drawn in square inserts with rhomboidal shapes. The reduction of the human body canon to pure geometrical forms was trialled by Dürer in 1528 and by Juan de Arfe in 1585[12]. Matyla Ghika, it must be remembered, in the 1920s, related some of Dürer's figures with Cubism. And, finally, in many of his numerous treatises on the human body, the already mentioned physician, anthropologist, inspiration of artists—and closet pornographer—Carl Heinrich Stratz, some of whose books Picasso may have known[13], schematised the human figure, in its various anthropometric possibilities, through triangles and rhomboidal figures, which, by the way, is an almost habitual way of proceeding in studies of proportions.

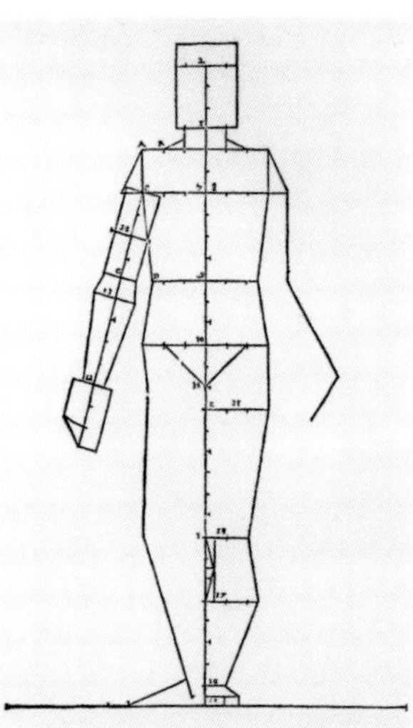

9. See: David Lomas, "In Another Frame: *Les Demoiselles d'Avignon* and Physical Anthropology" included in Christopher Green (ed.), *Picasso's "'Les Demoiselles d'Avignon"*, Cambridge University Press, Cambridge 2001, pp. 104–27. The first version of Lomas' text, "A Canon of Deformity: *Les Demoiselles d'Avignon* and Physical Anthropology" appeared for ▶

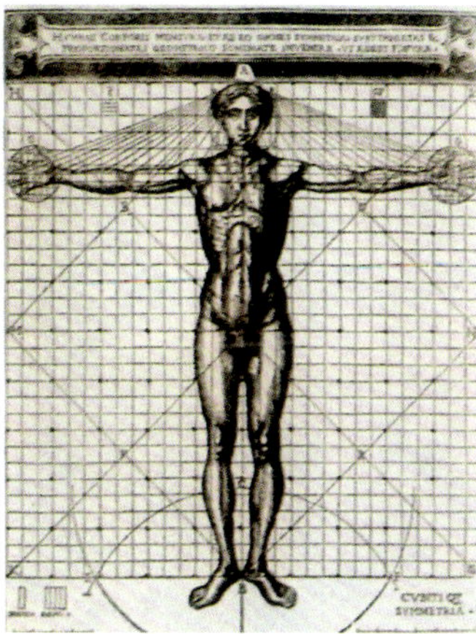

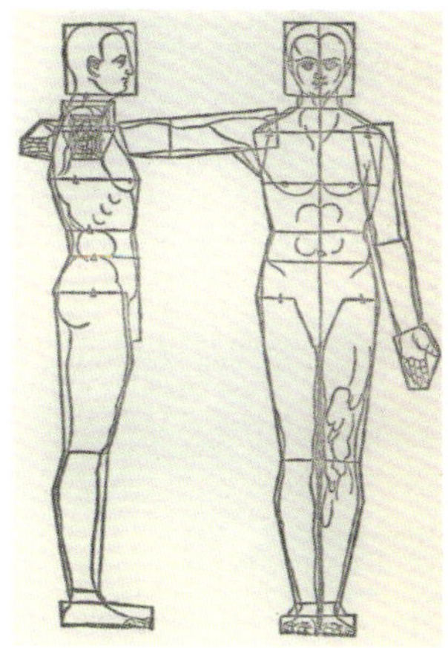

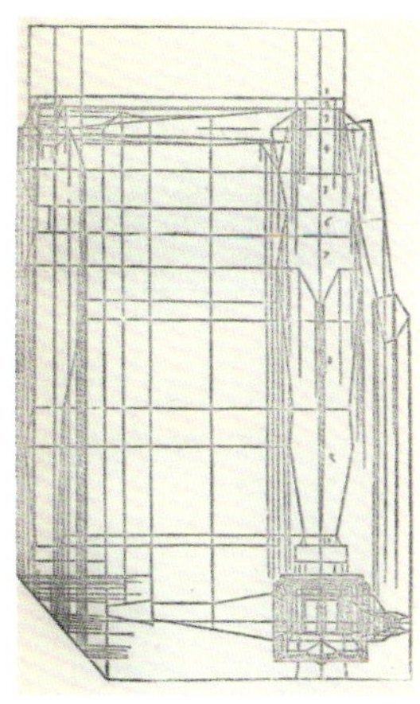

Pablo Picasso
Cahier no. 5, April-May 1907
Nude Standing with Hands Together
(*Study of proportions*)
PRIVATE COLLECTION

Villard de Honnecourt
Sketch from *Livre de portraiture*
13th century, edition from 1585

Juan de Arfe
Anthropometric sketch
De varia commesuración, 1585

Cesare Cesariano
Vitruvian Man in *De Architectura*, 1521

Albrecht Dürer
Hierinn sind Begriffen
*vier menschlichen Proportionen*1528
Cited by Arthur Jerome Eddy
in *Cubism and Postimpressionism*
A. C. McClurg & Co., 1919

Albrecht Dürer
Hierinn sind Begriffen
vier menschlichen Proportionen, 1528
Cited by Arthur Jerome Eddy
in *Cubism and Postimpressionism*
A. C. McClurg & Co., 1919

That is to say, Picasso works to find a canon, and not necessarily an African canon, because inside even what we could call *autochthonous or original African physiognomies* applied to art, the possibilities are various. In one of Stratz's treatises it can be proven that the canon of proportions of so-called *tribal art* is very different to the one developed by Picasso. What we could call, even generalising and simplifying too much, the *African canon* gives primacy to the size of the head, the trunk and the thorax over the legs. The primacy of the lower limbs that Picasso employs is more reminiscent of formulas of artistic treatment of the body in Ancient Egypt or the Greek Art of the archaic period. There even exists a drawing, conserved in the Picasso Museum in Paris and, undoubtedly, related to some of the contributions in *Cahier* no. 5, which divides the figure into sections in a similar way to what we find in the well-known *Lepsius Canon*, applied from the middle of the 19th century to the Egyptian art of the age of the pharaohs.

According to this view, Picasso creates, through superimposed rhomboidal figures, an elongated canon in which two conical figures, with the lower one upright from the knees and the upper one inverted, are secant cuts. The cut of the two forms creates a very narrow waist in the figure. In the upper part, the chest, which could be either male or female, stands on the inverted base of the upper cone. Both conical forms, being resolved on the plane, tend to become truncated triangles. The lower triangle, however, emulating the forms of the hips, curves its sides, offering an unusual bell shape. In these drawings the head is always oval. In some of these heads, Picasso has maintained a very lobed and disproportionate ear that has always been considered to have come from the pieces of Iberian Art the artist knew.

In short, Picasso tested the possibilities of a study of proportions that was based more on the recreation of Egyptian, Greek and Iberian archaic models than *African*. Picasso's triangular pattern can even be *related back* to well-known representations of the so-called Geometric Period of Ancient Greek Art, such as the art we find in the *Dipylon Burial Amphora*, in the Museum of Athens. But, above all, to small free-standing figures, such as the ceramic ivory-finish statuette, executed between the late 8th century and the early 7th century BC, today in the National Museum of Athens, or the well-known *Statuette of a Kneeling Youth*, executed between 630 and 620 BC, also in the National Museum of Athens. And regarding this figure, and regarding the coloured figures of the *Dipylon Burial Amphora*, it is worthwhile to indicate the similarities with drawing 3r in the way of conceiving the triangular torso jointed via the narrow waist to the

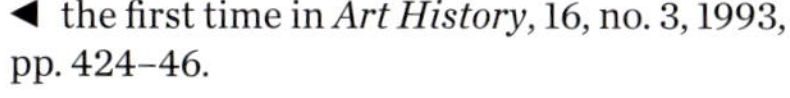

◄ the first time in *Art History*, 16, no. 3, 1993, pp. 424–46.

10. See: Christopher Green, "Looking for difference. The *demoiselles d'Avignon* again", in *Picasso: Architecture and vertigo*, Yale University Press, New Haven and London 2006 pp. 42–73.

11. In Spain, the first translation of *La figura humana en el arte* appeared in 1915, in Barcelona, by Editorial Salvat. This edition called itself the direct translation of the first German edition of the work. The author signs his text in The Hague; we can suppose, perhaps, that this German edition is from the early 20th century.

12. I wish to thank Prof. Dr. Carmen González Román and researcher Mara Portmann for the comments and suggestions contributed in this regard. On the other hand, I wish to mention the early relationship between Cubism and Dürer's treatises on the human figure, outlined by Arthur Jerome Eddy in *Cubist and post-impressionism*, A. C. McClurg & Co., 1919 (first edition from 1914).

13. Picasso may have known, in particular, C. H. Stratz, *Die Schönheit des weiblichen Körpers* (*La belleza del cuerpo femenino*), Verlag von Ferdinand Enke, Stuttgart 1905 (1898), since the French edition of the book existed, *La beauté de la femme*, published in Paris, 1905. This book contains numerous plates with studies of anthropometric canons and evocative photographs. Other books by Stratz, such as those devoted to Javanese young women or ethnographic beauties. On the other hand, some drawings by Picasso are related to photographs collected by Stratz in *Die Frauenkleidung*, Verlag with Ferdinand Enke, Stuttgart 1900.

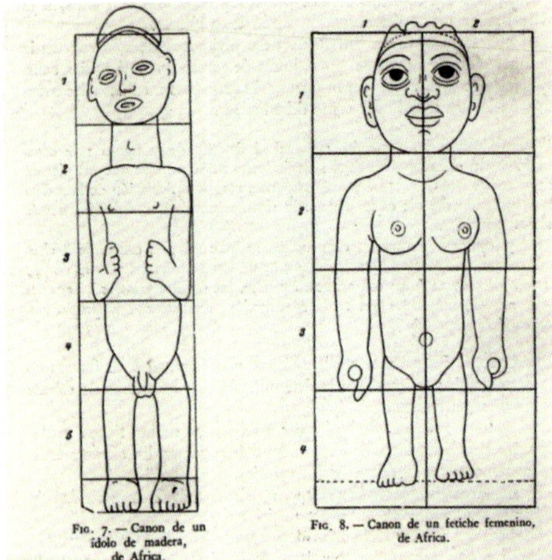

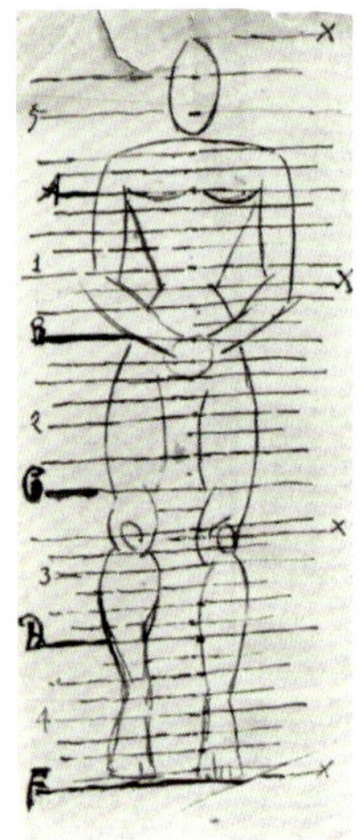

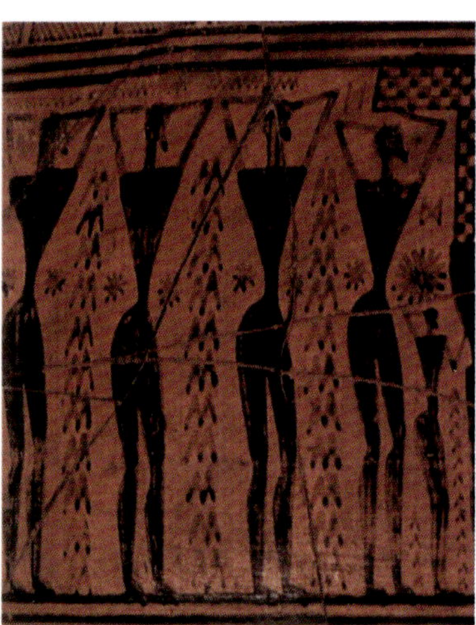

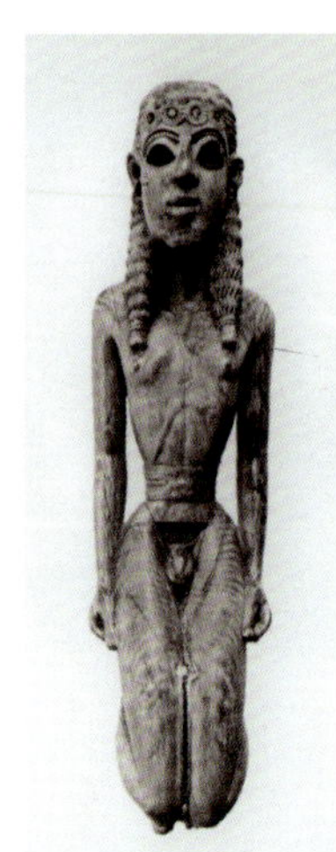

Proportional canon of African sculptures according to C. H Stratz, *La figura humana en el arte*, Salvat, Barcelona 1915. The most widespread German edition is from 1914, but diagrams of bodily proportions of African art drawn by Stratz were known prior to this date

Pablo Picasso, *Nude Standing* (*Study of proportions*), 1907
PARIS, MUSÉE PICASSO, MP 538

Dipylon burial amphora (detail), 7th century BC
ATHENS, NATIONAL ARCHAEOLOGICAL MUSEUM

Statuette of Young Man Kneeling, 630–20 BC
ATHENS, NATIONAL ARCHAEOLOGICAL MUSEUM

hips and thighs in an elliptic or flared way, with the *Statuette of a Kneeling Youth* marking a clear triangular pubis. It could be argued that the since these works are in Athens and were relatively recent discoveries, Picasso could not have seen them. However, Picasso could have seen similar pieces in the Museum of the Louvre, or in publications of the time. In any event, what it is interesting to highlight is that Picasso's work intended to attain the *primitive* could have prompted him to find solutions already foreshadowed in the Greek Art of the archaic period, to which Iberian Art may be associated, without the artist, in his most innovative or bold solutions, necessarily being indebted to so-called *black art*. And it is worth recalling now, as at the time, that Patrice Triboux related *Woman with Hands Clasped*, a work that interests us considerably, painted on *Le bourdel*, with the so-called Head of Dipylon, in the National Museum of Athens, a works executed in around 610 BC[14].

This model or this canon, and no other, was the one that the artist deposited in the female figure of *Cahier* no. 7, in drawing 3r, the complexity of which we have been commenting upon.

In a certain sense, the presence of this drawing in the more than revealing album supposes the presence of an enigma, and the enigma is accentuated if we observe the whole series of female figures that follow and close the notebook. Most of these other figures remained in pencil. This means that Picasso did not reconsider them. But they all relate to another composition on page 7 (7r), which has been named *Nude with Hands Crossed, Full-frontal*. If Picasso worked through the sheets of the notebook in order and consecutively, then it would be a contemporary of the female figure of drawing 3r that we have commented on so much. This female figure on the front side of page 7, the *Nude with Hands Crossed* in ink, is very similar to the female figure on the front side of page 57, in pencil. William Rubin identified this second figure with a Bambara figure from Mali. Today, sincerely, we find it difficult to see the resemblance. Initially, the *Nude with Hands Crossed* reminds us of the existence of figures with hands together in the Picasso of Gósol. Here the tone, however, is clearly anti-naturalistic, not abstract but unlikely from the physical point of view. The head and face of the figure are those we will find later in *Les Demoiselles*, but the union of shoulders, arms and hands describes a ring between the neck and the waist, while the hips and legs have a horseshoe shape. The figure is in front of drapery, but not integrated into it. We may understand that Picasso, rather than think-

14. See: "Works, no 16", in Various Authors, *Picasso and Greece*, Basil & Elise Goulandris Foundation, Museum of Contemporary Art, in association with the Picasso Museum of Paris and with the patronage of the Hellenic Culture Organization – Cultural Olympiad, Andros (Greece) 2004, no page ref.

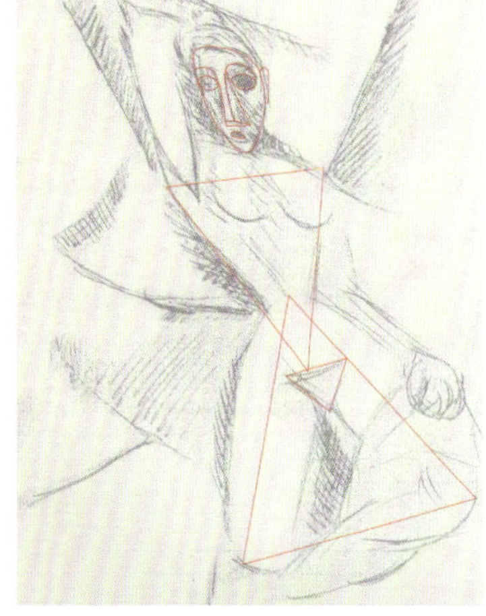

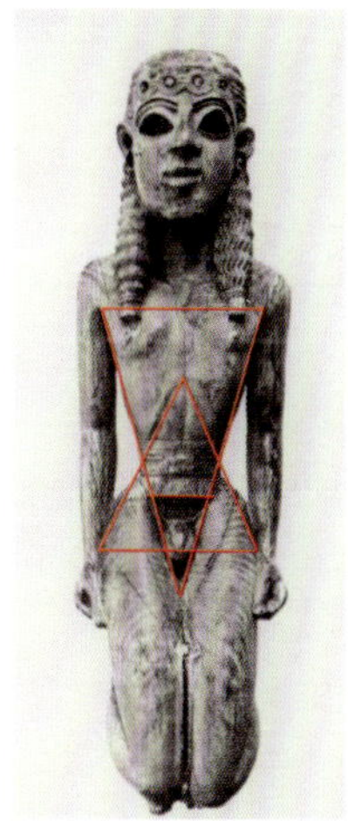

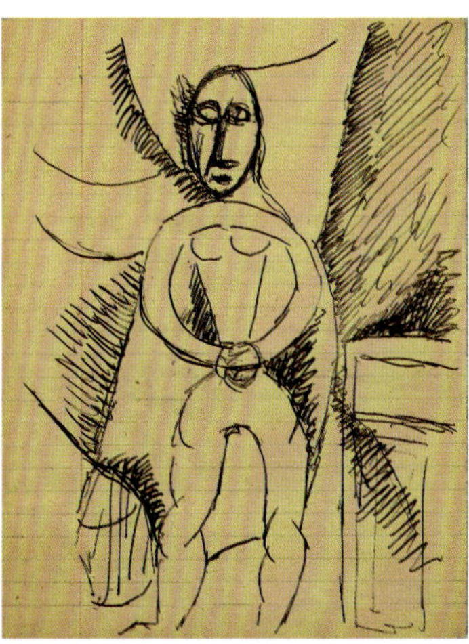

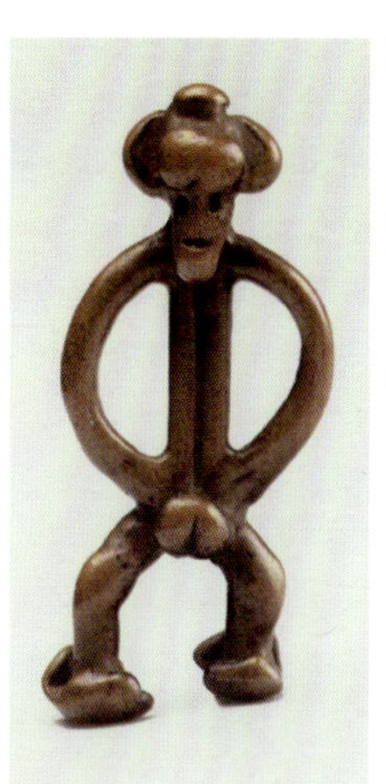

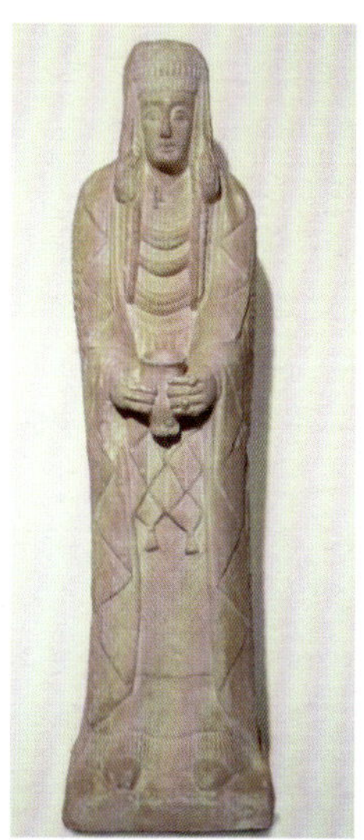

Graphic diagram on Figure of c. 3r
of *Cahier* no. 7. Grafismo, Maite Lavado

Graphic diagram on *Statuette of Young Man Kneeling*

Nude with Hands Crossed, Full-Frontal
Cahier no. 7, c. 7r
May–June 1907
MALAGA, COLLECTION OF THE PABLO RUIZ PICASSO FOUNDATION BIRTHPLACE MUSEUM

Figurine, executed between mid-19th and early 20th century
Senufo or Tussian Culture, Ivory Coast or Burkina Faso
NEW YORK, THE METROPOLITAN MUSEUM OF ART
THE MICHEL C. ROCKEFELLER MEMORIAL COLLECTION
LEGACY OF NELSON A. ROCKEFELLER

Dama del Cerro de los Santos, also known as *Gran Dama Oferente*, between 3rd and 2nd century BC
MADRID, MUSEO ARQUEOLÓGICO NACIONAL

ing about modular sequences and integrated relations between background and figure, was counting—it is worthwhile to express it in these terms—on the visual power of an icon outside of our visual imagination. This aspect is, again accepting the meaning of the term, *primitive.* But was it an invention?

With the exception of concrete data already presented years ago by some investigators, today it is difficult to reconstruct what Picasso could have known or in what he could find a source of inspiration. His visits to museums are always borne in mind, but iconic sources accessible in books and magazines are little considered. Going back over non-recent general summaries of the history of art, we encounter the ancestral idols of Papua New Guinea, such as the one conserved in the Field Museum of Chicago, which has a similar ringed forms of arms and shoulders to the female figure drawn by Picasso[15]. On the other hand, Carl Heinrich Stratz, in *Die Frauenkleidung,* a work translated into French at the beginning of the century, reproduces a photograph of a woman, whom he calls *suraustral* [literally *South Southern*] which shows some epithelial protuberances that end up forming an unusual body ring from the shoulders to the waist. The resemblance of both references with Picasso's drawing is remarkable. We know that the artist knew and even possessed objects from the so-called Polynesian art of the time. It is not unlikely that he knew of objects and images such as those we are suggesting. To arrive at knowing whether he knew them for certain means embarking on a meticulous study that requires time. And yet

15. I wish to thank Marie-Catherine Lambert for the contribution of documents and iconographic elements provided in this regard.

the iconographic similarity of the *Nude with Crossed Hands* with some anthropomorphous statuettes of the Senufo culture is striking. The Senufo developed in an area today divided between Ivory Coast, Burkina Faso and Mali. Some of these statuettes, the concrete ritual meaning of which is unknown, are held today in the collection of the Museum of Quai Branly coming from the former Museum of Man, in the Trocadero. These small figures were also present in the collection of Paul Guillaume and in some dealers' shops from the turn of the last century, who undoubtedly introduced them into US collections. Recently, in the beautiful exhibition *La Magie des images. L'Afrique, L'Ocèanie et l'Art Moderne*, held at the Beyeler Foundation, Oliver Wick and Antje Denner related some sculptures by the Senufo, very similar to those that we are commenting on here, to the well-known work by Cézanne, *Madame Cézanne in a Yellow Chair*. In this work by Cézanne, the model, the artist's wife, poses sitting with her hands together; her head is ovoid and her arms with hands interlinked almost form a circle. Did Picasso also have Cézanne in mind when giving shape to the peculiar iconography of *Nude with Crossed Hands*...?

What is certain, because we find it in *Cahier* no. 7, is that Picasso attempted an entire small series of realisations from this new plastic motivation. The drawings, as has already been anticipated, remained in pencil and this means that they were not able to become a *solid alternative* to the *high-priority* line previously commented upon. Even so, in these pencil compositions it is interesting to verify how the artist deduces a new type of anthropomorphic canon in which the tubular replaces the conical or in which the conical and triangular is stylised and becomes more angular and more pointed if this fits. The reference to the pubic triangle remains, although it no longer *modulates* the composition, and a specific shape is sought for the hips, while the legs get wider and become more voluminous, in the Polynesian or the African way. In some compositions of the series, the ring of shoulders, arms and hands superimposed on the trunk are substituted by a closed U-shape that unites shoulders, arms and hands over the head. These compositions are perhaps even more anti-naturalistic than the previous ones. They also harken back to the art of the Senufo people and to certain artistic creations by the natives people of today's Ivory Coast.

These compositions marked the encounter between so-called *black art* and *Cahier* no. 7. Although they did not mark the encounter of this *black art* with the major painting of the cycle or of the galaxy of *Les Demoiselles*. It is clear that Picasso sought the eclecticism or the syncretism of what was considered *primitive* and that this research is the meaning of *Cahier* no. 7. But the complexity of the artist's figurative thought was not prepared to make it easy for the contemporary commentator.

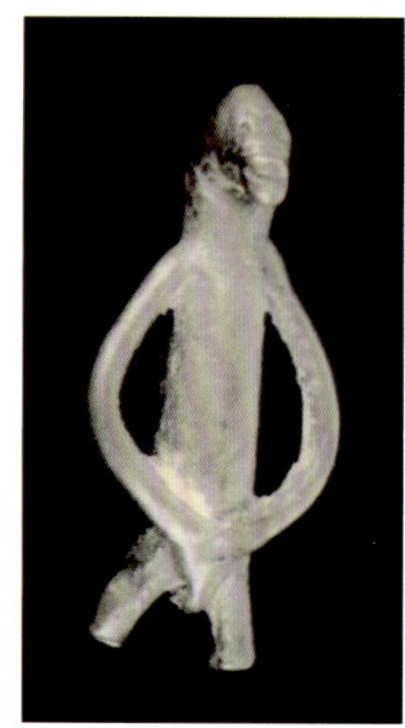

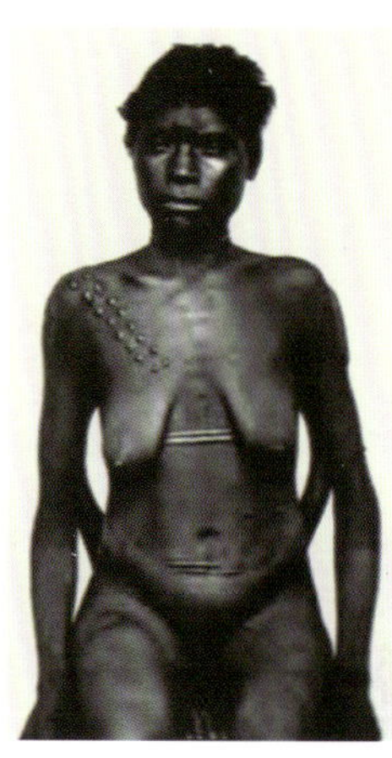

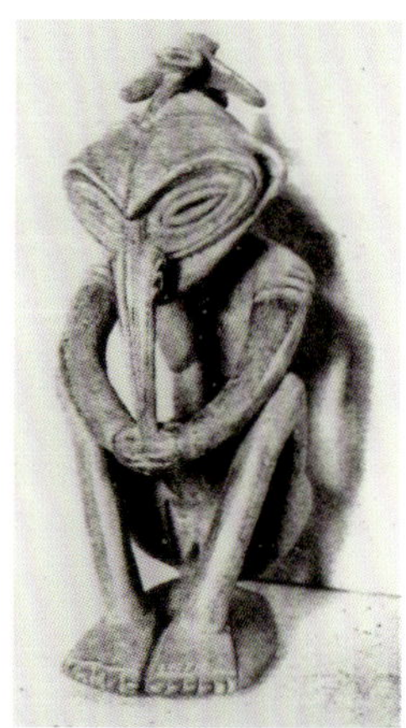

Anthropomorphic figurine
Senufo Culture, Ivory Coast
PARIS, MUSÉE DU QUAI BRANLY

Young "suraustral" [South Southern] woman with tattoos
ethnographic photograph from the Museum of Leiden included by C. H. Stratz in *Die Frauenkleidung*, Ferdinand Enke, Stuttgart 1900, p. 13

Figure
New Guinea
CHICAGO, FIELD MUSEUM

PICASSO, ORIGINS AND TRANSFORMATION

Before starting the great change, before he placed himself on the threshold of the Modern, Picasso was again in Barcelona. The spring was ending and he passed through there. The year was 1906 and, the very day before leaving for Gósol, his friend Joan Vidal i Ventosa, whom Picasso had painted in 1899 in the free and sketched style characteristic of Modernisme, took a photograph of him. This photograph, taken in Vidal's studio *El Guaiaba,* has been often reproduced. With a table covered with papers in front of him, Picasso, Fernande Olivier and Ramón Raventòs pose seated on a couch protected from the wall by a rustic tapestry. In the mirror, in the background, reproductions can be seen of well-known works of art and portraits of unknown people. In the foreground, in the bottom right corner, is a camera. Is this presence, perhaps not intended, a signal announcing something or something that speaks of another time? Picasso always knew how to look at the camera. He seems a young man, but he looks older than twenty-four, his age at the time. His gaze is, as has been commented on many times, profound, penetrating. Fernande, beside him, expresses her larger physical presence. She is wearing a hat like the one in which Matisse had painted his wife a year earlier. It is *Belle époque* clothing. Fauvism has already appeared in public; Picasso is about to cross the threshold of Modernity, and the photograph that has survived to leave a memory of that instant mixes the local, still in the echo of *fin de siècle,* the promising presence of the camera and the formal appearances of *la Belle époque.* One would not imagine the images of moments of change in this way. But major aesthetic changes have always taken place, perhaps, more silently and intimately than we imagine.

A few months before returning to Barcelona, Picasso had painted *Death of Harlequin.* Picasso was not often explicit in his works about the presences or absences of final full stops or turns of pages. Picasso painted without punctuation. He made ages coexist and mixed styles. Picasso warned his spectators little of his changes of direction. And yet, how can we not see in *Death of Harlequin* an announcement, a call or a farewell? Knowing Picasso, the harlequin would come 'round. He would come 'round several times. But he would do so with another *form* in his body and, therefore, with another psyche, with another meaning and another spirit. This harlequin that dies now, if we observe him closely, does not die completely: he joins his hands and says goodbye. The figures have their faces painted white and they tell us that every concluded personality is but a mask, a surface of painted skin that can be washed. When painting *Death of Harlequin* Picasso wants to leave behind something more than a style or a formula: he wants to leave behind an entire conception of art in the society of his time and a whole conception of being an artist. Picasso had already attempted this farewell before: and he did not achieve it. It was after the death of Casagemas, in 1901. The young Picasso very soon understood that modern art was measured in a constant pulse of transformation, that it was not enough to add to the already given, that the true artist found his own place if he modified the future of those historical proposals that never ceased to happen. Very soon the young Picasso understood that to build a new art, nihilism and the bohemian life had to be left behind. What Decaudin called

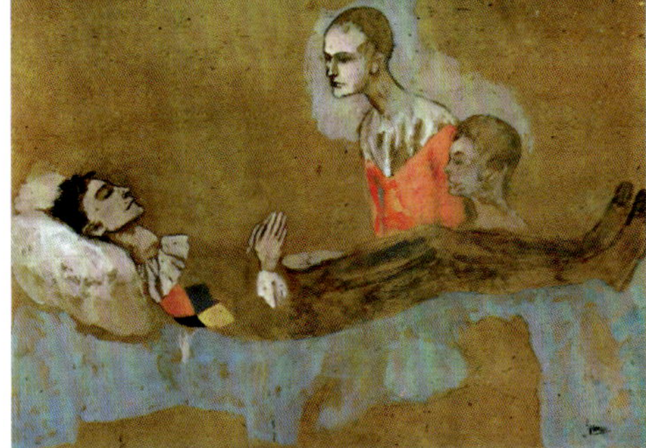

Pablo Picasso
Death of Harlequin, 1905 (1906)
PRIVATE COLLECTION

"the crisis of the Symbolist values" in France[1] was very soon felt by artists: long before most historians noticed. When organising the narrative of Modern painting starting from Cézanne they forgot other possible narratives and other complexities, more relevant even than the pro-Cézannian narrative, in which the young Picasso was involved. To recover these other narratives is to understand the young Picasso, and to understand the young Picasso is to understand the young Miró and the young Dalí, and from so much new understanding only one of the possible ways, among several, of understanding the rise of what we call Modern art arises.

In *Death of Harlequin* Picasso linked two compositional registers that were not completely absent from his works of those years, but that now, by bringing them together, they gain special relevance: drawing with a Classicist root and the union of autonomous and sketched marks under the principle of the "unfinished"[2]. Both resources were to return at the time of the Picasso called Classical. Picasso was regaining himself. The young Picasso remained in the mature Picasso. But in *Death of Harlequin* we find something more. The background, with a predominance of pink, or similar tones to pink, in immediately previous works, has moved towards ochre tones. It is the preamble to the "ochres of Gósol"[3]. After *Death of Harlequin* Picasso began a new stage in Paris. The evocation of a new Arcadia began: nude adolescents, horsemen, horses, sparse but gratifying nature: a landscape very similar to that of the mountains of Malaga. Picasso sensed in his own works the point of departure of a major change, the point of departure that would lead to something really different. Then he was thinking of a re-encounter with an original place. He had been told of a town rich in spring water and clean air where the country folk lived almost self-sufficiently, in full contact with a nature that was not wild or untameable, but man's friend. Something similar to what he had found in Horta in 1898. Thanks to Pallarés, Picasso arrived in Horta to recover from an illness. The myth was complete: the primitive place as source of health and regeneration. It was a romantic myth, yes, but also an idea that had taken root in the men of the Generation of '98 and then in those of the Generation of '14. Due to his age and birthplace, Picasso was between the two, although he trained in Barcelona, in the intellectual and cultural space of which the two generational concepts did not exist. Picasso was to take up the myth of the primitive through the enormous influence that Gauguin exercised on him. But he took some time to take it up, he took some time to understand it not as something literary but as his own thing, as something that could and should affect his person and his work. And in the same way that most of the Symbolist movement forgot the rarefied atmospheres, the decadent expressions and sophisticated rhetorical resources and sought sunlight and the re-encounter with Classicism, Picasso, independent of all context, abandoned the blue sadness and the rose melancholies for that same vital radiation and that same aesthetic climax. But Paris did not seem a suitable place to bring out the change. Gósol seemed a more appropriate setting. Finally, Gósol was the re-encounter with the primitive.

Picasso's work in Gósol was different. Of course it was. It was precisely when talking of Gósol that Palau i Fabre, after so many years devoted to the artist, expressed, amid admiration and consternation, praise and disorientation at the same time when presented with Picasso's diversity:

---

1. Michel Décaudin, *La crise des valeurs symbolistes. Vingt ans de poésie française, 1895-1914*, Slatkine, Gèneve and Paris 1981.

2. On the *unfinished* in Picasso, see José Ignacio Díaz Pardo, *Paradójico Pablo Picasso*, Terramar, Malaga 2008.

3. The expression "ochres of Gósol" is used by María Teresa Ocaña in *Picasso 1905–1906*, Electa, Barcelona 1992. I had the opportunity to present the variables in the language of Picasso in 1906 in the paper "De Gósol al Cubismo" presented at the conference *Gósol. El pròleg de l'aavant-gardea*, held in the Museu Picasso in Barcelona in 2006. Unfortunately the proceedings of this conference have not been published. Very interesting in this regard is the book by Jéssica Jacques Pi, *Picasso en Gósol. Un verano para la modernidad*, Antonio Machado y Visor, Madrid 2007.

> "It is almost impossible to detect an absolutely unitary stage in the work of Picasso. In spite of the manifest preponderance of some tendencies, Gósol does not escape this law. Picasso's diversity depends on various factors: the artistic intentions that attract him, the voluntary or involuntary influences he experiences, the things he has seen or lived at that moment, and the surprise factor. Picasso knows how to leave aside or do without the premises that he has accumulated, however important they are, when a vision surprises him. Their immediacy knows how to overcome the established schemata. This is how it happened in Gósol, where he spent just two and a half months, from early June to 15 August 1906"[4].

In Gósol we find resources that we could call Mannerist. In Gósol we find resources that we could deem to be in the sphere of a peculiar Realism. But still with all the exceptions that can be argued, what does not seem to be subject to debate is that there are two principal aesthetic references for Picasso in Gósol: Primitivism and Classicism. Referring to the young Picasso, as well as referring to the young Miró and Dalí, we are talking, through copulative conjunctions, of Primitivism and Classicism as though used to placing these terms in correspondence or as though there were a natural relationship between them. In fact, historically, from the perspective of concepts traced to the history of art and the history of aesthetic thought, they are antagonistic, at least opposite terms. In fact, today we know well that to consider any cultural proposal as primitive is anthropologically and ideologically unacceptable. But even so, we are going to accept it because Picasso—extraneous in his time, logically, to our cultural debate—knew about the word and the concept that he wanted to contain in the term primitive. We will also accept, from the formalistic point of view that there exists, in the manner of Wölfflin, in Western art, the artistic language that we define as Classical. This being the case, Classical would be what surpasses and reorganises the primitive *pro norma* and *pro forma*. And primitive would be what does not aspire to the formalising canon that Classicism imposes and to some extent offers itself as its other.

Between the primitive and the Classical, on the threshold of Modernity we therefore encounter a paradox. But if we are really on the threshold of Modernity, this paradox served to construct another perhaps even greater paradox. Understanding what *Modern* meant, not in the historical evolution of the term, but in its use, however variable, in Europe from the mid-19th century to the early 20th century, it was incomprehensible to want to be Modern favouring the aesthetic assumption of the primitive or of the Classical. Either it was incomprehensible or it was contradictory. Modernity was something else. Modernity was that of the scenes of the *petit bourgeois* life of the Impressionists. Modernity was urban strolling of Baudelaire's *flâneur*. Nobody would have thought that Modernity could be associated with Primitivism or the reconsidered Classicism. But this was the change that the young Picasso made. Let us give a starting point to this change. A point of departure, in the beginning.

Science and Charity, executed by the teenage Picasso in 1897, has always been understood as the great work of a precocious talent, as the genius's great promise. But there is something more in *Science and Charity*. Although it seems obvious, *Science and Charity* is actually a beginning. The theme aimed to be an

4. Josep Palau i Fabre, "El oro de Gósol", in Ocaña, *Picasso cit.*, p. 75.

illustrative or edifying one in an academic way. But the circumstances of chance, of necessary chance, meant that *Science and Charity* was given other possibilities. It is, in the first place, the figure of the father. It is always commented that Don José is simply a model: not an example but a figure in his son's paintings. He is probably much more. It is worth remembering what Picasso commented to Brassaï:

> "Every time I draw a man, I think, unintentionally, of my father... For me, man is "Don José" and it will be this way all my life. He had a beard... All the men I draw I see more or less with his features"[5].

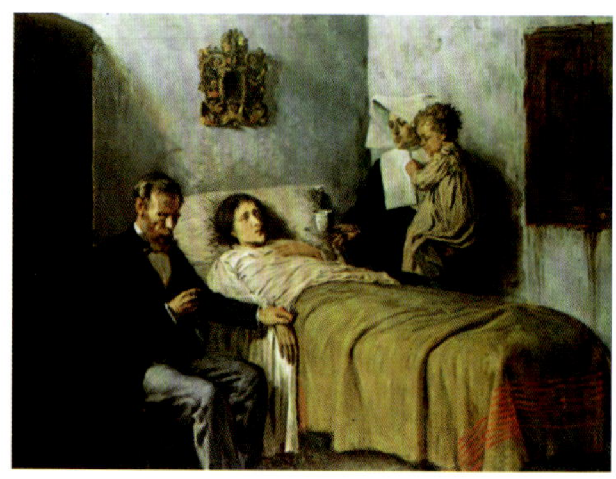

Pablo Picasso
Science and Charity, 1897
BARCELONA, MUSEU PICASSO

Perhaps Don José is a meaning that Picasso has to replace. He has to learn to replace. Picasso declared to Zervos that all his work until he arrived at Cubism had been just an "accumulation of destructions"[6]. Natasha Staller took good note of Picasso's statement and has drafted a study that it could be said combines psychological complexity and social anthropology[7]. Staller travels over the parameters of the Picasso in formation until he arrives at the Cubist moment. Picasso quickly burns stages. It is not pure exhaustion of entropic force. Each step is a challenge. But for the first time in a study on Picasso, we witness his Malaga origin and his relationship with his father as something that goes beyond the merely anecdotal. It is Don José, in his career as a professor who forces Picasso to be nomadic and, ultimately, an exile. And I understand an exile to be someone who sees himself continually needing to reflect on his origin and on his own constant movements. Later Picasso would give up his name. Picasso did not want to be called "Ruiz". Picasso commented to Brassaï that this choice was purely "cosmetic": the rarity of his mother's surname, the two "S"s as in Matisse. But the adoption of his maternal surname gave Picasso status as a foreigner. The Picassos were not a family of artists. The Ruiz family was. Picasso's exile is exile from "the name of the father".

The numerous sketches, drawings and oils in which the adolescent Picasso paints his father had a peculiar and significant continuity in the sketches for *Life*, the large work with great iconographic ambition that Picasso painted in Barcelona between late spring and early summer of 1903. In the final oil on canvas, the meaning of which is not concrete, and the possibilities of interpretation are not closed and are therefore multiple, Picasso placed a severe woman with a baby in her arms where in the sketches there was the drawing of an old painter. Most of the experts on the artist consider that this old painter in the sketches immediately reminds them of the figure of Don José. Also in the production of this oil Picasso swapped his own image, present in the preparatory works, for that of Casagemas. Very soon the young Picasso spoke of the painting from the painting; the creative process of *Life* is proof of that. The reflection on the human life cycle is *locked into* the study of a painter. And, in *Life*, Picasso replaces his father's failure with the failure of Casagemas. In the young Picasso, the anguish caused by the neurosis of failure was intimately linked with the general anguish that causes reflection on existential flowing in individuals.

Don José, therefore, or what Don José symbolises, dominates, so to speak, in an evident or underground way, from *Science and Charity* to *Life*, most of the work of the young Picasso. But in *Science and Charity*, which had been the point

---

5. Brassaï, *Conversations avec Picasso* (1964), Gallimard, Paris 1997.

6. In Christian Zervos, "Conversations avec Picasso", in *Cahiers d'Art*, Paris, 1935, pp. 173–8.

7. Natasha Staller, *A sum of destructions: Picasso's cultures and the creation of cubism*, Yale University Press, New Haven and London 2001.

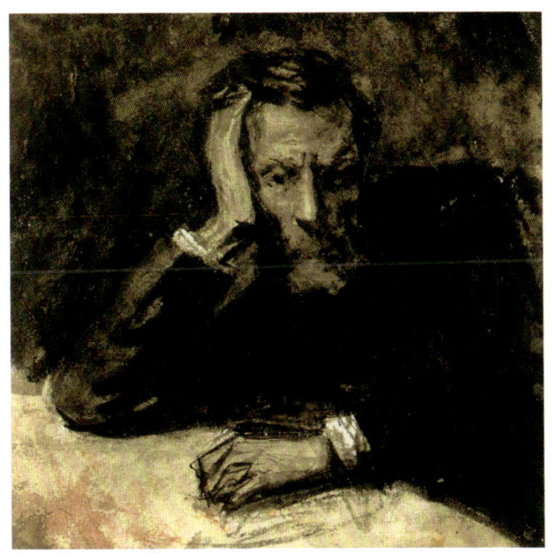

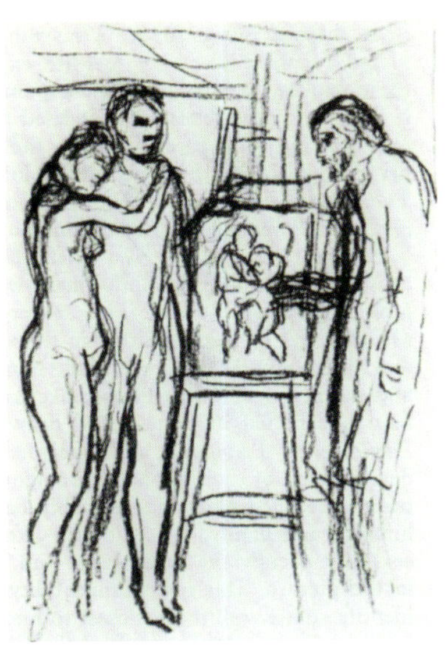

Pablo Picasso
Don José Ruiz Blasco, 1895
BARCELONA, MUSEU PICASSO

Pablo Picasso
Sketch for Life, 1903
BARCELONA, MUSEU PICASSO

of departure of this reflection, there is still something more. The painting received awards. Picasso soon built up the relationship with his work awaiting the recompense, but, at the same time, the young Picasso very soon also had to experience the psychic tension involved in not wanting to be what the others, mainly those who have given an award, expect somebody to be. In any event, when saying that in *Science and Charity* there is something more, the reference was not intended to be psychological again, but of another type. In *Science and Charity* Picasso crystallised a concept: to develop a painting was not only to establish some variables of technique and language but it was also to give a powerful iconographic meaning. That was why, although Picasso attempted the absolute of pure painting in 1910, he resisted it. And that was also why in his work always, or practically always, the presence of the figure is transferred into that of the icon.

But, in addition to what he learned from his father (of what he learned in *Science and Charity*), Picasso also expanded something more in his work: the encounter of a skilled figurative dialectic between the outline of a physiognomy, which ends up being comparable to that of other physiognomies, and the capturing of the particular. In reaching this achievement the artist's virtuosity had special importance, it is true, but, in any event, to know how to establish a graphic sketch that condensed the general giving space to the particular was the secret and the difference of Picasso with respect to his contemporaries in the foundation of Modern art. In Matisse, in Braque or in Derain, the synthetic reduction of forms, characteristic of the first moment of -isms, provided general outlines of figures and objects. In Picasso these general outlines always involved the expression of some detail, whether already in the innate physiognomy of the thing represented or in what distinguished one character from another. And this can be observed, again, at the moment when Cubism comes closest to abstraction, in the portraits of Vollard, Uhde and Kahnweiler, executed, although there is debate over the dates by the specialists, between the spring and autumn, or the autumn and winter, of 1910.

These apprenticeships and these abilities imply others. The young Picasso, skilled in passing over the delicate limits between the figure and the icon, and also skilled in the treatment of physiognomies from the general to the particular, goes to develop a special interest in the grasping of types. There would remain for the future Picasso's capacity, through a type, to develop an entire figurative theme with which to sustain a painting. When Picasso was a teenager, the grasping of types was a characteristic resource of the painting of manners. Picasso, in around 1895 or 1896, aged barely fourteen or fifteen, was to take on the subject in another way, perhaps more through intuition than through other types of reasons. The teenage Picasso contrasts academic learning with the capacity to capture physiognomies and poses that, although at first sight could seem conventional, strictly speaking they are not. In *Portrait of a Man with a Beard*, for example, the hair and black beard, and the concealment of the face by the pose, already force the teenage Picasso to establish the sensation of volume and form through a single colour, the black of the hair, while from the whole assembly we deduce the capacity to capture a mood that cannot be transmitted by the face, because the face is shown looking down. Picasso therefore converts the poses into gestures. In *Old Man with a Cloak*, a watercolour painted by Picasso in 1895 devoted—and, significantly, to a master of the Malaga 19th century school, Antonio Muñoz Degrain—Picasso, who signs as Pablo Ruiz Picasso, achieves the *tour de force* of giving bodily sensation not through the representation of the body in itself, but by means of a volume, locked into the fabric of the blanket, which we could consider abstract.

The horizon of this teenage Picasso is located in 1900. His painting *Last Moments* was included in the Universal Exposition in Paris. There is a line that joins together *Science and Charity* and *Last Moments*. The latter piece has not been conserved, but from the sketches and preparatory works related to it we can sense that the academic moralism of *Science and Charity* has given way to the intense dramatism that had—it must be admitted—a certain capacity for denunciation, but that above all was a strikingly effective blow. In the preparatory studies for this work there has remained an almost unavoidable reference to charity, but the science, undoubtedly introduced into the work of 1897, as concept, by the Liberal and Regenerationist Don José, has disappeared. Picasso was apparently thinking of a work to conquer Paris and, partly, achieved this. Because what we sense of *Last Moments* is very different from the elegant and even sophisticated tone with which the young Picasso, emulating Ramón Casas, presented himself in El Quatre Gats[8]. That *Last Moments* was a strategy perhaps lies at the basis of the fact that the artist erased it to paint *Life* over it. Mary Mathews Gedo[9] has analysed the fact from psychoanalytical perspectives, arriving at interesting conclusions. It is true that the obsession with death and illness would end up becoming constant references in Picasso's work. But the strong desire to paint over a work that meant success is a type of negation that reveals other evidence. In the first place, the evidence of *Last Moments* as a manoeuvre. And, in second place, the evidence that Picasso felt himself more in *Life* than in the painting from 1900 that opened the gates of the French capital for him.

Although Paris was well worth a strategy. The effect of the encounter with Paris was slow. Picasso still moved incessantly between Barcelona, Madrid, Paris again and, even, Malaga. In Malaga he unsuccessfully sought recognition. And in Malaga he also unsuccessfully sought to cure Casagemas of his nervous afflictions. But it is worthwhile to confirm that still, in 1900, Malaga was a vital reference for a Picasso in the process of transformation. Picasso was not to settle in Paris until 1904. The work, executed by Picasso between 1900 and 1904, has been related to Degas, Renoir, Pissarro, Toulouse-Lautrec and Gauguin on one hand, and with Anglada-Camarasa and Nonell on the other. With regard to the latter, there is a burning question of dates to elucidate debts and loans or shared spaces. With regard to the former, the only thing we need to ask is why a young painter in 1900 with Paris in his head would not have them as a reference. This young Picasso who sought to be himself by interpreting others is reminiscent of the young Dalí at a similar juncture. But Dalí overcame the challenge by being imitative and interposing between all his references, as we have seen, a strict principle of art *pro norma* and *pro forma*. Picasso, rather than imitating, *cites*, recreates or reconsiders. And everything he does is proposed by a character that makes the references cited far away. This modifying character of Picasso has to do with his way of resolving the painting. But it also has to do—and this comes from the teenage Picasso and arrives up to *Les Demoiselles d'Avignon*—with the way of understanding the themes to be handled. It is always thought that the Picasso's revolution only has to do with languages, but it undoubtedly also has to do with the way of approaching topics or with the way of selecting them and with the way of proposing them. In Picasso the gallant tends to rove around the sordid; the erotic

8. For this topic see: Marilyn Mccully, *Els Quatre Gats: art in Barcelona around 1900*, N.J., Art Museum, Princeton University, Princeton 1978. See also: María Teresa Ocaña (ed.), *Picasso i els 4Gats*, Lunwerg, Barcelona 1995, with texts by María Teresa Ocaña, Francesc Fontbona, Cristina Mendoza, Malén Gual, Lluis Bagunyà, Marilyn McCully, Claustre Rafart i Planas, Merè Doñate, Vinyet Panyella and Josep Palau i Fabre.

9. In Mary Mathews Gedo, *Picasso: Art as autobiography*, University of Chicago, Chicago 1980.

tends in him towards lasciviousness or concupiscence; the intimate towards the ironic and the almost risqué. Are his scenes devoted to such burning topics as loving encounter, the kiss and the hug not surrounded by this game of ambiguities? The Picasso of 1900 wanted to challenge the aesthetic category of beauty, in the inherited sense of the meaning; an inherited sense that was still so important in some founders of the Modern, such as Matisse, Braque or Derain.

The capacity for impact of a painting began to be measured in other terms, and what made a work of art interesting could also be something disturbing or harrowing. Picasso combined this with another factor that offers a retrospective gaze. In a certain way, his diversity of registers could end up being so potent or so marked that the cataloguing methods of the critics and historians of art found it difficult to establish narrative structures of any type for his work. This today may appear, in spite of everything, acceptable, but in 1900 it was inconceivable when presented with the work of any artist. At the same time that in the School of Vienna the notion of style was being forged, Picasso broke it. We have also had to approach the diversity of Dalí and, to some degree, to a lesser degree, that of Miró. But what in Dalí was a desire for self-affirmation, in Picasso was the need to make changes that allowed him to gain drive.

At no time in his work did Picasso appropriate the poetics of diversity so much as in the year 1901: the year that in itself could constitute a whole chapter of his work. Already in 1900 Picasso had attempted to assimilate his Post-Impressionist chromatic conquests to topics that we could call Spanish. Some commentators have seen in this expression the desire to captivate some French buyers who enjoyed Spanish-ness as a genre. This would be the case were it not for the fact that bullfighting was associated with Picasso from his first drawings as a child. On many occasions the bull and bullfighting in Picasso were a means to experiment with plastic language, and there are some compositions from 1900 that seem to inaugurate this trend. In them, Picasso synthesises form in this way and the colour stands out with such intensity that Pierre Daix has spoken of Pre-Fauvism[10]. It is necessary to talk of Pre-Fauvism, it is true, but it would almost be better to talk of Fauvism *avant-la-lettre*, because it is certainly a Fauvist intensity that we find in *Spanish Dancer* from the Nahmad Collection and the whole series of works relatable to those that Picasso executed in 1901. As is known, the artist ended up taking his Fauvist advance to the portrait. In his *I, Picasso* the green mark deposited on the face starts from a daring reading of some portraits by Renoir, especially the self-portrait, painted in around 1875, that the painter presented in the second exhibition of the Impressionists. In fact, the vases of peonies, or peonies and roses, were another of the themes cultivated by Renoir. In them Renoir tended towards exuberance; in Picasso's vases, on the other hand, without abandoning the Post-Impressionist freedom, the concentration, as shown by Picasso's vases in the Nahmad Collection and in the National Gallery of Washington, curiously, in this whole series of vases that Picasso painted to a large extent for his exhibition in Vollard in 1901, the artist, rather than accentuating the transparencies and colouring of the shadows, sought to redefine Impressionism anticipating some notions linked to what would later be called pure painting, but concentrating the colour, not expanding it as in *Spanish Dancer*. This *Spanish Dancer*, like some other contemporary works and the saga, developed the expressive and ornamental possibilities of Divisionism, not to capture the optical representation of reality but to give rise

10. Daix has expressed this consideration in a number of publications; as a summary of these, see the content of *Diccionaire Picasso*, *cit*. This consideration is also contained in the *Catalogue raisonné* of the artist's work between 1900 and 1906, prepared with Joan Rosslet and edited by Ides et Calendes in 1966.

to a sensation of an especially impactful festive atmosphere. Picasso's vases, on the other hand, if they offer some references, as Palau i Fabre has already indicated[11], it is inasmuch as they refer to Modernisme, another of the substantial registers of the Picasso of the year 1901. It is a modified Modernisme, a Modernisme that begins to be Post-Modernisme, but that the painter expanded in a unique way. First he shared it in Barcelona with other creative artists. Then he transferred it to Madrid, founding the magazine *Arte Joven* and exhibiting *Lady in Blue*, which is today in the collections of the Museo Reina Sofía, in the Spanish capital. *Lady in Blue* has always been linked with the Infanta Margarita of *Las Meninas*. But undoubtedly it is a crossing of paths. As shown by *Woman with Big Hat* reproduced in *Arte Joven*, Picasso recreates fashions of *la Belle époque* that come to coincide with Baroque crinolines. But Picasso always plays with the knowing or not knowing of the spectator's gaze. What in some paintings from Barcelona are middle class women, in the *Lady in Blue*—the background of which anticipates the abstraction of colour fields—it is a dress that is worn by a courtesan that does not deceive us when we discover her lips and her expression, or elegant characters and misunderstandings that, as in *Conversation*, comment ironically on the modes of urban culture in its private salons.

And how different this environment is from the one we find in *The Two Acrobats* in the Pushkin Museum. In 1901 Picasso took the Synthetism of Gauguin to the setting of bohemian life and exchanged Gauguin's concise plasticity for a contained Mannerist gesture. In this register Picasso began to paint solitary women at a table in a bistro and in this register Harlequin arrived in his painting to stay. Does Picasso locate the scene in the Age of Carnival or does he give Harlequin the status of a real character? Did Picasso already identify Harlequin as his *alter ego*? And another even bigger question than the two previous ones: did Picasso think that the primitive innocence that Gauguin found in Breton and Tahitian women was translatable into moral equality, at least in the solitary night characters that consumed their lives drinking absinthe? Withdrawn and intense, Picasso deposited an ineffable fondness in these characters. Harlequin's elongated fingers make us suspect that El Greco is already latent in some of these compositions and transmit to us some unexpected sensations of lightness and spirituality. Picasso painted nine works in this register. A short number for a series, but a large number of pieces in view of the limited weeks in which they were produced. The beings represented in these works are creatures on the margins, but the drama is still not in them. The drama, however, would not take long to appear. *Mother and Son* and *Woman Ironing* take us to the *blue* Picasso. *Mother and Son* is the antechamber to this other Picasso of 1901. It was almost certainly a painting from early summer. *Woman Ironing*, as Sabartés reminded Daix, is from the end of the year[12].

Picasso's blue can be explained in various ways. But, perhaps, we still do not have a sufficiently convincing explanation. Did Picasso not say on one occasion that blue was the colour of colours? And did not Apollinaire comment that Picasso's blue had the humidity of bottom of the abyss and the lament? Sabartés, on the other hand, added that Picasso had always believed that art was the child of sadness and pain and that sadness led to meditation while pain was the background of life[13]. Does this mean that in the sadness of blue Picasso was, better than in other registers from 1901, truly Picasso? Picasso himself confirmed that he moved to blue after Casagemas's death. But the chronology complicates

11. Josep Palau i Fabre, *Picasso Vivo*, Polígrafa, Barcelona 1980, p. 256.

12. In Daix, *Catálogue raisonné*, *cit.*, p. 202.

13. In Jaume Sabartés, *Portraits et souvenirs*, Louis Carré et Maximilien Vox, Paris 1946.

this statement a little. Casagemas died on 17 February 1901 when Picasso was in Madrid. Barely a month before they had been together in Malaga. A whole misogynistic story put the blame on Germaine Florentin. Just a few years later Picasso would comment to Brassaï on the extreme situation of his friend as the true cause of his death. But after Casagemas' death, Picasso remained in Madrid. He published *Arte Joven* in March and ended up planning another publication. In late April the painter was in Barcelona and only at the end of May did he return to Paris, to occupy the studio that Casagemas had occupied. But not for this reason did Picasso's painting change. From May to June he prepared his exhibition in Vollard with Iturrino, an exhibition that, incidentally, was a success with the critics and in terms of sales. Only at the end of the summer, when painting *Evocation*, did Picasso begin to treat Casagemas' death and only then did his painting become blue. Was it, in almost Freudian terms, a *deferred action*? One could say that it was, above all, a choice. Picasso painted Casagemas dead with Post-Impressionist intensity and he also painted Casagemas dead in blue. He chose the second possibility. But undoubtedly he chose it to remember his dead friend as much as to offer a painting solution. The exhibition in Vollard was a success, as has already been said. Picasso made money. But the critics, although favourable, stressed his debt to an artistic generation immediately prior to his own. Picasso chose blue because blue was only Picasso. Picasso had discovered himself. And it is true that he chose a path of return. Chromatism took him to the heart of Fauvism and to anticipate the proposals of the Parisian avant-garde. Blue made him return to a figurative world that did not seem the right path for plastic innovation. Picasso began a long march, but along his own path. There are several locations of the blue Picasso. It has always been said that the most intense blues are those of Barcelona, those that correspond to works such as the *Portrait of Ángel Fernández Soto* and *Barcelona, Riera de Sant Joan at Dawn*. But several registers of the blue Picasso also existed. In the first instance it may not be noticed, but the blue Picasso is as complex and varied as Picasso himself in 1901. In his blue period Picasso attempted realism in the figures, but he also investigated Abstract simplification of forms, the effects of volumes on the plane, faces as masks, the combined view of the front and profile and the arbitrary deformation of bodies to achieve plasticity. And does the *Woman's Head* in the Metropolitan that seems to anticipate the best compositions in Gósol not possess a sweet and underlying Classicism? Is this piece not related to *Bust of a Woman with her Left Hand Raised* (*Fernande Olivier*)?

On the iconographic plane, Picasso invented new types and opened the chapter of his relations with the old masters: borrowings from El Greco, Morales "el divino" and even Murillo and Raphael. It is surprising to see Picasso rely on religious iconography to give space in painting to those who have nothing, the dispossessed, the wretched beings, those who live without hope. Picasso made his blue emerge from an ideological position. It has been considered that at this time Picasso was clearly close to anarchism and that his painting would translate it[14]. This view has resonated. Certainly it is attractive to give this explanation. But the issue is complex. In Europe, anarchist thought very soon coexisted with and was related to the Symbolist bohemian. In Catalonia the power of Anarcho-Syndicalism was intense and decisive until the Spanish Civil War of 1936. However, when we see the book *La musa libertaria*[15] relating to the arts we see that this relationship is very different from the one outlined

14. The fundamental study on this point of view is the one by Patricia Leighten, *Re-ordering the Universe, Picasso and Anarchism, 1897–1914*, Princeton University Press, Princeton, N.J. 1989. Also see: Robert S. Lubar, "Barcelona Blues" in *Picasso the Early Years, 1892-1906*, New Haven and London, Yale University Press and Washington, National Gallery of Art 1997, pp. 87-101.

15. For the relations in Spain between anarchism and art, see Lily Litvak, *La mirada roja: estética y arte del anarquismo español (1880–1913)*, Serbal, Barcelona 1988, and also *Musa libertaria. Arte, literatura y vida cultural del anarquismo español (1880–1913)*, Fundación Anselmo Lorenzo, Madrid 2001. Also see the writings by Javier Navarro in *Tierra y Libertad. 100 años de anarquismo en España*, edited by Julián Casanova, Crítica, Madrid 2010.

by Picasso. A creator imbued with the awareness that anarchist thought would have imbued in him would never have proposed to represent the dispossessed in their own depression without any outlet or hope. He would have represented them as rebellious and with the ambition to change a socially unjust situation. At least the painter, as before certain heirs of Realism and as some artists of the Weimar Republic did afterwards, he would in some way have shown us the signs of his critical conscience. Picasso only displays these impoverished beings; he only encounters them. Does it not say in the Gospel of Saint Mathew that only in the meek can the presence of God be found? Is the presence of the Kingdom of Heaven not in the *anawin* [poor]? With his exhibition in Vollard Picasso met with a success that was also an economic success. He was about to turn twenty when he exhibited in Vollard and he had already been successful in Paris. He could have continued along this path, but he chose another. In 1901, Picasso lived his own *psychomachia* as an artist. He could have chosen the easy path that led to success. He had found a formula that assured it for him. But he chose a winding and difficult path: in the fixing of blue, which abandoned the Post-Impressionist chromatic attractions, and in the constant reflection on the image of the dispossessed, he found a *truth*, the principle of a *truth* that separated the world of art from that which it had served. With his technical choices and with his choices of theme, the young Picasso, the twenty-year-old painter, aspired to re-found the experience of the artistic, nothing more and nothing less. He could only do so by placing himself on the side of those who had nothing. The attempt lasted years, but he attained it. The boy genius fulfilled his promise, although it was an unexpected promise. The acrobats and circus characters, metaphors of his own world of art, in the fullness of their lives, filled with risk and creation, but with limited and disillusioned recompense, replaced the dispossessed. In them, in a way that Picasso only knew, the artist discovered drawing and the profiles of a renovated Classicism, extraneous to the determinants of History. Picasso knew then that what he sought was in the reflection on form. And when, between 1906 and early 1907, the artist saw that the secret of form was the secret of the art of primitive peoples, then, and only then, could the young Picasso invent Modern art. ■

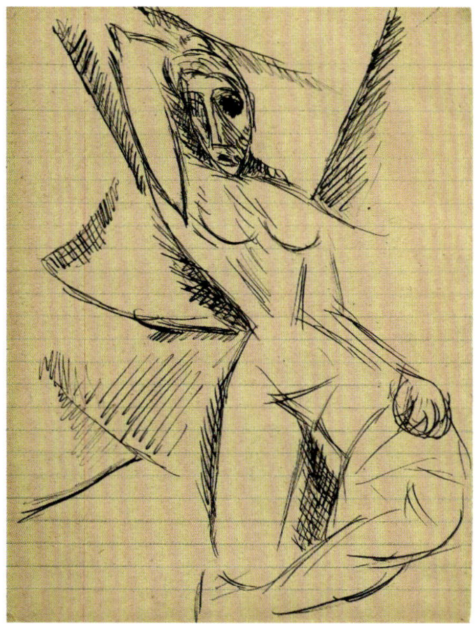

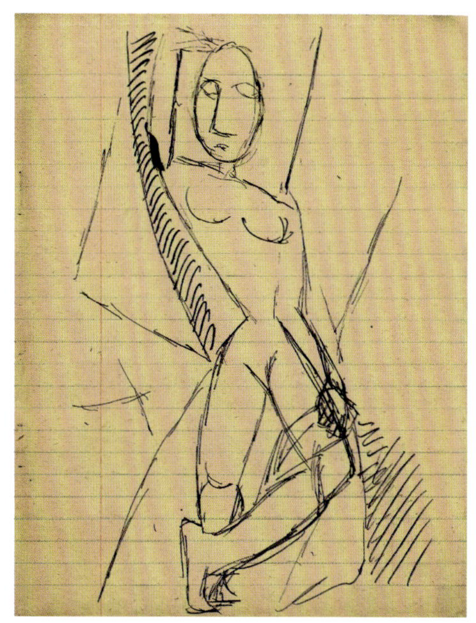

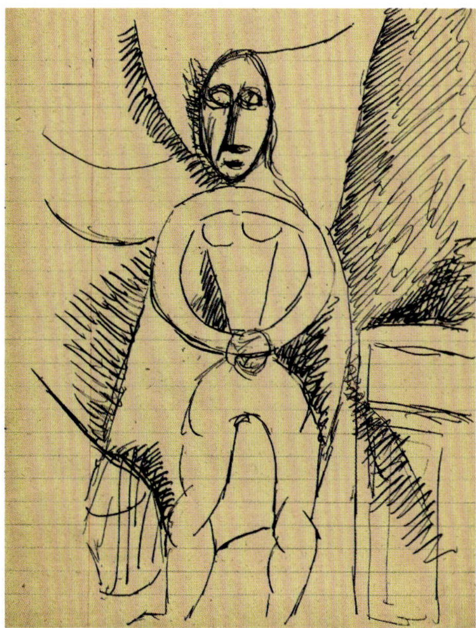

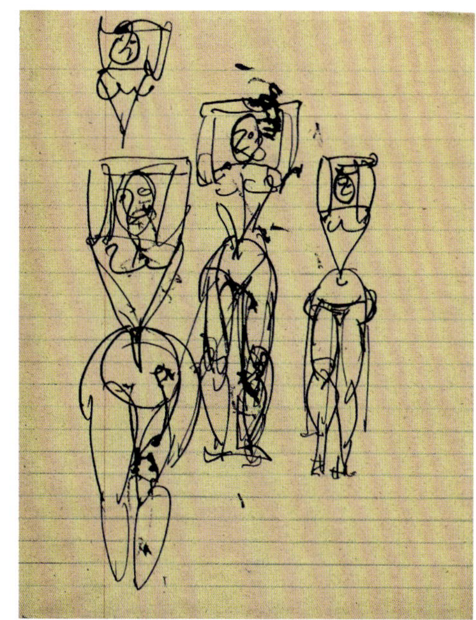

4.1a Pablo Picasso
Study for the Seated Girl: Nude with Drapery
Cahier no. 7
MALAGA, COLLECTION OF THE PABLO RUIZ PICASSO FOUNDATION - BIRTHPLACE MUSEUM. FPCN: 2037, C. 3R

4.1b Pablo Picasso
Study for the Seated Girl: Nude with Drapery
Cahier no. 7
MALAGA, COLLECTION OF THE PABLO RUIZ PICASSO FOUNDATION - BIRTHPLACE MUSEUM. FPCN: 2037, C. 5R

4.1c Pablo Picasso
Nude with Hands Crossed, Full-Frontal
Cahier no. 7
MALAGA, COLLECTION OF THE PABLO RUIZ PICASSO FOUNDATION - BIRTHPLACE MUSEUM. FPCN: 2037, C. 7R

4.1d Pablo Picasso
Study for the Girl with Raised Arms: Nudes with Raised Arms, Full-Frontal
Cahier no. 7
MALAGA, COLLECTION OF THE PABLO RUIZ PICASSO FOUNDATION - BIRTHPLACE MUSEUM. FPCN: 2037, C. 11R

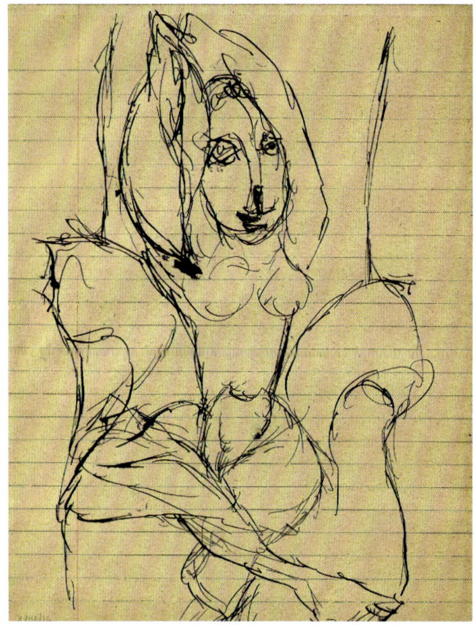

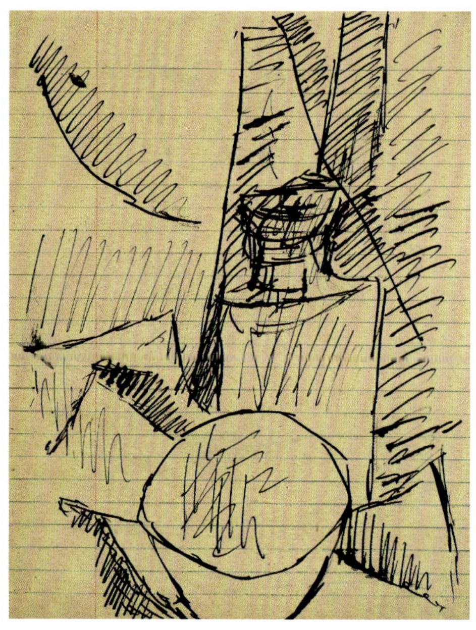

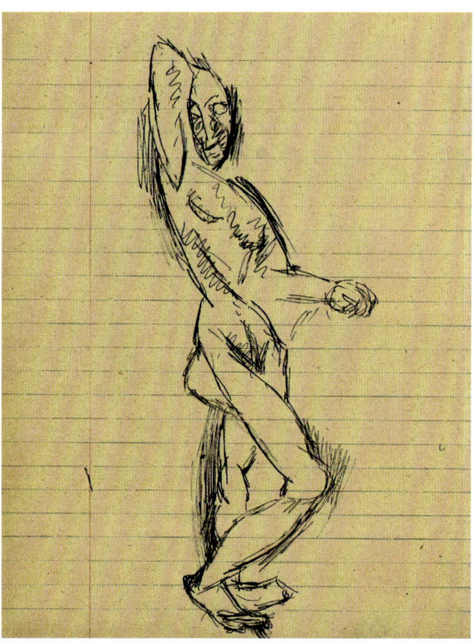

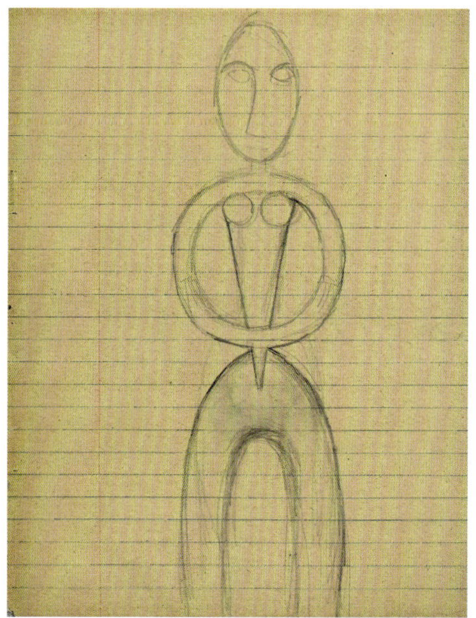

4.1e Pablo Picasso
Study for the Seated Girl: Nude Seated on a Armchair
Cahier no. 7
MALAGA, COLLECTION OF THE PABLO RUIZ PICASSO FOUNDATION - BIRTHPLACE MUSEUM. FPCN: 2037, C. 15V

4.1f Pablo Picasso
Study for *Still Life with Bananas*: Jug and Bowl with Towel
Cahier no. 7
MALAGA, COLLECTION OF THE PABLO RUIZ PICASSO FOUNDATION - BIRTHPLACE MUSEUM. FPCN: 2037, C. 43R

4.1g Pablo Picasso
Study for *Nude with Drapery:* Nude from the Side with Arm Raised
Cahier no. 7
MALAGA, COLLECTION OF THE PABLO RUIZ PICASSO FOUNDATION - BIRTHPLACE MUSEUM. FPCN: 2037, C. 52R

4.1h Pablo Picasso
Study for the Girl with Raised Arms: Nude with Arms Crossed
Cahier no. 7
MALAGA, COLLECTION OF THE PABLO RUIZ PICASSO FOUNDATION - BIRTHPLACE MUSEUM. FPCN: 2037, C. 57R

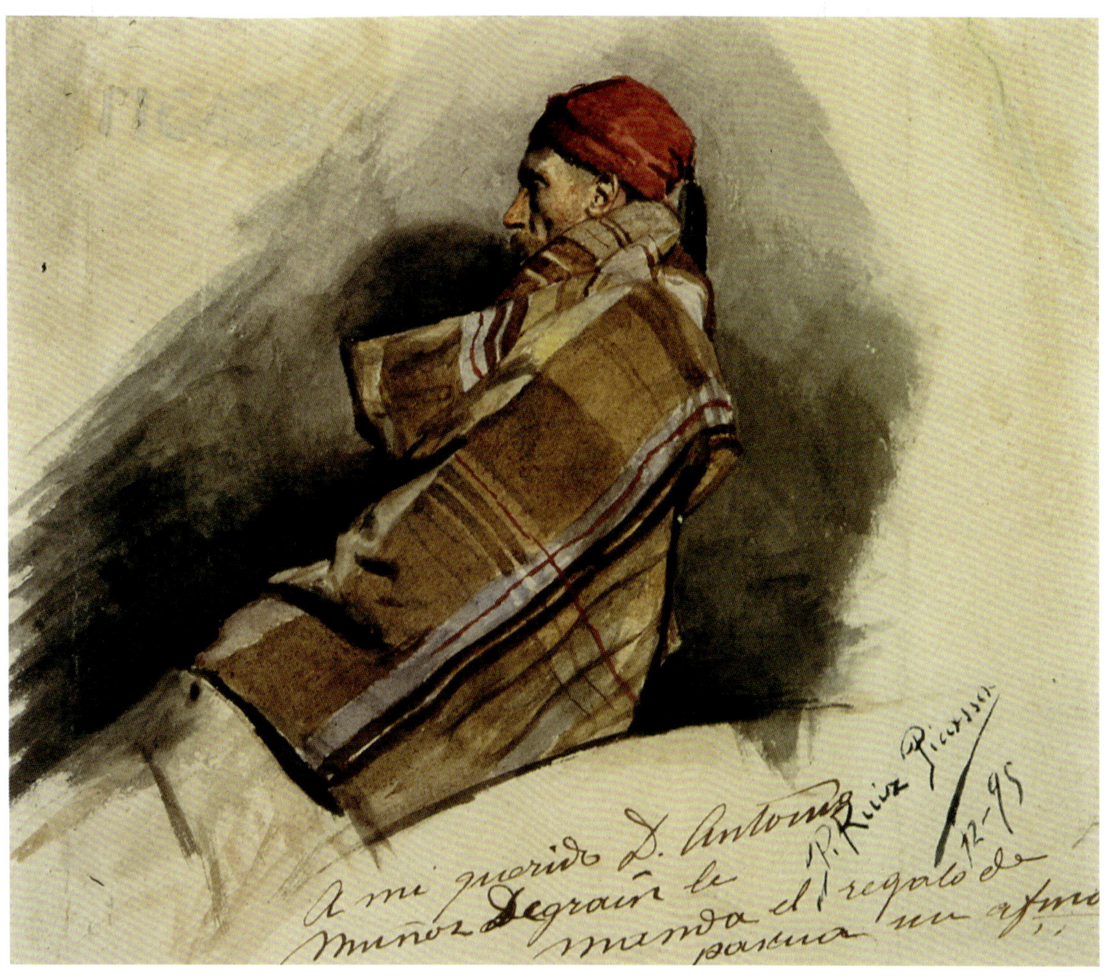

4.2 Pablo Picasso
Old Man with a Cloak (D. José Ruiz Blasco)
[El viejo de la manta (D. José Ruiz Blasco)]
La Coruña 1895

MALAGA, MUSEO DE MÁLAGA. BA/CE00344

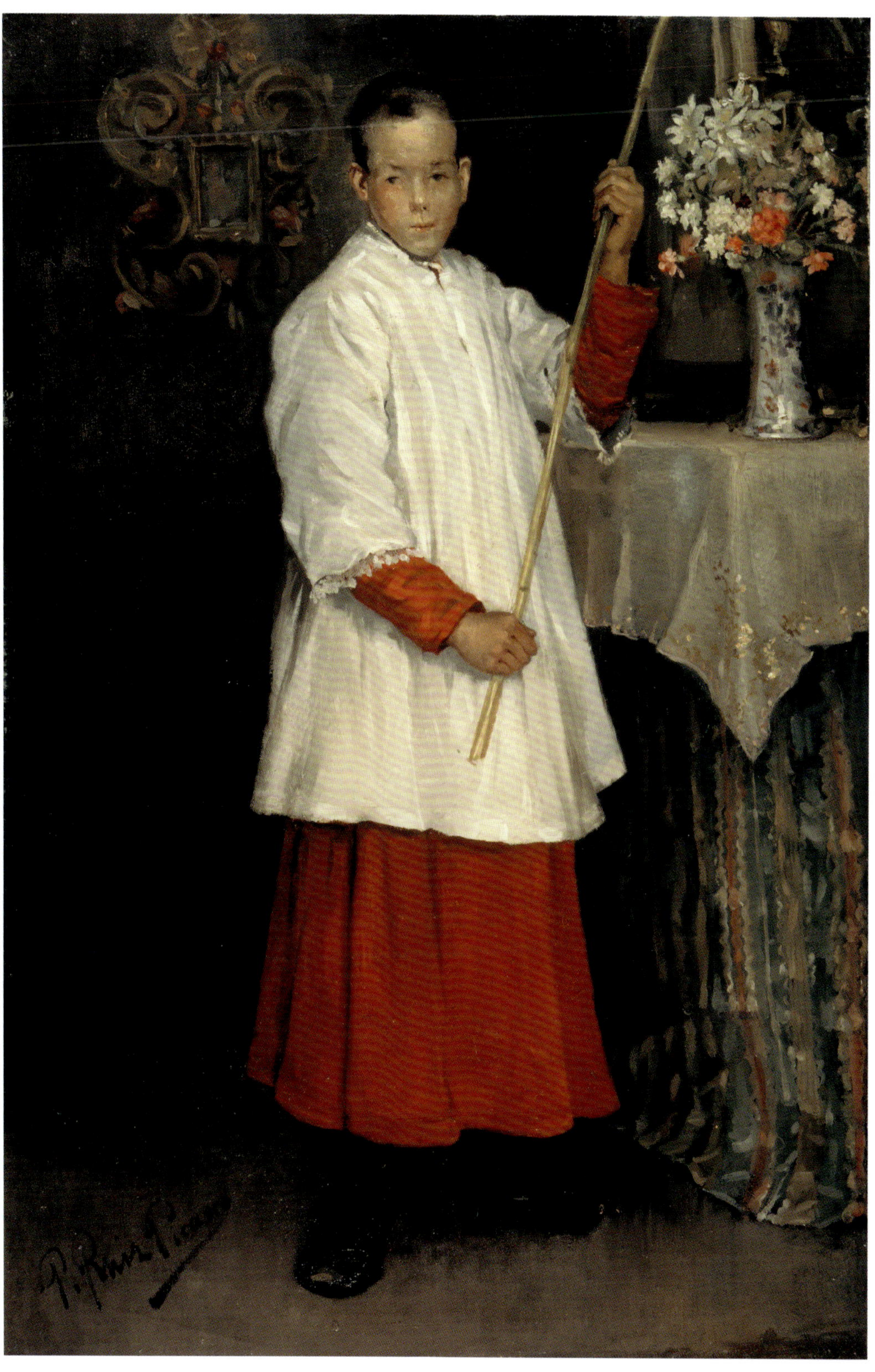

4.3 Pablo Picasso
Altar Boy
[L'Enfant de chœur]
1896
MUSEU DE MONTSERRAT. DONATED BY J. SALA ARDIZ. R.N. 200.503

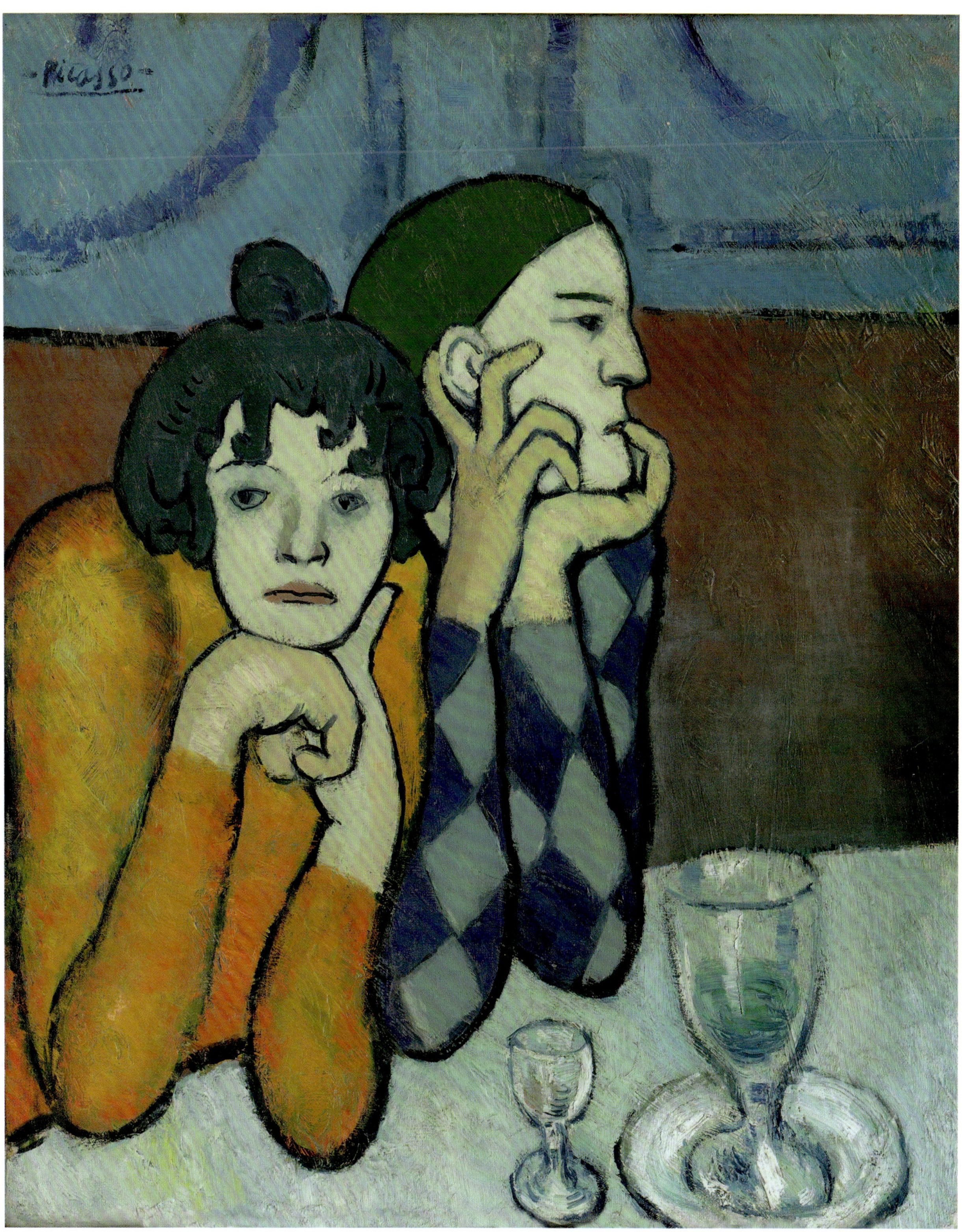

4.4 Pablo Picasso
The Two Acrobats (Harlequin and his Companion)
[Les deux saltimbanques (Arlequin et sa compagne)]
September–October 1901
MOSCOW, THE STATE PUSHKIN MUSEUM OF FINE ARTS. 3400

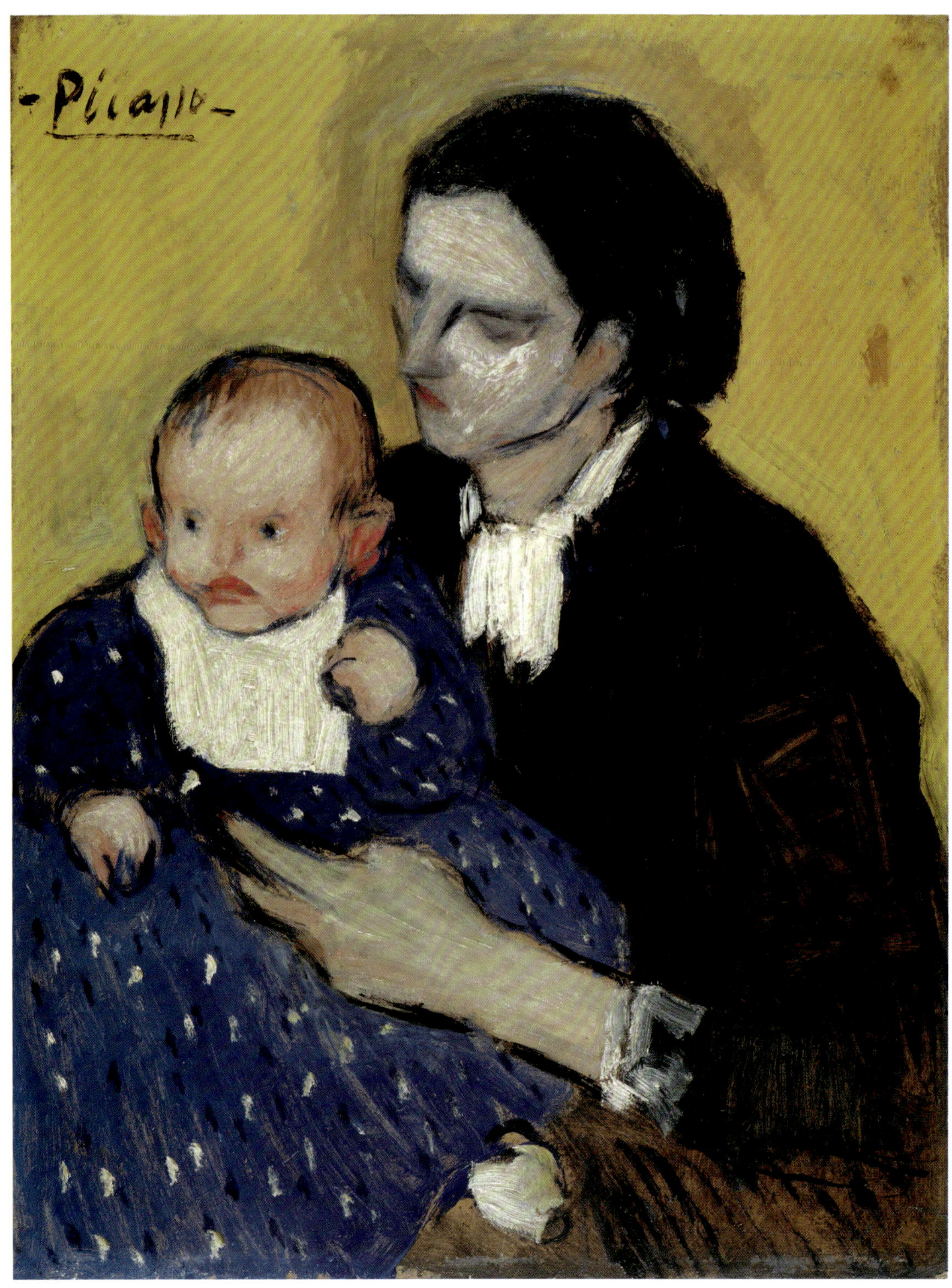

4.5 Pablo Picasso
Mother and Child
[Mère et enfant]
1901
BERN, KUNSTMUSEUM BERN, LEGAT GEORGES F. KELLER 1981

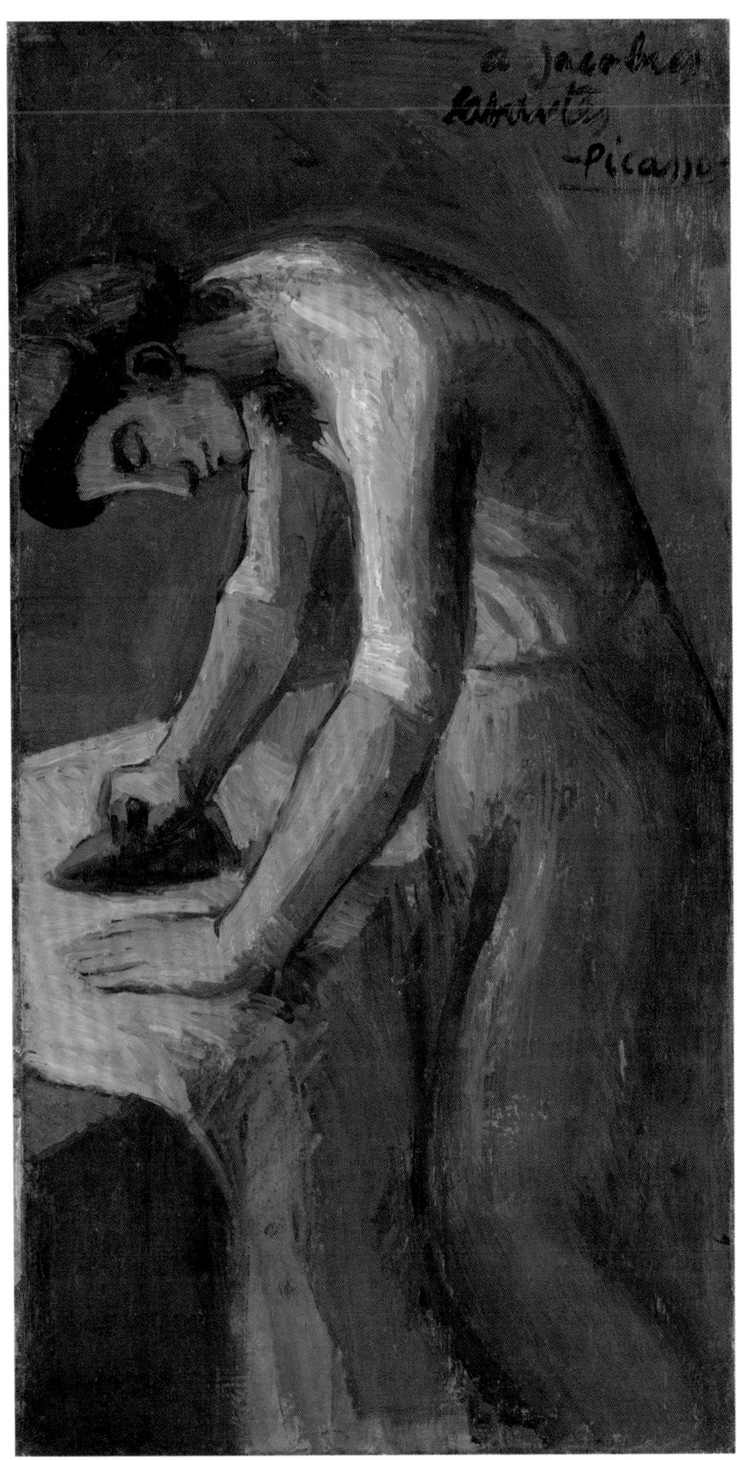

4.6 Pablo Picasso
Woman Ironing
[La Repasseuse]
1901
NEW YORK, THE METROPOLITAN MUSEUM OF ART, ALFRED STIEGLITZ COLLECTION. 1949, 49.70.2

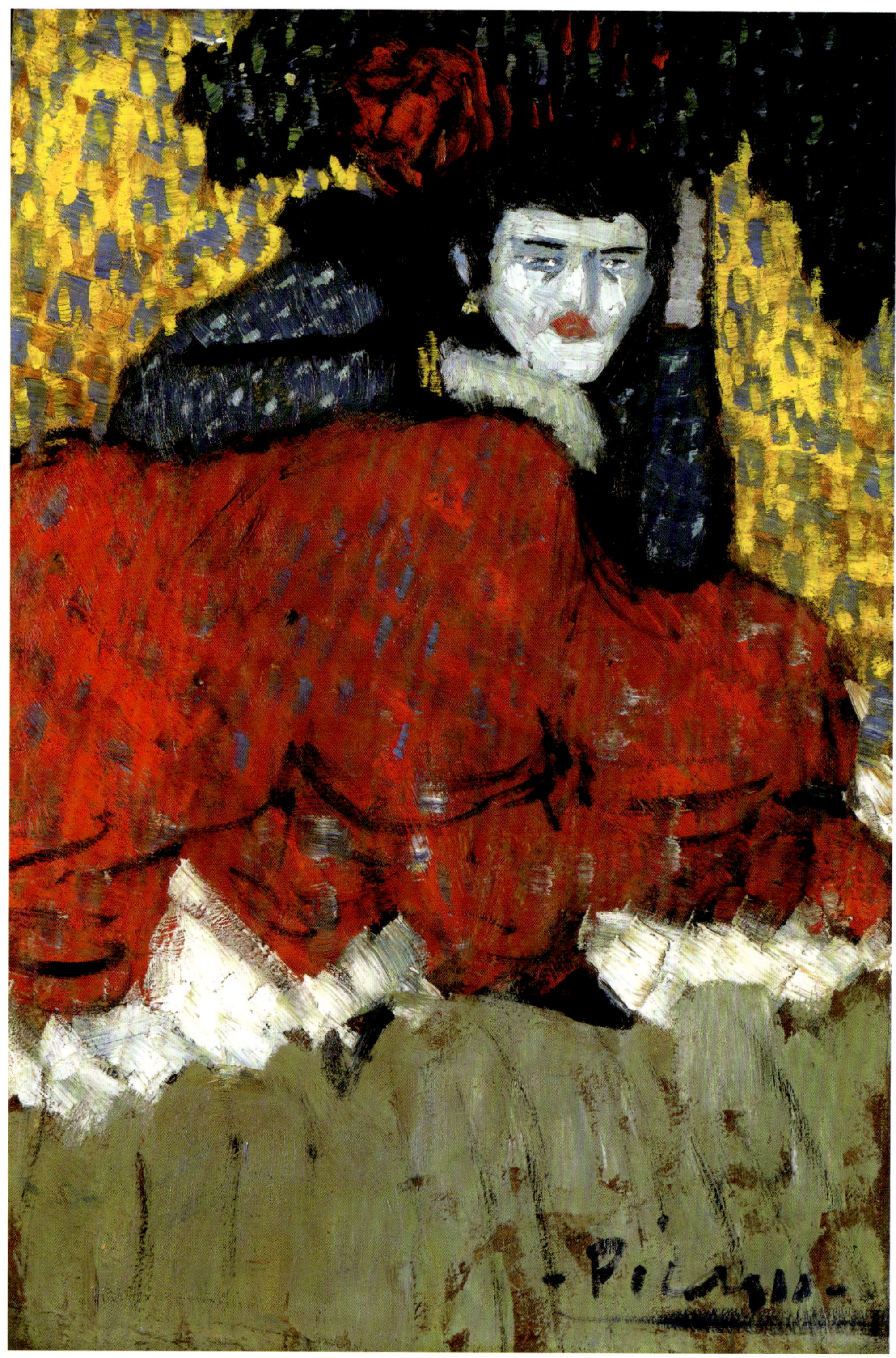

4.7 Pablo Picasso
Spanish Dancer
[Danseuse espagnole]
1901
SWITZERLAND, NAHMAD COLLECTION

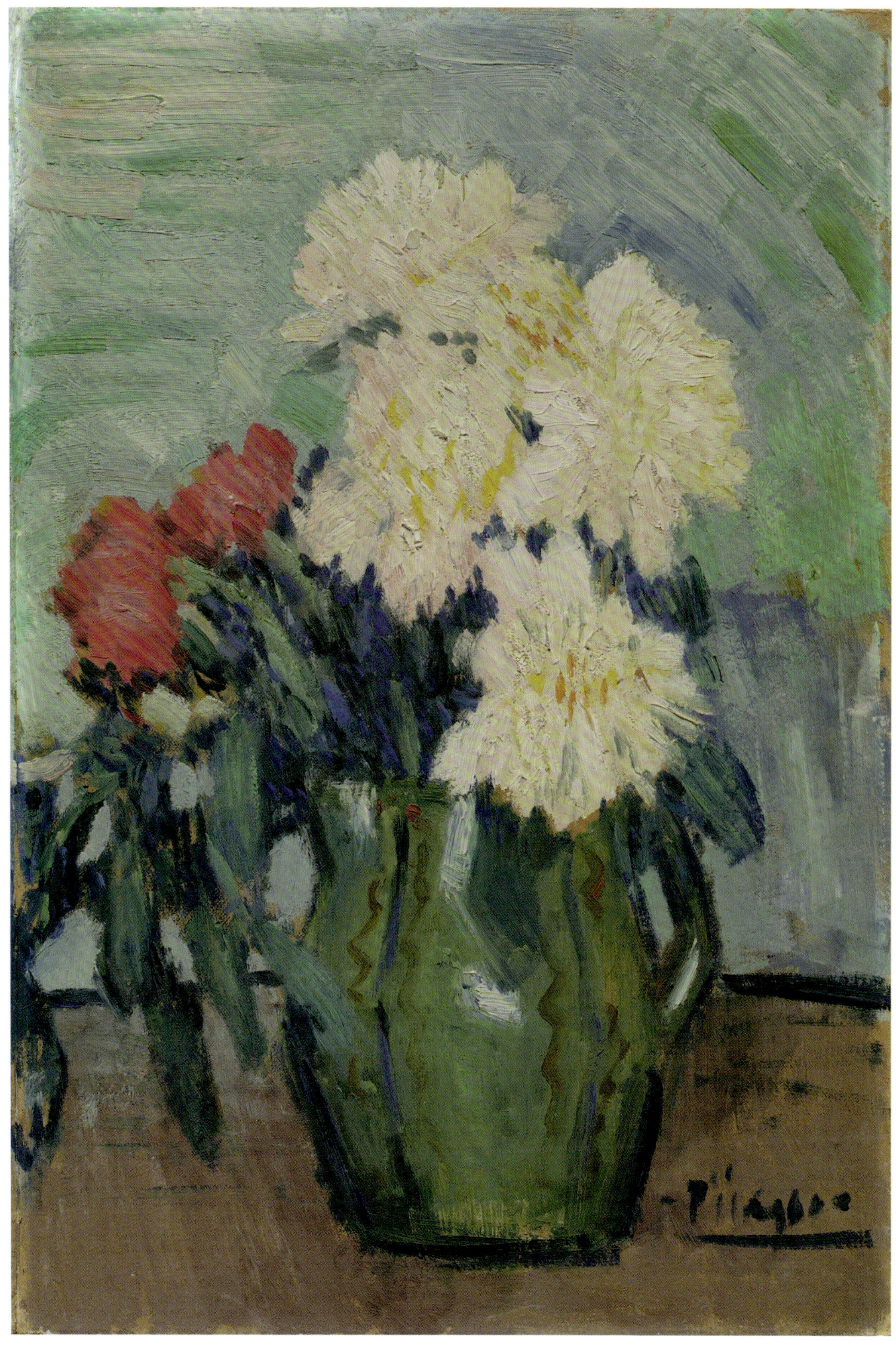

4.8 Pablo Picasso
Peonies
[Peonies]
1901
WASHINGTON, NATIONAL GALLERY OF ART, GIFT OF MRS. GILBERT W. CHAPMAN, 1981.41.1.(2847)

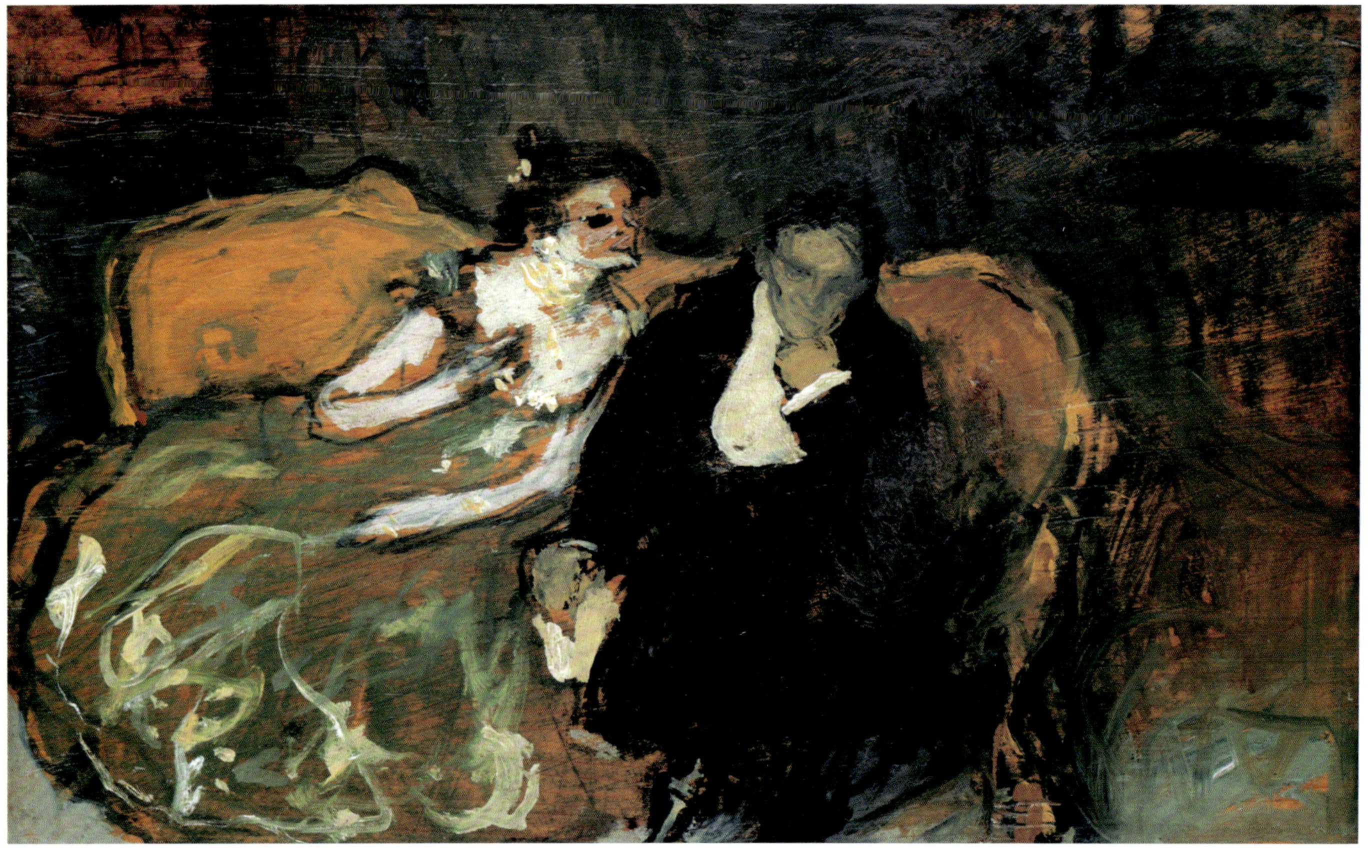

4.9 Pablo Picasso
The Conversation
[La Conversation]
1901
KÜNZELSAU, WÜRTH COLLECTION

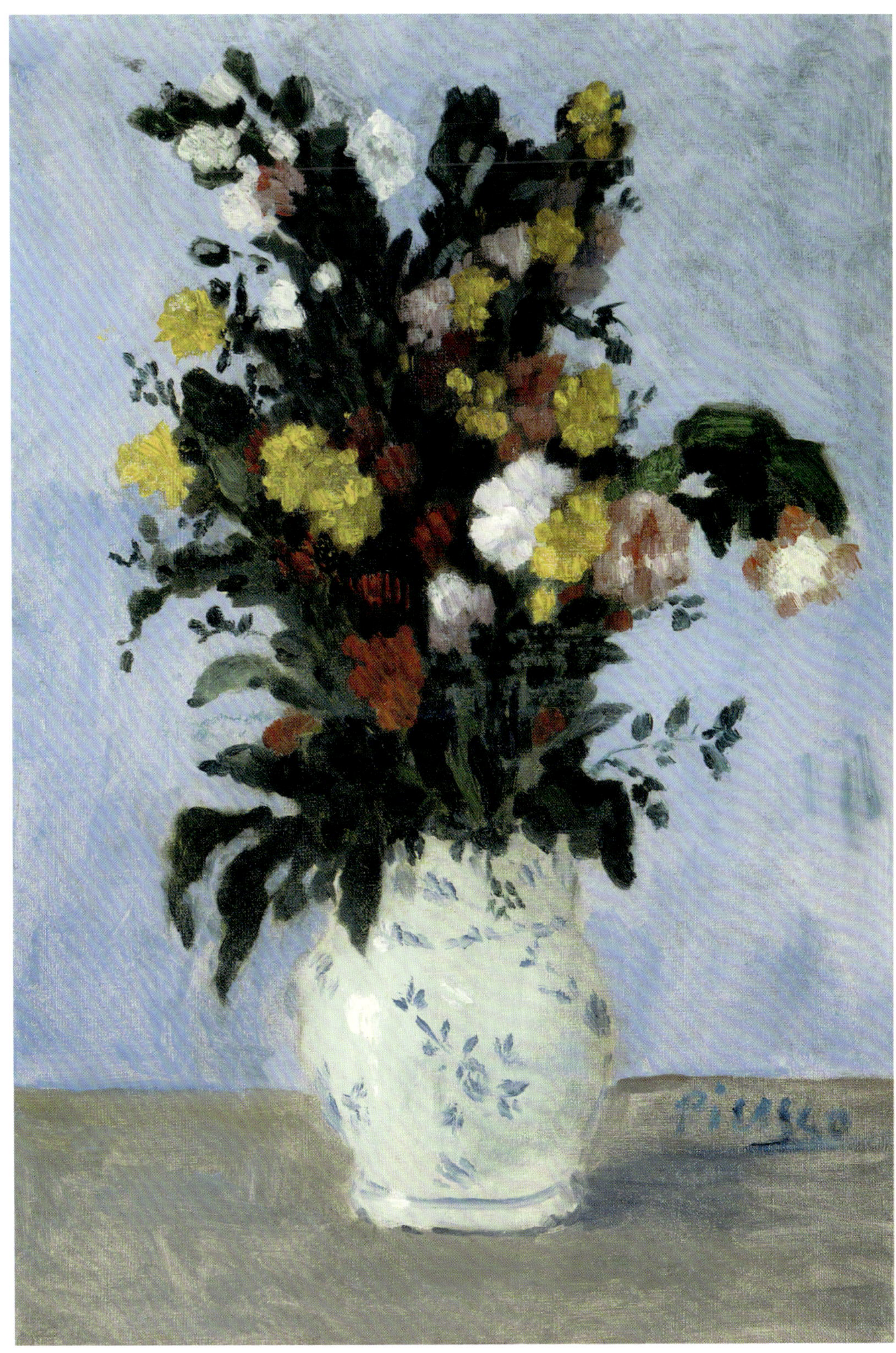

4.10 Pablo Picasso
Vase with Flowers
[Vase de fleurs]
1901
SWITZERLAND, NAHMAD COLLECTION

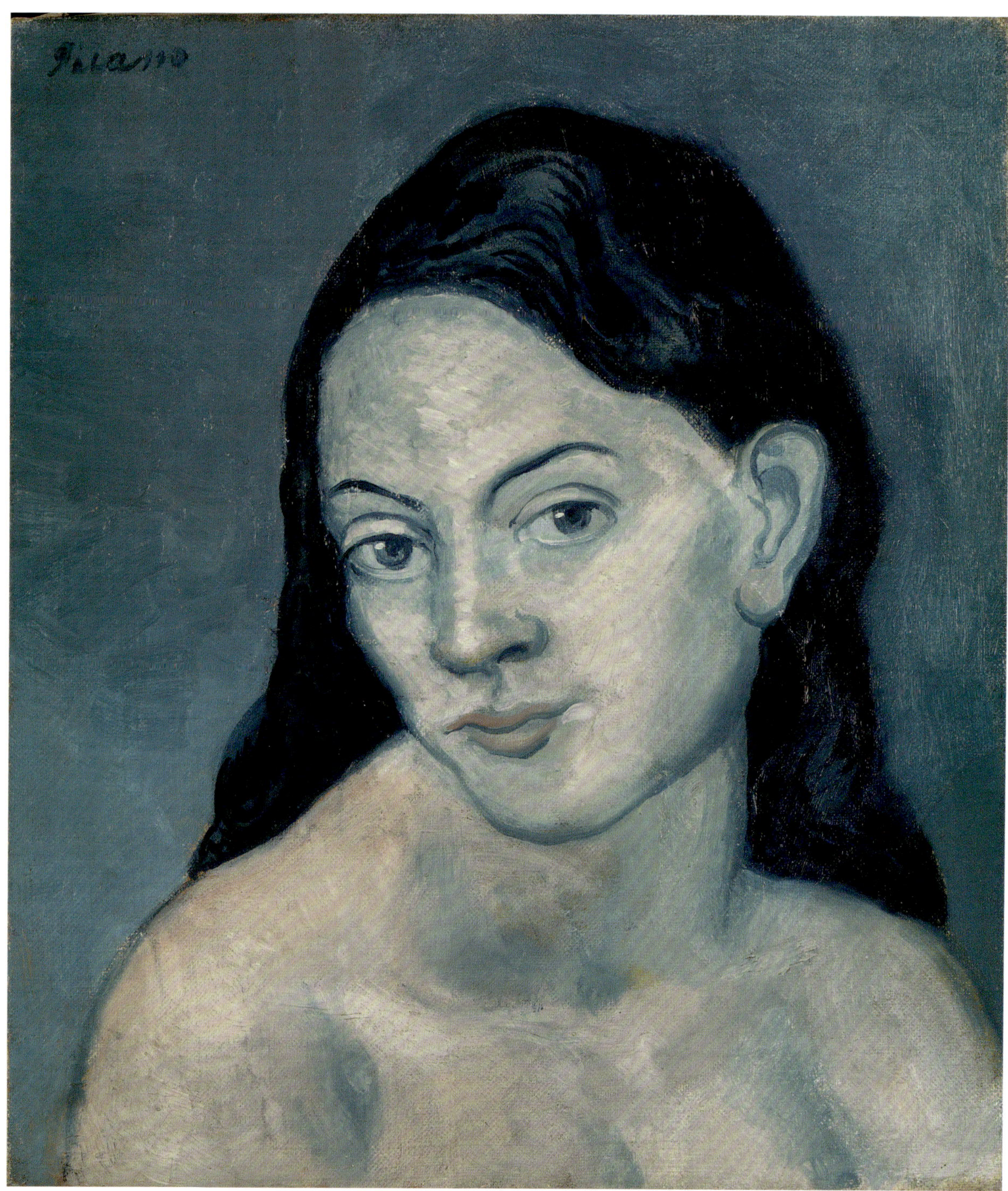

4.11 Pablo Picasso
Head of a Woman
[Tête de femme]
1903
NEW YORK, THE METROPOLITAN MUSEUM OF ART, BEQUEST OF MISS ADELAIDE MILTON DE GROOT, 1967, 67.187.91

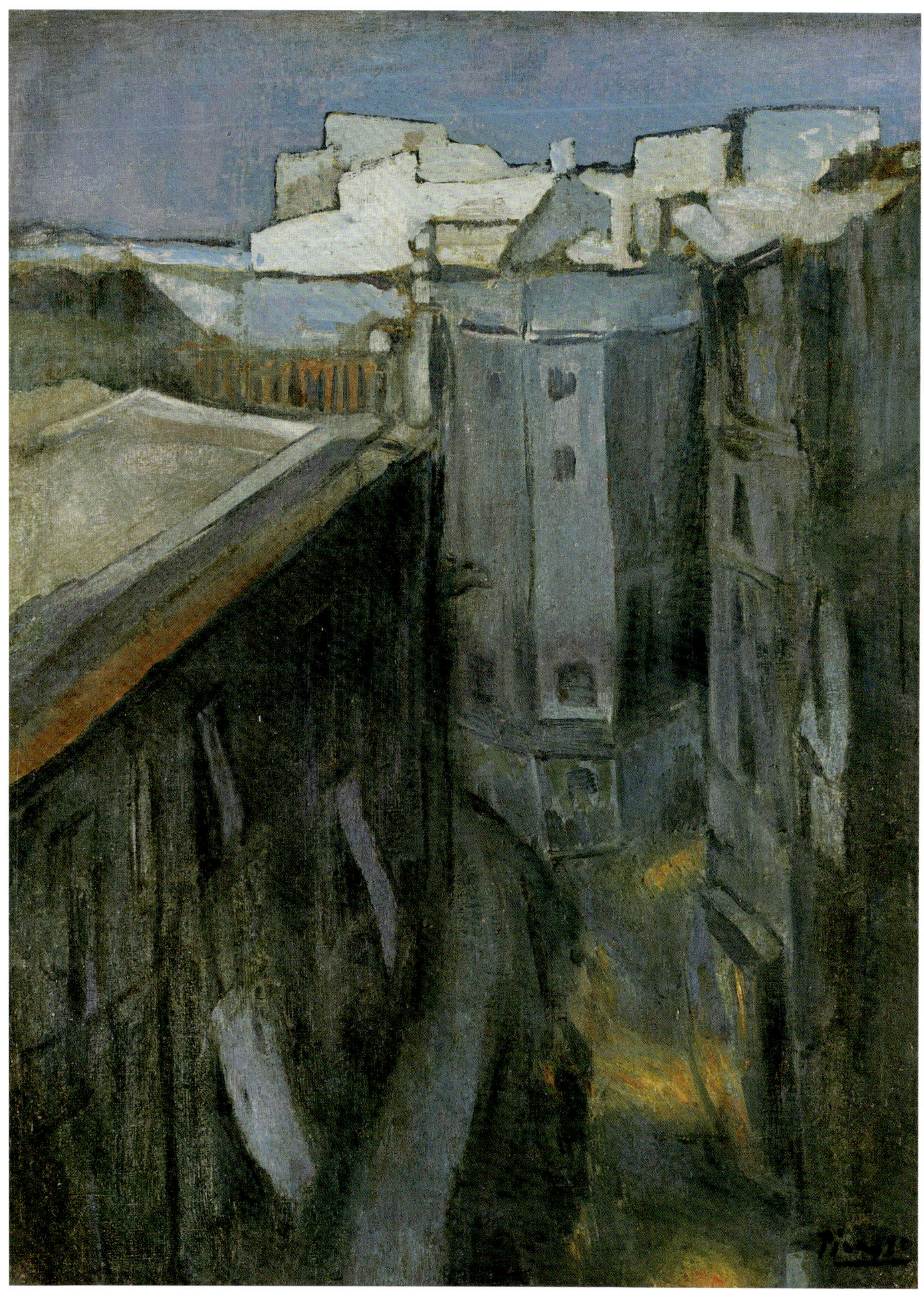

4.12 Pablo Picasso
Barcelona, Riera de Sant Joan at Dawn
[Barcelona. Riera de Sant Joan à l'aube]
1903
SWITZERLAND, PRIVATE COLLECTION

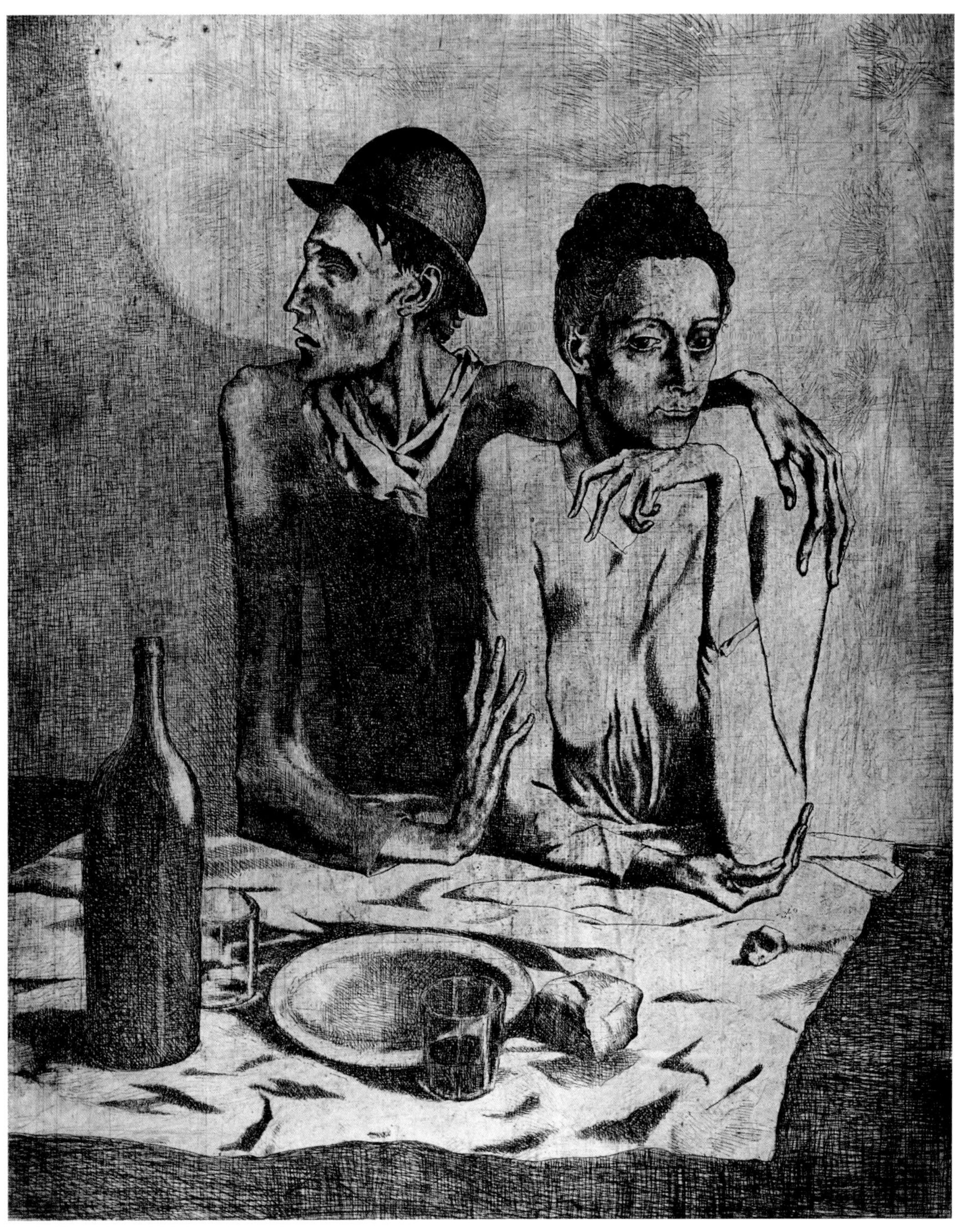

4.13 Pablo Picasso
The Frugal Meal
[Le Repas frugal]
1904
BERN, E.W.K.

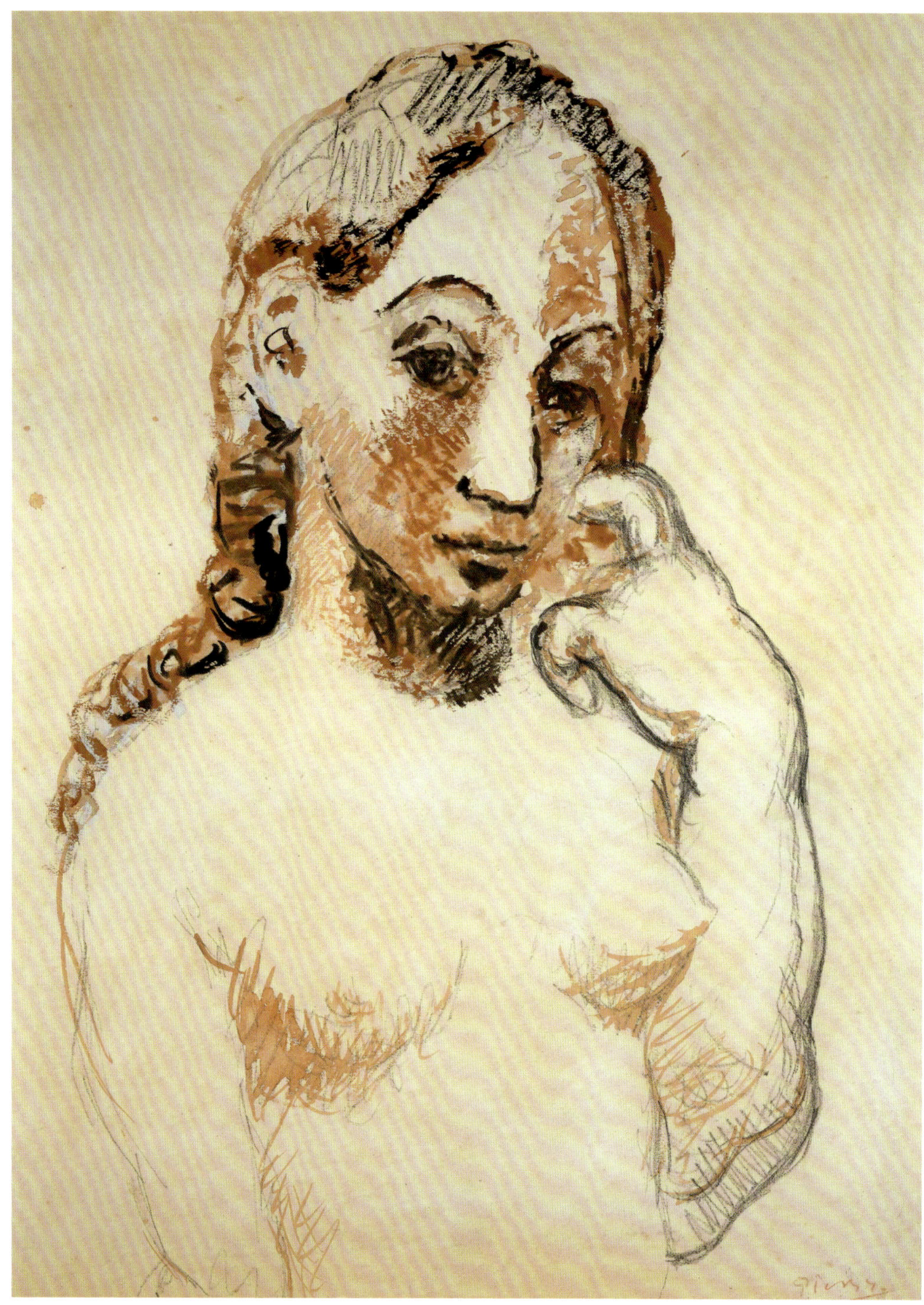

4.14 Pablo Picasso
Bust of a Woman with her Left Hand Raised (**Fernande Olivier**)
[Buste de femme la main gauche levée (Fernande Olivier)]
c. 1905–6
COURTESY ACQUAVELLA GALLERY. WORK NOT ON DISPLAY

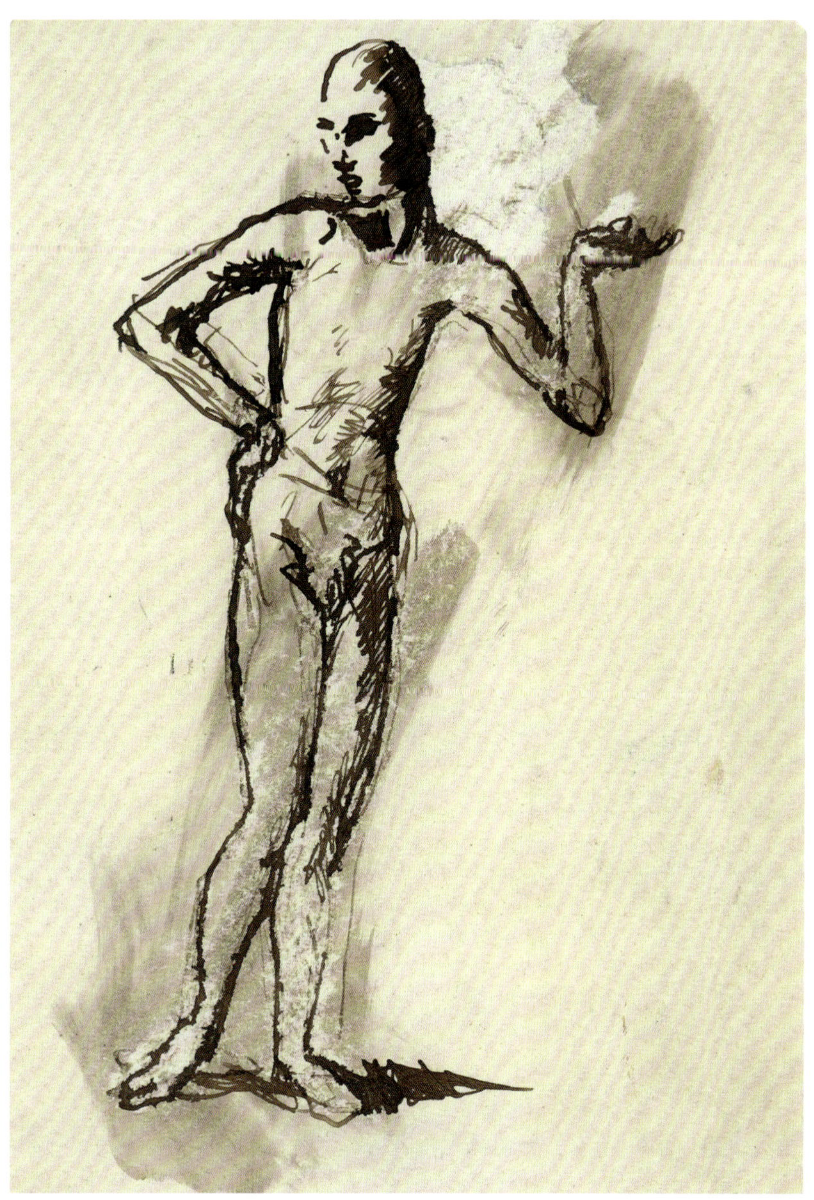

4.15 Pablo Picasso
The Actor
[L'Acteur]
1904
KÜNZELSAU, WÜRTH COLLECTION

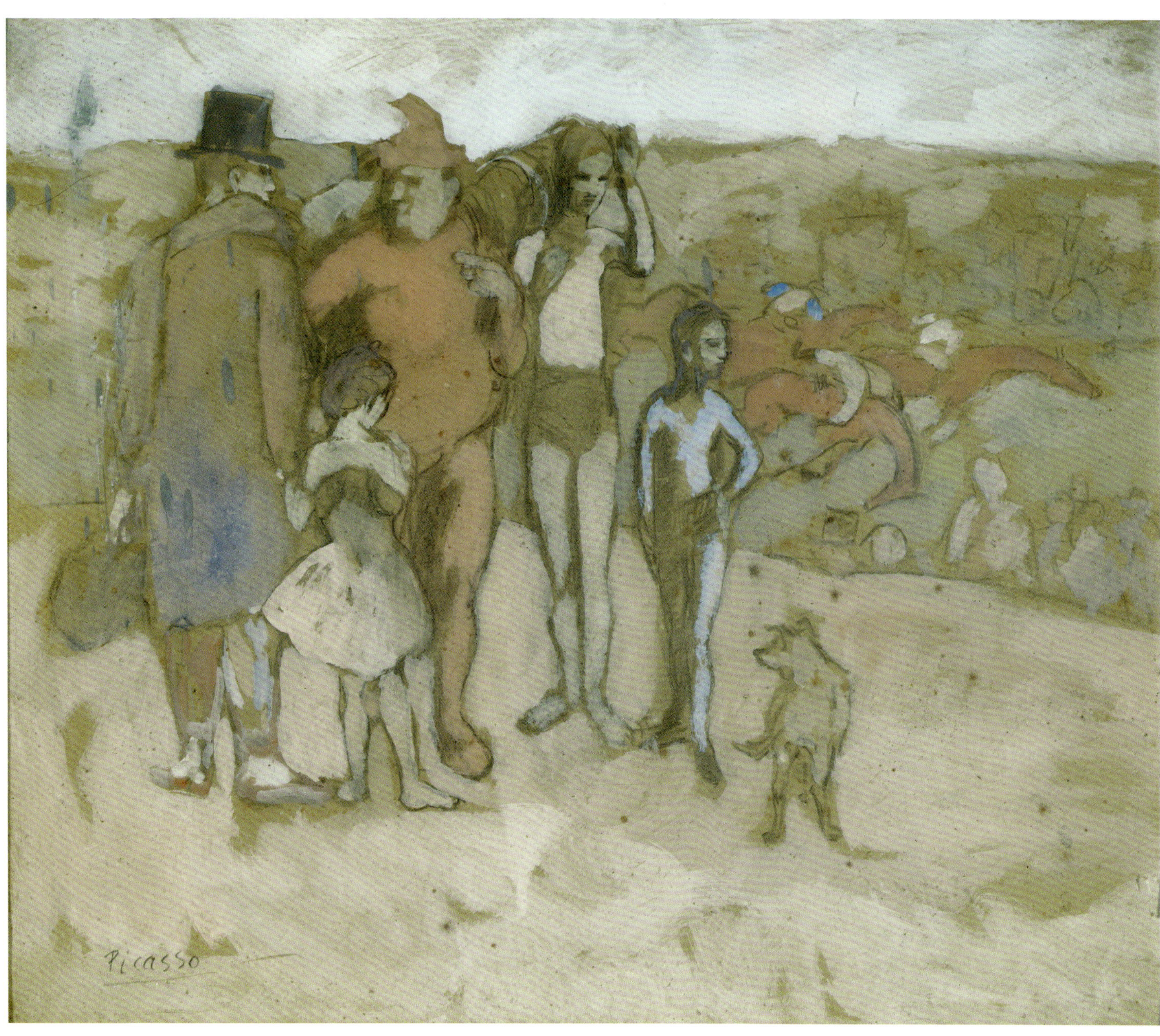

4.16 Pablo Picasso
Family of Acrobats
[Famille de saltimbanques]
Spring 1905
MOSCOW, THE STATE PUSHKIN MUSEUM OF FINE ARTS. WORK NOT ON DISPLAY

EPILOGUE

5.1 Pablo Picasso
The Weeping Woman
[La Femme qui pleure]
1937

RIEHEN/BASEL, FONDATION BEYELER. 98.3

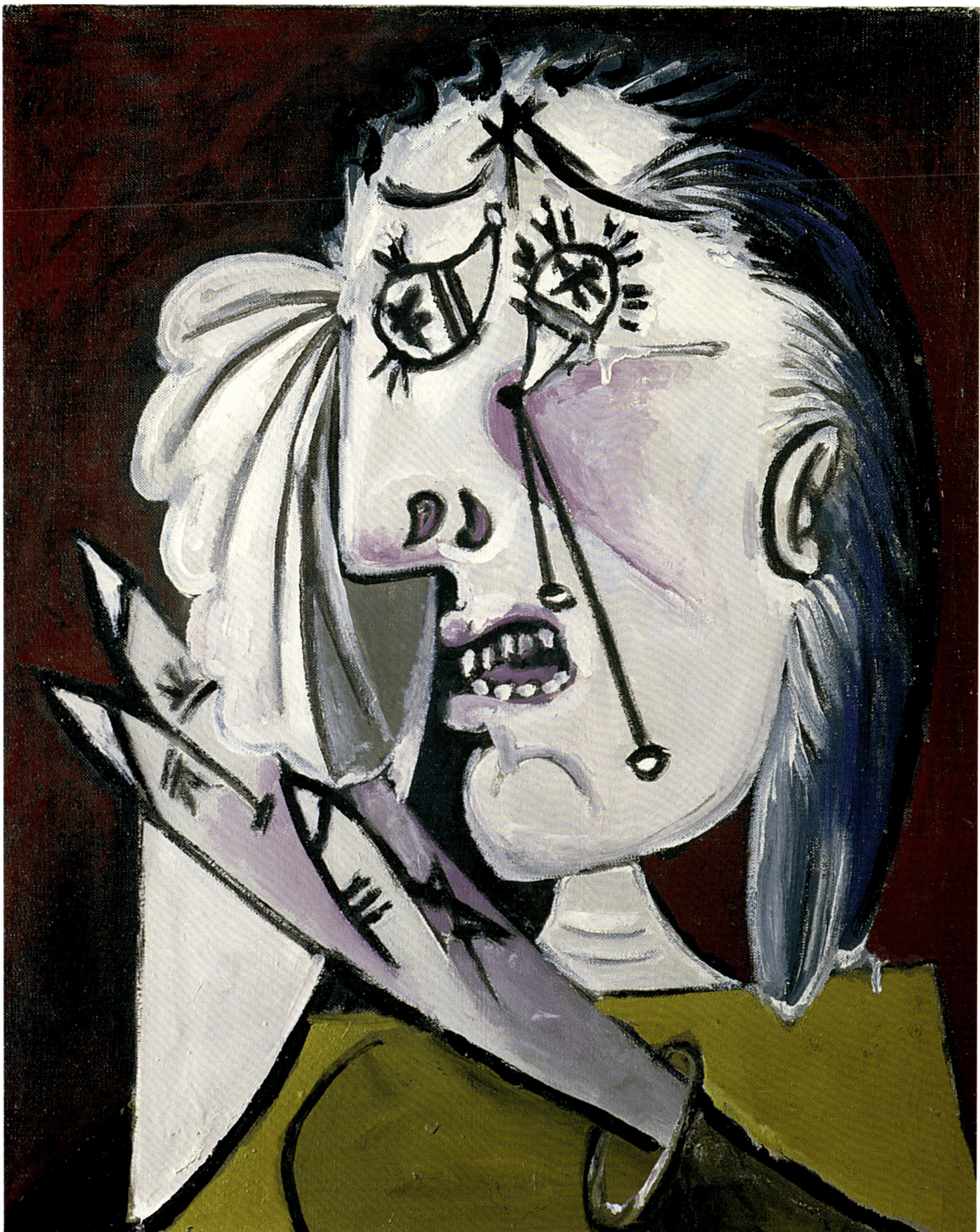

5.2 Joan Miró
Composition (Little Universe)
[Composition (Petit Univers)]
1933

RIEHEN/BASEL, FONDATION BEYELER. 72.4

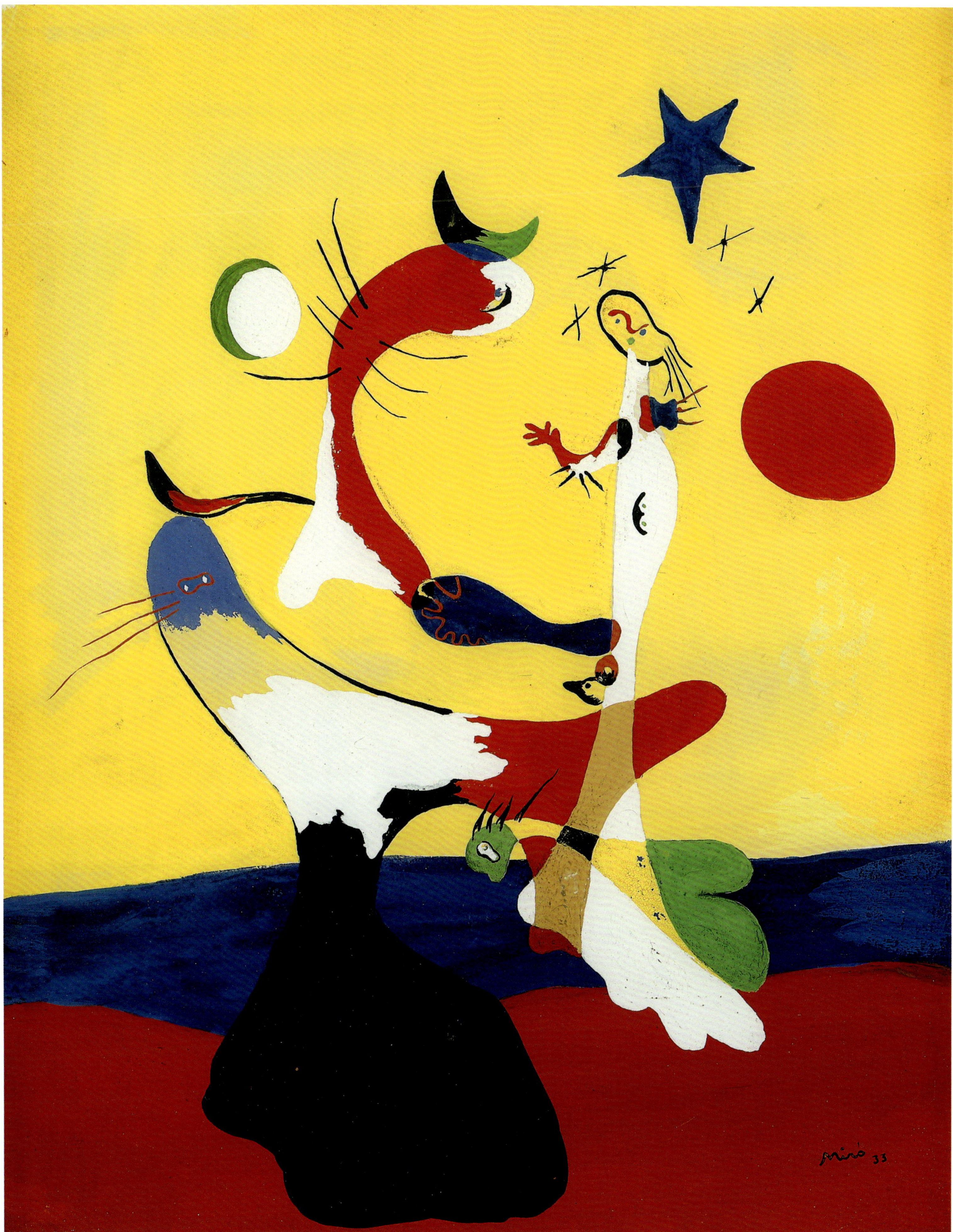
miró 33

5.3 Salvador Dalí
The Bleeding Roses
[Las rosas ensangrentadas]
1930
LA CORUÑA, COLLECIÓN CAIXA GALICIA

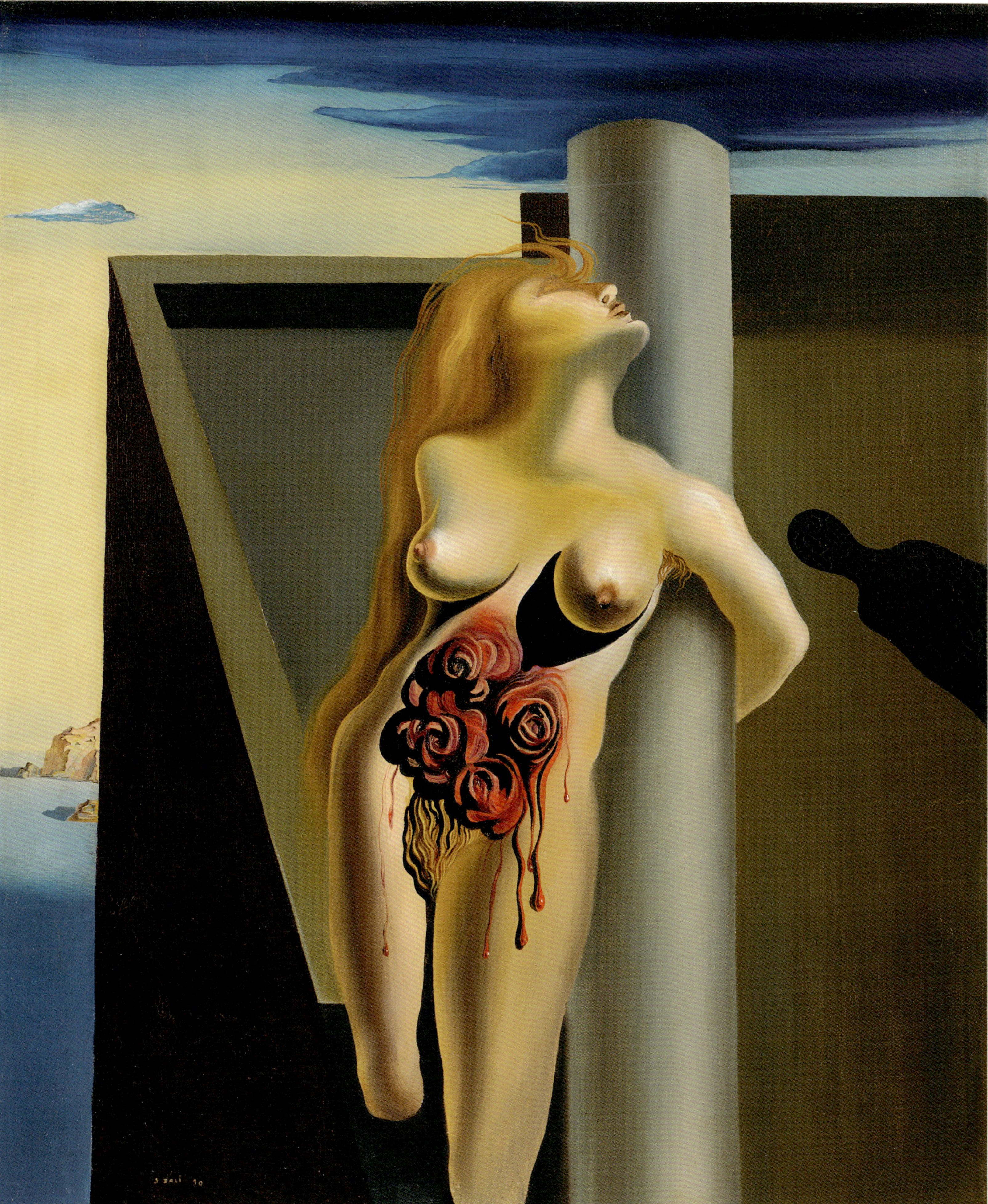

CHECKLIST

1ST CONSIDERATION
PSYCHOMACHIA

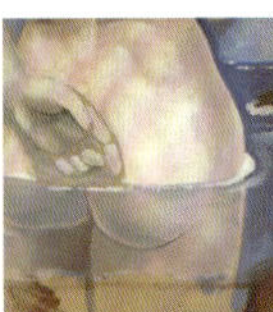

1.1 Salvador Dalí
Nude in the Water
[Nu a l'aigua
Desnudo en el agua]
c. 1924
oil on paperboard
50.5 x 47 cm
MADRID, MUSEO NACIONAL
CENTRO DE ARTE REINA SOFÍA
DE01567

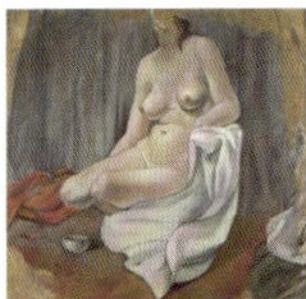

1.2 Salvador Dalí
Nude
[Nu / Desnudo]
1924
oil on cardboard
46 x 48.5 cm
MADRID, MUSEO NACIONAL
CENTRO DE ARTE REINA SOFÍA
DE01566

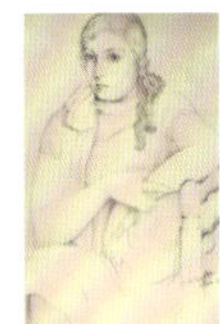

1.3 Salvador Dalí
Previous Sketch for "Portrait of Maria Carbona"
[Estudi per el "Retrat
de María Carbona"]
1925
leadpoint on paper
49 x 32 cm
MUSEU DE MONTSERRAT
DONATED BY J. SALA ARDIZ
R.N. 200.413

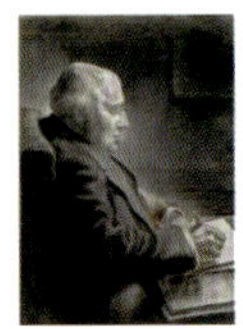

1.4 Salvador Dalí
Portrait of Artist's Father
[Retrat del pare de l'artista
Retrato del padre del artista]
c. 1925
charcoal and pastel on paper
43.4 x 31.3 cm
MUSEU DE MONTSERRAT
DONATED BY J. SALA ARDIZ
R.N. 200.575

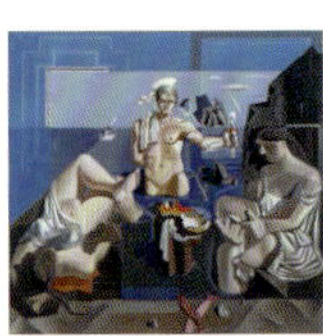

1.5 Salvador Dalí
Composition with Three Figures. Neocubist Academy (The Sailor. Neocubist Academy)
[Composició amb tres figures.
Acadèmia neocubista
(El mariner. Acadèmia neocubista)
Composición con tres figuras.
Academia neocubista
(El marinero. Academia
neocubista)]
1926
oil on canvas
190 x 200 cm
MUSEU DE MONTSERRAT
DONATED BY JOSEFINA CUS
R.N. 201.390

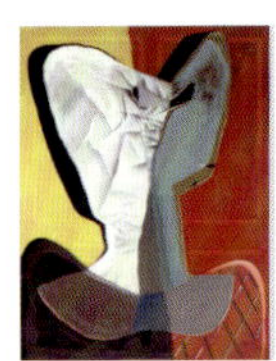

1.6 Salvador Dalí
Harlequin
[Arlequí / Arlequín]
1926
(although dated 1927
by the artist)
oil on canvas
196.5 x 150 cm
MADRID, MUSEO NACIONAL
CENTRO DE ARTE REINA SOFÍA
AS07488

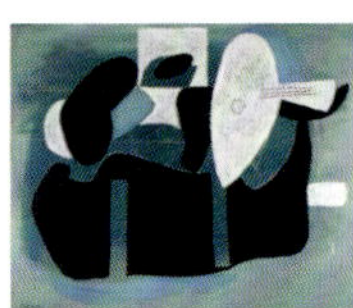

1.7 Pablo Picasso
Musical Instruments on a Table
[Instruments de musique
sur une table]
1925–6
oil on canvas
162 x 204.5 cm
MADRID, MUSEO NACIONAL
CENTRO DE ARTE REINA SOFÍA
AS10615

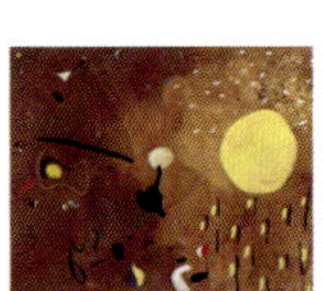

1.8 Joan Miró
Composition
[Composition]
1926
oil on canvas
72.5 x 92 cm
THYSSEN-BORNEMISZA
COLLECTIONS 1975.38

1.9 Joan Miró
Painting-Poem (Music, Seine, Michel Bataille and I)
[Peinture-poème
(Musique, Seine, Michel
Bataille et moi)]
1927
oil on canvas
80.8 x 100 cm
SWITZERLAND
VOLKART FOUNDATION

2ND CONSIDERATION
GENIUS LOCI

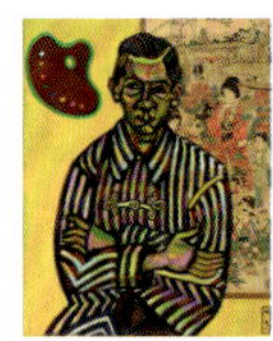

2.1 Joan Miró
Portrait of Enric Cristòfol Ricart
[Retrat
d'Enric Cristòfol Ricart]
Winter 1916
or early spring 1917
oil on pasted paper on canvas
81.6 x 65.7 cm
NEW YORK,
THE MUSEUM OF MODERN ART
FLORENCE, MAY SCHOENBORN
BEQUEST 822.1996

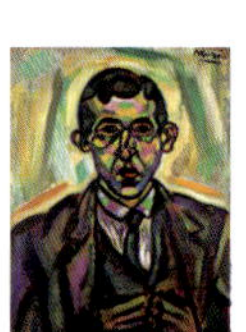

2.2 Joan Miró
Portrait of Josep F. Ràfols
[Retrat de Josep F. Ràfols]
1917
oil on paper mounted on panel
76 x 54 cm
ST. LOUIS,
MILDRED LANE KEMPER ART MUSEUM
WASHINGTON UNIVERSITY IN ST. LOUIS
GIFT OF MR. AND MRS. SYDNEY
M. SHOENBERG, JR., 1961

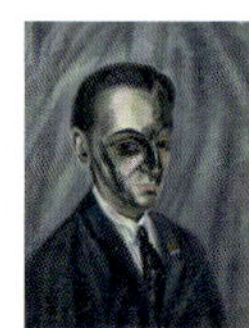

2.3 Salvador Dalí
Portrait of Joan Torres i Darnis
[Retrat de
Joan Torres i Darnis]
c. 1922
oil on canvas
49.5 x 39.5 cm
BARCELONA, MNAC
MUSEU NACIONAL D'ART
DE CATALUNYA 043720-000

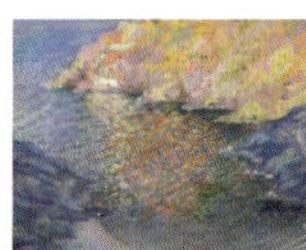

2.3 verso **Nans Cove. Cadaqués**
[Cala Nans. Cadaqués]
c. 1920

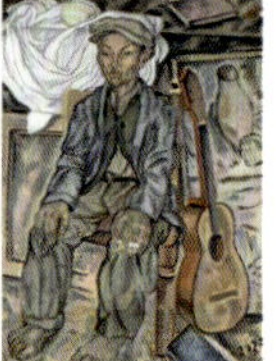

2.4 Salvador Dalí
Figueres Gypsy
[Gitano de Figueres]
1923
oil and gouache on paperboard
104 x 75 cm
MADRID, MUSEO NACIONAL
CENTRO DE ARTE REINA SOFÍA
AS11129

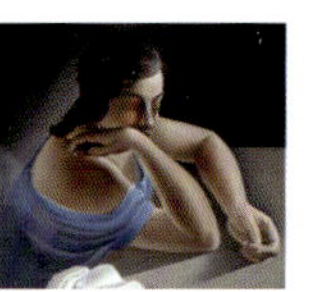

2.5 Salvador Dalí
Figure at a Table (Anna María Dalí)
[Figura en una taula
(Figura en una mesa
Anna María Dalí)]
1925
oil on paperboard
mounted on wood
46 x 48 cm
MILAN, PRIVATE COLLECTION

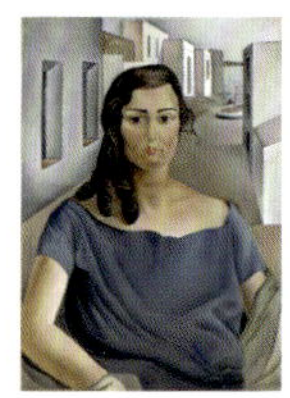

2.6 Salvador Dalí
Portrait of my Sister
[Retrat de la meva germana
Retrato de mi hermana]
1925
oil on canvas
92 x 65 cm
FIGUERES
FUNDACIÓ GALA-SALVADOR DALÍ

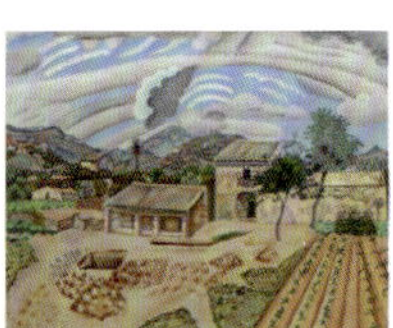

2.7 Joan Miró
Tile Factory in Mont-roig
[Tuilerie à Mont-roig]
1918
oil and collage on canvas
65 x 81 cm
NEW YORK, PRIVATE COLLECTION
COURTESY OF MDP & ASSOCIATI,
LUGANO

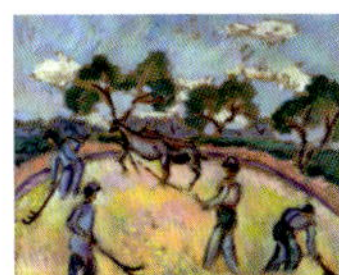

2.8 Joan Miró
Threshing
[Battage du blé]
1918
oil on canvas
45 x 56 cm
PARIS, COLLECTION MAEGHT
BAC 2242

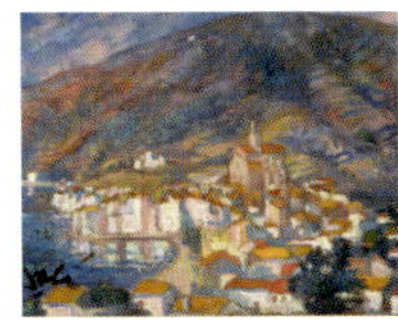

2.9 Salvador Dalí
Landscape of Cadaqués
[Paisatge de Cadaqués
Paisaje de Cadaqués]
1920–1
oil on canvas
41.5 x 52 cm
OVIEDO, COLLECCION MASAVEU
C/TV.136

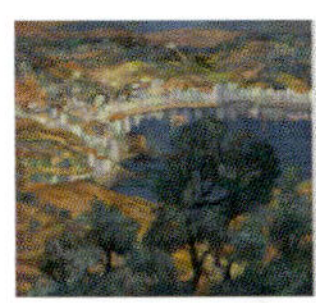

2.10 Salvador Dalí
Landscape of Cadaqués
[Paisatge de Cadaqués
Paisaje de Cadaqués]
c. 1921
oil on canvas
31.2 x 34 cm
BERN, KUNSTMUSEUM BERN
BEQUEST OF GEORGES F. KELLER 1981

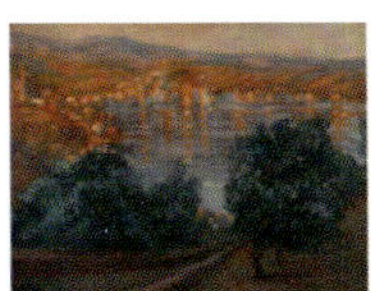

2.11 Salvador Dalí
Landscape of Cadaqués
[Paisaje de Cadaqués]
c. 1921
oil on canvas
39.5 x 51 cm
BERN, KUNSTMUSEUM BERN
BEQUEST OF GEORGES F. KELLER 1981

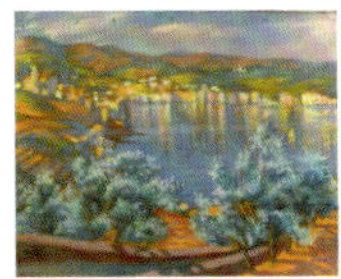

2.12 Salvador Dalí
Landscape of Cadaqués
[Paisatge de Cadaqués
Paisaje de Cadaqués]
c. 1921
oil on canvas
45 x 52 cm
PRIVATE COLLECTION

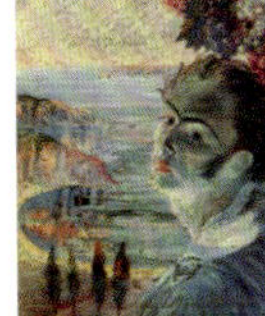

2.12 verso
Self Portrait
[Autoretrat
Autoretrato]
c. 1920

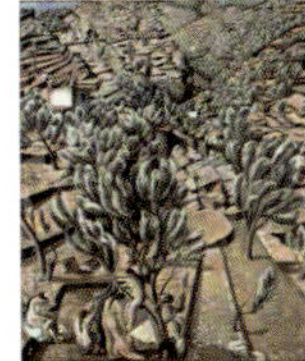

2.13 Salvador Dalí
The Jorneta Stream
[El torrent de la Jorneta
El torente de la Jorneta]
c. 1923
oil on canvas
122.8 x 99.5 cm
DEPOSIT OF PRIVATE COLLECTION, TENERIFE
CABILDO INSULAR DE TENERIFE, TEA
TENERIFE ESPACIO DE LAS ARTES. DG2010-01

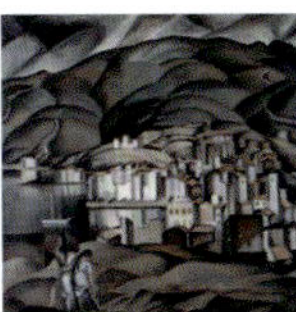

2.14 Salvador Dalí
**Cadaqués Seen
from the Tower of Creus**
[Cadaqués vist des de la Torre
de Les Creus / Cadaqués visto
desde de la Torre de los Creus]
c. 1923
oil on canvas
100 x 98 cm
FIGUERES
FUNDACIÓ GALA-SALVADOR DALÍ

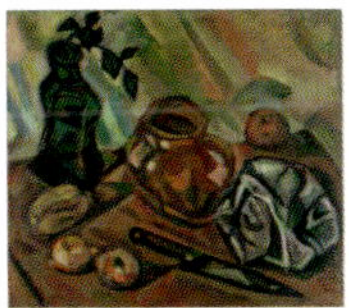

2.15 Joan Miró
Still Life with Knife
[Nature morte au couteau]
1916
oil on cardboard
mounted on panel
59.5 x 68.5 cm
SWITZERLAND, NAHMAD COLLECTION

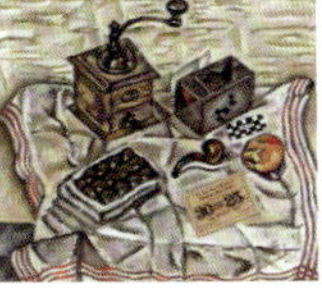

2.16 Joan Miró
The Coffee Mill
[Le Moulin à café]
1918
oil and collage on canvas
62.5 x 70.5 cm
NEW YORK, PRIVATE
COLLECTION. COURTESY OF MDP
& ASSOCIATI, LUGANO

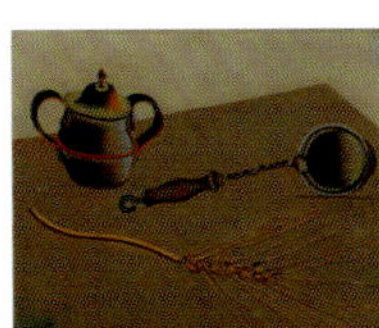

2.17 Joan Miró
**Still Life I
(The Ear of Corn)**
[Nature morte I
(L'Épi de blé)]
1922–3
oil on canvas
37.8 x 46 cm
NEW YORK
THE MUSEUM OF MODERN ART
PURCHASE, 12.1939

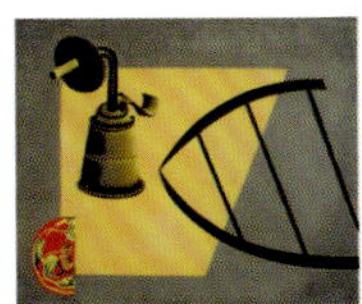

2.18 Joan Miró
**Still Life II
(The Carbide Lamp)**
[Nature morte II
(La Lampe à carbure)]
Mont-roig and Paris 1922–3
oil on canvas
38.1 x 45.7 cm
NEW YORK
THE MUSEUM OF MODERN ART
PURCHASE, 1939

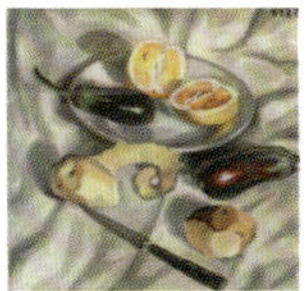

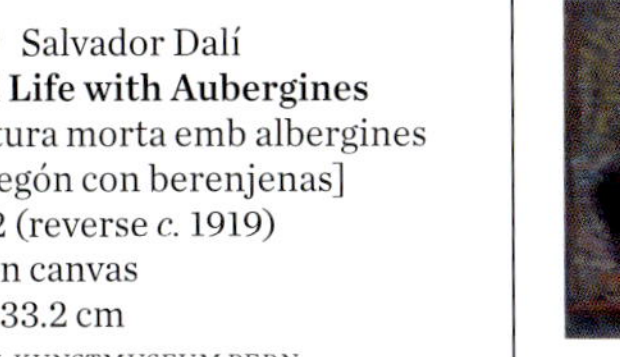

2.19 Salvador Dalí
Still Life with Aubergines
[Natura morta emb albergines
Bodegón con berenjenas]
1922 (reverse *c.* 1919)
oil on canvas
31 x 33.2 cm
BERN, KUNSTMUSEUM BERN
LEGAT GEORGES F. KELLER 1981

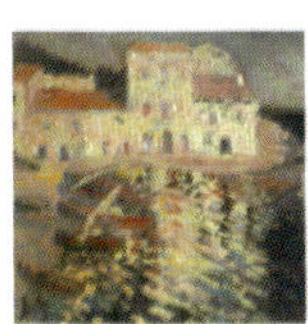

2.19 verso
Cadaqués
c. 1919

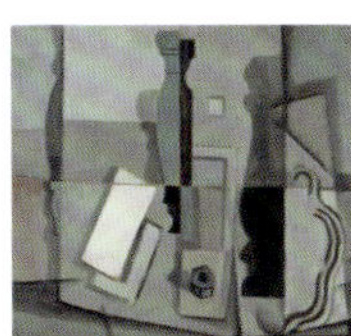

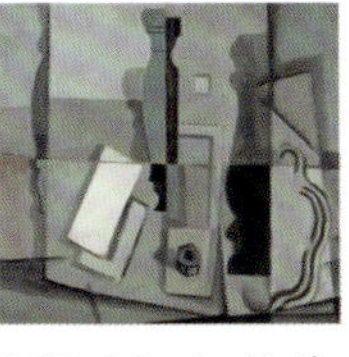

2.20 Salvador Dalí
Still Life
[Natura morta
Naturaleza muerta
Bodegón]
1923
oil on cardboard
50 x 65 cm
MADRID, MUSEO NACIONAL
CENTRO DE ARTE REINA SOFÍA
AS11132

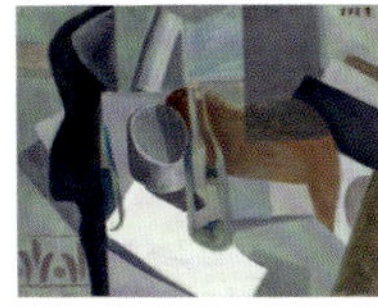

2.21 Salvador Dalí
Still Life
[Natura morta
Naturaleza muerta]
1923
oil on cardboard
50 x 56 cm
MADRID, MUSEO NACIONAL
CENTRO DE ARTE REINA SOFÍA
AS11130

3RD CONSIDERATION
WHEN MIRÓ ALMOST MET PICASSO

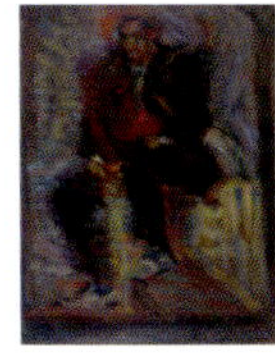

3.1 Joan Miró
The Peasant
[Le Paysan]
1915
oil on canvas
65 x 50 cm
PARIS, COLLECTION
MAEGHT. BAC 4085

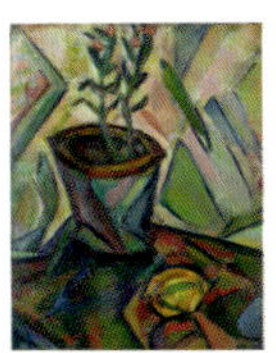

3.2 Joan Miró
Vase of Flowers with a Lemon
[Le Pot de fleurs et le citron]
1916
oil on cardboard
63.8 x 50.8 cm
MADRID, JOSÉ LLADÓ

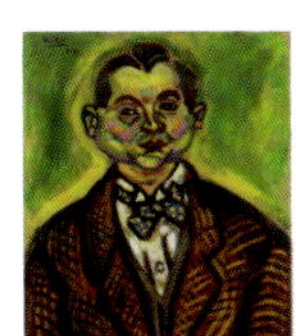

3.3 Joan Miró
Self Portrait
[Autoretrat / Autoretrato]
1917
oil on canvas
61 x 50 cm
NEW YORK, PRIVATE COLLECTION
COURTESY OF MDP & ASSOCIATI,
LUGANO

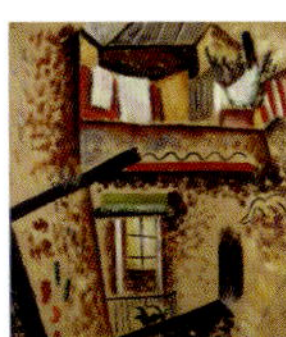

3.4 Joan Miró
The Balcony below Sant Pere
[El balcó, Baixa de Sant Pere]
1917
oil on canvas
40 x 35 cm
PARIS, COLLECTION MAEGHT
BAC 2241

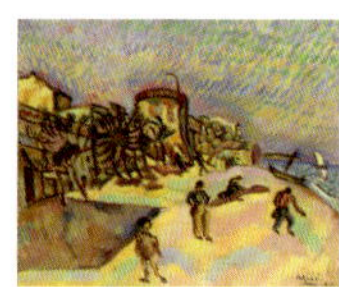

3.5 Joan Miró
The Beach at Cambrils
[La Plage à Cambrils]
1917
oil on canvas
60 x 73 cm
SWITZERLAND
NAHMAD COLLECTION

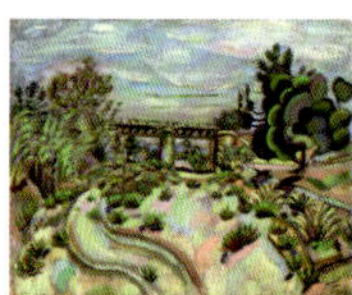

3.6 Joan Miró
Mont-roig: The Bridge
[Mont-roig: le pont]
1917
oil on canvas
46.5 x 58 cm
SWITZERLAND
NAHMAD COLLECTION

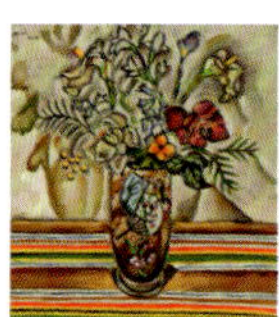

3.7 Joan Miró
Flowers
[Fleurs]
1918
oil on canvas
72.07 x 63.98 cm
MILWAUKEE
MILWAUKEE ART MUSEUM
GIFT OF MRS. HARRY LYNDE BRADLEY
M1977.124

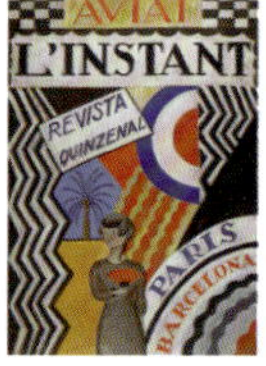

3.8 Joan Miró
Poster designed for "L'Instant" magazine
[Projet d'affiche pour l a revue "L'Instant"]
1919
oil on cardboard
107 x 76 cm
VALENCIA, IVAM
INSTITUT VALENCIÀ D'ART MODERN
1996.019

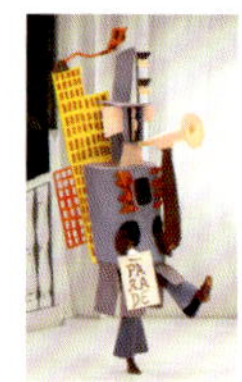

3.9
Parade:
The American Manager
[Parade:
costume de manager américain]
modern reproduction of the 1917
original to a drawing
by Pablo Picasso
painted cardboard and clothes
200 x 100 x 80 cm
BORDEAUX
OPÉRA NATIONAL DE BORDEAUX

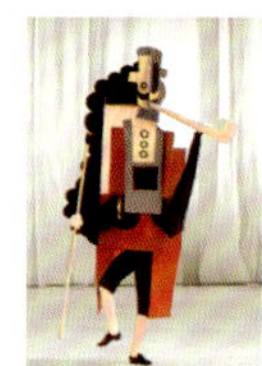

3.10
Parade:
The French Manager
[Parade:
costume de manager français]
modern reproduction of the 1917
original to a drawing
by Pablo Picasso
painted cardboard and clothes
200 x 100 x 80 cm
BORDEAUX
OPÉRA NATIONAL DE BORDEAUX

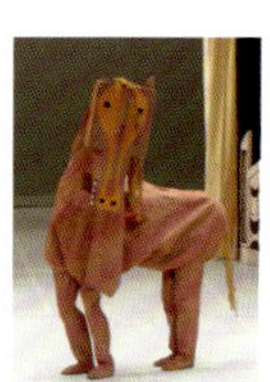

3.11
Parade: Horse
[Parade: costume du cheval]
modern reproduction of the 1917
original to a drawing
by Pablo Picasso
BORDEAUX
OPÉRA NATIONAL DE BORDEAUX

4TH CONSIDERATION
ON THE THRESHOLD OF MODERNITY

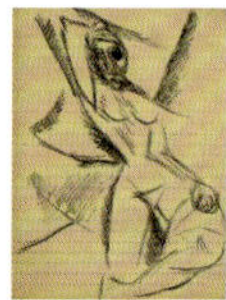

4.1a Pablo Picasso
Study for the Seated Girl: Nude with Drapery
Cahier no. 7
May–June 1907
220 x 170 mm
MALAGA, COLLECTION OF THE PABLO RUIZ PICASSO FOUNDATION - BIRTHPLACE MUSEUM. FPCN: 2037, C. 3R

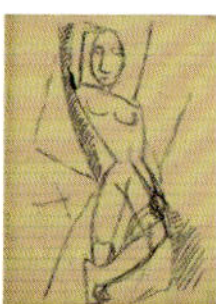

4.1b Pablo Picasso
Study for the Seated Girl: Nude with Drapery
Cahier no. 7
May–June 1907
pen and ink on paper 220 x 170 mm
MALAGA, COLLECTION OF THE PABLO RUIZ PICASSO FOUNDATION - BIRTHPLACE MUSEUM. FPCN: 2037, C. 5R

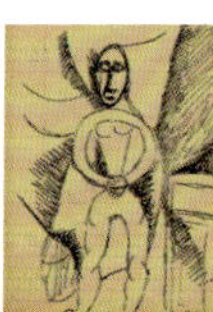

4.1c Pablo Picasso
Nude with Hands Crossed, Full-Frontal
Cahier no. 7
May–June 1907
pen and ink on paper 220 x 170 mm
MALAGA, COLLECTION OF THE PABLO RUIZ PICASSO FOUNDATION - BIRTHPLACE MUSEUM. FPCN: 2037, C. 7R

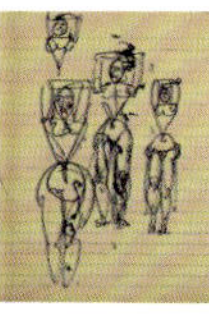

4.1d Pablo Picasso
Study for the Girl with Raised Arms: Nudes with Raised Arms, Full-Frontal
Cahier no. 7
May–June 1907
pen and ink on paper
220 x 170 mm
MALAGA, COLLECTION OF THE PABLO RUIZ PICASSO FOUNDATION - BIRTHPLACE MUSEUM. FPCN: 2037, C. 11R

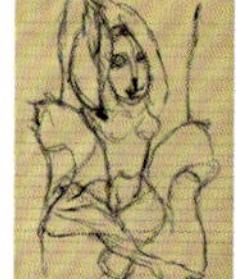

4.1e Pablo Picasso
Study for the Seated Girl: Nude Seated on a Armchair
Cahier no. 7
May–June 1907
pen and ink on paper
220 x 170 mm
MALAGA, COLLECTION OF THE PABLO RUIZ PICASSO FOUNDATION - BIRTHPLACE MUSEUM. FPCN: 2037, C. 15V

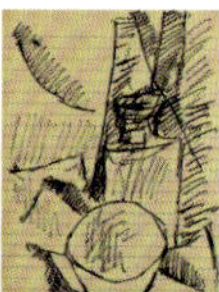

4.1f Pablo Picasso
Study for *Still Life with Bananas*: Jug and Bowl with Towel
Cahier no. 7
May–June 1907
pen and ink on paper
220 x 170 mm
MALAGA, COLLECTION OF THE PABLO RUIZ PICASSO FOUNDATION - BIRTHPLACE MUSEUM. FPCN: 2037, C. 43R

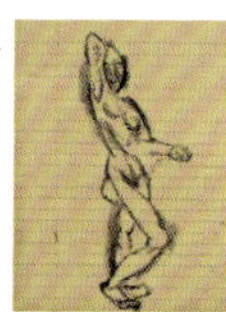

4.1g Pablo Picasso
Study for *Nude with Drapery:* Nude from the Side with Arm Raised
Cahier no. 7
May–June 1907
pen and ink on paper
220 x 170 mm
MALAGA, COLLECTION OF THE PABLO RUIZ PICASSO FOUNDATION - BIRTHPLACE MUSEUM. FPCN: 2037, C. 52R

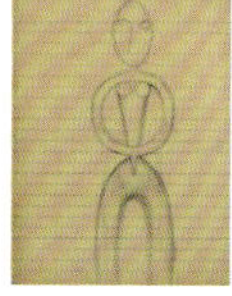

4.1h Pablo Picasso
Study for the Girl with Raised Arms: Nude with Arms Crossed Cahier no. 7
May–June 1907
pencil on paper
220 x 170 mm
MALAGA, COLLECTION OF THE PABLO RUIZ PICASSO FOUNDATION - BIRTHPLACE MUSEUM. FPCN: 2037, C. 57R

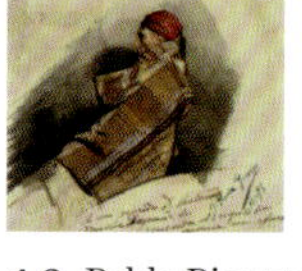

4.2 Pablo Picasso
Old Man with a Cloak (D. José Ruiz Blasco)
[El viejo de la manta
(D. José Ruiz Blasco)]
La Coruña, 1895
watercolour on
260 x 320 mm
MALAGA, MUSEO DE MÁLAGA.
BA/CE00344

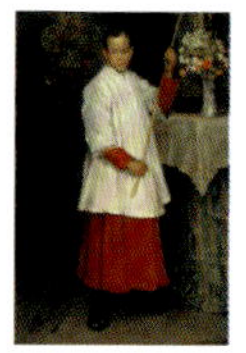

4.3 Pablo Picasso
Altar Boy
[L'Enfant de chœur]
1896
oil on canvas
75 x 50.5 cm
MUSEU DE MONTSERRAT
DONATED BY J. SALA ARDIZ
R.N. 200.503

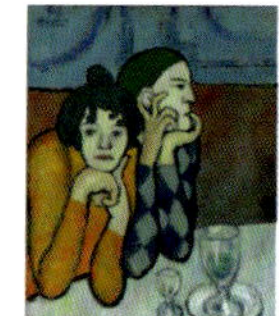

4.4 Pablo Picasso
The Two Acrobats (Harlequin and his Companion)
[Les deux saltimbanques
(Arlequin et sa compagne)]
September–October 1901
oil on canvas
73 x 60 cm
MOSCOW, THE STATE PUSHKIN MUSEUM OF FINE ARTS. 3400

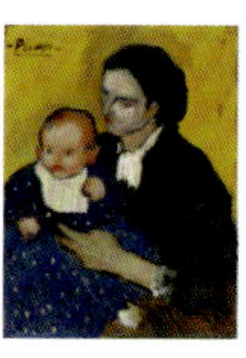

4.5 Pablo Picasso
Mother and Child
[Mère et enfant]
1901
oil on cardboard
67.5 x 52 cm
BERN, KUNSTMUSEUM BERN
LEGAT GEORGES F. KELLER 1981

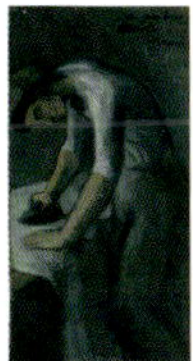

4.6 Pablo Picasso
Woman Ironing
[La Repasseuse]
1901
oil on canvas, mounted
on cardboard
49.5 x 25.7 cm
NEW YORK, THE METROPOLITAN MUSEUM OF ART, ALFRED STIEGLITZ COLLECTION 1949, 49.70.2

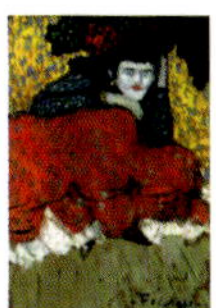

4.7 Pablo Picasso
Spanish Dancer
[Danseuse espagnole]
1901
oil on cardboard
50.8 x 35.8 cm
SWITZERLAND
NAHMAD COLLECTION

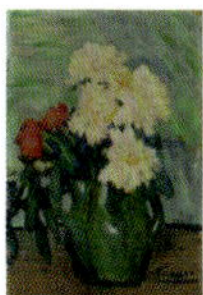

4.8 Pablo Picasso
Peonies
[Peonies]
1901
oil on hardboard mounted on
plywood
57.8 x 39.3 cm
WASHINGTON, NATIONAL GALLERY OF ART, GIFT OF MRS. GILBERT W. CHAPMAN 1981.41.1.(2847)

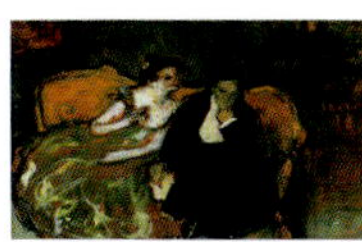

4.9 Pablo Picasso
The Conversation
[La Conversation]
1901
oil on panel
13.5 x 22.5 cm
KÜNZELSAU
WÜRTH COLLECTION

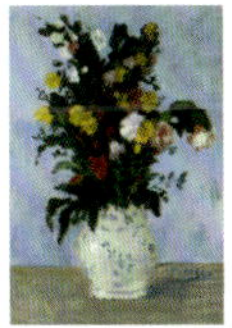

4.10 Pablo Picasso
Vase with Flowers
[Vase de fleurs]
1901
oil on canvas
66 x 46.5 cm
SWITZERLAND
NAHMAD COLLECTION

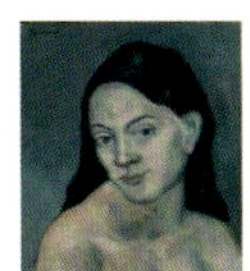

4.11 Pablo Picasso
Head of a Woman
[Tête de femme]
1903
oil on canvas
40.3 x 35.6 cm
NEW YORK, THE METROPOLITAN MUSEUM OF ART
BEQUEST OF MISS ADELAIDE MILTON DE GROOT, 1967, 67.187.91

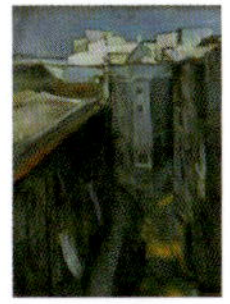

4.12 Pablo Picasso
Barcelona,
Riera de Sant Joan at Dawn
[Barcelona.
Riera de Sant Joan à l'aube]
1903
oil on canvas
54 x 45.5 cm
SWITZERLAND
PRIVATE COLLECTION

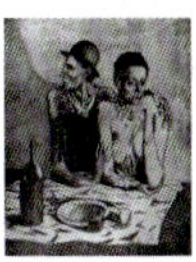

4.13 Pablo Picasso
The Frugal Meal
[Le Repas frugal]
1904
engraving
46.3 x 37.7 cm
BERN, E.W.K.

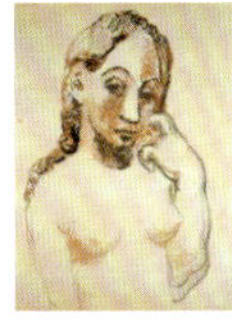

4.14 Pablo Picasso
Bust of a Woman
with her Left Hand Raised
(Fernande Olivier)
[Buste de femme la main gauche
levée (Fernande Olivier)]
c. 1905–6
gouache, watercolour, brush
and ink and graphic on paper
laid down on card
63.5 x 48.26 cm
COURTESY ACQUAVELLA GALLERY
WORK NOT ON DISPLAY

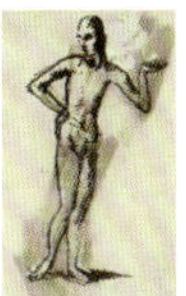

4.15 Pablo Picasso
The Actor
[L'Acteur]
1904
India ink and gouache on paper
16 x 11 cm
KÜNZELSAU
WÜRTH COLLECTION

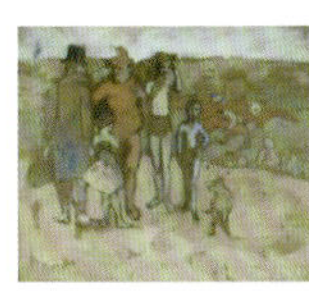

4.16 Pablo Picasso
Family of Acrobats
[Famille de saltimbanques]
Spring 1905
gouache and charcoal on cardboard
51.2 x 61.2 cm
MOSCOW, THE STATE PUSHKIN MUSEUM OF FINE ARTS

WORK NOT ON DISPLAY

EPILOGUE

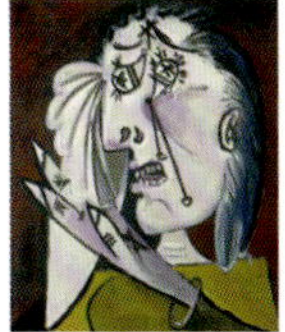

5.1 Pablo Picasso
The Weeping Woman
[La Femme qui pleure]
1937
oil on canvas
55 x 46 cm
RIEHEN/BASEL, FONDATION BEYELER. 98.3

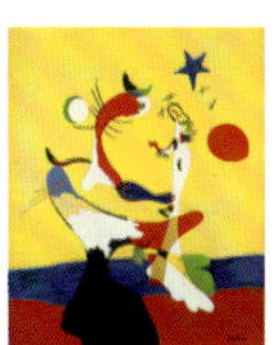

5.2 Joan Miró
Composition (Little Universe)
[Composition (Petit Univers)]
1933
gouache on card
39.5 x 31.5 cm
RIEHEN/BASEL
FONDATION BEYELER. 72.4

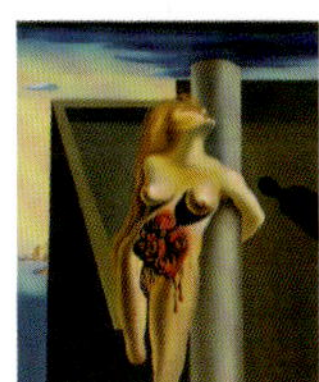

5.3 Salvador Dalí
The Bleeding Roses
[Las rosas ensangrentadas]
1930
oil on canvas
61 x 50 cm
LA CORUÑA
COLLECIÓN CAIXA GALICIA

CAHIER NO. 7

Pablo Picasso
Paris, May–June 1907
220 x 170 mm

MALAGA, COLLECTION OF THE PABLO RUIZ PICASSO FOUNDATION BIRTHPLACE MUSEUM. FPCN: 2037

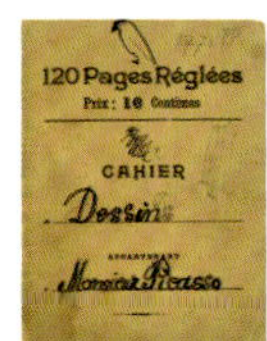

cover
Eagle and Printed Text
pen and ink on paper

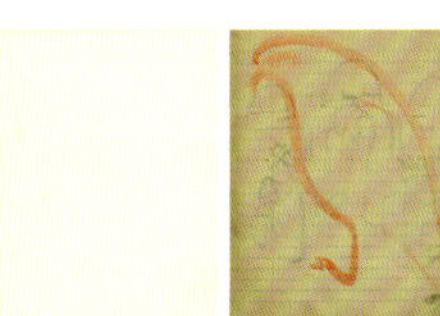

inside front cover
blank page
f. 1r Interior Scene and Eagle
pencil and red gouache on paper

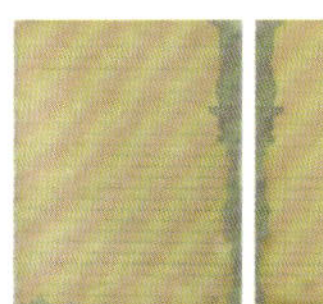

f. 1v blank page
f. 2r Legs
pencil on loose sheet; may originally have been situated between f. 4v and f. 5r

f. 2v blank page
f. 3r Study for the Seated Girl: Nude with Drapery
pen and ink on paper

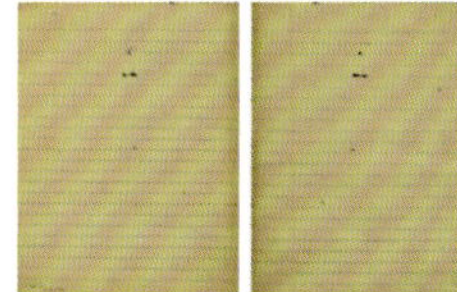

f. 3v blank page
f. 4r blank page

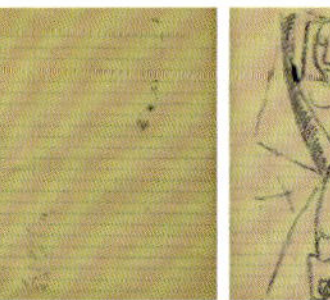

f. 4v blank page
f. 5r Study for the Seated Girl: Nude with Drapery
pen and ink on paper

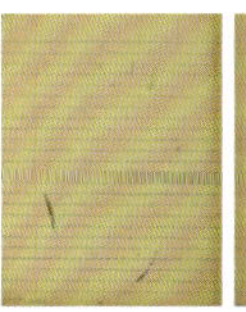

f. 5v blank page
f. 6r Study for the Seated Girl: Nude with Drapery
pen and ink on paper

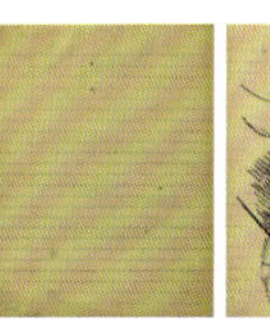

f. 6v blank page
f. 7r Nude with Hands Crossed, Full-Frontal
pen and ink on paper

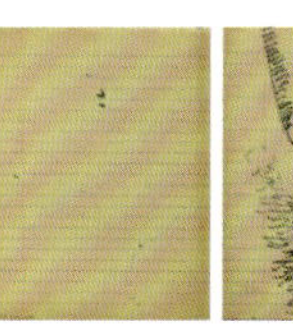

f. 7v blank page
f. 8r Study for the Girl with Raised Arms (?): Nude with Raised Arms, from the Side
pen and ink on paper

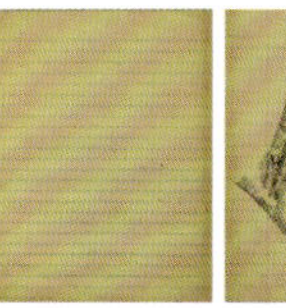

f. 8v blank page
f. 9r Nude with Raised Arm from the Back
pen and ink on paper

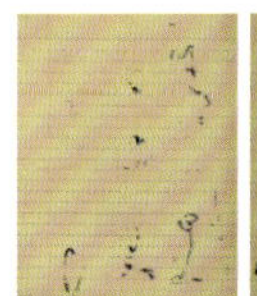
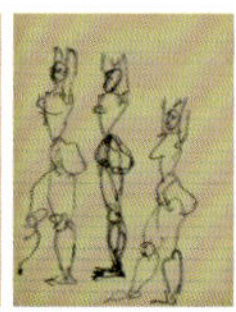

f. 9v blank page
f. 10r Study for the Girl with Raised Arms: Nudes with Raised Arms from the Side
pen and ink on paper

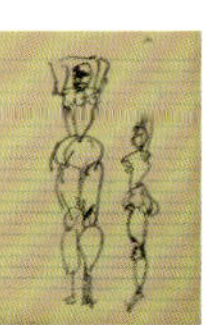

f. 10v Study for the Girl with Raised Arms: Standing Nudes with Raised Arms, Full-Frontal and from the Side
pen and ink on paper
f. 11r Study for the Girl with Raised Arms: Nudes with Raised Arms, Full-frontal
pen and ink on paper

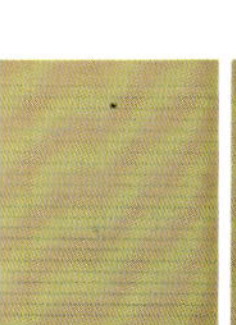

f. 11v blank page
f. 12r Profile of a Woman with a Bun
pencil on paper

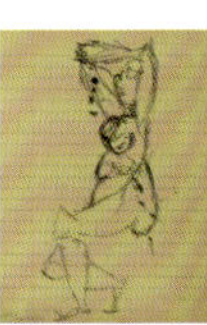

f. 12v Nude, Leaning with Raised Arms
pen and ink on paper
f. 13r Bust of Nude with Raised Arms and Standing Nude
pen, ink and pencil on paper

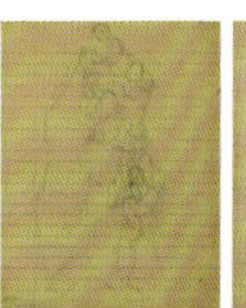

f. 13v Pyramid of Nudes with Curtain
pencil on paper
f. 14r Pyramid of Nudes
pencil on paper

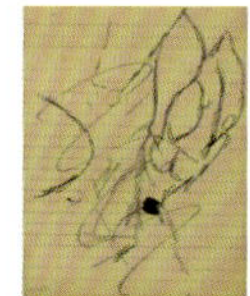

f. 14v Study for the Seated Girl: Bust of Nude with Raised Arms
pen and ink on paper
f. 15r Pyramid of Nudes
pencil on paper

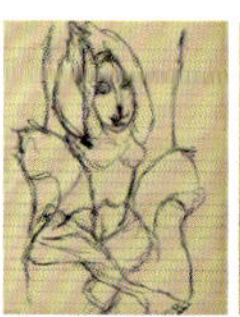

f. 15v Study for the Seated Girl: Nude Seated on a Armchair
pen and ink on paper
f. 16r Standing Nude with Legs Apart and Arms by his Side
pencil on paper

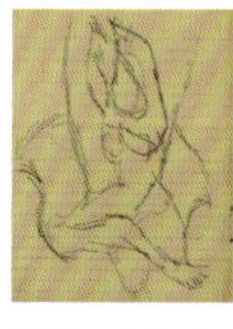

f. 16v Study for the Seated Girl: Nude Seated on a Armchair
pen and ink on paper
f. 17r Standing Nude with Legs Apart and Arms by his Side
pencil on paper

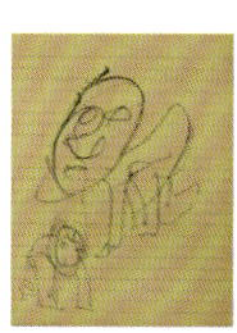

f. 17v Caricature: Two Figures on All Fours
pen and ink on paper
f. 18r Climbing Nude
pencil on paper

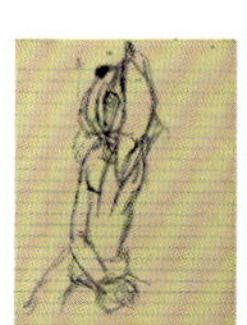

f. 18v Study for the Seated Girl: Seated Nude with Arm Raised
pen and ink on paper
f. 19r Climbing Nude
pencil on paper

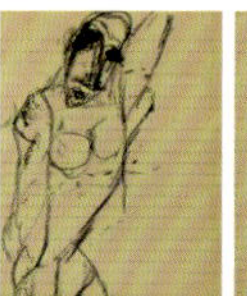
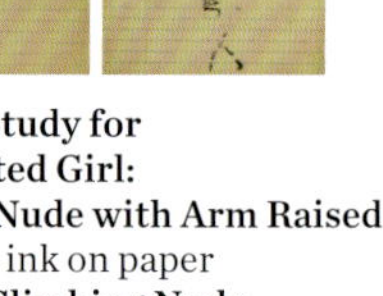

f. 19v Study for the Seated Girl: Seated Nude with Arm Raised
pen and ink on paper
f. 20r Climbing Nude
pencil and ink on paper

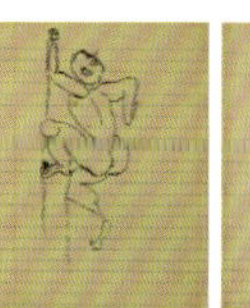

f. 20v Climbing Nude
pen and ink on paper
f. 21r Climbing Nude
pencil and ink on paper

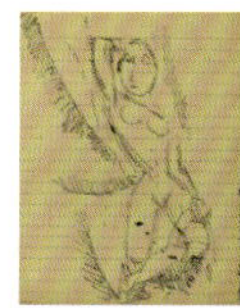
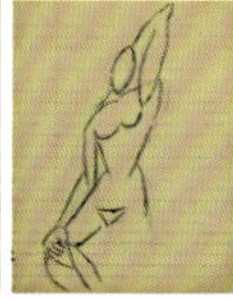

f. 21v Study for the Seated Girl: Nude with Drapery
pen and ink on paper
f. 22r Study for the Seated Girl: Nude with Arm Raised
pencil, pen, and ink on paper

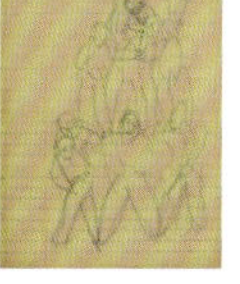

f. 22v blank page
f. 23r Pyramid of Nudes
pencil on paper

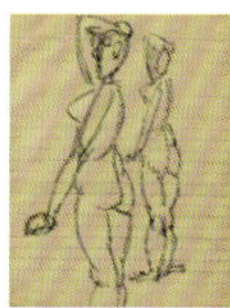

f. 23v Study for the Standing Girl on the Right (?): Nudes with Arm Raised from the Side
pen and ink on paper
f. 24r Pyramid of Nudes
pencil on paper

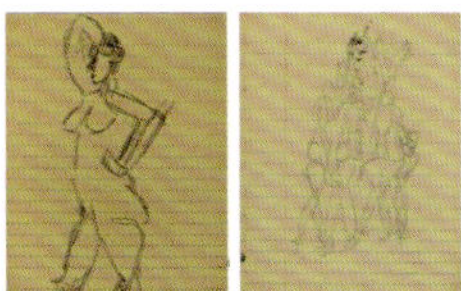

f. 24v Study for the Standing Girl on the Right: Nude with Arm Raised from the Side
pen and ink on paper
f. 25r Pyramid of Nudes and Nude, Leaning
pencil on paper

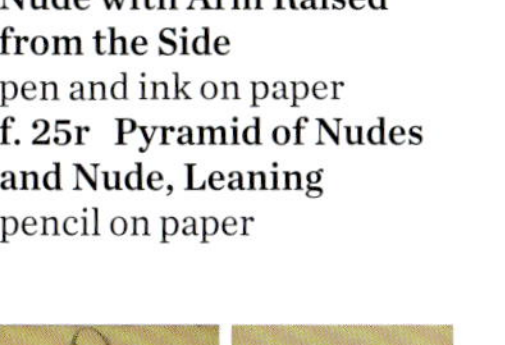

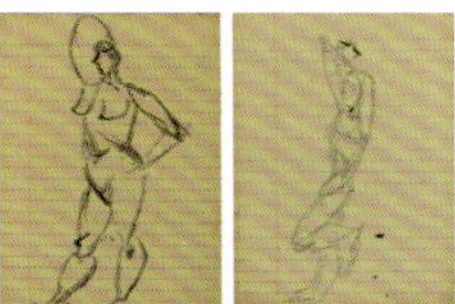

f. 25v Study for the Standing Girl on the Right: Nude with Arm Raised from the Side
pen and ink on paper
f. 26r Nude, Leaning, with Raised Arms
pencil on paper

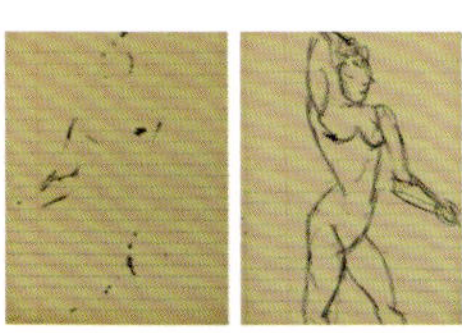

f. 26v blank page
f. 27r Study for the Standing Girl on the Right: Nude with Arm Raised from the Side
pen and ink on paper

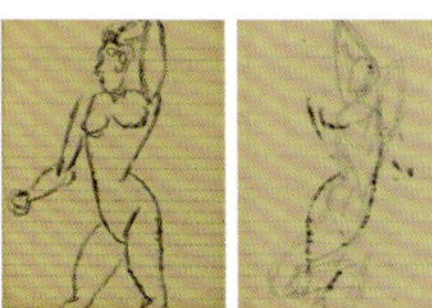

f. 27v Study for the Standing Girl on the Right: Nude with Arm Raised from the Side
pen and ink on paper
f. 28r Nude, Leaning with Arm Raised
pencil and traces of ink on paper

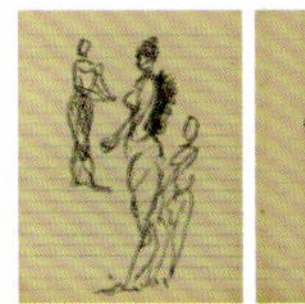

f. 28v Study for the Standing Girl on the Right: Nudes, from the Side
pen and ink on paper
f. 29r Study for the Seated Girl: Seated Nude with Arm Raised
pencil on paper

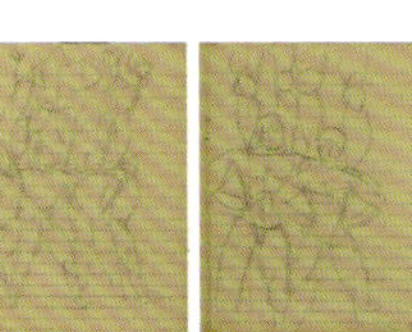

f. 29v Pyramid of Nudes
pencil on paper
f. 30r Pyramid of Nudes
pencil on paper

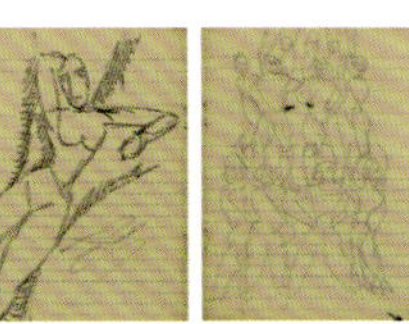

f. 30v Study for the Seated Girl: Reclining Nude with Drapery
pen and ink on paper
f. 31r Pyramid of Nudes
pencil on paper

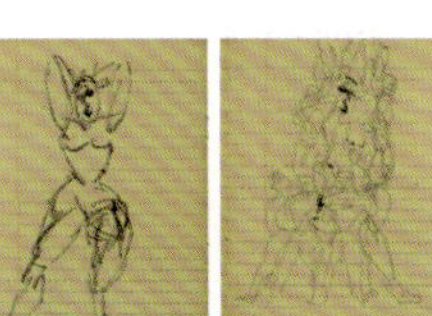

f. 31v Study for the Seated Girl: Seated Nude with Raised Arms
pen and ink on paper
f. 32r Pyramid of Nudes
pencil on paper

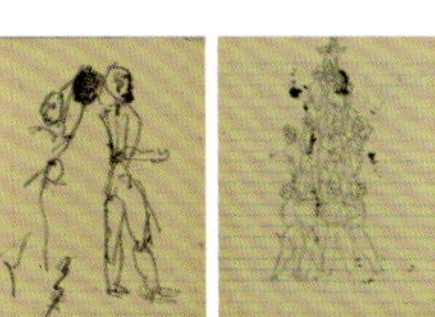

f. 32v Nude, Leaning from the Left, and Standing Nude, from the Right
pen and ink on paper
f. 33r Pyramid of Nudes
pencil on paper

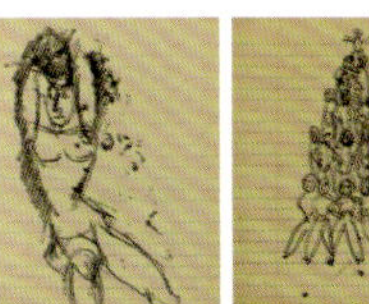

f. 33v Study for the Seated Girl: Seated Nude with Raised Arms
pen and ink on paper
f. 34r Pyramid of Nudes
pen and ink on paper

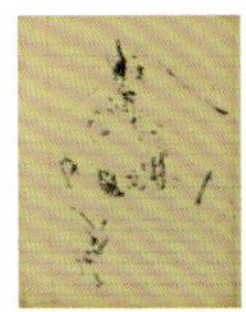

f. 34v blank page
f. 35r Pyramid of Nudes and Study for the Standing Girl on the Right
pen and ink on paper

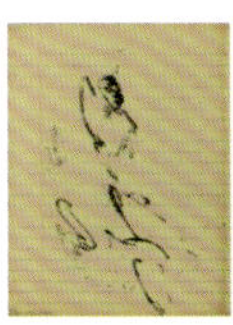

f. 35v blank page
f. 36r Nude, Leaning with Raised Arms
pen and ink on paper

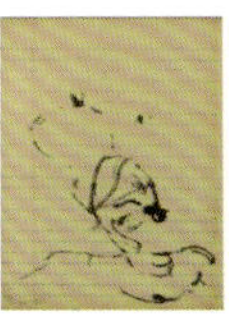

f. 36v blank page
f. 37r Study: Bust with Large Ear Climbing Nude and Full-Frontal Nude with Arms by his Side
pen and ink on paper

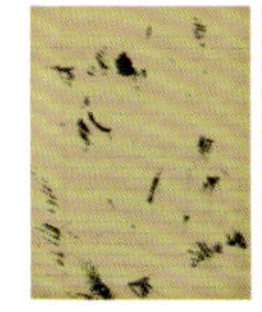

f. 37v blank page
f. 38r Study for *Still Life with Bananas:* Coffee Pot with Towels
pen and ink on paper

f. 38v blank page
f. 39r Portrait of a Young Girl (Raymonde?)
pen and ink on paper

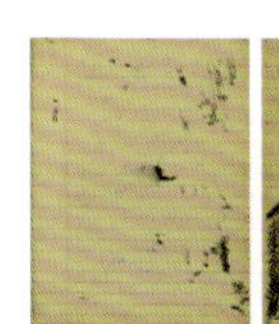

f. 39v blank page
f. 40r Study for *Jug Jar and Lemon:* Jug with Towels
pen and ink on paper

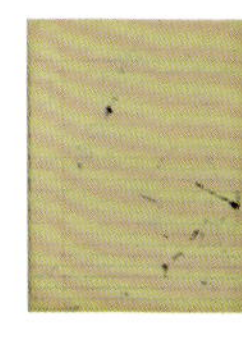

f. 40v blank page
f. 41r Study for *Jug, Jar and Lemon:* Jar
pen and ink on paper

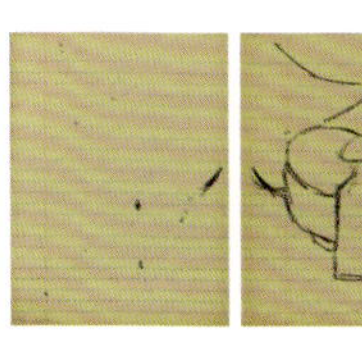

f. 41v blank page
f. 42r Study for *Jug, Bowl and Lemons:* Jug and Bowl with Towels
pen and ink on paper

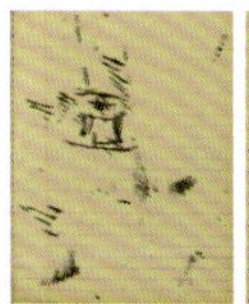

f. 42v blank page
f. 43r Study for *Still Life with Bananas:* Jug and Bowl with Towel
pen and ink on paper

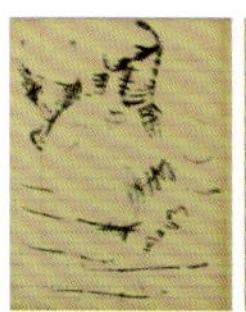

f. 43v blank page
f. 44r Study for *Jug Jar and Lemon:* Jug and Bowl on Tablecloth
pen and ink on paper

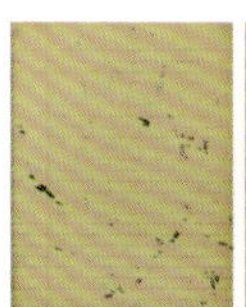

f. 44v blank page
f. 45r Still Life with Lemon
pen and ink on paper

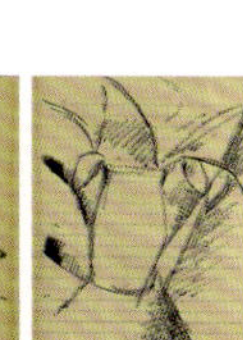

f. 45v blank page
f. 46r Jug and Lemons with Towels
pen and ink on paper

f. 46v blank page
f. 47r Study for the Seated Girl: Seated Nude with Arm Raised
pen and ink on paper

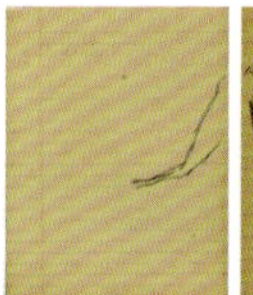
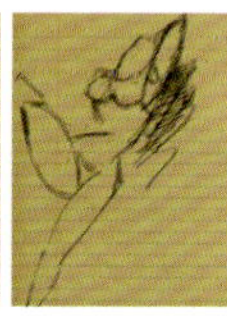

ff. 47v e 48r
Study for the Seated Girl: Reclining Nude
pen and ink on paper

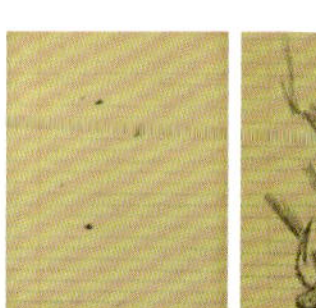

f. 48v blank page
f. 49r Study of a Hand
pen and ink on paper

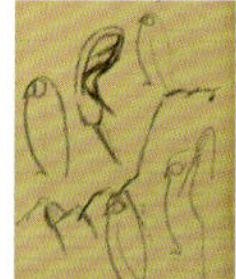
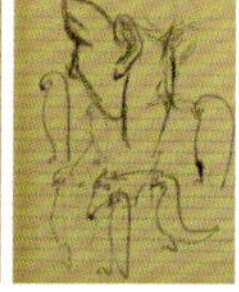

f. 49v Study: Owl, Ear and Heron
pen and ink on paper
f. 50r Study: Profile of a Woman, Owls, Dog, Bird
pen and ink on paper

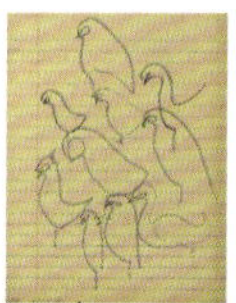
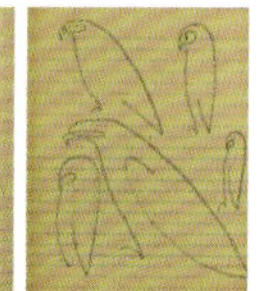

f. 50v Study: Chickens, Eagles, Owls, Birds
pen and ink on paper
f. 51r Study: Eagles and Owls
pen and ink on paper

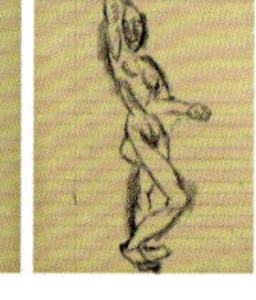

f. 51v blank page
f. 52r Study for *Nude with Drapery:* Nude from the Side with Arm Raised
pen and ink on paper

f. 52v blank page
f. 53r Study for the Seated Girl: Nude with Raised Arms
pencil on paper

f. 53v blank page
f. 54r Study for the Seated Girl: Nude with Raised Arms
pencil on paper

f. 54v blank page
f. 55r Study for the Seated Girl: Nude with Raised Arms Seated on a Armchair
pencil on paper

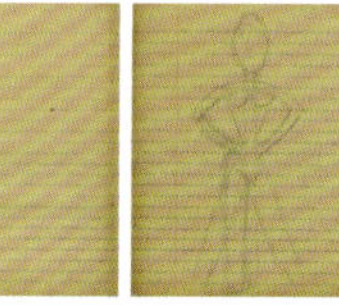

f. 55v blank page
f. 56r Study for the Girl with Raised Arms: Nude with Arms by her Side
pencil on paper

f. 56v blank page
f. 57r Study for the Girl with Raised Arms: Nude with Arms Crossed
pencil on paper

f. 57v blank page
f. 58r Study for the Girl with Raised Arms: Standing Nude with Arms Crossed
pencil on paper

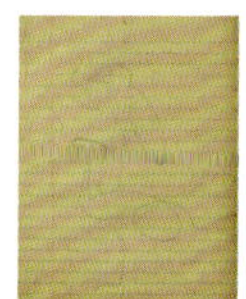
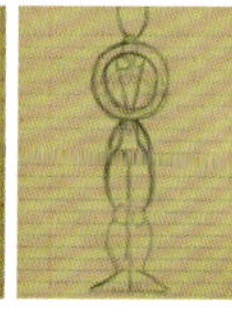

f. 58v Study: Birds
pencil on paper
f. 59r Study for the Girl with Raised Arms: Standing Nude with Arms Crossed
pencil on paper

f. 59v blank page
f. 60r blank page

f. 60v Study: Eagle, Owl and Crocodile
pencil on paper
inside back cover
blank page

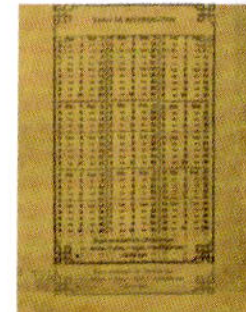

outside back cover
printed tables

(from *Listado de obras y catalogacíon, in Picasso y la escultura africana. Los orígenes de Las Señorita de Avignon,* TEA Tenerife Espacio de las Artes, Artemisa Ediciones Colodión, pp. 327–335)

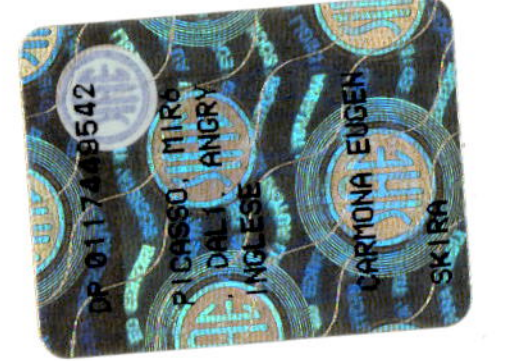